A Pictorial Record of
Great Western Engines

A Pictorial Record of GREAT WESTERN ENGINES

by
J. H. Russell

(Volume Two)

Haynes

Oxford Publishing Company

ISBN 0 86093 399 7

A FOULIS-OPC Railway Book

Published by:
Haynes Publishing Group
Sparkford, Near Yeovil, Somerset. BA22 7JJ

Haynes Publications Inc.
861 Lawrence Drive, Newbury Park, California 91320, USA

The author and publishers wish to point out that these volumes do not claim to be a complete history of Great Western engines but are a pictorial record only. (The historic documentation of this fascinating subject can be found in the R.C.T.S. publications concerning Great Western locomotives.)

Many of the line drawings and sketches are taken directly from official Swindon originals and due to the age of these the reproduction is not as clear as they would wish. The drawings have been reduced to 4mm scale as near as possible, but again, due to the condition of some of the drawings, variation in scale may exist.

Preface

In the first part of this collection, the designs of Gooch, Armstrong and William Dean were predominant, covering the years from 1835 to the turn of the century, with several G.J. Churchward engines placed on the concluding pages to make a transition from Part One to Part Two. As with the companion volumes on Great Western Coaches, the second part is of necessity larger because, as time passed, and the Great Western Railway developed and expanded, so did the stock, style and variety of locomotives increase.

This second part deals with the engines designed by the last three Chief Mechanical Engineers of the old G.W.R., namely G.J. Churchward, C.B. Collett, and finally F.W. Hawksworth. Accent has again been placed upon the 'work-a-day' engines, rather than the express passenger classes, which have already been covered by more capable authors than myself. Nevertheless, I have striven to include examples of every pure Great Western class, in order to give the work some continuity. Also, there are a few of the absorbed engines which were converted to a 'Swindon' outline at the factory, after 1922, plus several of the internal combustion machines, which after all, came under the aegis of the Locomotive Department, and so are worthy of their place here.

I have been fortunate enough to gain access to the official Swindon "Locomotive Diagram Book No. 2" from which many of the enclosed diagrams are reproduced. A guide to these diagrams and Lot numbers can be found on the final pages of Part One, where a Lot index has been printed. Unless stated to the contrary, the drawings are all to the 4m/m to 1 foot scale, for the benefit of modellers.

Finally, I would like to acknowledge all the photographers both official and unofficial, whose work appears in these books. Many have of course long since departed but their efforts live on, and continue to delight all of us who still find interest in the erstwhile "Great, Western Railway". To them, known and unknown, I, on your behalf, say "thank you sincerely".

JIM RUSSELL. 1975.

General Index

Class Index Part II

G.W.R. 4300 Class passing Kings Sutton in 1921

Starting Part Two with a pure Churchward design, we begin on this page with the 4-4-0 light passenger "3300" class. Developed from the 'Duke' Class, the first 'Bulldog' to appear with a domeless boiler was No. 3352 *Camel.* In 1899 this curved frame engine was turned out with the Standard No. 2 boiler and Belpaire firebox to *Diagram H* as seen in *Figure 1.* Unusual too was the siting of the number plate on the smokebox and the oval nameplate with the coat of arms in the centre. This was fixed to the cab side sheets. Nineteen 'Dukes' with their curved frames were also reboilered later and joined the 'Bulldog' series, being renumbered 3300 to 3319 (this included No. 3310 *Bulldog* herself) so that with *Camel,* and 20 new curved framed engines of the class built in 1900, the whole series totalled forty. One of this series was *Laira* No. 3338, and it is this engine which is illustrated in *Figure 2.*

The drawing in *Figure 3* is of the same curved frame class as at 1936 after being fitted with a superheater. The diagram was A. 25 for the 4-4-0 class as issued from Swindon drawing office. For the *Diagram H* of the class (as built) see *Figure 5A,* Page 2.

Figure 1

Figure 2

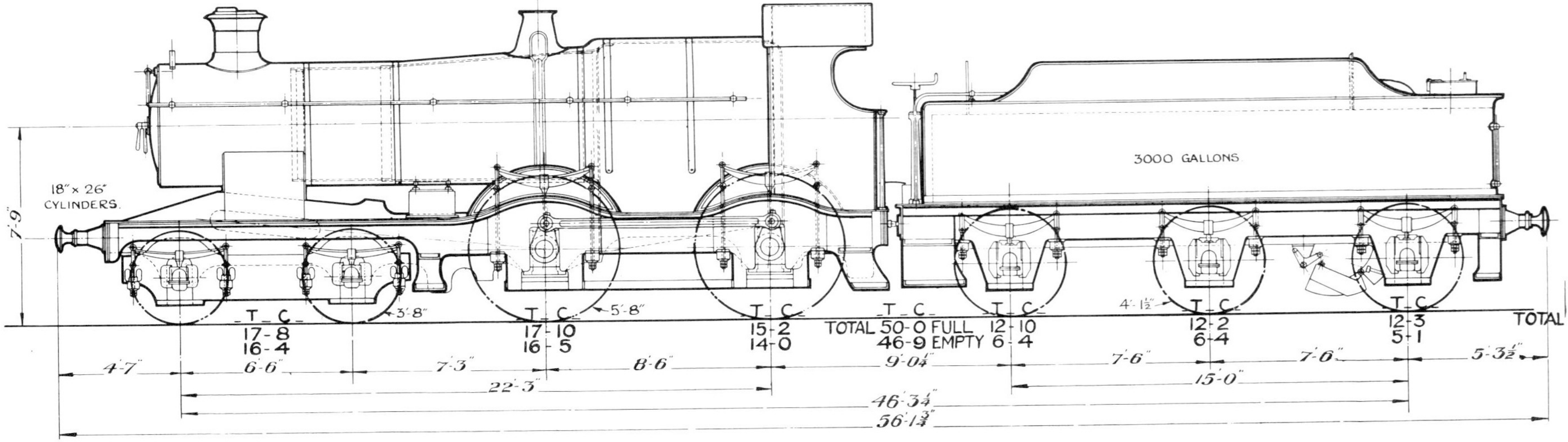

Figure 3

Figure 5

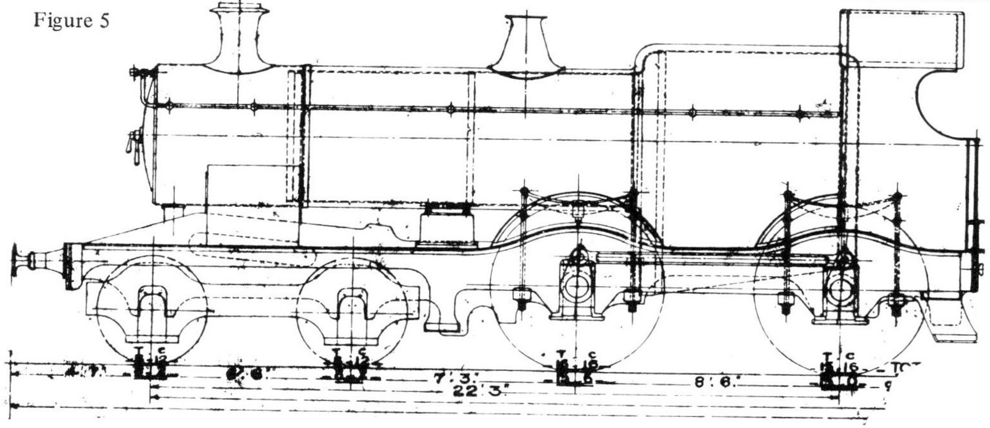

Figure 4

Figure 5A

Figure 6

Figure 7

The cabs on the '3300' class were really wide and roomy affairs, and definitely again the hand of Churchward; gone was the narrow cramped style with the regulator in the 'up and over' position, which meant the driver always had to stand. In the new design, there was a seat provided, large windows to give a view forward even in the sitting position, and the regulator was of a pattern which could also be handled whilst seated. There was a dual system of brakes, steam and vacuum, and reversing was also by steam cylinder. This gear was operated by the small lever on the right-hand cab side sheet, and the setting of the valves could be observed by the graduated scale just to the left of the driver's window. Although the principle was sound, in practice the gear kept drifting and wanted constant adjustment, and the only class to keep the steam reversing was the '2600' 'Aberdare' series, but as I can vouch, it was more nuisance than advantage.

Figures 5 and *6* show two examples of the curved frame 'Bulldogs', with the different designs of nameplate. *Maristow* seen in the 1920's has the curved nameplate, and the lettering now correctly spelt, whereas *Pegasus* No. 3331, still has the oval cab-side combined plate. Both engines lasted until 1934 before being withdrawn. *Figure 5A* shows the engine built to the original *Diagram H.*

The engine in the top illustration, No. 3300, started out in May 1895, as the second to be constructed of the 'Duke' class. She was rebuilt into the 'Bulldog' series in November of 1908, and was until 1923 named *Pendennis Castle.* The building of the 'Castle' class by C.B. Collett however, would have meant duplication, therefore the nameplates were removed, and No. 3300 henceforward was nameless until her withdrawal in 1936.

No. 3306 seen in *Figure 8* also had a varied history, she was the first 'Duke' to be converted to the 3300 series. In 1902, when so rebuilt, she carried straight nameplates on the boiler sides, but finally reverted to the normal curved style as seen in the photograph. In her 43 years service, she carried seven types of boiler, starting with S4 in 1896, to D2 in 1906, to D3 in 1910, back to D2 in 1912, D3 again in 1914, and finally Standard 3 in 1933.

These two pictures show both sides of the engine and should prove useful to modellers. Note the small cover on the firebox in the lower picture, which covered the screw reversing gear, and replaced the original steam reversing apparatus.

Figure 8

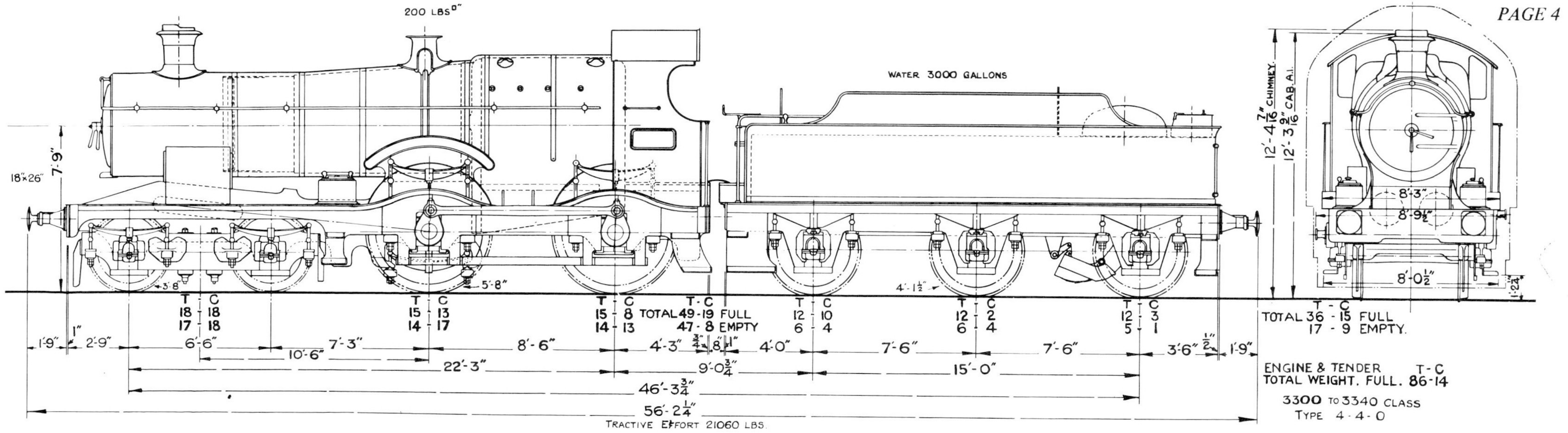

Figure 9

Two Swindon drawings on this page, both of the 'Bulldog' class, but circa 1936. In *Figure 9* we have *Diagram A.42* which is of the '3300' class with curved frame and cast tapered chimney, fitted with superheater and D3 boiler. *Figure 10* is of the '3341' class which followed the '3300' to '3340' series, and shows the raised framing cut in a straight line, which was *Diagram A.23.* The origin of the curved framing was of course to clear the coupling rod heads, but by raising the running plate and squaring it off it was found that this design was easier to build and less expensive, so all other 'Bulldogs' were so fitted. They numbered from 3341 to 3380 and all started life with the parallel D.0 type of boiler.

Figure 10

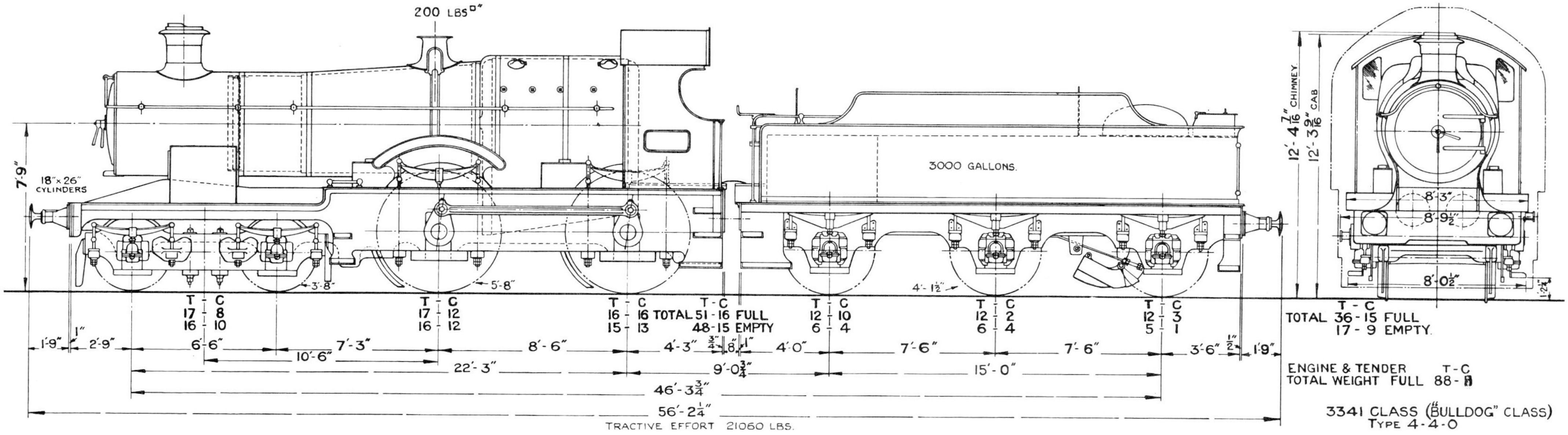

Figure 11

Figure 11 is an official Swindon photograph of the standard 'Bulldog' class as built in 1903. No. 3419 (later 3367) *Evan Llewellyn* is seen here with the taper chimney and parallel D.0 boiler, and still in the Works undercoat paintwork. She was fitted with a taper boiler in 1910, superheated in 1913 and withdrawn in 1935.

The next stage in the 'Bulldog' development can be seen in *Figure 12. Barbados,* No. 3466 has the built-up copper-topped chimney and the D.2 single ring taper boiler. Notice that the small round cab windows are still in place, as are the brass bands on the splashers.

The number was changed in 1910 to 3404 and *Figure 13* shows the engine in the 1930's, with a D3 boiler, superheater and large Collett tender. The date of withdrawal was 1937. Another picture of the final condition of the straight framed 'Bulldogs' is that of *Stanley Baldwin* as seen in *Figure 14.* Originally numbered 3701 when built, this engine carried her name from January 1909 until July 1937 when the plates were taken off to avoid duplication with the 'Castle' class.

Figure 12

Figure 13

Figure 14

Figure 15

A page depicting the 'Bird' Class (the 'Bulldog' class with the deeper frames). *Figure 15* shows *Chaffinch* as built in 1909 with the D3 boiler and in Works grey. *Cormorant* is seen in *Figure 16* as renumbered in 1910 to No. 3444. Her original number was 3734, and she survived until 1951, as did *Skylark* seen in *Figure 17.* Notice both engines are superheated, and have top feed to their boilers.

Figure 16

Figure 17

Figure 18

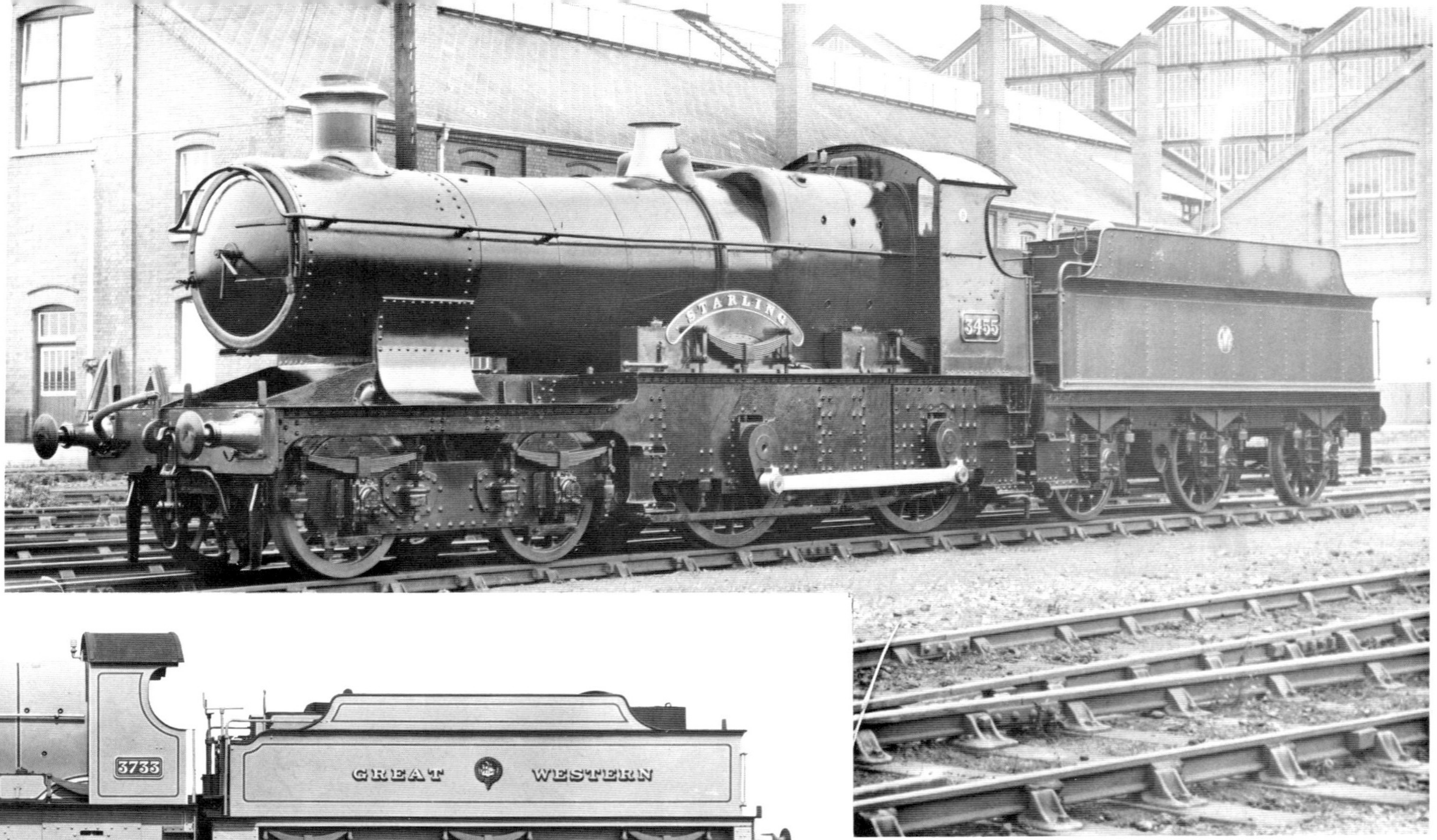

It means a jump ahead in time, but to keep with the 'Bulldogs' (if only to link up with the drawings on page 8), we must deal with the 'Bird' series, which were fifteen similar engines produced in 1909-10, to the same general design, but fitted as built with the D3 taper boiler, and with deep framing over the driving wheels. They numbered from 3731 to 3745 at first, but were later renumbered 3441 to 3455. Their names were as below.

Figure 19

No. 3731	Built	1909	*Blackbird*	later	3441	withdrawn	1949
No. 3732	”	”	*Bullfinch*	”	3442	”	1948
No. 3733	”	”	*Chaffinch*	”	3443	”	1949
No. 3734	”	”	*Cormorant*	”	3444	”	1951
No. 3735	”	”	*Flamingo*	”	3445	”	1948
No. 3736	”	”	*Goldfinch*	”	3446	”	1948
No. 3737	”	”	*Jackdaw*	”	3447	”	1951
No. 3738	”	”	*Kingfisher*	”	3448	”	1949
No. 3739	”	”	*Nightingale*	”	3449	”	1951
No. 3740	”	”	*Peacock*	”	3450	”	1949
No. 3741	”	1910	*Pelican*	”	3451	”	1951
No. 3742	”	”	*Penguin*	”	3452	”	1948
No. 3743	”	”	*Seagull*	”	3453	”	1951
No. 3744	”	”	*Skylark*	”	3454	”	1951
No. 3745	”	”	*Starling*	”	3455	”	1950

Shown on this page are *Starling* as at 1937; *Chaffinch* as built in 1909 (full broadside), and *Seagull,* awaiting the scrapman's torch in 1951.

Figure 20

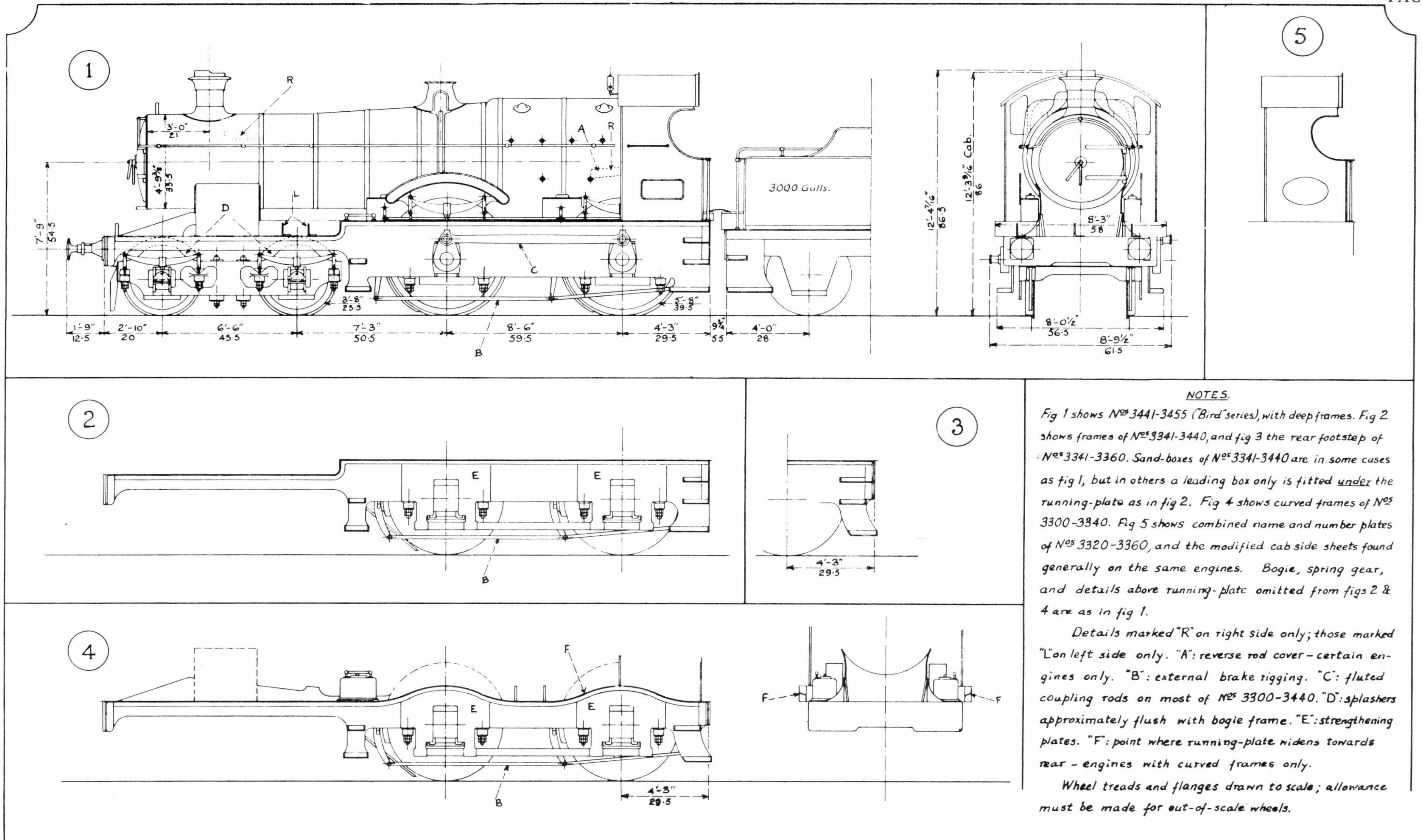

G. W. R. 3300 Class. Type 4-4-0.

Scale 4m.m = 1 foot.
Reduced from official drawings.

This comprehensive drawing of Colonel Templer gives all the three major frame details of the 'Bulldogs', and all the notes are appended in the panel on the right. All there is to add, is that the drawings are to 4m/m scale, feet and inches measurement are full size, and millimetre sizes are for 7m/m scale.

Figure 21

No. 3434, seen in *Figure 22*, was built in 1906, and originally carried the number 3724. She ran without nameplates until October 1917 when she was given the name *Joseph Shaw*. In 1913 (the date of this photograph) the engine was fitted with Westinghouse brake pump, and the extra hose can be seen on the front buffer beam. The pump itself was located on the front of the spectacle plate, below the window on the driver's side. What handsome little engines these were, and so useful, working all types of traffic from short distance fast passenger trains, to long distance coal trains. *Figure 23* features No. 3375 which was one of the 'Atbara' class, and really the prototypes of the famous 'Cities'. As can be seen, the outline of the engine follows closely that of the 'Bulldogs', but with the difference that they were fitted with 6′ 8½″ driving wheels instead of 5′ 8″. This is a fairly early picture of *Colonel Edgcumbe*, as can be seen by the parallel D.0 boiler carried (she was equipped with a taper D3 in 1906). Another rather unusual point about No. 3375 is that in her rather short career she carried four nameplates! She started with an oval cabside plate when named *Conqueror*, then changed to *Edgcumbe*, after this a 'Badminton' type plate was fixed to the boiler side, and finally the plate seen in the illustration. Her number was altered to 4122 in the renumbering.

Figure 23

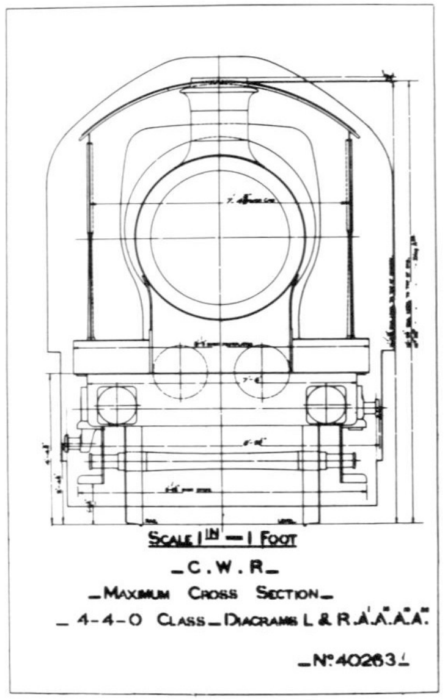

Figure 22

Two 'Atbara' class engines feature on this page. First *Colonel Edgcumbe* again in *Figure 25,* but fitted with the D3 taper boiler which, according to records, replaced the D.0 type in 1906, although the photograph is dated 1903!

The engine in *Figure 24* is No. 3374, and is one of the many examples of name changing for special occasions. Although named *Baden Powell,* the plates were removed and those from engine No. 3377 *Kitchener* were temporarily affixed to No. 3374, so that she could haul the special train, conveying the conquering hero home from the Boer War in July 1902. This was standard practice on the Great Western when a particular engine was not in a state of readiness for a specific duty, any available locomotive was commandeered, and rapidly renamed with the appropriate plates. One unusual feature of the old photograph in *Figure 24* is the impression it gives of the outside framing having no overhanging edge at the top. An optical illusion?

Figure 24

Figure 25

Figure 26

Figure 27

When the 'Atbaras' were first built, the Boer War was being fought in South Africa, and so it was thought fit to perpetuate the names which were so much in the public eye at that moment, therefore many of these engines received names which have gone down into our history books. Four such named engines are illustrated here, and all with their original oval combined name and number plate. *Figure 26* shows No. 3379 *Kimberley,* which has just been fitted with top feed, but still retains her original number. She was renumbered in 1912 to 4126. *Mafeking,* seen in *Figure 27,* had a very short life. She is seen in the illustration as built with the D.0 boiler, but was involved in an accident in 1911 and was consequently cut up.

The two other pictures show No. 3387 *Roberts* and No. 3374 *Baden Powell* both as constructed. These engines worked all the principal expresses at the turn of the century and so were 'top link'.

Figure 28

Figure 29

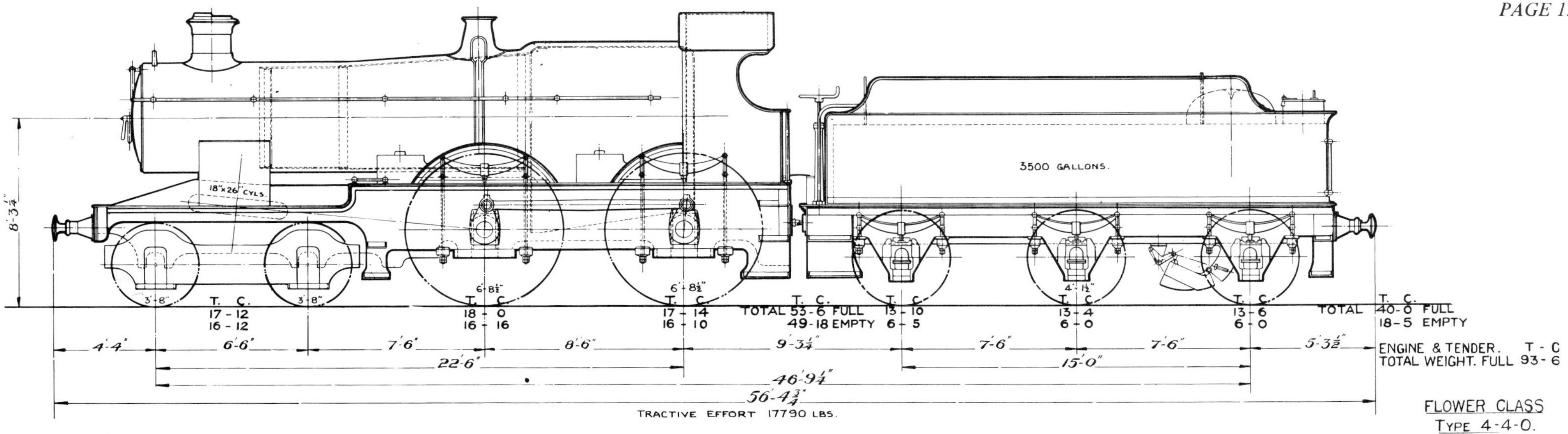

Figure 30

Figure 31

Most of the 'Atbara' class had outlived their usefulness by the late twenties, and in fact they were all withdrawn by 1930. The photograph in *Figure 31* of No. 4145 *Dunedin* shows the final condition of the engines before withdrawal as this picture is dated 1927 and *Dunedin* was scrapped in December of 1930. Before leaving this famous class of engine, it might be of interest to record what fast runners they were. *Rous-Martin* clocked 97.8 m.p.h. with one of them two years before *City of Truro* and they had many other moments of fame, often under false names. For instance, *Atbara* was renamed *Royal Sovereign* for the duty of hauling the funeral train of Queen Victoria. *Baden Powell* was renamed *Britannia* for another Royal journey to Kingswear, No. 3373 was renamed *Maine* for a military special in October 1900, and *Baden Powell* on a second train on the same day was called *Pretoria,* whilst a third train had *Powerful* at its head, which was in reality *White* No. 3392.

The development of the class resulted in the 'Flower' class in 1908. Twenty engines of identical dimensions to the 'Atbaras', but with deeper frames, and equipped with vacuum brake cylinders on the engines were built. The numbers ran from 4101-4120, later changed to 4149 to 4168. The drawing shown in *Figure 30* is the Swindon *Diagram A.19* and can be used for vital measurements, but note that the tender shown is one of the Collett type with long side plates. The photograph and drawing show well the difference in depth of frame between the 'Atbara' and 'Flower' class.

Again, apologies for being slightly out of sequence with building dates, as the 'Flowers' were not built until five years after the 'Cities', but the reason is that they do fit on to the 'Atbara' series both in dimension and numbering. In my opinion the names given to these engines were delightful, and worth inclusion of the following list.

Figure 32

Figure 33

No. 4101	*Auricula*	No. 4111	*Anemone*
No. 4102	*Begonia*	No. 4112	*Carnation*
No. 4103	*Calceolaria*	No. 4113	*Hyacinth*
No. 4104	*Calendula*	No. 4114	*Marguerite*
No. 4105	*Camelia*	No. 4115	*Marigold*
No. 4106	*Campanula*	No. 4116	*Mignonette*
No. 4107	*Cineraria*	No. 4117	*Narcissus*
No. 4108	*Gardenia*	No. 4118	*Polyanthus*
No. 4109	*Lobelia*	No. 4119	*Primrose*
No. 4110	*Petunia*	No. 4120	*Stephanotis*

Figure 32 shows *Begonia* as turned out of the factory in 1908 and *Stephanotis* (*Figure 33*) is seen on special train duty.

Figure 34

Figure 35

Here are two more illustrations of 'Flowers'. *Figure 35* shows *Campanula* in service and as built, numbered here as 4106, and without top feed, which would put the date of the photograph at approximately 1910. Note the polished buffer heads and smoke-box door hinges! *Marigold* seen in *Figure 34* was pictured at Tyseley shed in the 1920's, prior to hauling a saloon special from Birmingham to Paddington. Note that she now has superheated boiler and top feed, and also has been renumbered from No. 4115 to 4163.

So we now come to the historic 'Cities' of which there were only ten engines built as such, in 1903, the other ten in the class being rebuilt 'Atbaras'. The first prototype was *Mauritius* which was rebuilt in 1902 with the large No. 4 boiler and proved so successful that ten new engines were constructed likewise, given the numbers 3433 to 3442, and named after cities served by the railway. They were big engines for their time, weighing 92 tons complete, and this can be clearly seen in *Figure 36* (a lesser known picture of *City of Truro*). This illustration shows the engine as built, with the original boiler and number. The drawing (*Figure 37*) is of the class at a later date, after being superheated, the diagram being *A.17* of the Swindon classification.

Figure 36

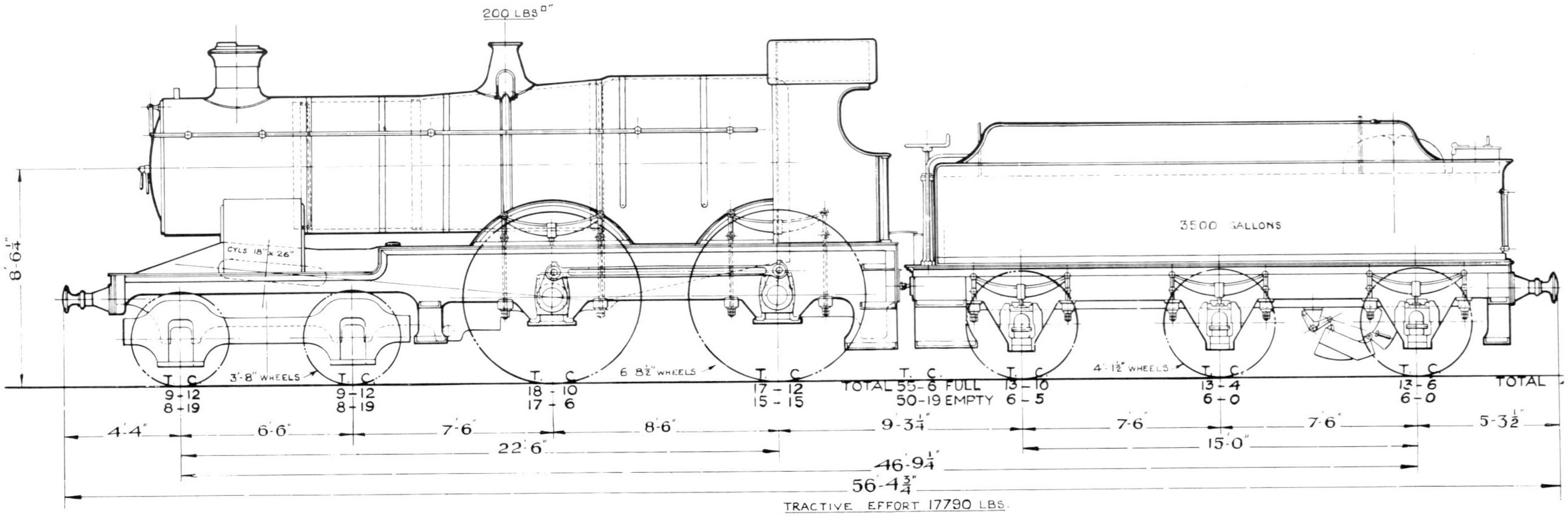

Figure 37

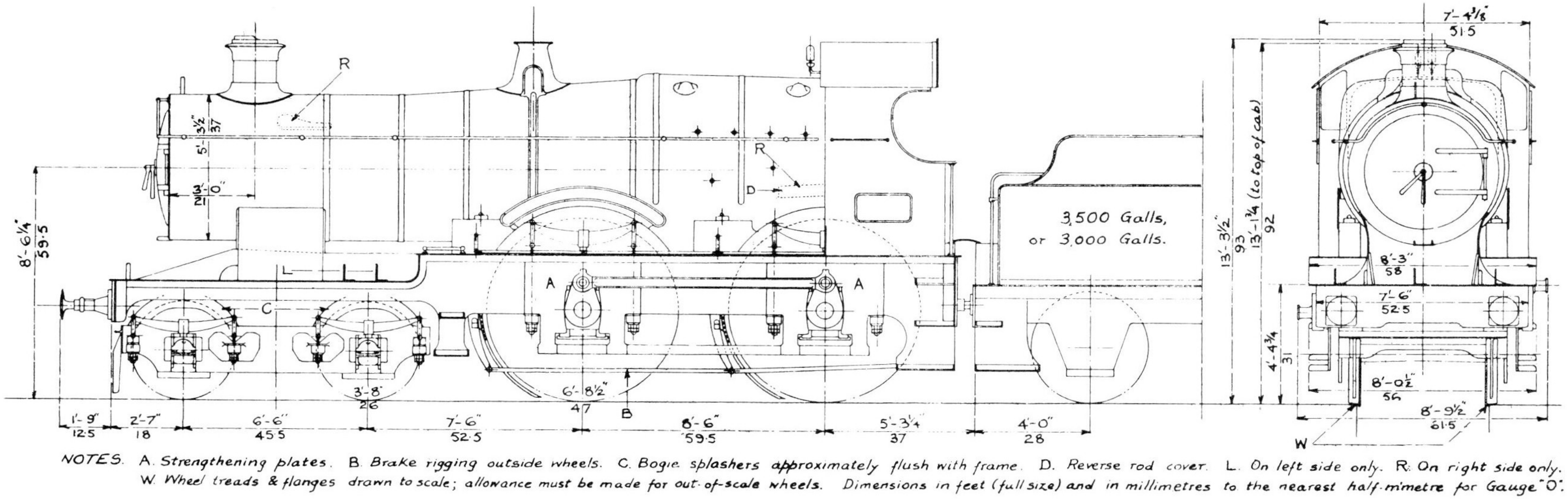

Figure 38

Much has been written of *City of Truro's* famous flight down Whitehall Bank, and the 102 m.p.h. said to have been attained in 1904, but if you believe it or not, these engines certainly were swift runners, and how nice it is to know that the historic engine was not cut up, but still exists in Swindon museum. Colonel Templer's drawing in *Figure 38* shows the measurements in feet for full size, and in millimetres for 7m/m scale, but shows the class as they appeared after being fitted with superheater and piston valves, similar in fact to *City of Bristol* seen in 1925, and numbered 3712 (*Figure 40*).

The same engine as she appeared when new can be seen in *Figure 39* and modellers should note the short smoke-box, the cast chimney, no top feed and the unstrengthened frames.

Figure 39

Figure 40

Figure 41

Wherever possible, the full frontal view of engines is shown, as, being a modeller myself, I know how necessary it is to know just what the smokebox-end looked like, as they were all different! *Figure 41* gives a good impression of No. 3713 *City of Chester* showing several points of note, for instance the height of the boiler above the frames, the centre line of which was 8′ 6¼″ above rail level. Also there was no provision for steam heating on the front buffer beam of the 'Cities' and finally, the vacuum pipe ran underneath the bogie frame.

A complete list of this class is given below

No. 3405	later	3705	*Mauritius*	rebuilt	1902	withdrawn	1928
No. 3433	"	3710	*City of Bath*	built	1903	"	1928
No. 3434	"	3711	*City of Birmingham*	"	1903	"	1930
No. 3435	"	3712	*City of Bristol*	"	1903	"	1931
No. 3436	"	3713	*City of Chester*	"	1903	"	1929
No. 3437	"	3714	*City of Gloucester*	"	1903	"	1929
No. 3438	"	3715	*City of Hereford*	"	1903	"	1929
No. 3439	"	3716	*City of London*	"	1903	"	1929
No. 3440	"	3717	*City of Truro*	"	1903	preserved	
No. 3441	"	3718	*City of Winchester*	"	1903	withdrawn	1927
No. 3442	"	3719	*City of Exeter*	"	1903	"	1929
No. 3400	"	3700	*Durban*	rebuilt	1907	"	1929
No. 3401	"	3701	*Gibraltar*	"	1907	"	1928
No. 3402	"	3702	*Halifax*	"	1908	"	1929
No. 3403	"	3703	*Hobart*	"	1909	"	1929
No. 3404	"	3704	*Lyttleton*	"	1907	"	1928
No. 3406	"	3706	*Melbourne*	"	1908	"	1929
No. 3407	"	3707	*Malta*	"	1908	"	1929
No. 3408	"	3708	*Ophir* later *Killarney*	"	1907	"	1929
No. 3409	"	3709	*Quebec*	"	1907	"	1929

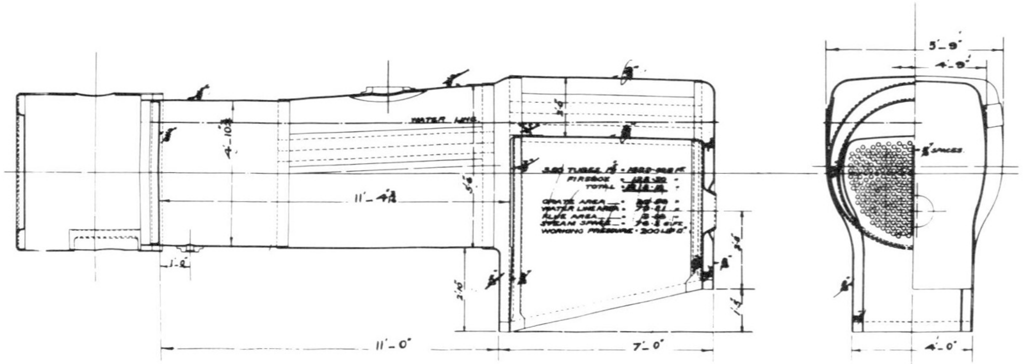

Diagram of No. 4 boiler fitted to 'City' class.

Figure 42

The year 1899 saw the advent of the remarkably ugly locomotive No. 2601, which is illustrated on this page (*Figure 42*). Being so undignified, the engine soon acquired the nickname of 'Kruger', who to the Boer War public was what Kaiser Bill and Hitler were to World Wars I and II respectively.

This massive engine, whose frames were similar to those of No. 36 described in Part One, possessed a domeless boiler which had a 3′ 6″ combustion chamber between it and the raised Belpaire firebox. This boiler was supported at the front end by the smokebox and at the rear by a cradle which stretched across the frames. The small pannier resting on top of the boiler was a sandbox, placed here to see if the heat of the boiler would keep the sand dry and so free-running; steps were placed on both sides of the smokebox for access to this sand container. The springing on this experimental engine was of the volute type in nests, as can be seen, and the bogie had spoked wheels with an inside frame. It should also be noted that the firebox sides were straight and not waisted, being a uniform width of 5′ 9″ and the length 7′.

She had a very short life, being withdrawn in December 1904.

Two years after the original 'Kruger' was constructed, a similar machine numbered 2602 was built, and differed from No. 2601 only in having a pony truck in place of the four wheeled bogie, and being fitted with laminated springs on the leading drivers, which was linked by a compensating beam on to the suspension of the pony wheels (*Figure 43*).

The only drawings I have of these two 'Krugers' are shown in 4m/m scale in *Figures 45, 46 and 47* and should suffice to enable a model to be made. *Figure 46* is the Swindon drawing to *Diagram A* of the subsequent 'Kruger' class, and shows clearly the family likeness to the first engine from which it was derived. *Figure 47* is the official *Diagram B* of No. 2601 whilst *Figure 45* shows another scale drawing of the same engine but minus tender. The picture in *Figure 44* shows the left-hand side of No. 2601.

Figure 43

Figure 44

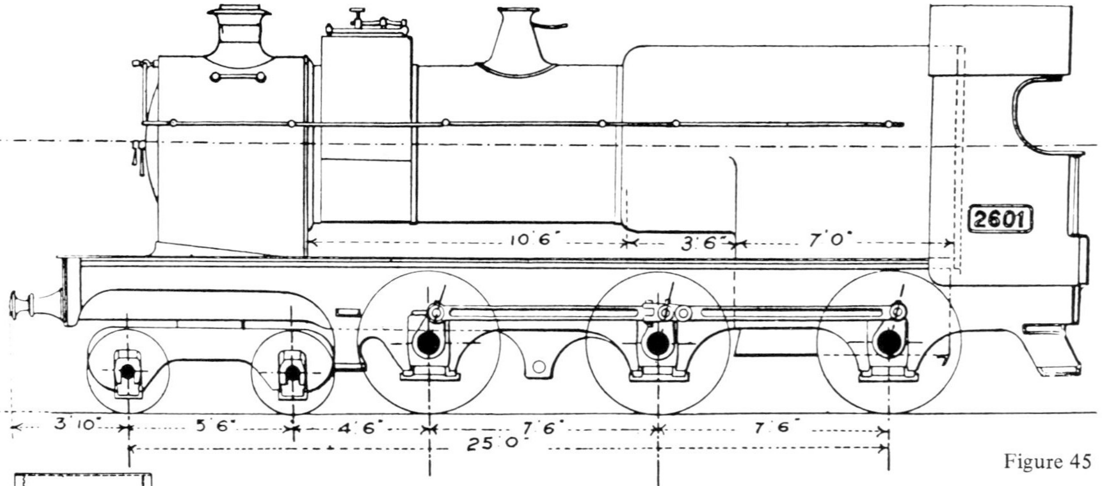

Figure 45

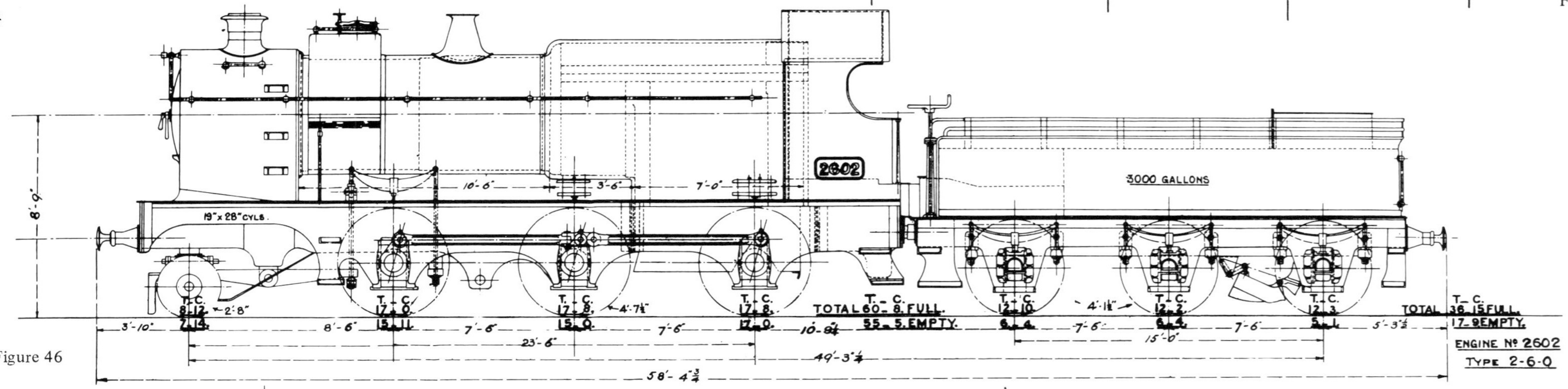

Figure 46

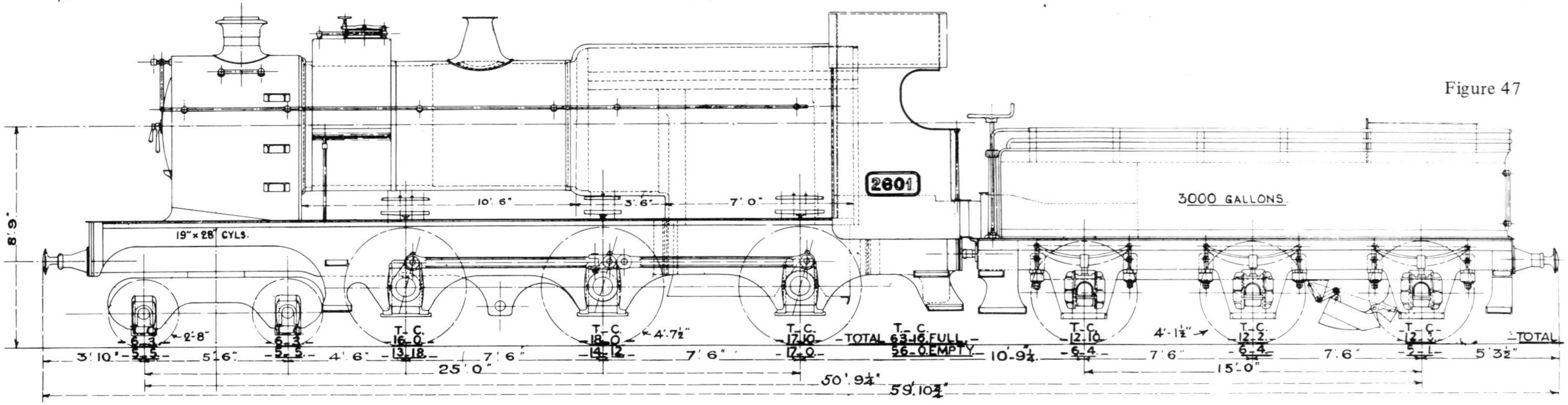

Figure 47

Figure 48

Figure 49

Figure 50

There were nine 2-6-0 'Krugers' built with the special boilers, numbering 2602-2610 and *Figure 50* shows one of these, No. 2610, just before being withdrawn. In this condition the engines only lasted a few years, all being taken out of service by January 1907. It is presumed that many parts were cannibalised for use in the 'Aberdare' class, the next series to bear the '26XX' numerical order.

The prototype engine for the 'Aberdare' series, was No. 33 which was built in 1900 and although similar in outward appearance to the 'Krugers', was a smaller and much neater design altogether. Fitted with the parallel D.0 boiler, and 18″ cylinders in place of the 19″ of the 'Kruger' class, the stroke was also reduced from 28″ to 26″. Weight and length were also reduced and resulted in the useful design seen in *Figures 48 and 49.* No. 33 eventually became 2600 in 1912 and was always slightly different from the subsequent '26XX's' in that the leading driver spring hanger was vertical, all others in the class were inclined.

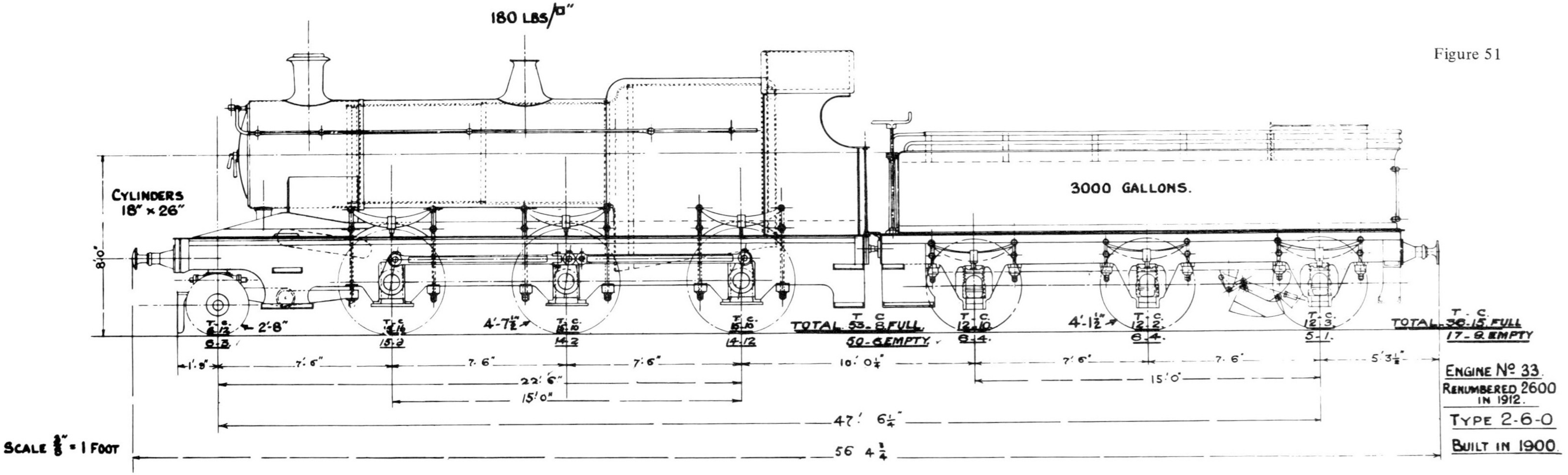

Figure 51

The two diagrams on this page show the small difference between the prototype engine No. 33 (later 2600) seen in *Figure 51,* to *'B' diagram,* and the earliest '2621-60' Class as built with the D.0 boiler to *Diagram 'C'* in *Figure 52.* This difference was in the springing of the leading drivers, the hangers being vertical in the prototype, but changed to oblique in the subsequent engines.

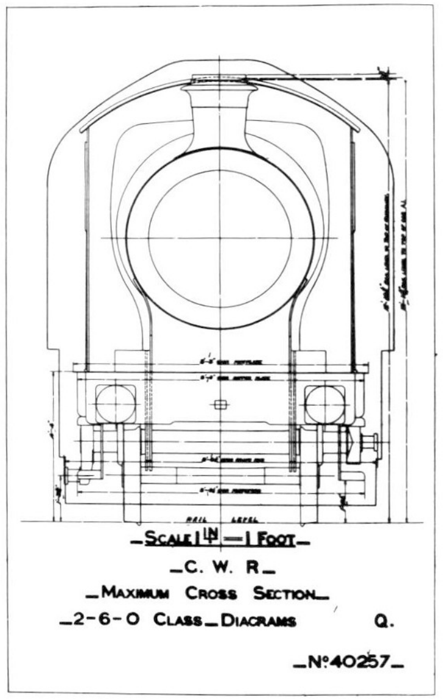

Figure 52

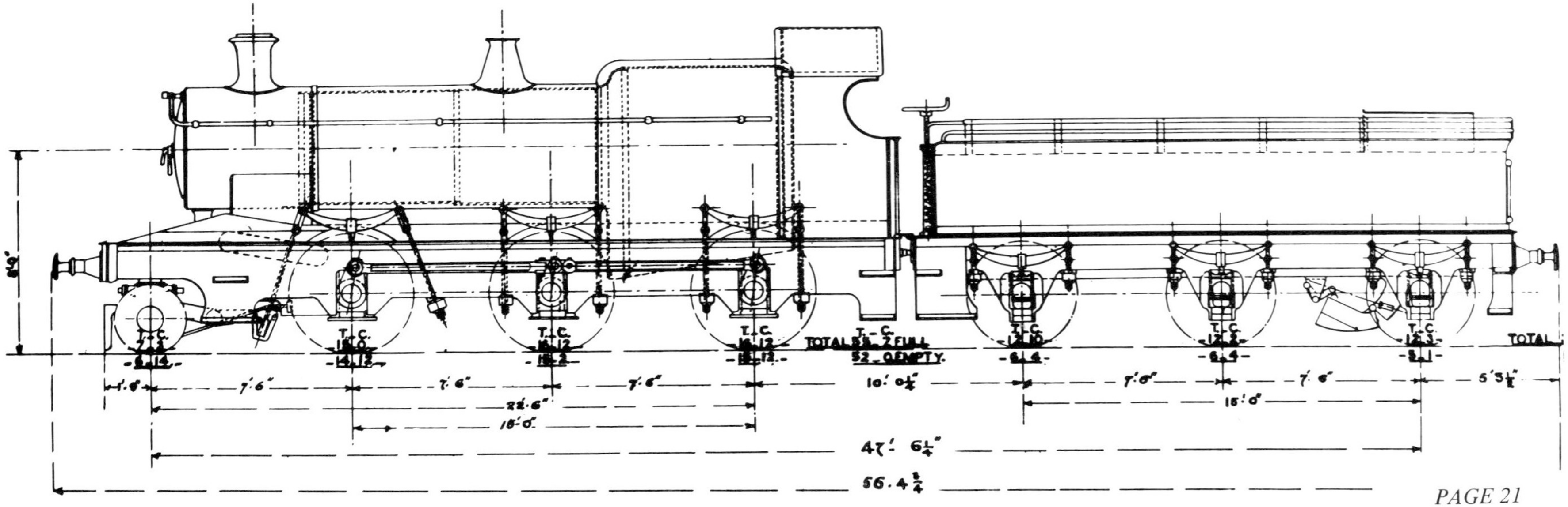

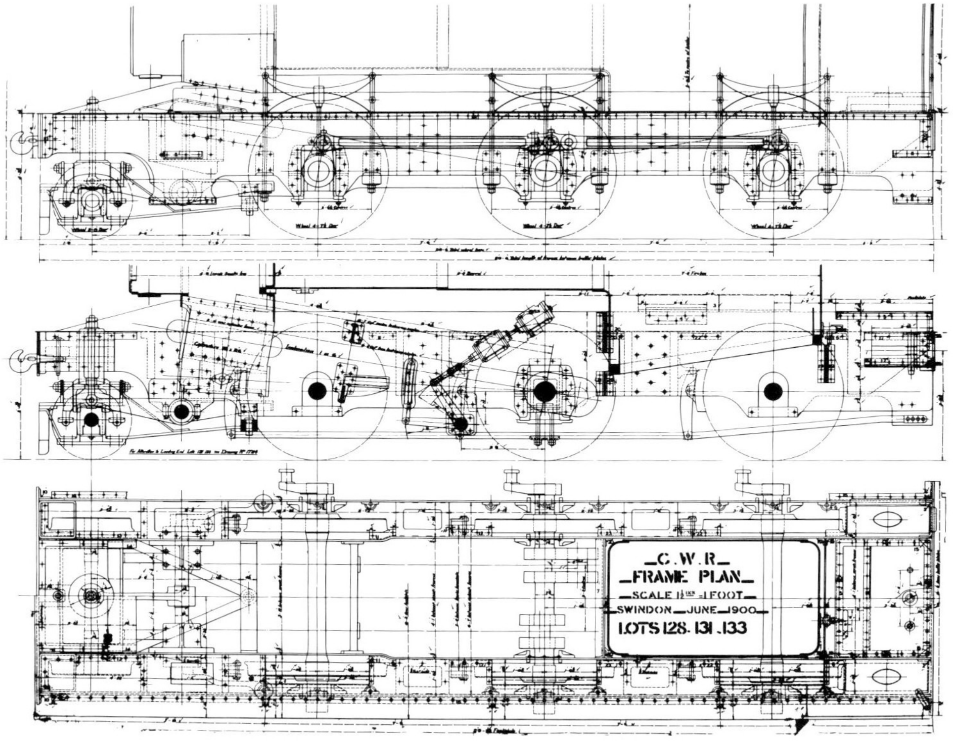

Figure 53

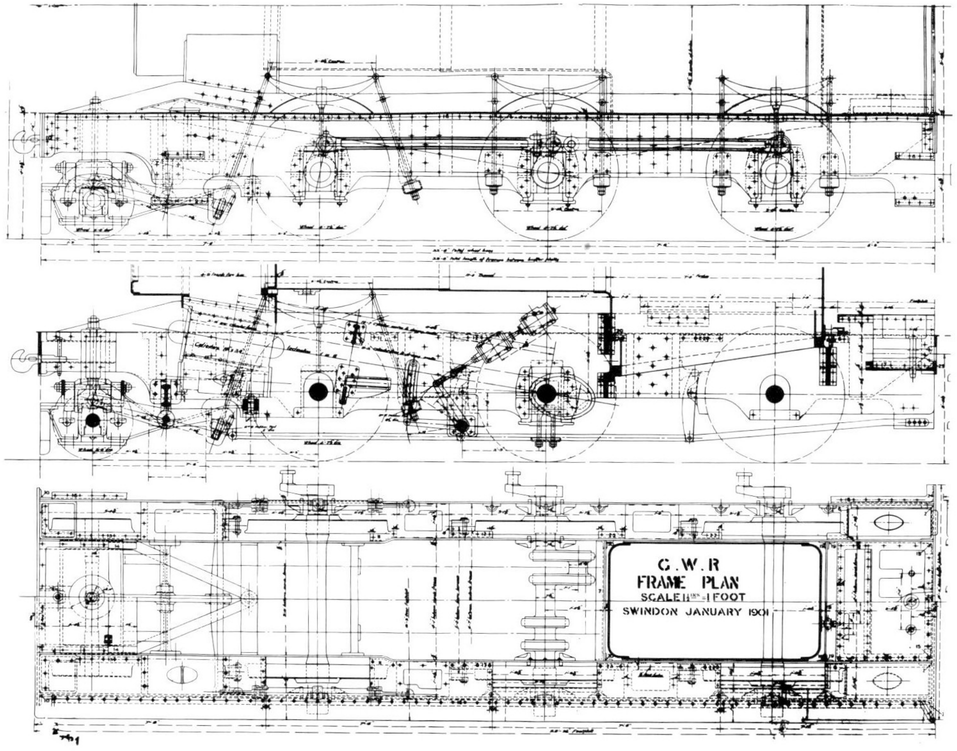

Figure 54

Two of the official 'Frame Plans' have been reduced to 4m/m scale, and are shown in *Figures 53 and 54.* To make this leading driver springing change quite clear large copies of these works drawings can be obtained from the Publishers.
Figure 55 is the official *Diagram F* of the '26XX' class and illustrates the rebuilding with the standard 4 boiler without top feed and with the standard Great Western tender.

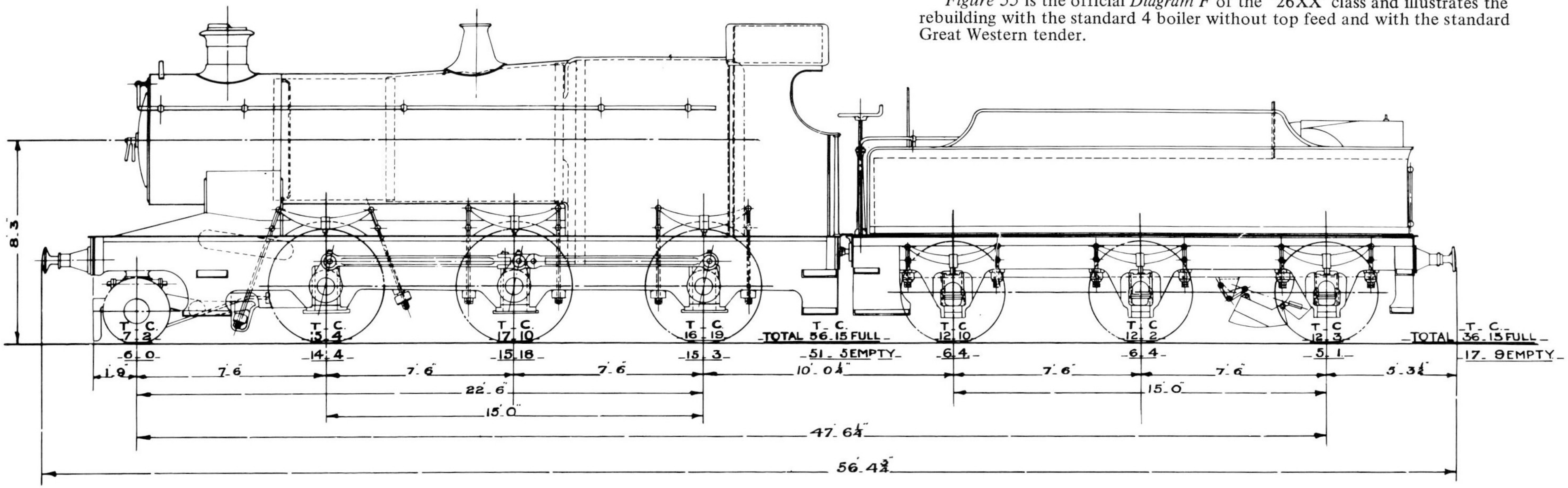

Figure 55

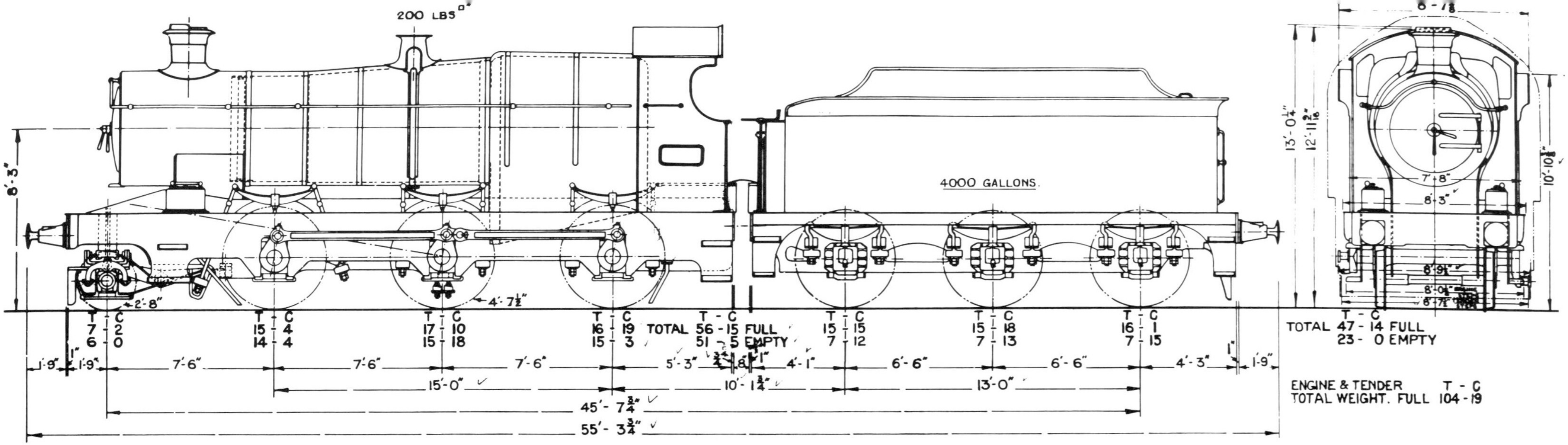

Figure 56

Figure 57

The inclination of the leading spring buckles again can be clearly seen in both the drawing and the 1912 picture of No. 2607 (*Figure 57*). This picture is of particular interest as it proves that several engines in this class were fitted with a copper topped chimney of unusual shape. It should be noted that Nos. 2602 to 2610 were built in 1906-7, the last nine to be constructed, and took over the numbers of the withdrawn 'Krugers'. It is probably of interest to note that these two illustrations all show the 26XXs each with different style tender, *Figure 56* is of *Diagram Q* showing the class as finally rebuilt with standard No. 4 boiler and coupled to the ex-R.O.D. tender.

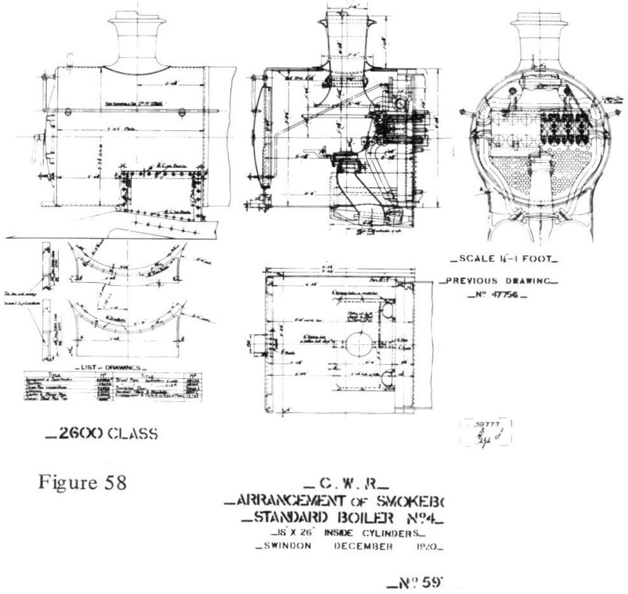

Figure 58

Figure 59

The name 'Aberdare' was given to these engines because their main duty was the hauling of coal trains from Aberdare to Swindon, and many of the class remained on this work until relieved by the heavier 2-8-0 class.

Many of the engines were fitted later in life with the large R.O.D. tenders, and it was in this condition that I knew and worked with them. Powerful engines they undoubtedly were, being classified as 'D' blue routeing, but their Achilles heel was the steam reversing gear, very easy to work, but it had a tendency to drift, so that a continual watch had to be kept on the setting. *Figure 59* features No. 2632 straight out of 'shops' after a major overhaul in 1924, and shows the small tender with the plain 'GREAT WESTERN' transfer thereon. One small point, note that the take-off cock for the steam lance is on the right hand side of the smoke-box, it was usually on the left! *Figure 58* shows the 1902 condition of No. 2659 with the scroll crest on the tender, and makes a good example of 'as built' and 'rebuild' of some twenty years later.

Figure 60

Figure 60 illustrates the 1912 condition of the 'Aberdares'. No. 2632 is seen with the garter crest on the standard 3000 gallon tender, and links up nicely with the Swindon *Diagram I* shown in *Figure 61*. However, note, the tenders are not identical, several differences can be identified.

Figure 61

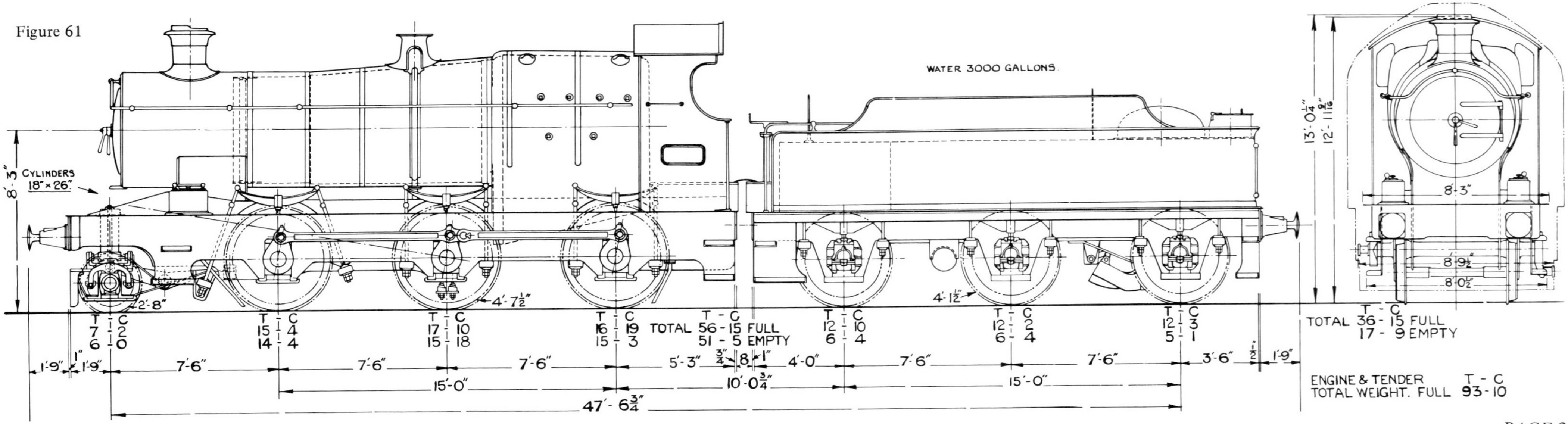

Figure 62

Finally, some close-up detail pictures of No. 2602 taken in 1933 just before the engine was withdrawn. *Figure 62* illustrates the back end of the engine and the front of the R.O.D. tender, the metal box by the footsteps contained the batteries for the A.T.C. gear. Note also, there was no water pick-up gear on these ex-G.C. Rly tenders.

Figure 64 shows the middle section of the engine, and in particular the hinged lever which passed behind the firebox clothing and was the operating gear for the reversing cylinder. *Figure 63* gives many details of the front end, including that inclined spring hanger, Dean type sandbox, and lubricator on the frame extension. What a strange mixture they were, showing influences of both Dean and Churchward.

Figure 63

Figure 64

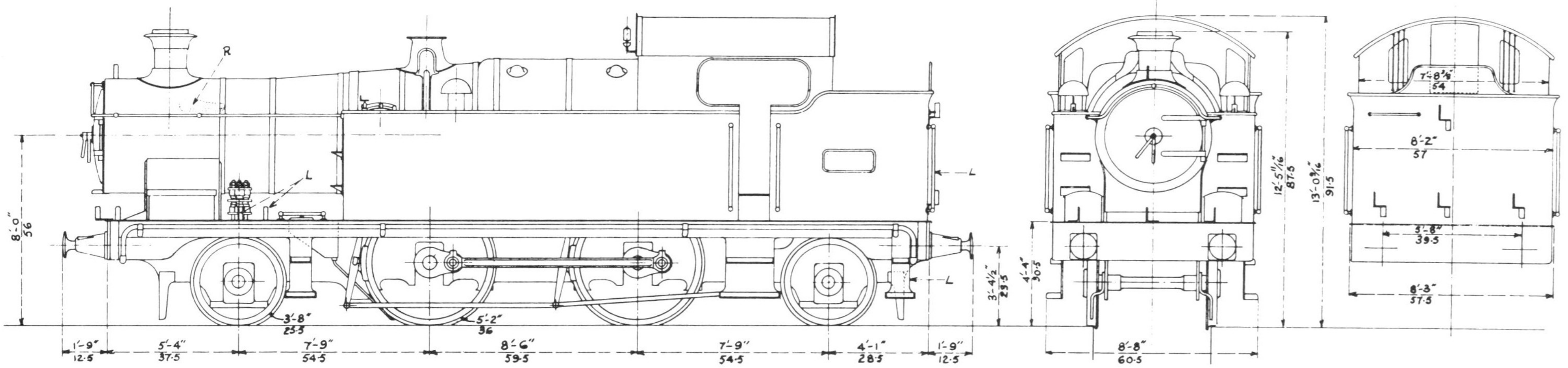

Figure 65

NOTES. Details marked "L" on left side only: those marked "R" on right side only. Wheel treads and flanges drawn to scale; allowances must be made for out-of-scale wheels. Dimensions in feet (full size), and in millimetres to nearest half-millimetre for Gauge O.

Figure 66

The year 1900 saw the advent of an unusual type of engine for the Great Western, namely a 2-4-2 tank. Only one locomotive had been constructed to this Great Western configuration before this, which was No. 13 for the standard gauge. The only other G.W. engine, apart from this series, ever to run with a four coupled wheel arrangement, plus a pair of carrying wheels fore and aft, was No. 3593, a converted 'Metro' already described in Part One (this does not take into account the absorbed engines).

The new design started with one engine, number 11, and closely resembled the Lancashire and Yorkshire Railway's Aspinall tank of that time, in having large side tanks, inside cylinders and radial axleboxes for the leading and trailing carrying wheels. A shortened version of the 'Camel' boiler was fitted with safety valve on the second ring, without a dome. Steam operated reversing gear was used, and also steam-powered water pick-up apparatus was installed, enabling the engine to pick up water in either direction.

Figure 67

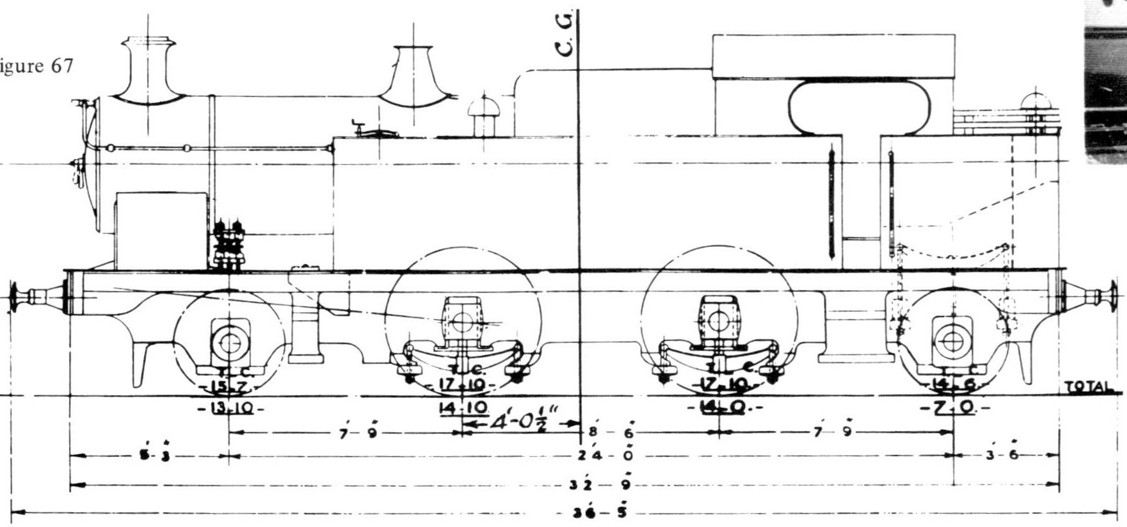

Cast iron taper chimneys were fitted originally, but copper topped design replaced these in 1907, only to be superseded again on eighteen of the class from 1923 onwards. The design proved a success, working initially on the Birmingham to Wolverhampton and Leamington Spa local trains, so that in 1902 a further twenty were ordered, and numbered 3601 to 3620. The prototype carried her number 11 until 1912, when she was brought into line with the series and renumbered 3600.

Figure 66 shows No. 3611 and the design as built in 1902, whereas the drawing by Colonel Templer shows the class later in life, fitted with D.3 boiler and superheated, plus the curved-sided bunker and minus the round spectacle windows. The official *Diagram A* in *Figure 67*, is No. 11 (later No. 3600) as built in 1900 with the D.0 boiler, the actual prototype of the class.

These two pictures illustrate the '36XX' class as built. The photographs are dated April 1902 and it is possible to see that the livery was still that of green topsides and Indian red for the framing. Modellers should note that the early engines had several points of difference to those of later date. For instance, the engine's main design was for running backward as easily as forwards, and with this in mind large rear windows were fitted into the high steeple cab and a sliding shutter was installed in the roof. It was on account of this huge arched cab that these engines became known as 'Birdcages'!

Figure 68

The prototype No. 11, whilst picking up water at Rowington, did so with such violence as to split the sidetanks open like a sardine can! This led to the fitting of much bigger mushroom vents, not only in the side tanks but also in the bunker. After approximately five years in service, the steam operated pick-up gear was altered to hand crank, and round about 1921 the scoops were removed altogether, which meant small vents reappearing on the water tanks.

Figure 69

Figure 70

Figure 71

As can be seen in *Figures 70 and 71* all the class were eventually superheated and were fitted with the taper D.3 boiler with top feed. They also received the distinctive built up chimney, which was always so reminiscent of the later 56XX class. Trouble was also experienced with coal breaking the bunker windows, so that these were reduced in size, and had bars fitted on the outside.

It should also be noted that the leading wheels were fitted with volute springs, whilst the trailing pair used the leaf type. The official *Diagram G* from Swindon covers the first batch. The last ten 3621-30 built in 1903 were covered later by *Diagram H.* The small sketch shows the large vent fitting in the bunker. All were withdrawn by 1934.

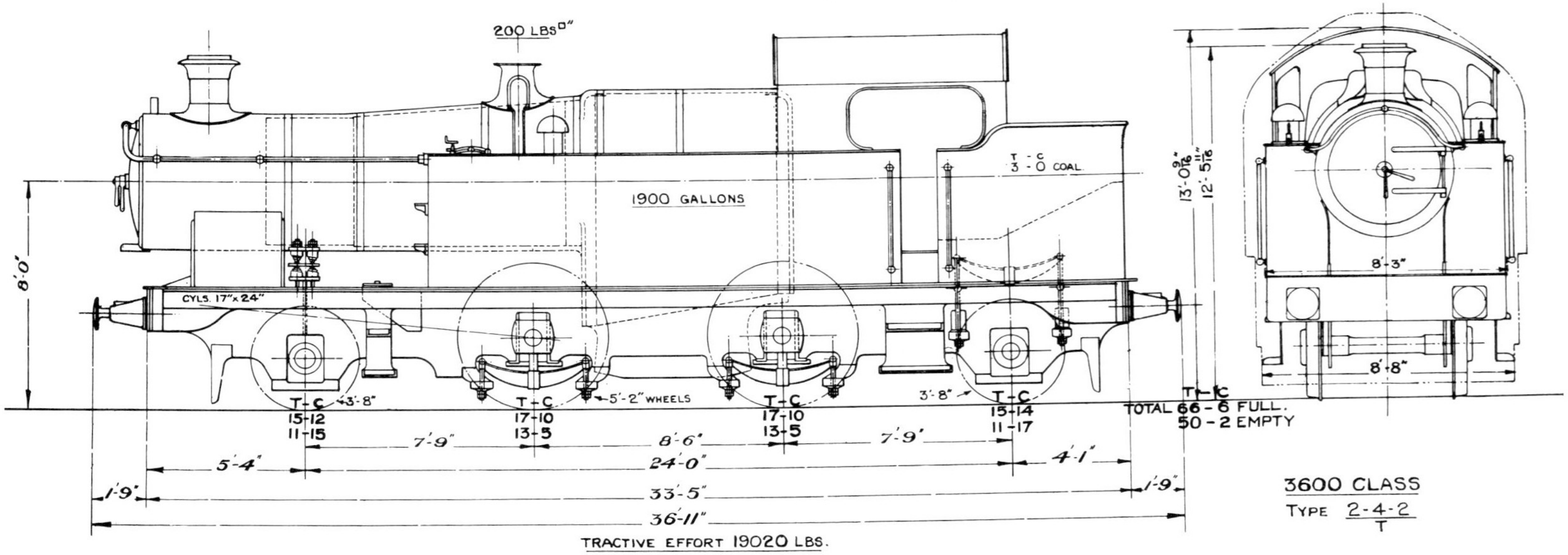

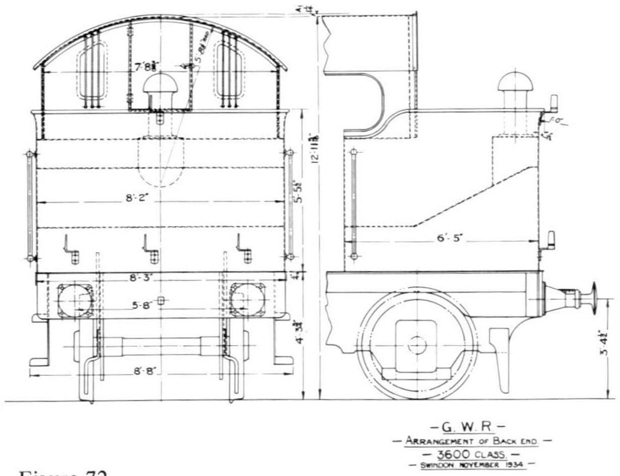

Figure 72

Figure 73

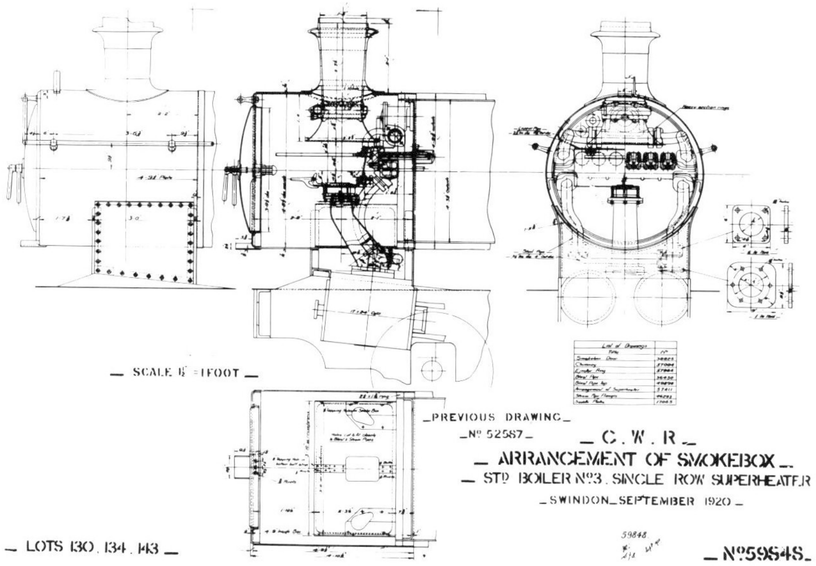

Figure 73A

Two pictures of the '3600' class feature here. *Figure 73* gives a full frontal view of No. 3603 seen at Tyseley lifting shop in 1930. The two large frontal tool boxes can be seen on the running plate, as can the high smokebox saddle. In *Figure 73A* No. 3629 can be seen at Leamington Spa in 1910. Note that the engine still has the smokebox damper steam cylinder on the right-hand side of the smokebox.

Figure 73B

The first engine to carry outside cylinders on the Great Western was the Churchward designed express engine No. 100. This 4-6-0 express design came out of Swindon shops in February of 1902 just a few months before the retirement of William Dean.

The whole layout of this stark machine broke new ground, in fact the outline of the engine was very similar to American practice of that time, with the long boiler, exposed wheels, outside cylinders with inside valves worked with Stephenson link motion. The bogie frames were of the American bar-frame type and the smokebox was carried on a saddle. Piston valves with double ports were operated indirectly and differently to later engines. The piston stroke was also unusual in having a 30 inch length and the big ends were the first to have the solid eye design. All of this meant that Churchward, upon assuming command at Swindon, had produced his prototype engine, from which standardization and indeed locomotive design on the Great Western followed slavishly from here on. *Figure 74* shows the engine as built in 1902 with an accompanying drawing in *Figure 75.* In June of the same year No. 100 was named *Dean* which was changed in November to *William Dean* on a curved plate around the leading splasher (see *Figure 73B*). In 1904, standard nameplates were fitted but still on the leading splasher, as in *Figure 76,* and finally in 1906 the plates were moved to the driving splashers, which set the pattern for all others.

The drawing in *Figure 75* is the only one I have been able to find of No. 100 in her original condition, but it does at least give the leading dimensions and is reproduced here to 4m/m scale.

Figure 74

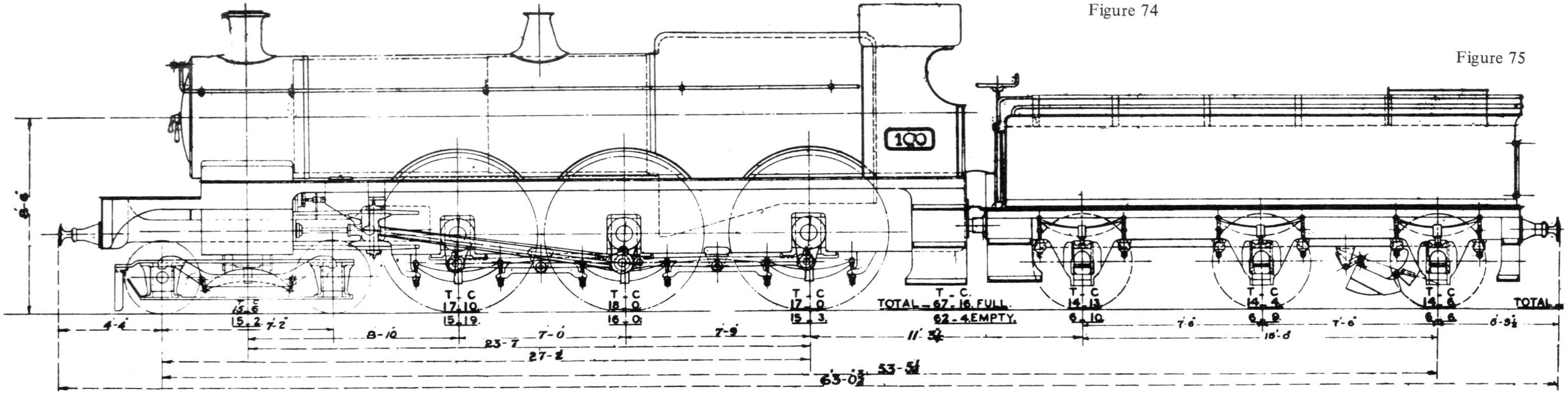

Figure 75

Two early official drawings from the Swindon diagram book which serve to illustrate these prototype 4-6-0 engines of Churchward.

In *Figure 77* the first engine No. 100 is seen when renumbered '2900' and rebuilt with Swindon No. 3 superheater. This drawing links up with the photograph on Page 33, *Figure 80.* The diagram is *'P'.*

The other diagram is *'D'* and shows No. 98 as built originally, a photograph of which can be seen on Page 34 in *Figure 82.*

Figure 76

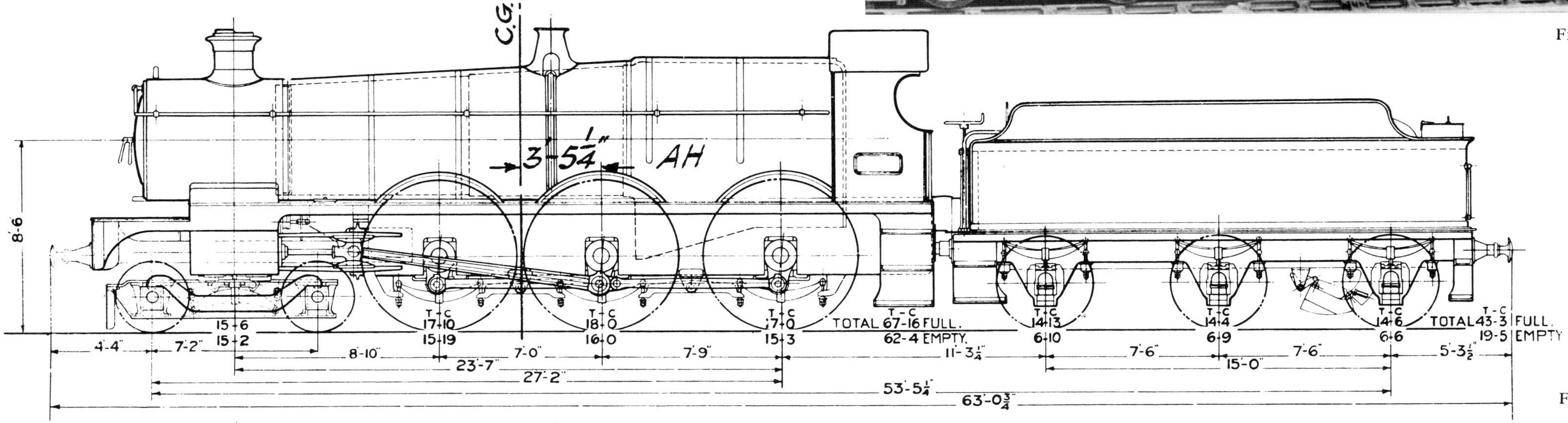

Figure 77

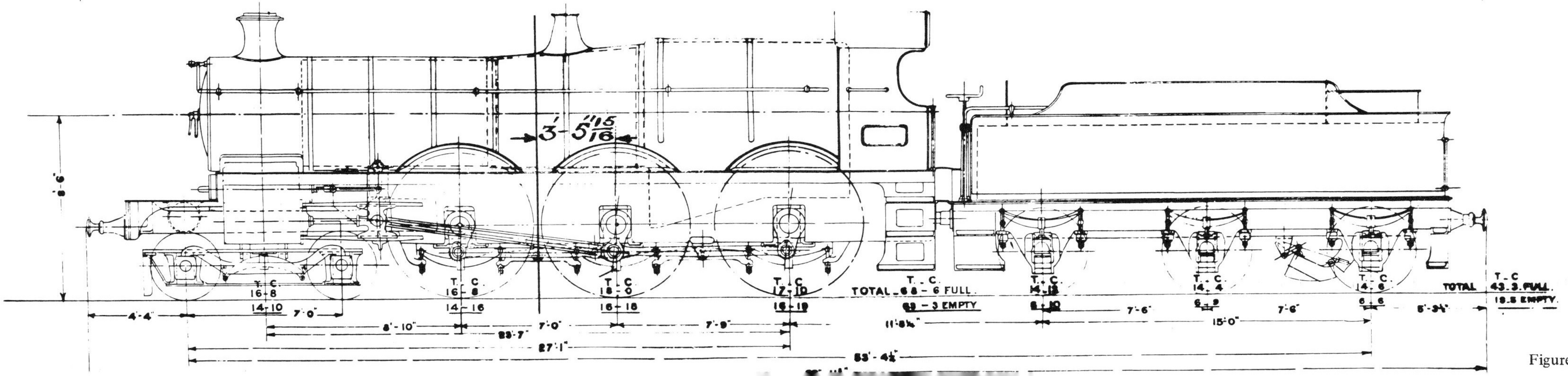

Figure 78

Figure 79

William Dean (seen above) was of course the predecessor of that long line of distinguished engines, the 'Saints', to my mind as a practical railwayman, the finest express engines ever produced by the Great Western. The 'Stars', 'Castles', 'Kings' and 'Counties' were after all, only derivations and enlargements of this, the original design, and that they all stemmed from this original Churchward prototype can be seen clearly on this page.

Figure 80 illustrates No. 100, in 1921, after being fitted with top feed, long coned boiler, and 3,500 gallon tender. She was renumbered into the 'Saint' class at the end of 1912 and became 2900, but could always be identified by the non-standard cylinder cover.

This class of engine was always subject to experimentation as will be illustrated in the next few pages, and one such was *Viscount Churchill* originally No. 175, which was renamed and renumbered *Sir Ernest Palmer* No. 2975 in 1924 (*Figure 79*). This machine was equipped with extended valve spindles and the guides were housed in protruding cylindrical covers which can be seen under each side of the smokebox. No. 2975 ran until 1944, before being withdrawn, whereas *William Dean* went to scrap in 1932.

Figure 80

Returning to 1903, the second express 4-6-0 engine was No. 98, which came out of shops in March of that year. She was really the first one hundred per cent Churchward standard locomotive with all the characteristics enthusiasts have come to know and admire over the past seventy years! *Figure 82* is the official photograph of this machine at her first steam trials. The front end differed from No. 100 in that the two cylinders were cast complete with half of the smokebox saddle, so that when bolted together the whole unit formed a very strong structure, to which the frame extension could be affixed. Large piston valves of 10″ diameter were fitted, with 18″ diameter cylinders, which had the long stroke of 30″. In order to avoid any possibility of fouling the low narrow part of the loading gauge, the centre line of the cylinders was 2½″ above that of the driving wheel centres.

Two other engines were designed at the same time as No. 98, namely No. 97, the forerunner of the 2800 class, and No. 99, the first of the long line of 2-6-2 side tanks for mixed traffic. All three engines had the same standard features, and the cylinders set the 2½″ above the axle centre line.

No. 2803 illustrated in *Figure 81* is placed here, to show the great similarity between the two engines, although the prototype No. 97 can be seen on Page 35, in diagram form.

Figure 81

Figure 82

Returning to No. 98, this engine ran un-named for four years and then received plates showing the name *Vanguard,* but after only nine months she was renamed *Ernest Cunard* as shown in *Figure 83*. When the class was finally renumbered into the 2900 series *Ernest Cunard* became 2998, and survived until 1933.

Figure 83

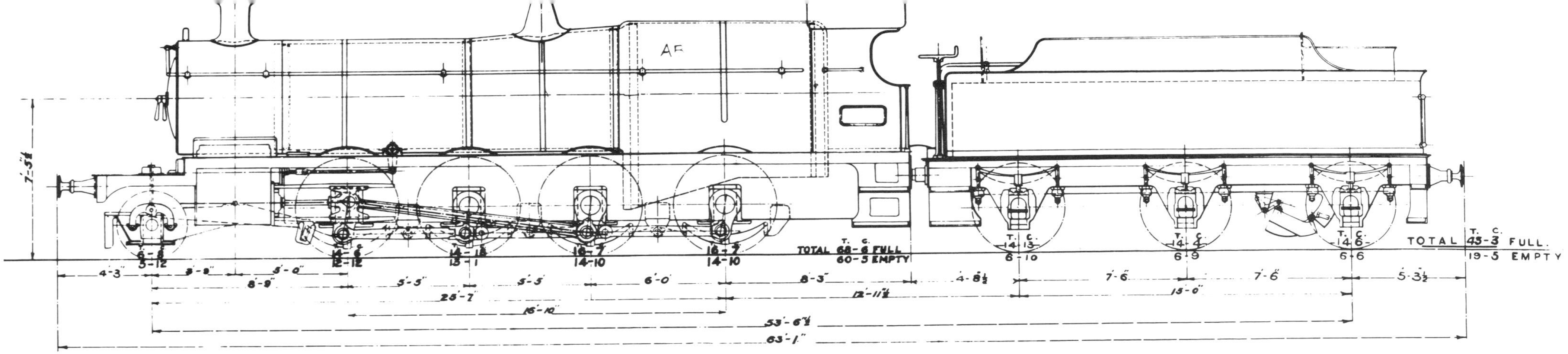

Figure 84

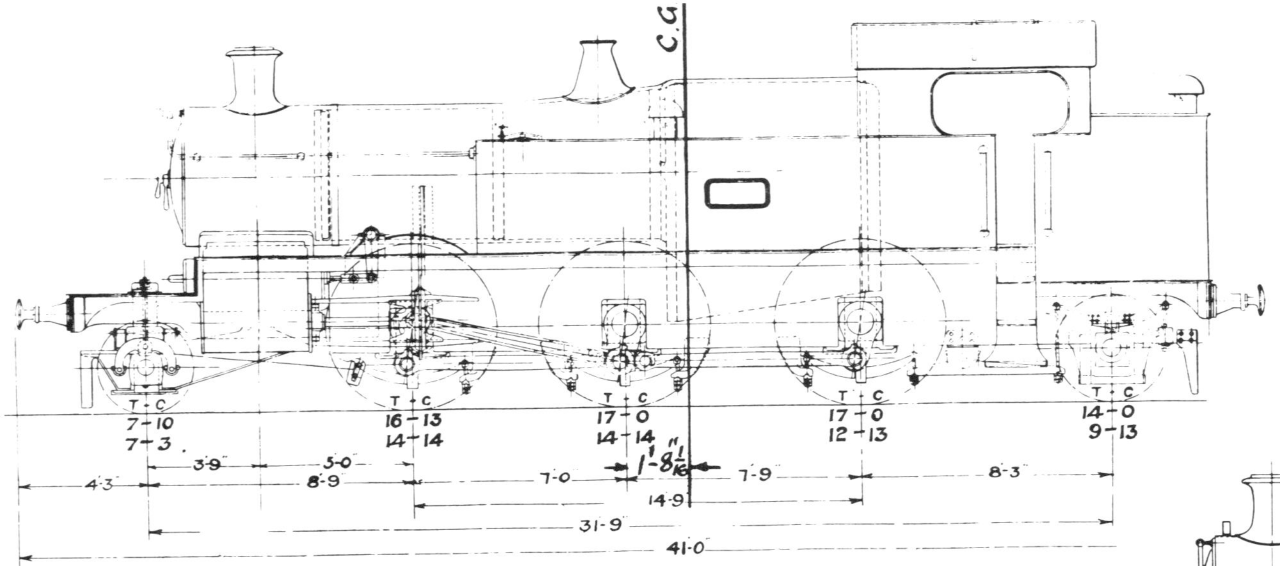

Figure 85

Gathered together on this page are three of the early diagrams of the prototype 'Standard' classes. At the head of the page is *Diagram A* of *Lot 139.* This was the original engine No. 97 (later 2800) shown as built under *Lot 139* with 18″ cylinders, D.2 low pitched boiler, non-superheated, and with non top feed of course.

Figure 86 is *Diagram C* of the small-wheeled branch tank type, of which No. 115 was the first. At first the rest were numbered 3101-10, but later they became 4400-10. The drawing shows the engine as built, and complements the picture in *Figure 90.* Lot numbers were *144 and 147.*

The middle drawing is of the first large-wheeled 2-6-2T to be built, No. 99 which is to *Diagram A.* This original drawing links with *Figure 88* on page 36.

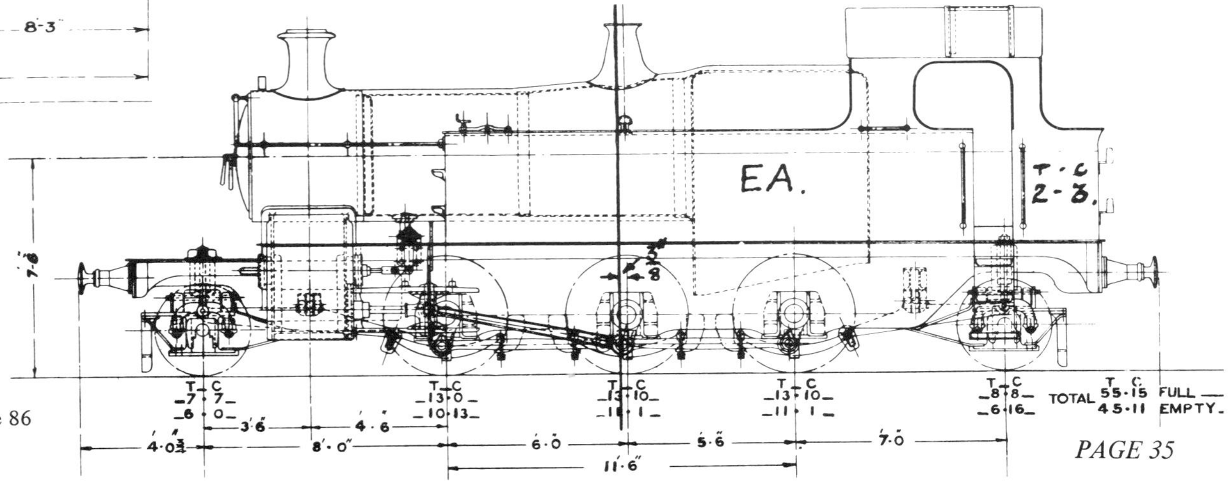

Figure 86

As briefly referred to on the previous page, one of the three prototype standard engines built by Churchward in 1903 was the 2-6-2 side tank version No. 99, which is illustrated in the photograph (*Figure 88*). The practice at Swindon was to give these prototypes a full trial, extending over several years and then, if they proved successful, to proceed with the building of a series. So it was with the large 'Prairie' tanks. No. 99 ran for two years as the lone example, showed the soundness of the design, and was followed in 1905/6 by thirty-nine others, and in the years 1906 to 1908 a further forty-one engines were built with larger boilers and were numbered as '3150' class. No. 99 formed the nucleus of the '3100' class which was eventually changed to '5100's in 1929.

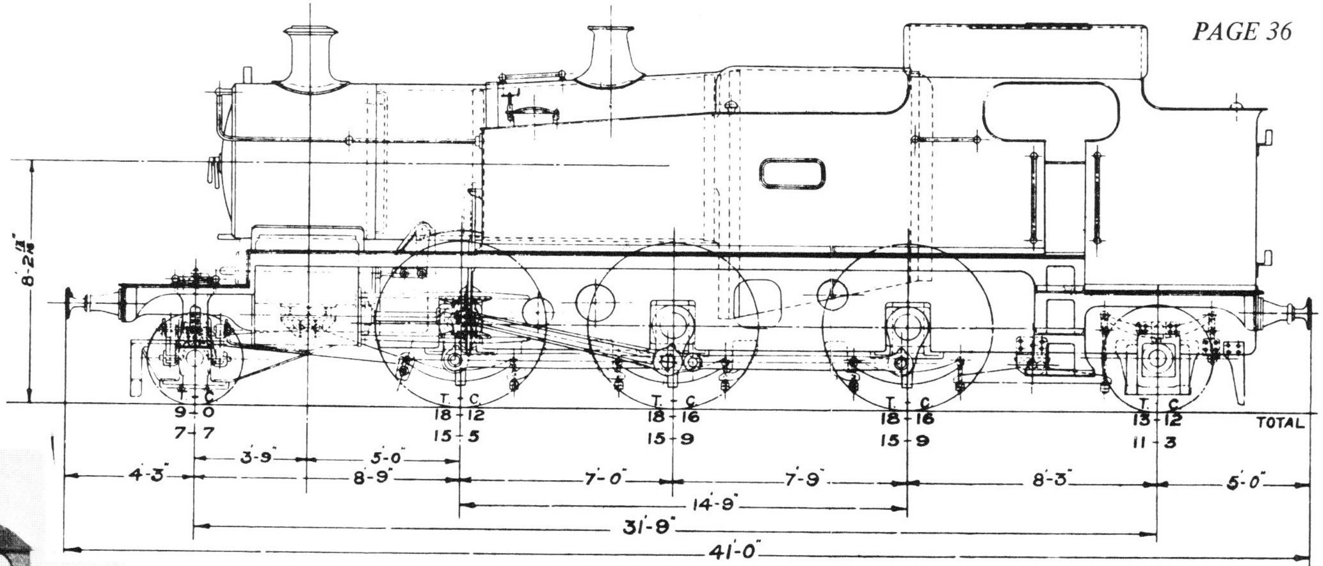

Figure 87

The smaller-boilered series were numbered from 3111 to 3149, and from these original engines the 2-6-2 side tanks with large wheels went on and on, right up to 1949, when a total of 290 locomotives had been constructed. The class numbering was changed in the 1928/29 period and became the well-known 4100's, 5100's and 6100's, about which further details can be seen on page 198.

Figure 88

Figure 89 illustrates the 1905, '31XX' class as fitted with the two-way water pick-up gear, and the taper boiler. Note the position of the tool boxes over the cylinders, later changed to inside the cab, when the water scoop arrangement was dispensed with. Also at this date no strengthening struts were fixed to the front buffer beam, as these came later in 1909. The drawing in *Figure 87* is of the '3150' class which was practically identical to the early '3100' series, with the exception of having a boiler of 4′ 10¾″–5′ 6″ diameter in the place of the smaller 4′ 5⅛″–5′ 0½″.

The *Diagram H* shows several structural differences i.e. the height of the cab front plate, and its side apertures.

Figure 89

A natural follow-on to the large Prairie tanks just described, was the series of smaller 2-6-2T's known to present day enthusiasts as 44XX's and 45XX's. The whole fleet of these attractive little engines began as usual with one prototype, namely No. 115, built in 1904 by Churchward, as a scaled down version of No. 99. She was an immediate success, proving her worth over the hilly branch lines in the West Country and Wales, so much so in fact that only one year after being built, a further ten were ordered on a Swindon Lot number (147), but were actually built at Wolverhampton.

The class became 3101-10 in numbering, which was eventually changed to 4401-10, and No. 115 the prototype engine became 4400.

Figure 90

The logical sequence to these ten small-wheeled Prairies built at Wolverhampton between 1905-1906 was a similar class, but with slightly larger driving wheels, namely 4′ 1½″. This made a very effective and efficient little machine for branch line work, and so the well-known '4500's came into being. Originally numbered 2161 to 2190, the first twenty were constructed at Wolverhampton but all the rest were built at Swindon factory, the last, No. 5574, being turned out in 1929! These small 2-6-2T's were renumbered into the 45XX class in 1912 and ran on into the 55XX series. *Figure 90* shows the original No. 115 prototype of the class, whilst *Figure 91* illustrates one of the early larger-wheeled variety of No. 2164 which eventually became 4503. More details of the 45XX class will be found on Pages 141-146 as development took place.

Figure 91

Figure 92

Always alive to the locomotive development in other countries, Churchward in early 1903 noticed records of particularly good work being performed in France by the De Glehn 4-cylinder compounds, and so the C.M.E. persuaded the Board to purchase one of these engines for comparative trials on the Great Western Railway.

La France was taken into stock in October 1903 and allotted the number 102. She first started her trials on the 11th October after being fitted with various equipment to allow her to run on the Great Western.

The importation of *La France* to England and in particular to Swindon, had a marked effect on the locomotive designs of the Churchward engines which lasted up to, and beyond Nationalization. Much has been written about the impact these Compounds made, and one of the best sources is O.S. Nock's book, *Stars, Castles & Kings, Part I.* Suffice it to say here that the main object of the exercise was to hold comparative trials between a 4-cylinder compound of 4-4-2 wheel arrangement, and a 4-6-0 express locomotive worked as a high pressure simple engine. The divided drive, balanced motion, with fluted connecting rods, double slide bars, and the De Glehn bogie, were all bonuses, of which Churchward took full advantage. *Figure 92* shows the engine as first running at Bristol Temple Meads and in the original livery of black, with red and white lining. In the lower photograph No. 102 is seen painted in the green and indian red style of the later period, and fitted with standard top feed and larger tender.

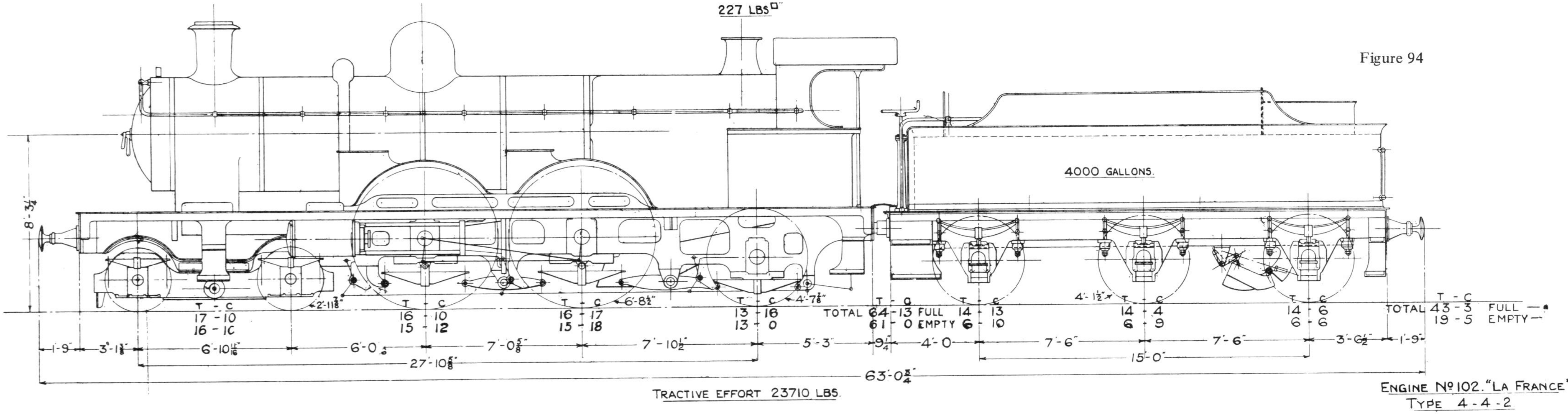

Figure 94

For those enthusiasts who feel tempted to model the French engines, this page shows the original design of No. 102. *Figure 94* is the official drawing from Swindon to *Diagram A* which shows the engine as built, whereas *Figure 95* illustrates the Churchward version of a 2-cylinder simple 4-4-2 express engine, with which the locomotive department ran comparative trials. This is *Daigram B* of *Lot 154* which shows the 'Atlantic' as first built. Numbers ran from 171 to 190 (*see later pages*).

The main difficulty in constructing a model of the Frenchmen in 4m/m scale is the very fine motion and valve gear fitted, even Churchward himself remarked that it was 'watchmaker's work'! Also the driving wheels, like the Great Northern Railway's 'Atlantics' were placed so close together, as to make it almost impossible to get the fingers between the two separate flanges! Try translating this to 4m/m scale. Nevertheless, these engines do make interesting models and perhaps one day some enterprising firm will produce a good kit.

It would perhaps be worth adding that the large pipe encircling the boiler just ahead of the dome was not the top feed as later, but the steam supply to the outside high pressure cylinders.

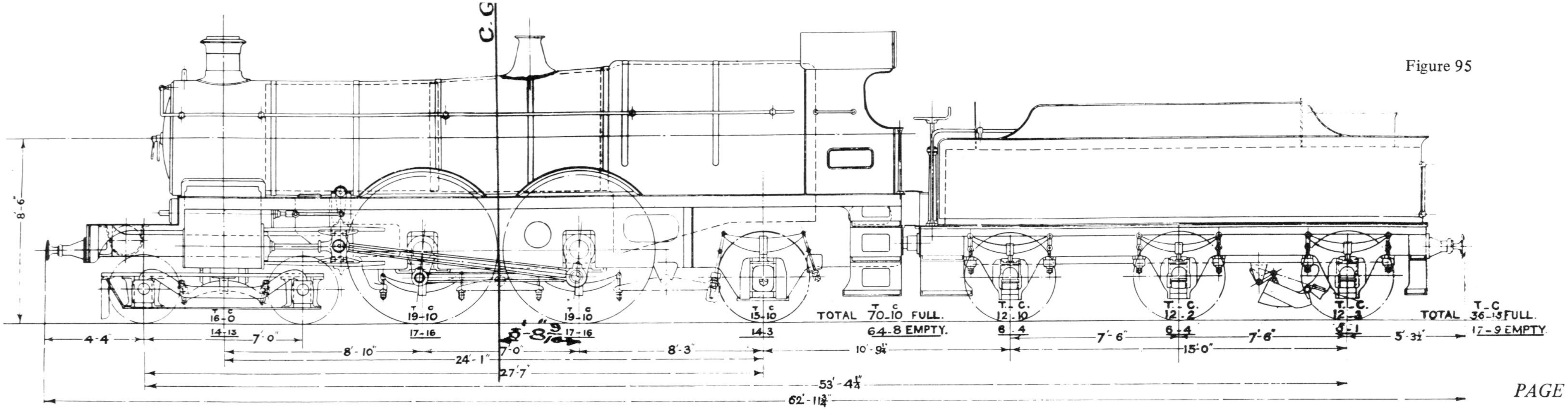

Figure 95

Figure 96

The Great Western Railway always seemed to have a knack of making just the right gesture on any important occasion, and so it was with the Churchward's engine which was used as a comparison against *La France.* No. 171 was built in December of 1903 as a 4-6-0 similar to No. 98, but with a boiler pressure of 225 lbs. and *Figure 97* shows her in this condition and given the appropriate name of *Albion* in February 1904. The locomotive ran in this condition for nine months, and then, being chosen by the C.M.E. to act as a representative for the simple type of engine against the compound design of De Glehn, and to achieve a more balanced comparison, No. 171 was altered to the 4-4-2 classification. This was achieved by simply removing the trailing drivers and substituting in their place a pair of 4′ 1½″ carrying wheels with outside axleboxes located on an extended subframe, riveted on to the main frame.

Figure 96 illustrates *Albion* running as an 'Atlantic' which she continued to do until July of 1907. One odd phase was from March 1907 until July of the same year, when she was re-converted back to a 4-6-0. During this period, for some unknown reason, she was named *The Pirate,* and it is in this unusual guise that I have made my model of No. 171. If any reader knows of a photograph of this engine running as *The Pirate,* I would be very grateful to learn of the whereabouts, if only to check the authenticity of my small miniature. *Albion* as later numbered 2971, was shedded in her last days at Banbury, and I knew her well, with that curious small close fitting nameplate. She was finally sent to scrap in 1946. Note in the photo in *Figure 96* that *Albion* was the only 'Atlantic' to have upright spring hangers on the trailing wheels under the cab. The diagram in *Figure 98* is the official '*F*' of the 'Atlantics' built after *Albion.*

Figure 97

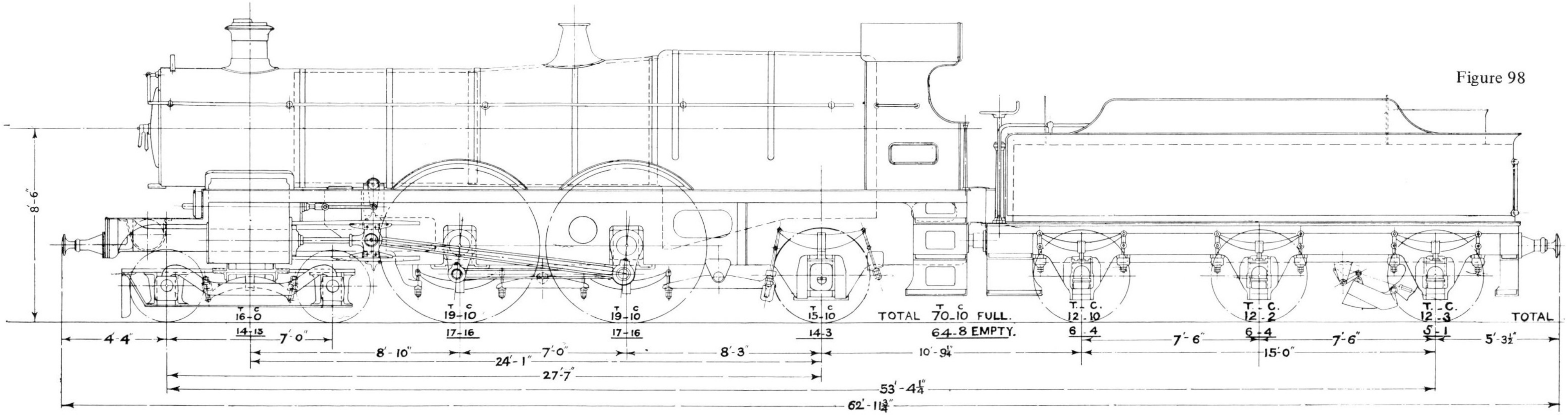

Figure 98

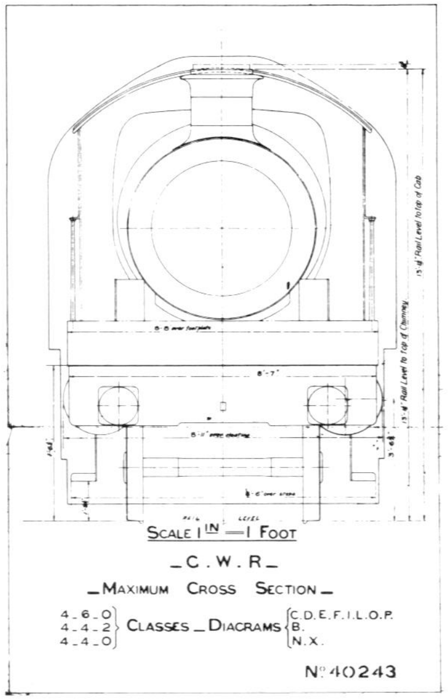

Figure 99

Five months after *Albion* was altered to the 4-4-2 arrangement, Churchward authorised thirteen more 'Atlantics' to be built, most of which were given names from the Waverley novels of Scott. Nine of the names had previously been borne by the 4-4-0 broad gauge engines ordered by Gooch, which might explain the brief naming of *The Pirate.* Also, several of these engines had their names changed over the years. One, however, who carried her name throughout without any alteration, was No. 181, *Ivanhoe* seen, as built, in *Figure 99.* She was constructed in June of 1905, ran for two years unnamed, and then received her plates in 1907 which she retained until being withdrawn in 1951. The works photograph shows *Ivanhoe* as she appeared in 1907, still unsuperheated but with nameplates and in undercoat livery for photographic records. The engine was superheated in 1910 whilst still an 'Atlantic', and the official drawing in *Figure 98* gives all the salient measurements, the only difference between *B* and *F* diagrams being the length of the smokebox, and shape of chimney. Note at this date the framing still had the square ends which as altered in the case of *Albion* to the more gracious curved style in July of 1912. *Figure 100* shows the '29XX' class under *Diagram E* which was the superheated 4-6-0 version of the series when converted.

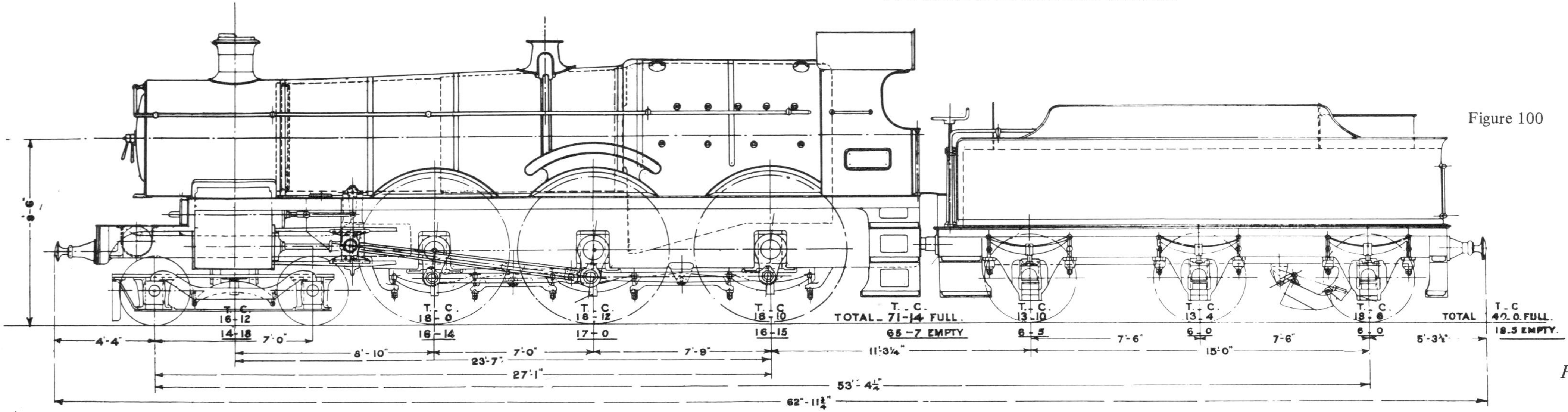

Figure 100

At the same time as the 'Atlantics' were running, several identical engines in the series were outshopped as 4-6-0's, and always remained as such. These were Nos. 173 to 178 inclusive, amongst them being No. 175. She was built in 1905, named *Viscount Churchill* in 1907, superheated in 1911, renamed *Sir Ernest Palmer* in 1924, and finally became *Lord Palmer* in 1933, which name she carried until withdrawal in 1944. (*Figure 102*)

Figure 101

Figure 102

Figure 101 illustrates No. 190 as built in 1905, and gives good comparison with the 4-6-0 No. 175 in the lower picture. No. 190 was named *Waverley* in 1906, was converted to a 4-6-0 in 1912, and ran on until 1939 before being withdrawn. Modellers should note that all the 'Atlantics' with the exception of No. 171 had sloping spring shackles and anchorages on the trailing carrying wheels under the firebox. *Albion's* were straight up and down, also these engines started life with the long lever and quadrant reversing gear, but were later fitted with screw-crank type which gave finer valve setting and was much easier in handling than the huge heavy lever.

Figure 103

At the risk of boring repetition, I am enclosing as many pictures as possible of the 'Scott' class 'Atlantics', because they do not seem to have received their full share of publicity in the past, and this seems a good opportunity to rectify this.

Figure 104

Figures 104 and 105 show No. 179 from the rear and front end respectively, both pictures illustrating the left-hand side and the early condition of the engine. Notice that the nameplates are of the same pattern as those of *Albion,* namely, small and close-fitting on to the splasher. These plates were only carried for two years, 1905 to 1907, the engine being renamed *Quentin Durward* in 1907. *Magnet* or rather 2979 *Quentin Durward,* was altered to a 4-6-0 in August 1912 and lasted until 1951 before being scrapped.

Figure 103 illustrates No. 182. As built to the 4-4-2 configuration, and unnamed, she received plates in 1906 as *Lalla Rookh,* and was re-built as a 4-6-0 in 1912.

Figure 105

This last page of the 'Scott' class illustrates the three different phases the series went through as time passed. *Figure 106* shows No. 185 at that time named *Winterstoke* (later *Peveril of the Peak*) and as built in 1905. *Figure 107* is of No. 188 'Rob Roy' at Old Oak Common in 1910, after being fitted with superheater and larger chimney. Finally in the lower photograph we see *Red Gauntlet* No. 183 in 1912, just after being altered to a 4-6-0 engine, and with the more gracious dropped curves to the framing in place of the stark right-angles. This engine had the name made into one word *Redgauntlet* in 1915, and ran until 1946. Hoping readers will find these engines as interesting as I do, I am adding a list of names and numbers of this series showing the various changes over the years:–

Figure 106

Figure 107

No. 171 built 1903 named *Albion* 1904 renamed *The Pirate* 1907. *Albion* restored 7/07
No. 172 built 1905 named *Quicksilver* renamed *The Abbot* in 1907
No. 179 built 1905 named *Magnet* renamed *Quentin Durward* in 1907
No. 180 built 1905 unnamed. Named *Coeur de Lion* in 1907
No. 181 built 1905 unnamed. Named *Ivanhoe* in 1907
No. 182 built 1905 unnamed. Named *Lalla Rookh* in 1906
No. 183 built 1905 unnamed. Named *Red Gauntlet* in 1906, altered to *Redgauntlet* in 1915
No. 184 named *Churchill* altered to *Viscount Churchill* in 1906, renamed *Guy Mannering* in 1907
No. 185 unnamed in 1905, named *Winterstoke* in 1906, renamed *Peveril of the Peak* in 1907
No. 186 unnamed in 1905, named *Robin Hood* in 1906
No. 187 named *Robertson* in 1905, renamed in 1907 *Bride of Lammermoor*
No. 188 unnamed in 1905, named in 1907 *Rob Roy*
No. 189 unnamed in 1905, named in 1906 *Talisman*
No. 190 unnamed in 1905, named in 1906 *Waverley*

Figure 108

Figure 109

After this Scott series of 4-4-2 express engines, there were only three more 'Atlantic' class locomotives with tenders used on the Great Western, namely two more French engines and the famous 4-cylinder *North Star.*

Historians have always pondered over just why Churchward ordered two more De Glehns, as, although these engines were slightly larger than the initial '102' the only apparent reason for having two more compound locomotives on the stock was possibly to get greater experience and so widen comparisons with the Scott 'Atlantics'. In any event 1905 saw the importation of Nos. 103 and 104, which were named *President* and *Alliance* respectively in 1907.

Figure 110

The main differences externally between No. 102 and her two sisters was that the cab had side windows and a greater arc to the roof. Also the larger engines had bogies with inside frames, against those of No. 102 which were of the outside type.

Again, as this book does not set out to be technical, let it suffice to state that these trials between the compound engines of the Nord & Paris-Orleans railways of France and the high pressure simples from Swindon resulted in the fact that no economy was proved for the more complicated engines, and so from hence forward all Great Western locomotives were of the simple design. Nevertheless many features of the French machines were adopted, as will be shown later.

These three photographs show, at the top, No. 102 as built in 1903, in the centre No. 104 as received in 1905, and in the lower illustration No. 103 in 1914, generally 'Westernized' with copper topped chimney, Swindon boiler and fittings, and larger tender.

Figure 111

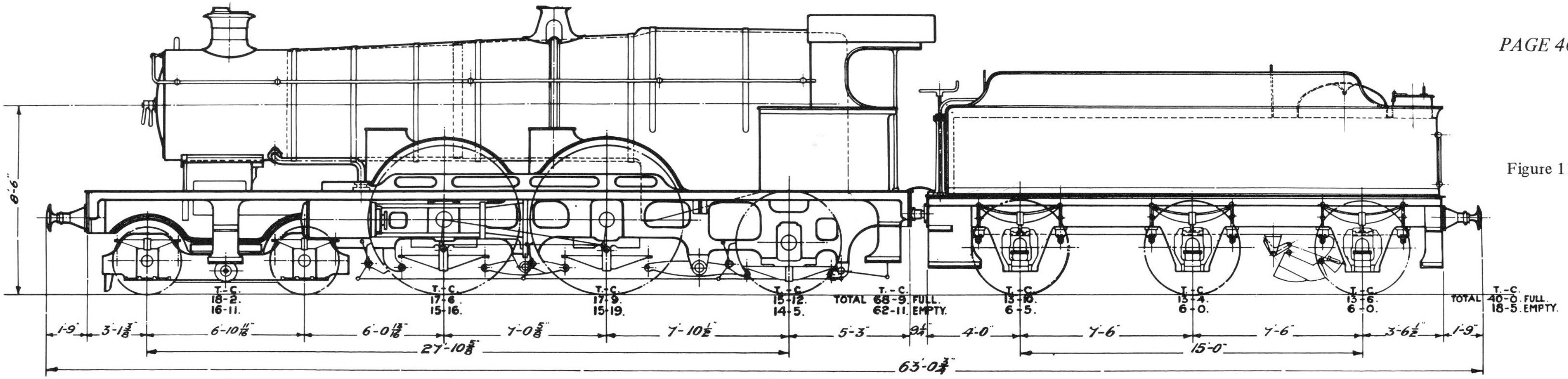

Figure 112

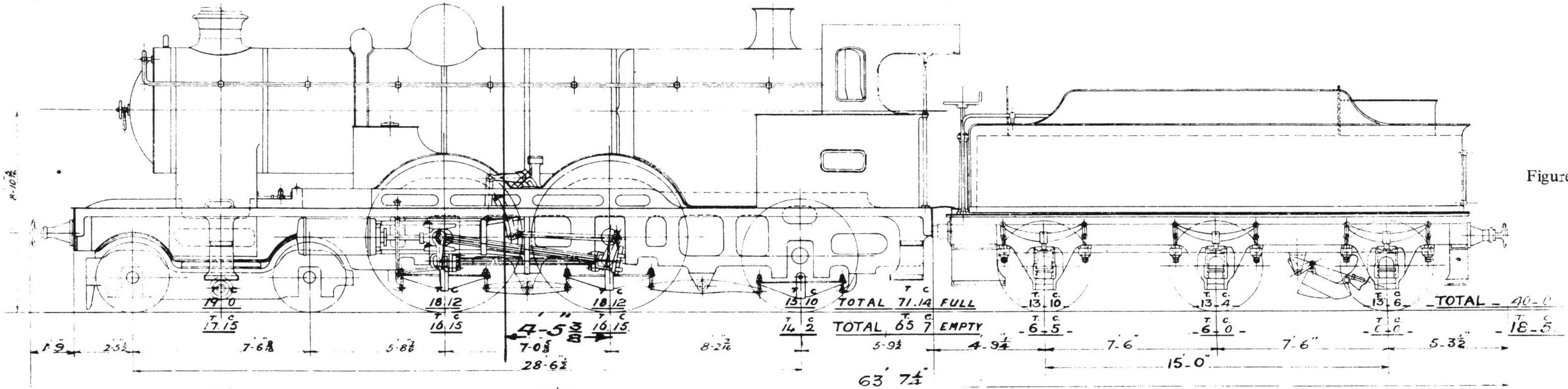

Figure 113

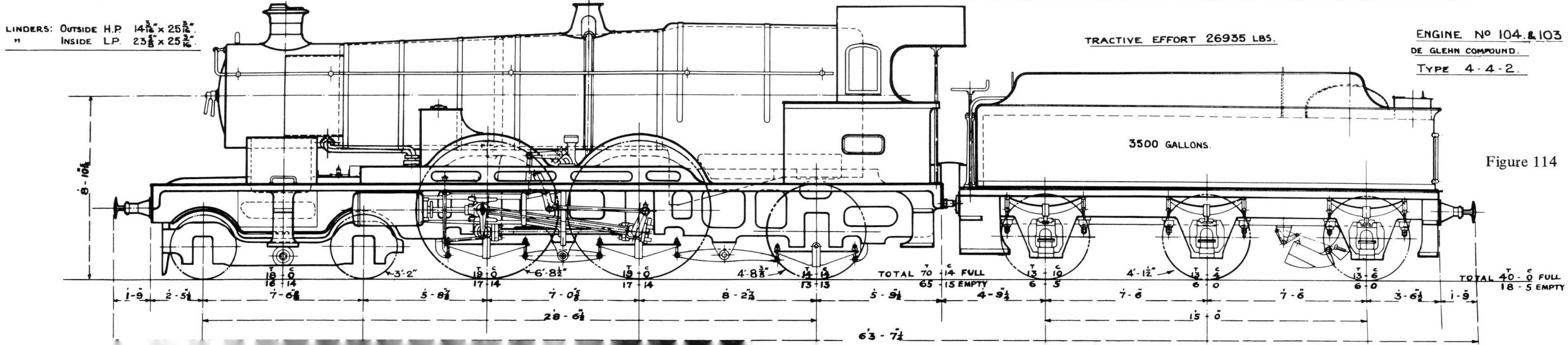

Figure 114

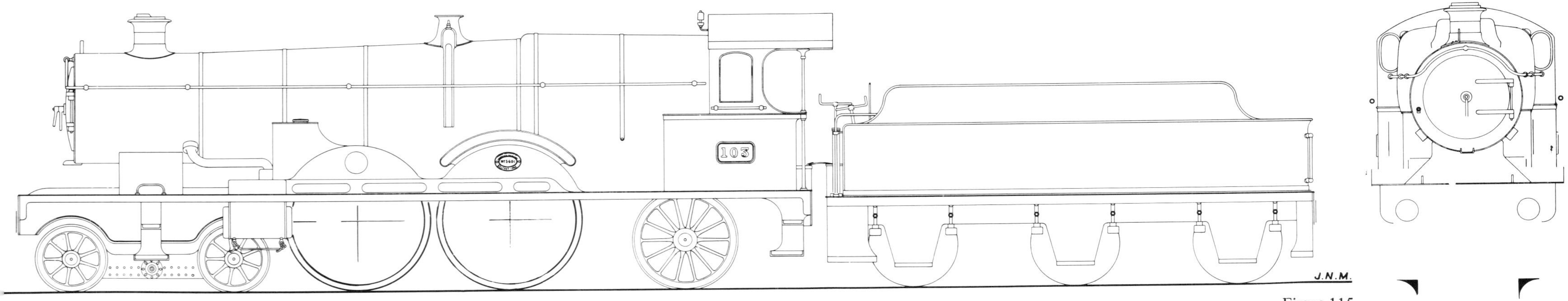

Figure 115

Three conditions of the De Glehn compound engines are illustrated above in drawings. All three are the official diagrams, and in *Figure 112* we see No. 102, the first French engine purchased, as *Diagram I,* rebuilt with a Standard 1 boiler in 1916.

Figure 113 shows the second pair of French engines as they were built in 1905, and as received by the Great Western in June of that year.

Finally, in *Figure 114*, we see the final rebuild of these two compounds, as reconstructed with the Standard 1 boiler and with a superheater.

It is also of interest to note the different tenders shown in the diagrams.

For those modellers who feel tempted to build a model of either one of the larger 'Frenchmen', this uncomplete drawing of J.N. Maskelyne gives many of the relevant measurements and shows the differences between these engines and the first compound No. 102.

Figure 116 illustrates the right-hand side of *President* in the 1914 condition, and it is possible to see the superheater damper, the reducing valve, and the outside steam pipes at the front end of the locomotive. The latter had to be fitted when the French engines received new boilers, and were surely the origination of the 'Castle' style of characteristic curved steam pipe used by Mr. Collett in 1925.

In their last workings these three engines were shedded at Oxford, and I knew them well as a 'youthful' name collector. They were often seen on Birmingham trains passing through Banbury, and were always conspicuous by their quiet graceful progress.

Modellers may refer to *Great Western Portrait* by Adrian Vaughan for other pictures of these engines, published by Oxford Publishing Co.

Figure 116

Figure 117

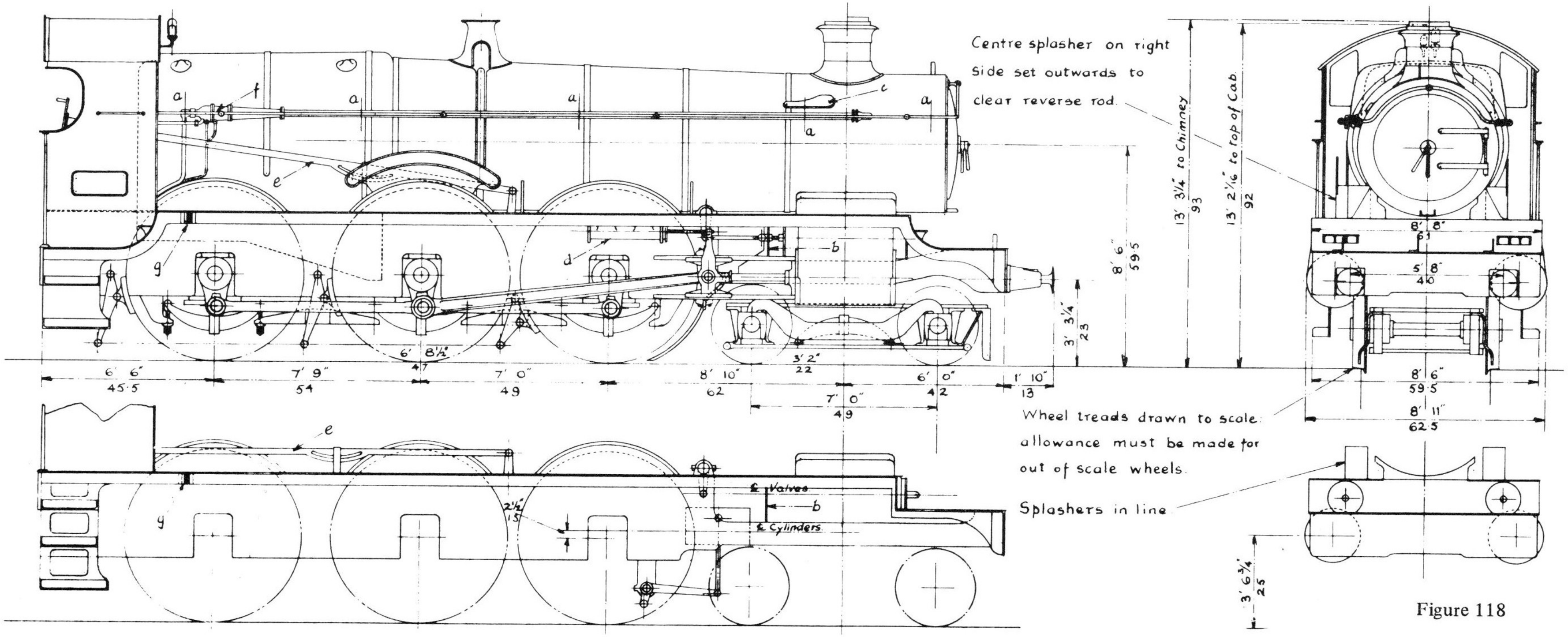

Figure 118

Apart from those engines already referred to in the previous pages, the first 'Saint' class proper were the 'Ladies'. This odd remark is explained by the fact that the '2900' class, which finally numbered 76 with the inclusion of the 21 Scotts and William Dean contained in its name list, ten 'Ladies', twenty 'Saints', and twenty-five 'Courts'. Although these 2-cylinder 4-6-0's contained such a diversity of names they were always affectionately known to enthusiasts as 'Saints'. Amongst railwaymen, these express engines were known as 'twenty-niners', and were always regarded as fast runners, even if a little on the rough side from the point of view of footplate comfort.

Figure 117 is a works photograph of No. 2902 *Lady of the Lake* in the 1910 condition superheated, but with no top feed. The drawings are by Colonel Templer, and show both the square-ended and the curved running plate.

When No. 2902 was first seen at Paddington, a well-wishing enthusiast tossed a horse shoe on to the footplate, and when this gesture came to the attention of G.J. Churchward he had a suitable mount made for the shoe, and the engine carried the talisman in the cab until the end of her days!

Three drawings of the 'Saint' class are shown on this page. *Figure 119* is the official Swindon drawing *L* of the series of No. 2922, as it was fitted with No. 2 superheater. Note the running plate is square and ends at the cab end, with the long cab ladder, whereas in Mr. Maskelyne's lovely drawing of *Saint David* the two ends of the framing have now been swept

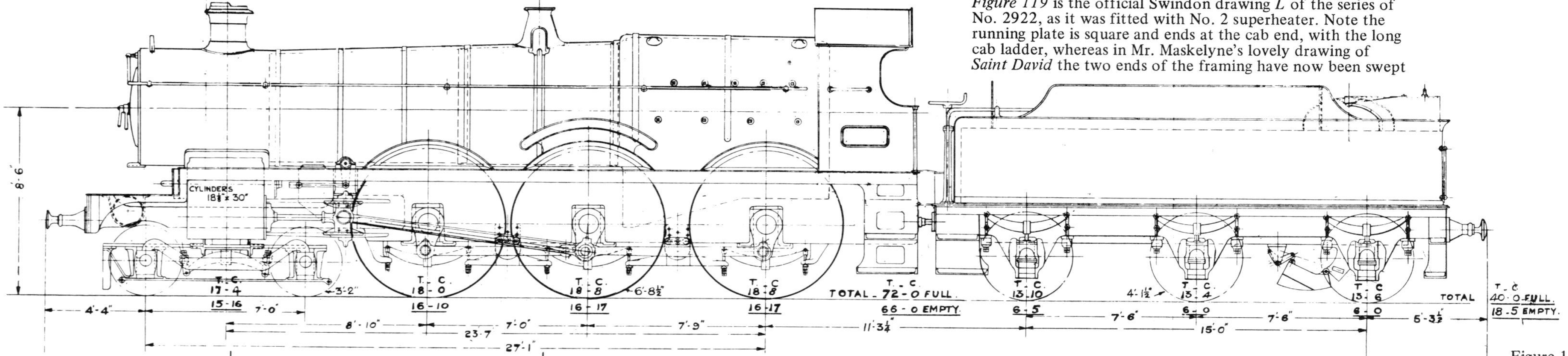

Figure 119

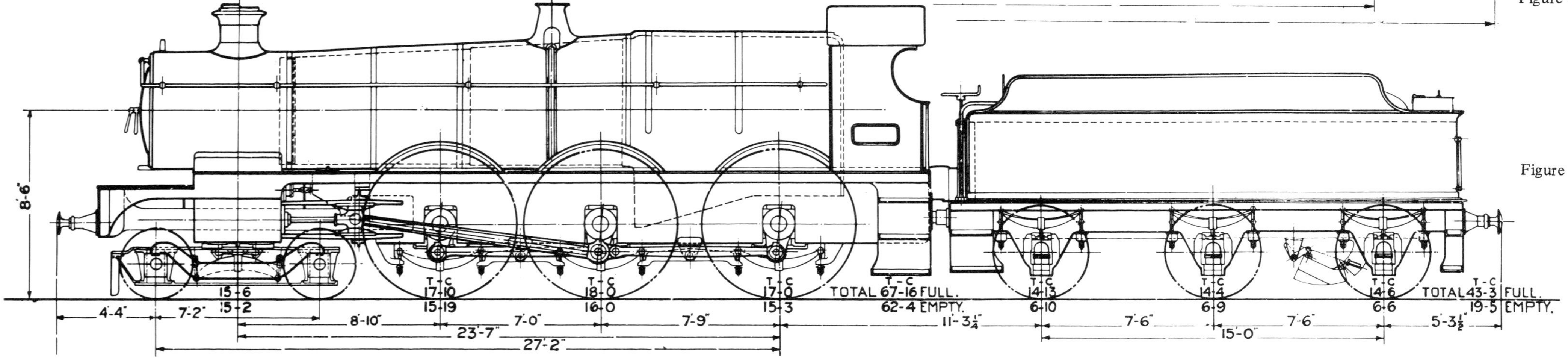

Figure 120

down in curves, the engine has been fitted with No. 4 superheater and in fact is in the 1935 condition (*Figure 121*). In *Figure 120* the engine No. 2900 is seen with the No. 3 superheater. Built to *Diagram P*.

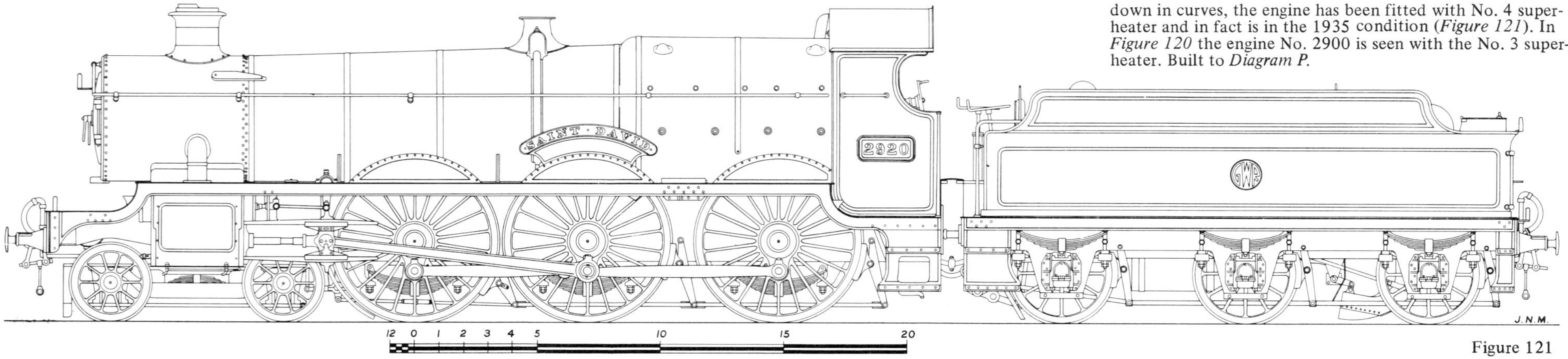

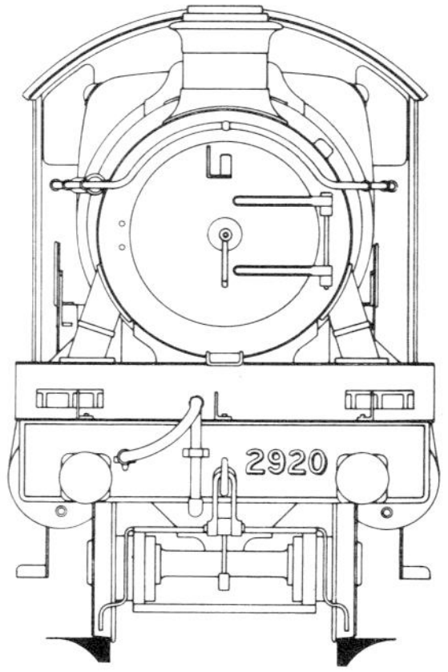

Figure 121

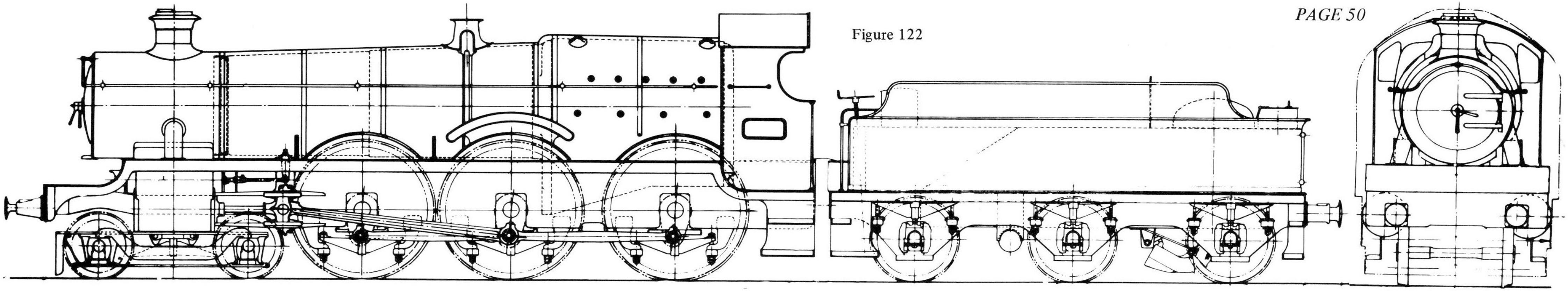

Figure 122

Figure 123

Figure 124

Figure 125

Three more 'Saints' feature on this page. In *Figure 123* No. 2923 *Saint George* is seen in 1908 at Old Oak Common. *Figure 124,* also at the same location but in the 1920's, is No. 2920 *Saint David* fitted with the larger tender, as is *Saint Cuthbert* No. 2919 illustrated in *Figure 125.* This engine was named *Saint Cecilia* until late 1907 when the name was changed. The engine was withdrawn in 1932. The official drawing in *Figure 122* is the Swindon *'V'* diagram which shows the 29XX class with standardised 18½" cylinders.

Figure 126

Figure 126 shows *Lady of the Lake* in immaculate condition on one of the Birmingham-Paddington expresses just prior to the 1914-18 War, with small tender and superheater damper on the smokebox. *Figure 127* is another study of *Saint George* but at a later date, in fact, at her last shopping in 1932; withdrawal came two years later in 1934. *Butleigh Court* No. 2934 is seen in the works grey official photograph in *Figure 128,* and *Titley Court* in *Figure 129* is a picture taken in 1947 at Swindon by myself on this engine's last shopping.

Figure 127

Figure 128

The point of the four pictures on this page shows the class at four evenly spaced periods in time, namely 1912, 1925, 1932 and 1947. Note that No. 2953 in *Figure 129* was destined for Chester shed, as can be seen on the left-hand side of the front buffer beam.

Figure 129

Figure 130

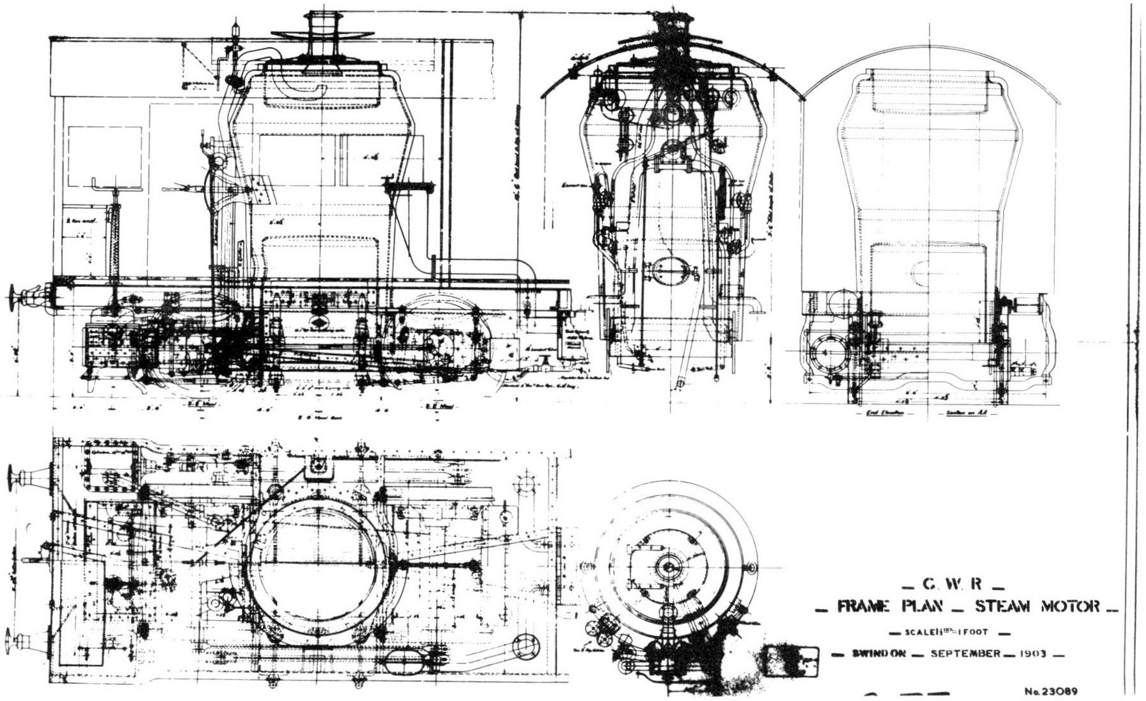

Figure 131

Great Western Railway.

Locomotive, Carriage & Wagon Department

DRAWING OFFICE,

Swindon, Wilts,

October 19th, 1906.

1st Cars.	Two built at Swindon Oct: 1903, to designs of Mr Churchward. 57'.0" long, 52 seats, 3'.6" wheels, other particulars as given in table P 8. Put to work in Stroud Valley.
Results.	Speedily justified further expenditure in this direction. At present time 80 Motor Cars, & 34 Trailer Cars in service, 34 Motors 70'.0" long & majority of remainder 59'.6" long.
Original.	Cars open end to end, later cars more elaborate. Motor, luggage, smoking & non smoking compartments, centre vestibule & drivers compartment at end.
Cars.	Running on different parts of the system on gradients varying from 1 in 35 (Coed Poeth), 1 in 42 (Hemerdon) for 3 miles to 1 in 100, haul when required 2.70'.0" trailers.
Motor.	And trailer cars fitted with regulator & brake handles, & whistle gear, so that they may be driven from either end.

Researching around, amongst the C.M.E. archives, I came across three typewritten sheets, referring to the first steam rail cars to be built by the Great Western and as they were so interesting I have reproduced them here and in the next few pages in facsimile, as the headed notepaper is of some interest. The text speaks for itself, note the date October 19th 1906! In *Figure 130* is seen the first of the cars so built, No. 1, and in *Figure 131* is seen the official frame plan of No. 1.

Figure 132

Here is a continuance of the assessment of the Steam Rail Motor Cars (*Figure 133*) and *Figure 132* is a photograph of No. 7 showing the next stage in the development of the cars.

Great Western Railway.

Locomotive, Carriage & Wagon Department,

DRAWING OFFICE,

Swindon, Wilts,

190

450 Galls. are carried, & under ordinary conditions motor car without trailer runs about 30 miles, including stops without taking water.

Typical service for motor cars is that between Chalford & Stonehouse, on the main line between Swinden & Gloster. Population of this valley estimated at 40000, & with exception of Stroud & Stonehouse is fairly distributed. It is a shuttle service of 7 miles with 9 stops, actual run 25 mins, giving 5 mins at each end, for looking round engine etc.
Average run about 200 miles per day, & works out to about ¾ mile per stop, a fairly heavy service. It will be seen that a fairly high acceleration & deceleration is necessary to maintain this. Average acceleration from actual tests is about 1 4 7 say 30 M.P.H. in 30 secs taken at 60% cut off.

Maintenance greatest trouble have been due to bad water causing tubes, but this is gradually being overcome, as the different water softening plants now being installed come into operation.

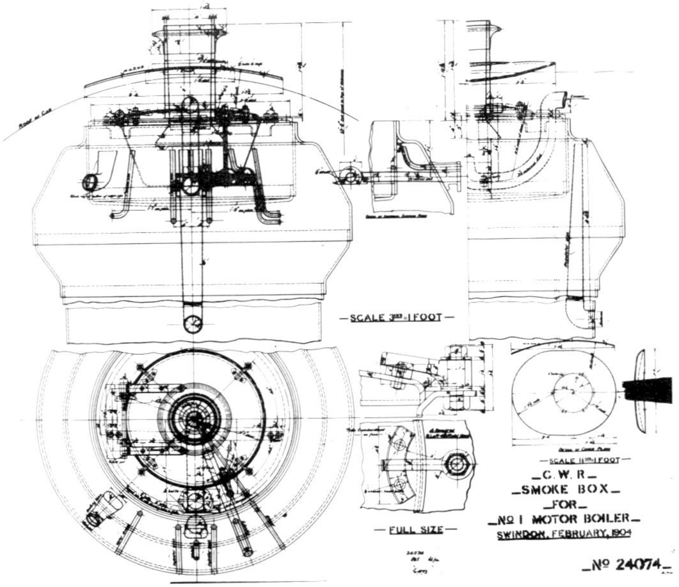

Figure 133

Figure 134

Great Western Railway,
Locomotive, Carriage & Wagon Department,
DRAWING OFFICE,
Swindon, Wilts,
190

Another trouble has been due to the frames. No diagram in paper, but the engine arranged similar to G.C. car P 14.

Outside cylinders 12" x 16" drive on to trailing coupled wheels, this produces a racking action, (principally at cylinder end) between the frames & the frame stiffeners work loose, overcome by stiffeners having stouter plate & angle irons, the trouble gradually disappearing. Earlier cars 3'.6" wheels, later cars 4'.0" wheels, at the same speed, less No of revs, & reduces the wear & tear on engine.

Repairs boiler detached from frame carrying brackets & lifted through roof by overhead crane. Engine is then run out underneath, this operation is only necessary in case of heavy repairs, which are done at a station having proper facilities.

Recent developments have been more in the direction of using a separate small loco: 0.4.2. class of which we have a great number, & which would otherwise be cut up. They are fitted with special regulator gear, & run with with trailers attached - approximate to ordinary

Figure 135

Swindon 29/9/05

Great Western Railway

RAIL MOTOR CARS

Cost of the engine £850: of the 55ft body £884 and of the 70ft body £1010 (total £1734 and £1860 respectively for 55ft and 70ft cars)
The complete cars are built at the Company's Swindon Works, but some have been bought from outside firms. Power is not transmitted by spur wheels, and a speed change is not fitted.
There is space on the engine for 15 to 18 cwts of coal and 450 gallons of water.
The main line is laid with rails 97 lbs per yard, and the branches with rails not less than 75 lbs per yard.
Trailers are attached to the cars when necessary, the cars being capable of hauling one trailer up a gradient of 1 in 40, and one trailer and four horse boxes or milk trucks up a gradient of 1 in 100.
59'6" trailers cost £856 and 70 ft trailers £1186.
Two men are employed to operate the engine, a driver and fireman. One man is employed to attend to passengers, both when the car runs alone and with a trailer attached.
Enginemen are paid 5/6 per day when running on branches, with 6d extra for main line work. Firemen receive 3/- and 3/6 respectively. A car is not turned for the return journey. When a trailer is attached, this is pushed.
The maximum grade over which the cars run is 1. in 40, extending for $2\frac{1}{2}$ miles.
The maximum load hauled is 1 trailer up 1 in 40, and 12 horse boxes on the level.
12 m.p.h. is developed up 1 in 40: 50 m.p.h. on the level. The average speed is 35 m.p.h.
The mileage of the cars per day varies from 100 to 200 miles and the mileage per stop from $\frac{3}{4}$ to $4\frac{1}{2}$ miles.
The coal consumption is 18.45 lbs per mile.

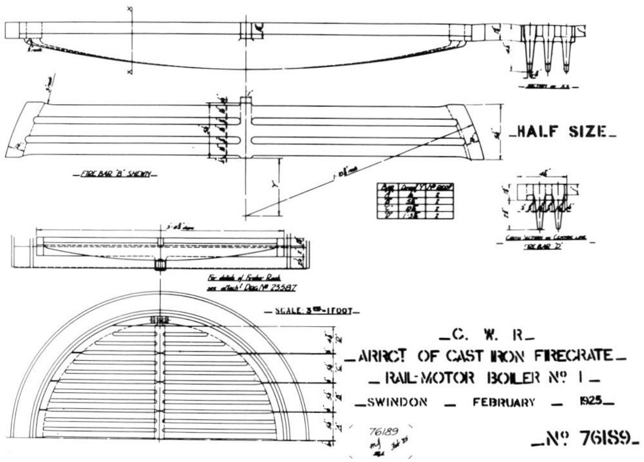

I am including the last of Swindon write-up of the early Steam Rail Cars (*Figure 135*), and in *Figure 134* is Car No. 67, one of the privately built bodies of the later series.

Also on this page, another facsimile of a letter from the drawing office to the C.M.E. in 1905, which makes interesting reading nearly seventy years on, especially in relation to the running costs and wages!

The car in *Figure 137* is No. 75, one of those whose bodies were made by the Gloucester Carriage & Wagon Co.

Figure 136

Figure 137

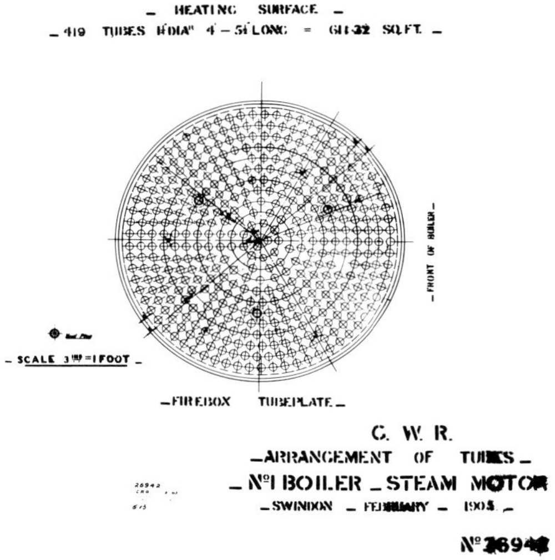

Figure 138

From a traffic angle, the steam rail cars are dealt with fully in the companion volume *A Pictorial Record of Great Western Coaches – Part II* but the actual engines used in these carriages find a place in this work on locomotives. Hitherto model makers have had to guess what the motive power unit of the 'cars' looked like or measured, and I hope that in covering these little engines thoroughly it will help to correct this lack of information.

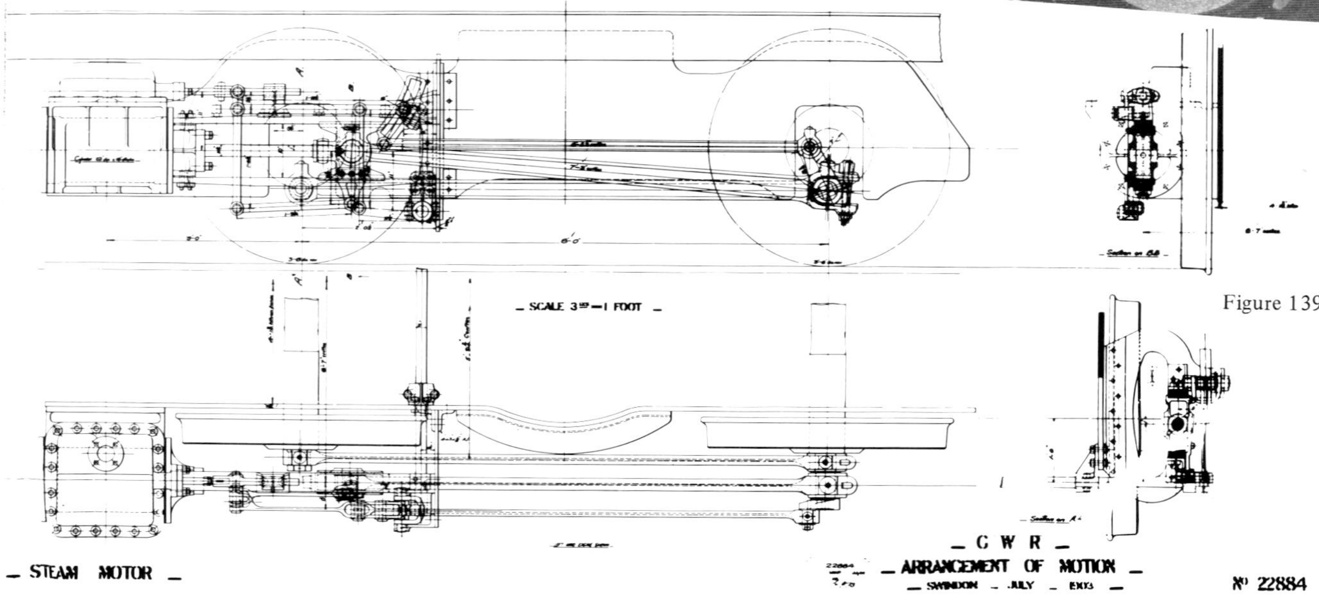

Figure 139

All the four-wheeled steam units were interchangeable, which allowed for major servicing, although to withdraw the engine from the coach meant, first lifting the boiler high with a crane, and secondly running the engine chassis out from under the car, in order to make the mechanical part accessible. *Figure 138,* a photograph loaned by kind permission of Mr. Wheeler, illustrates two of these little engines at Swindon awaiting attention, and the main features are laid bare. An upright boiler with copper firebox is supported on the frames by angle irons riveted to the shell and held down by bolts. Weighing 6 tons they were rather unstable, and not only set up a swaying motion at speed, but also a fore and aft 'hunting' oscillation. These small engines were the first on the Great Western to use outside Walschaerts gears, and not only does this show well on the photographs, but is also illustrated in three views in the official drawing *Figure 139* of the steam motor's motion.

Figure 140 shows in clearer detail the layout of the special Walschaerts gear for the steam rail cars with the connections to the reversing quadrant. A plan view of the engine unit is seen in *Figure 142* and together with the photograph in *Figure 141* it can be seen that the whole weight of the front end of the vehicle is supported and pivots upon the four scroll irons and double transverse beams. A side elevation of this engine unit appears on page 32 of *A Pictorial Record of Great Western Coaches – Part II.*

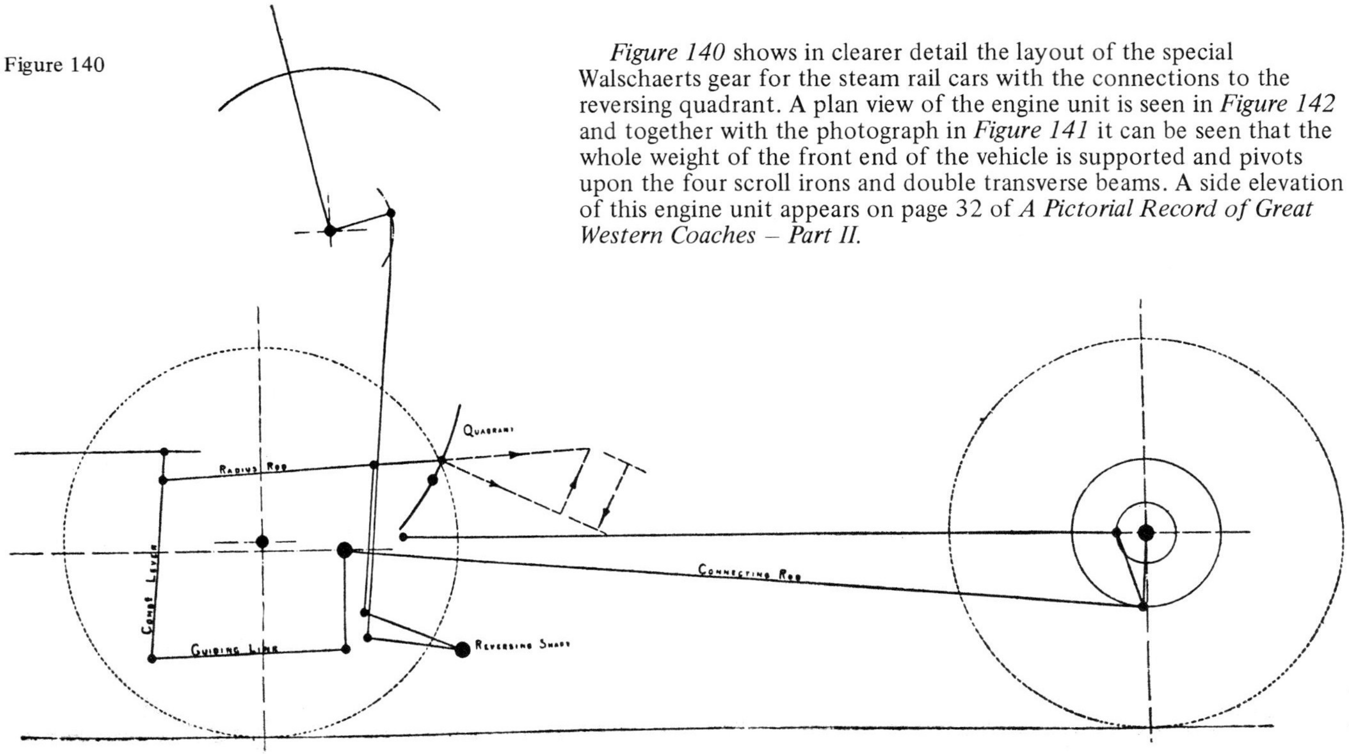

Figure 140

Figure 141

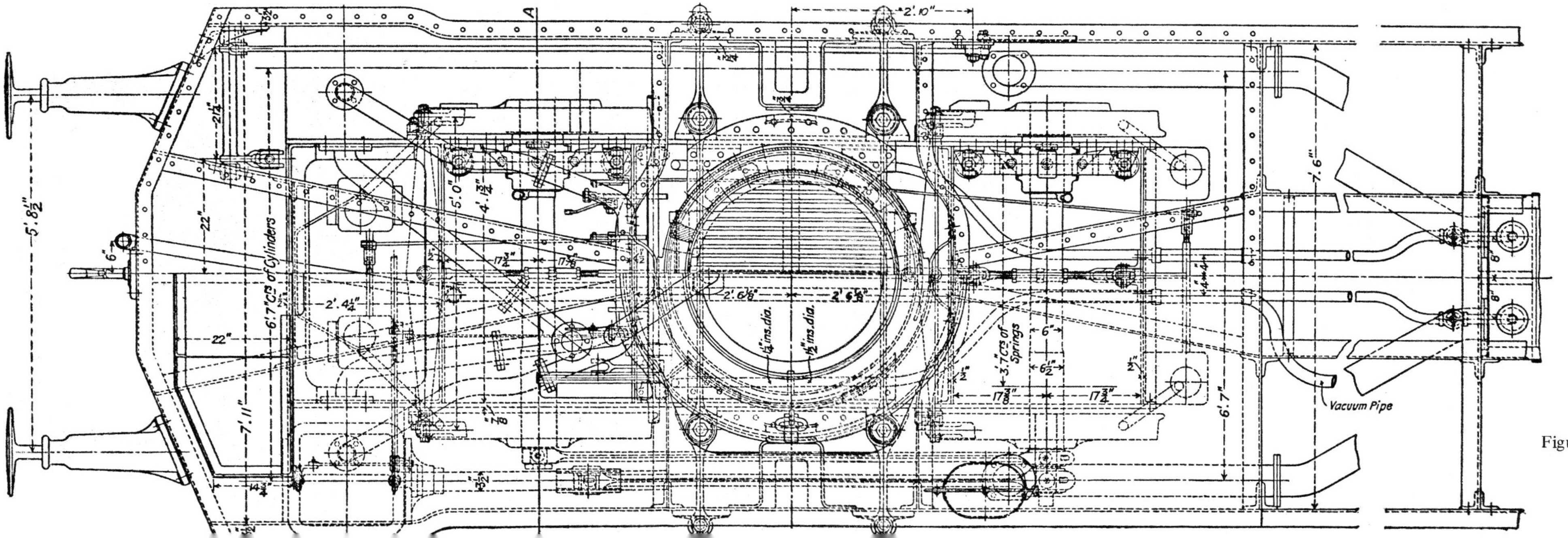

Figure 142

Figure 143

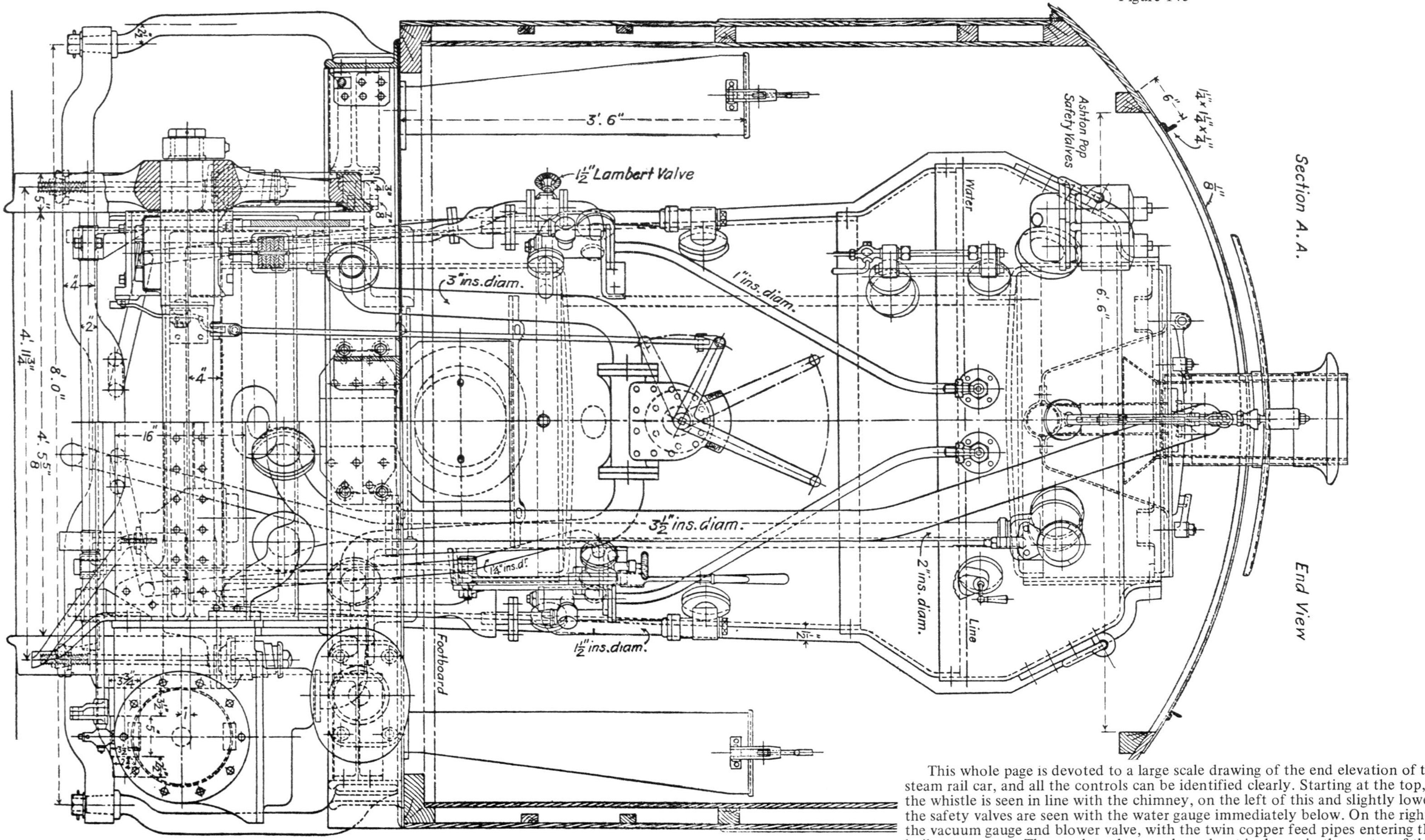

This whole page is devoted to a large scale drawing of the end elevation of the steam rail car, and all the controls can be identified clearly. Starting at the top, the whistle is seen in line with the chimney, on the left of this and slightly lower the safety valves are seen with the water gauge immediately below. On the right is the vacuum gauge and blower valve, with the twin copper feed pipes entering the boiler top centre. The regulator lever and quadrant is shown in the centre of the drawing with the reversing lever on the right. Just above the firehole door on each side are the two injectors and controls, and at the extreme width of the car, left and right, are shown the two water filler intakes, with screw-down lids. The long extension rod from the regulator is for control from the front end of the car, and was detachable.

Two official diagrams of the first 4-4-2T class tanks built in 1905-6, and the only one small-wheeled 4-4-2T No. 4600, built in 1913.

The diagram in *Figure 144* is the Swindon *Diagram A* of Nos. 2221-29 and 2231-40 as built with short smoke-box, no superheater, and early boiler fittings. The drawing in *Figure 145* is of No. 4600 to *Diagram D* which shows the locomotive as built. Later in 1917, the bogie centre was extended forward four inches.

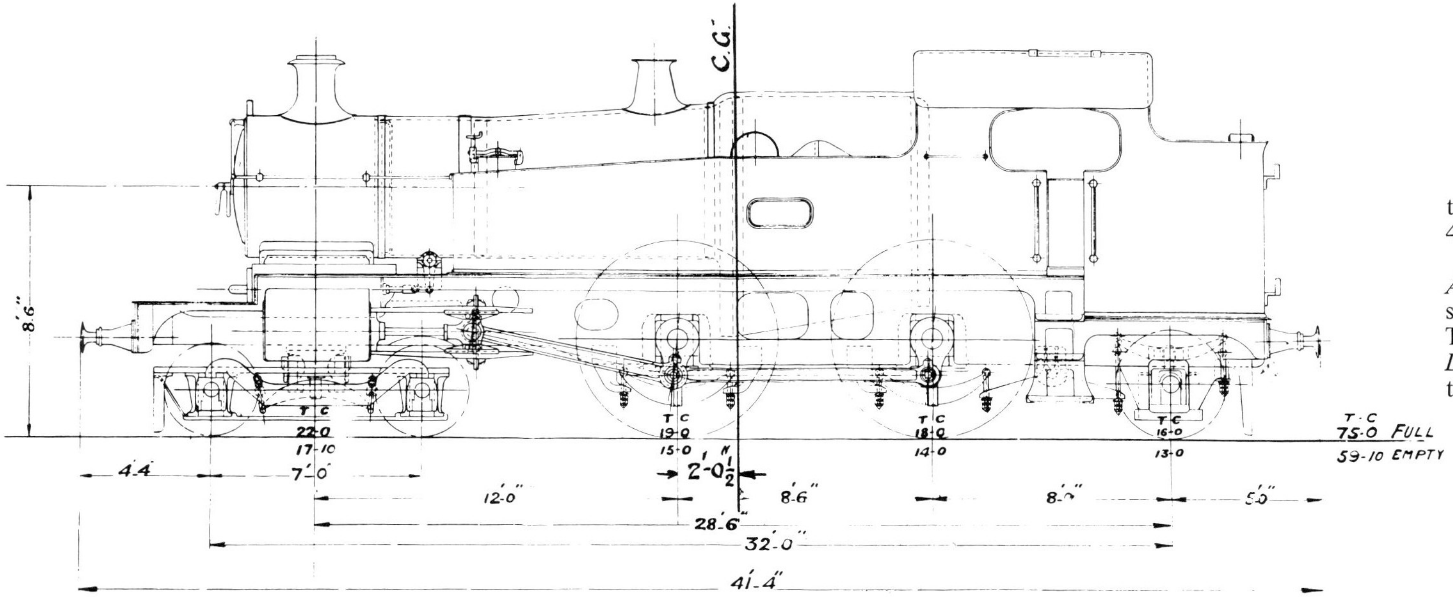

Figure 144

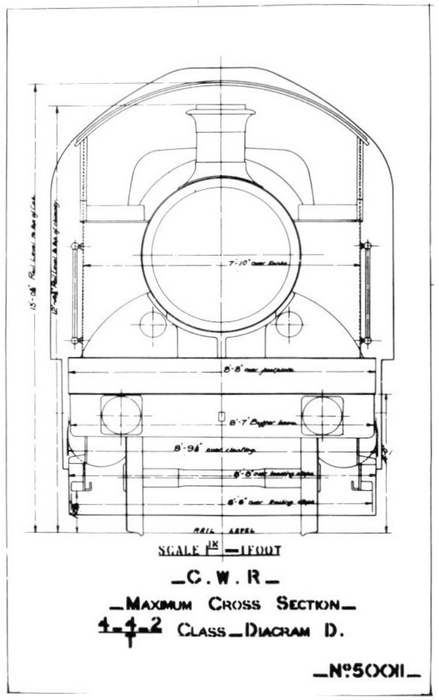

Figure 145

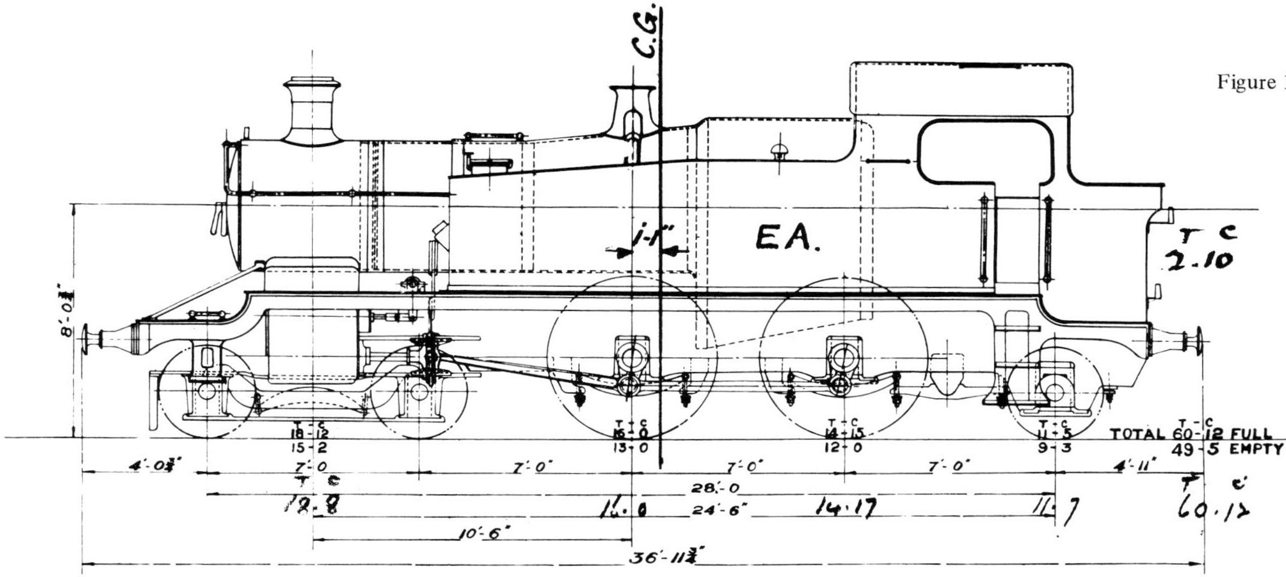

Figure 146

In 1905 these large-wheeled 'County' tanks were introduced to gradually supersede the much smaller 2-4-2T, '3600' class already described.

The 22XX series were big, high standing heavy engines, their full weight tipping the scales at 75 tons. They were of the 4-4-2T classification with their driving wheels the largest ever used for tank engines on the standard gauge, namely 6′ 8½″ diameter.

The first of the series to be constructed under *Lot 151* was No. 2221 seen in *Figure 146,* and this one engine was slightly different to all her sisters in that the number plates were mounted on the tank sides and the cab side sheets were flush with the bunker and water tank sides. The other original small feature No. 2221 had was steam sanding gear, but this fitment only lasted for six months before being removed. The whole class was equipped with two-way water scoop, which remained on the engines until the early 'twenties.

Figure 147

No. 2230 illustrated in *Figure 147* was another oddity, in that she was originally fitted with a larger No. 4 boiler when built, but it proved too heavy and a standard No. 2 replaced the No. 4, which meant a packing piece had to be used on the smokebox saddle to make up the difference. This can clearly be seen in the 1907 photograph. Both engines were withdrawn before the end of 1933.

Figure 148

The first twenty engines in the 'County' tank class had two major differences from the final ten of the series, the first being that the running plate in the 2221-40 series was of the square-ended drop type, whereas in the 2241-50 batch, this was curved at the front end. Secondly, the first series had their cylinder centre line 2½" above that of the driving wheels. Also, the second batch came out of the factory already fitted with top feed, whereas the previous twenty had this improvement added to them during heavy repairs. *Figure 148* shows No. 2237 as at 1925, with superheater and top feed, and water scoop removed.

Colonel Templer's drawings illustrate the differences between the two series, and no further comment is needed (*Figure 149*).

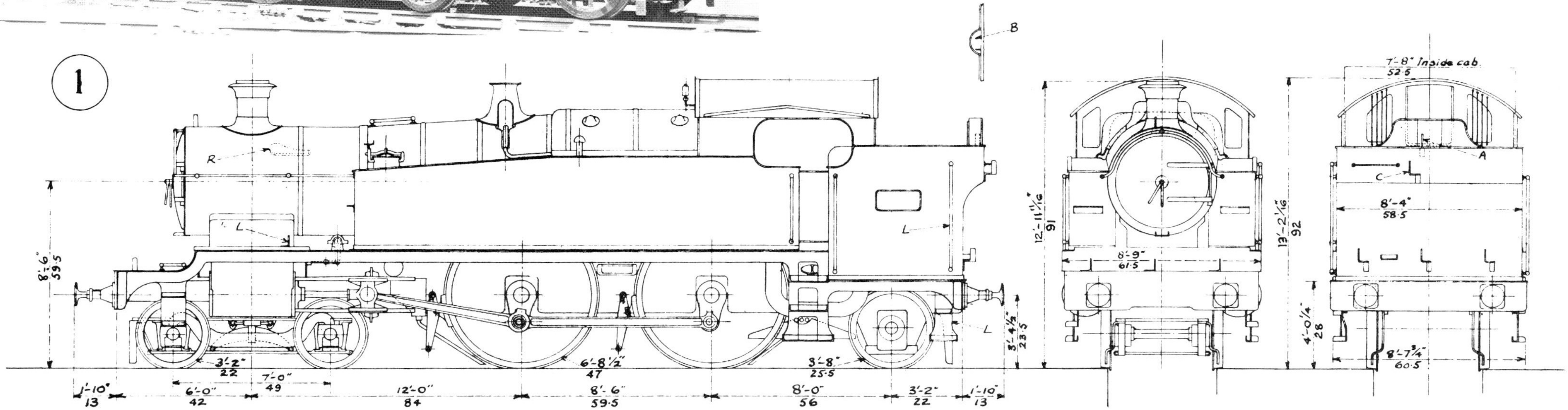

Nos. 2241–2250 thus, with vacuum pump on right side as shown at 'X' in fig 2, but with crosshead extension arm 2½ inches longer, to compensate for cylinder c/l being lower.

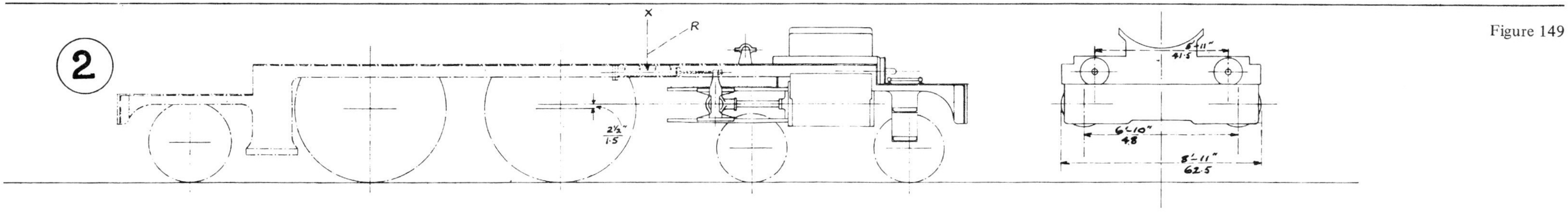

Figure 149

Nos. 2221–2240 thus to full lines, otherwise as fig. 1, except cab of No. 2221 which was wider, with side sheets in one with tank & bunker sides. Note particularly centre line of cylinders is 2½ inches above that of coupled wheels.

The official photograph in *Figure 150* shows No. 2243 just after being shopped in 1924, and in the final stage of the class, with the extended bunker, top feed and superheated boiler. This engine was withdrawn in December of 1934, but lingered on at Old Oak Common for many years as a stationary boiler.

The official drawing of the class seen in *Figure 151* is the Swindon *G Diagram,* and whilst all the dimensions are no doubt correct, modellers should beware of the chimney outline and cab window size. If one refers to the photograph above, the point will be abundantly clear!

Figure 150

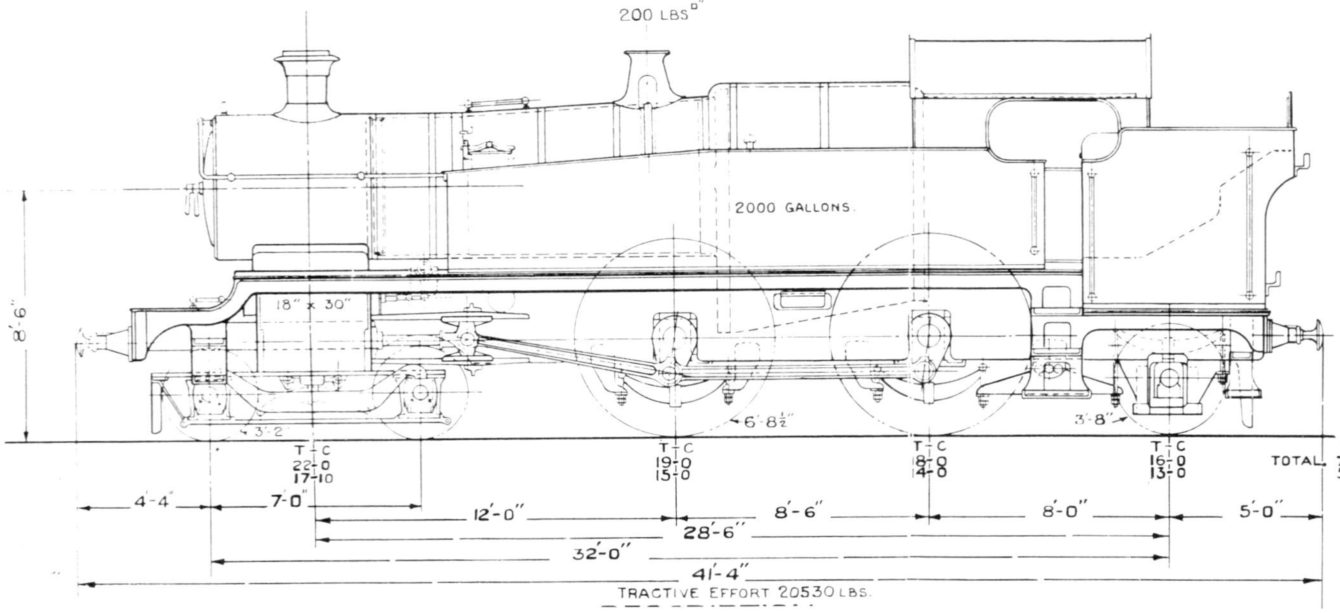

Figure 151

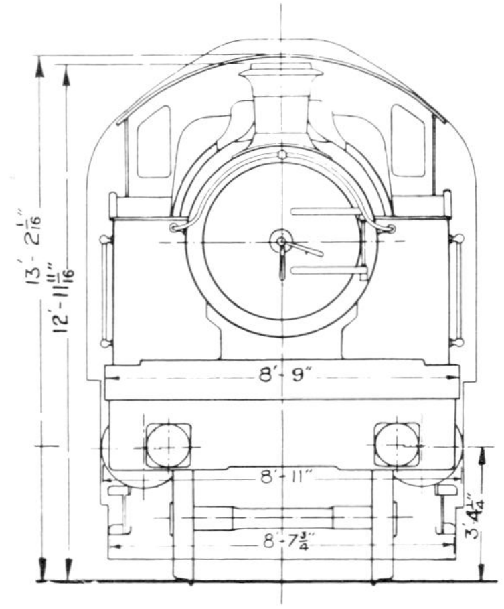

2221 CLASS
TYPE 4-4-2 T

Figure 152

Figure 153

Some of the class of 'County' tanks were fitted with the cast taper chimney, as can be seen in the bunker-end picture of '2242', but in the main these engines were fitted with the built-up, copper-topped variety. *Figures 152 and 153* illustrate two of the last batch to be built, Nos. 2242 and 2249 as running in the early thirties but originally constructed to *Lot 188* in 1912. *Figure 154* shows No. 2243 again, but in the 1912 condition with flat-ended bunker, the garter insignia, and still fitted with the two-way water scoop. They were big handsome engines, but inclined to be rough riders due to the large reciprocating masses, and had comparatively short lives, as they were superseded by the '61XX' 2-6-2T's in 1931, on their London suburban duties.

Figure 154

Figure 155

Another oddity was No. 4600, built in 1913 with the idea of taking over the 'Metro' class light suburban duties, and branch line work. Events proved however that the 2-6-2T type of locomotive with the smaller wheels was more flexible and could handle this traffic much easier than the small Atlantic tank, so that she remained the only example of her class.

I have a model of this engine, which visitors are always confusing for the 'County' tank, so to clarify the position, here are the two types shown in side view for comparison. It will be seen immediately that '4600' is a scaled-down version of the larger tank, with 5′ 8″ driving wheels in place of the 6′ 8½″ type on the 2241 series, and a wheelbase of 28′ as compared to the 32′ of the larger engines.

One small point to note is that this engine was the only example of the bogie tanks to be fitted with struts at the front buffer beam. She spent the early years of her life shedded at Tyseley, but later on found service in West Wales until being withdrawn in 1925. The 4m/m drawing is by J.N. Maskelyne.

Figure 156

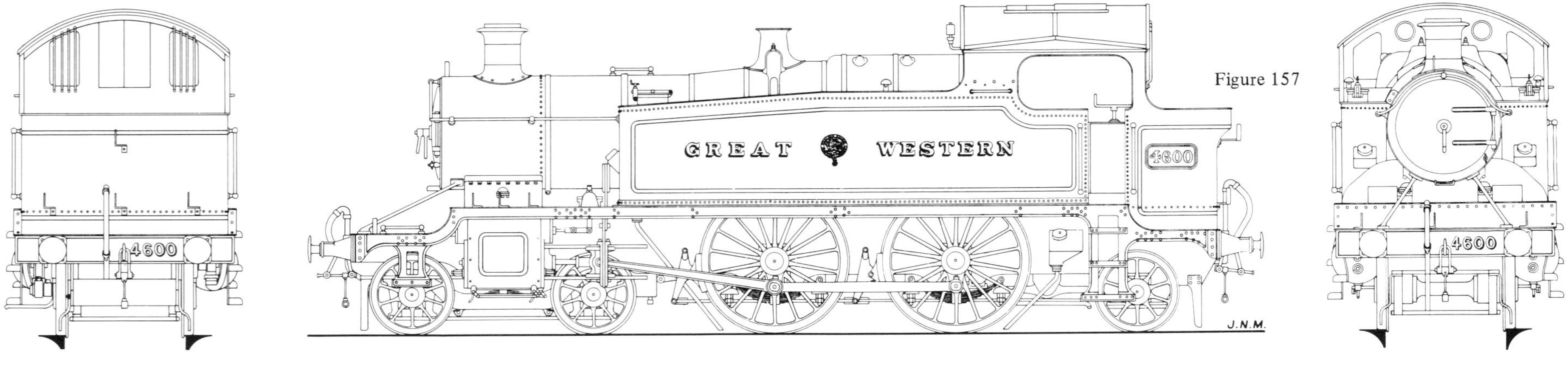

Figure 157

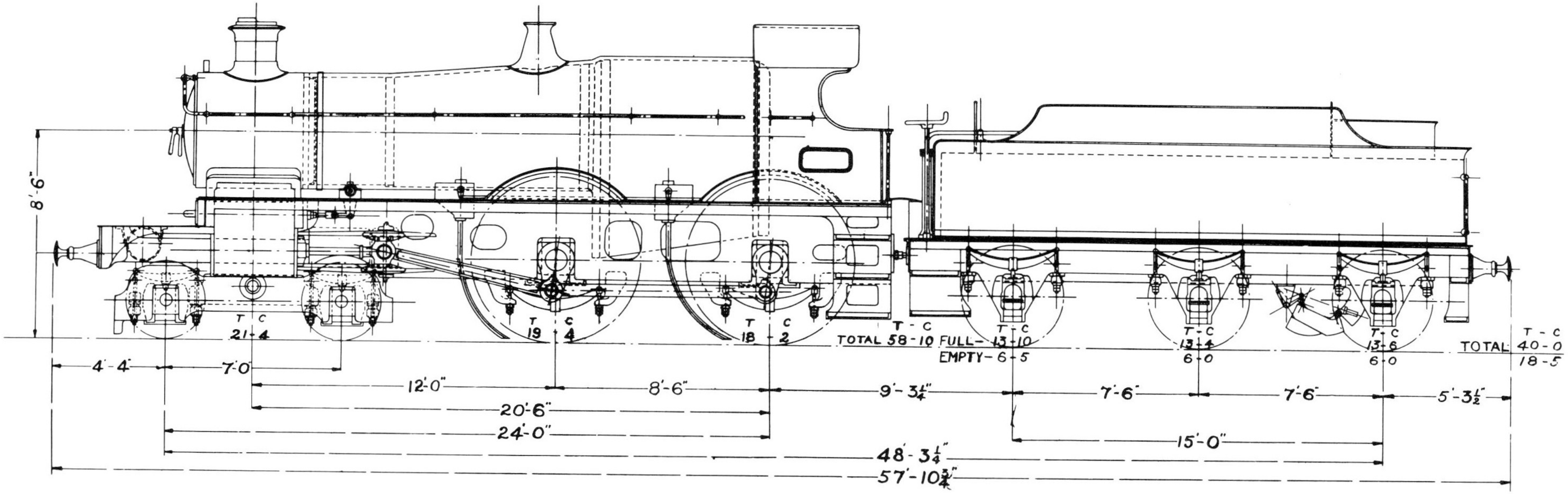

Figure 158

Known to Western men as 'Churchward's Rough Riders', the 'County' class of 4-4-0 express engines was a series of moderately sized passenger locomotives with inside frames, and looking very much like a shortened version of the 'Saint' class. It has been suggested that the reason behind the design was to work cross-country services over the Shrewsbury-Hereford line, where 4-6-0's were not allowed. The first batch of ten were constructed in 1904 under *Lot 149,* and were numbered 3473-82 (later in 1912, altered to 3800, 3831-9) and the names given to the engines were those of Counties through which the Great Western passed. More engines were built in 1906 and 1912, so that like the 'Halls' many years later, the nomenclature had perforce to range beyond the boundaries of the railway. The line drawing in *Figure 158* gives a good side elevation for measurements, and the photograph of No. 3478 in *Figure 159* shows the original condition of the 'County' class in 1904. Note the neat Dean type copper-topped chimney, the squared frames and the lettering on the tender. *County of Devon* was the sole engine to carry these experimental initials, grouped into one panel like this.

Figure 159

Figure 161

Figure 160 illustrates *County of Radnor* in works grey. One of the second batch of 1906, the chimney is of the cast iron tapered type, and the brake rigging is now behind the driving wheels, instead of in front as before. These twenty locomotives were numbered 3801-20 and the first ten received Irish county nameplates. Note that the sandboxes are now above the running plate, and on both drivers instead of one, as on the first batch. Brakes were fitted to the bogie wheels, but eventually this fitting was removed, following the practice of the larger express engines.

Two photographs on this page illustrate well the differences between the 'County' class as built, and the design as finally constructed. No. 3480 *County of Stafford* (seen in *Figure 161*), is as originally turned out of the factory in 1904 with squared framing, Dean type chimney and scroll insignia on the tender. *County of Oxford* the last in the series to be built in 1912, is depicted in *Figure 162* at Leamington Spa during the First World War years with crimson lake stock, on a Birmingham-Paddington express. *Figure 163* shows No. 3824 *County of Cornwall* on station pilot duties at Weymouth just before being withdrawn in 1931. Note that No. 3802 (*Figure 166* on page 67) has a pole reverser, whereas on No. 3824 the screw gear was fitted.

Figure 162

Figure 163

Figure 164

County of Bedford features in *Figure 164* as outshopped at Swindon in 1924, fitted with top feed, screw reverser and large tender, this being the final form of the series. The drawing (*Figure 165*) by Colonel Templer, gives many of the variations of the class; both the square-framed type and the later drop-ended style are shown, together with both sides to show the reversing lever and vacuum pump on the right-hand elevation. The notes thereon speak for themselves.

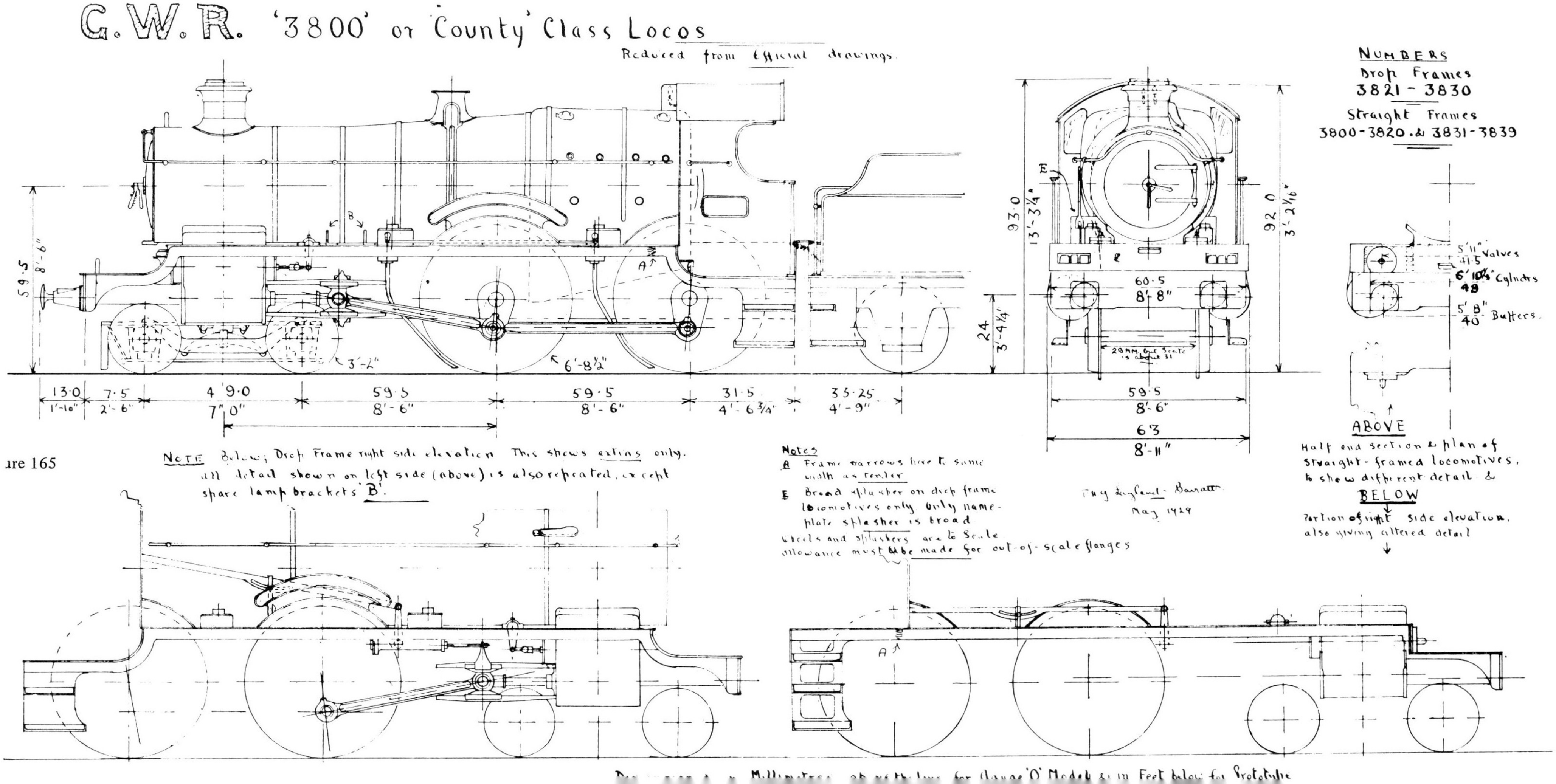

Figure 165

Figure 166

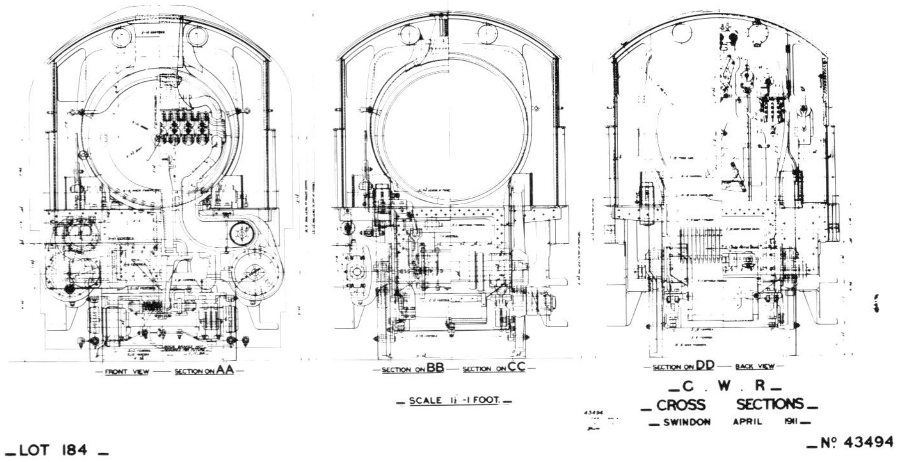

Two more straight-framed 'Counties' feature on this page. In *Figure 166,* No. 3802 *County Clare,* one of the Irish series, is seen at Old Oak Common in the 'twenties, after having worked an express up to Paddington. Although still retaining the pole reverse, the bogie brakes have been removed, and she is superheated and fitted with top feed. By courtesy of my friend Maurice Earley, I am privileged to show in *Figure 167 County of Devon* on an up Worcester express approaching Sonning Cutting in April of 1928. Note that the engine still retains the brake rigging outside the driving wheels, has flush fitting sandboxes and no bogie brakes. One small feature for modellers to watch, is that the cab ladder had two apertures in the top two steps, but was solid in the lowest one.

Figure 167

Figure 168

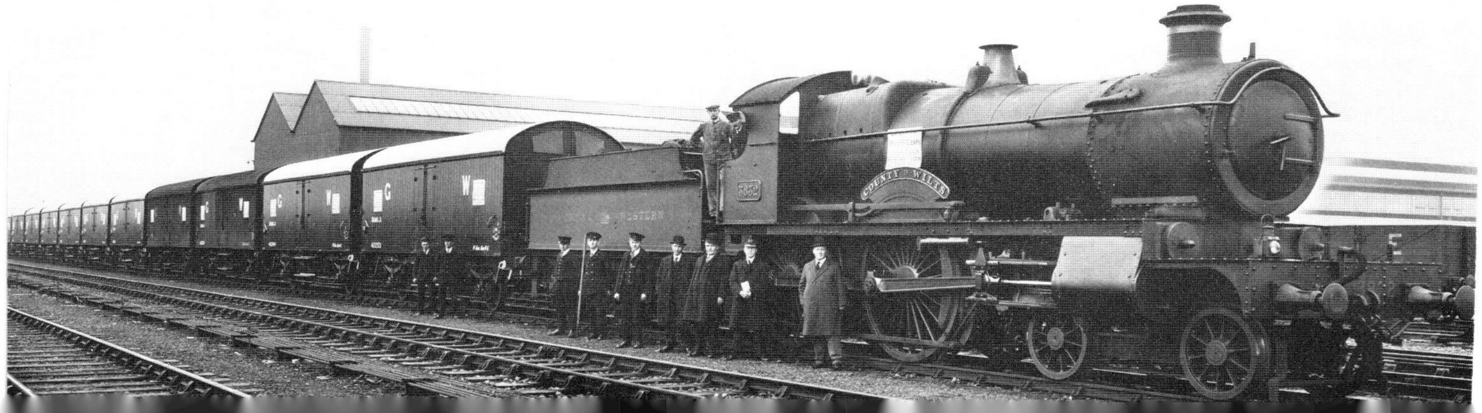

Two latter day 'Counties' in lowly service. No. 3822 *County of Brecon* is seen in *Figure 168* at Paddington in February of 1928 at the head of a train of milk churn empties. This superb official photograph shows the front curved running plate well, and all the fittings thereon. Notice particularly the reflection of the nameplate in the small puddle! The engine is carrying 'C' headlamps which could have meant, that the train was fully vacuum braked, or at least, one third of it.

In *Figure 169 County of Wilts,* No. 3832, is shown at Morris Cowley factory in 1929 with a special train of 'DAMO A's which was labelled *'Morris Cars' for the Scottish Motor Exhibition, Morris Cowley – Glasgow, Express.* One point strikes me as odd, the engine is heading east towards Princes Risborough; was the train going via Willesden Junction as all the car trains I knew went via Oxford? Again note the difference between the 1904 engine in *Figure 169* and the 1911 type in the upper illustration. A very fine kit of this class of engine is available in 4m/m scale.

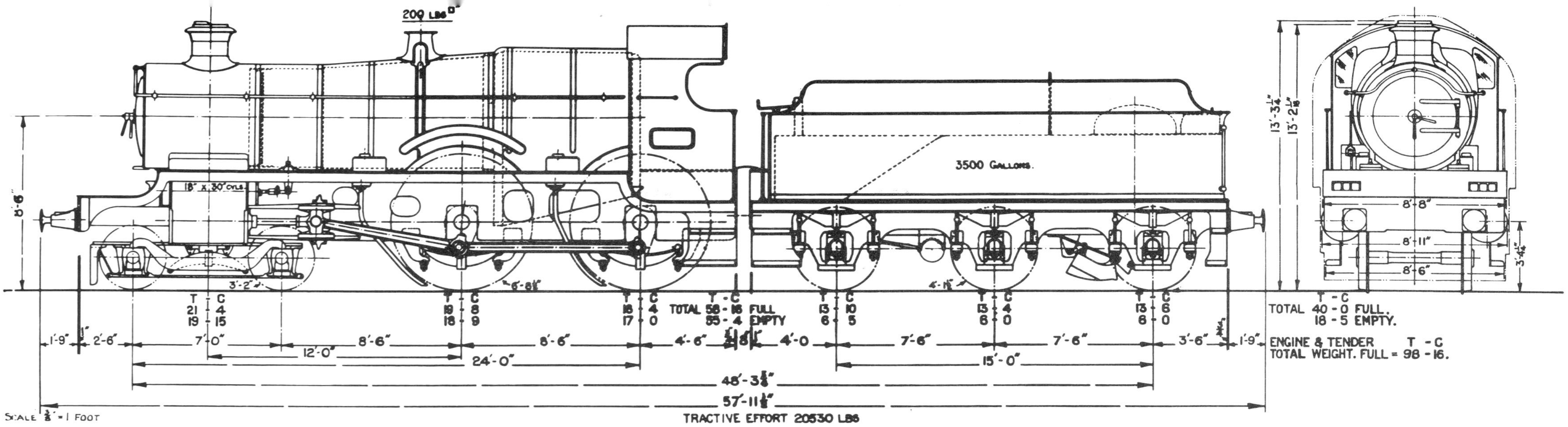

Figure 170

Diagram A.28 shown in *Figure 170* is of the 'County' class with curved frames and No. 4 standard boiler. *Figure 171* gives the comparison with the *Diagram N* illustrating straight frames with No. 4 boiler and non-superheated.

Figure 171

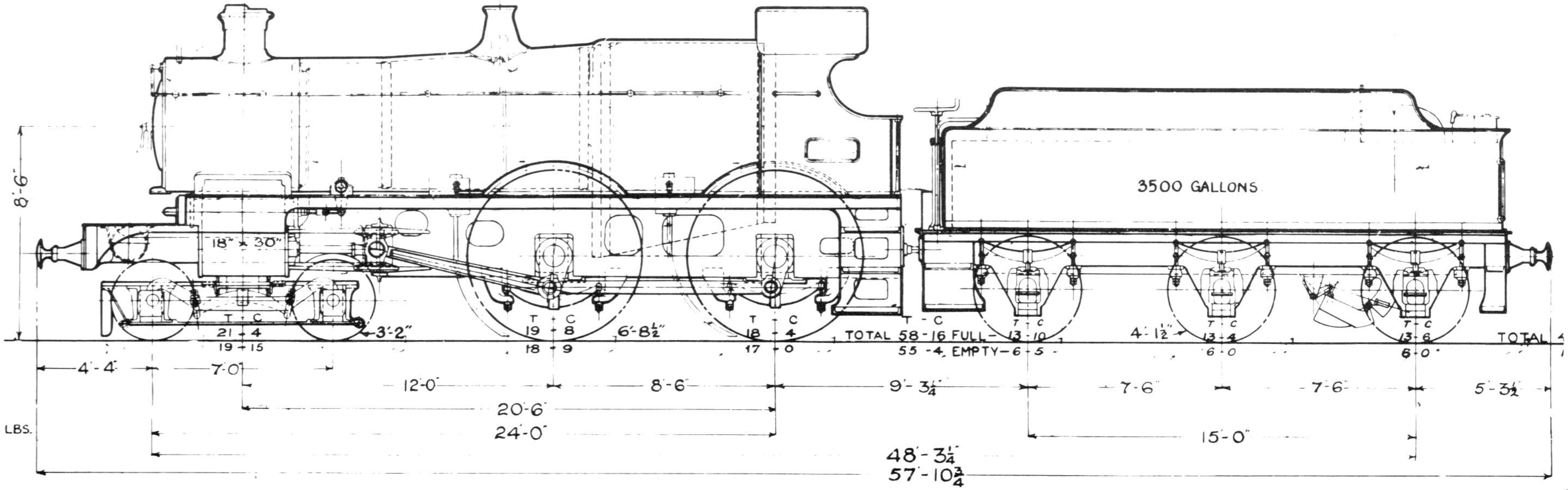

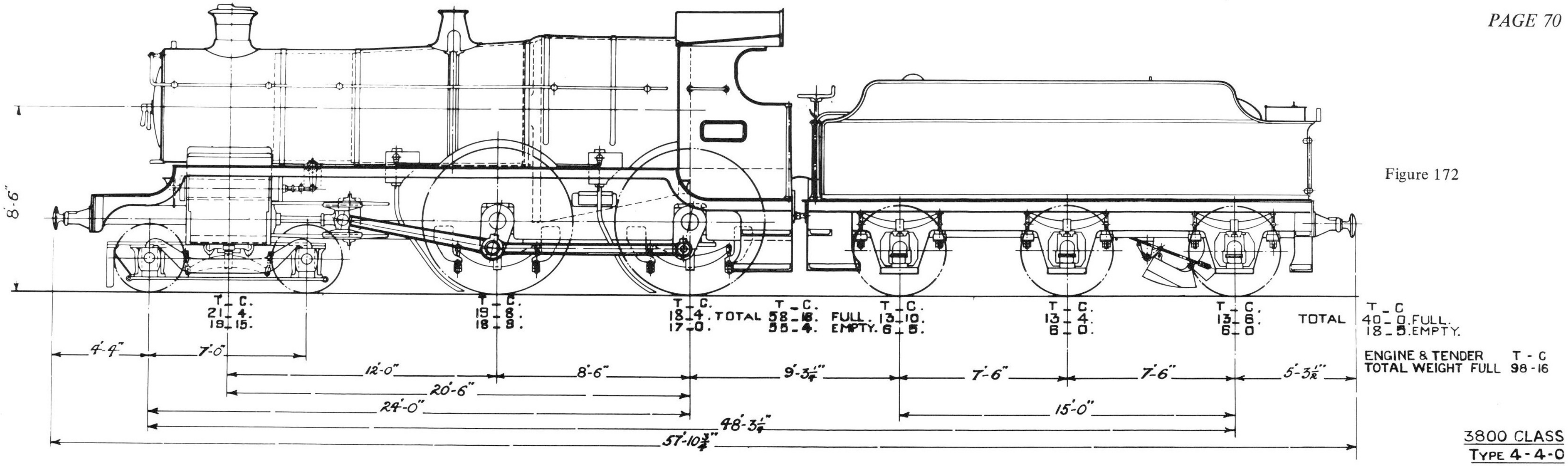

Figure 172

Here we have the same engine as in *Figure 169* but fifteen years earlier. *County of Wilts* is seen in this photograph of 1913, with 'E' headlights, heading a special train of heavy timber baulks. Note that she is running with the small early tender with handrails outside, and has the superheater damper on the outside of the smokebox. Also the cab ladder has apertures in each step back. For those interested in rolling stock, the first three wagon numbers are 32273, 32274 (close-coupled) and Macaw 70711.

The drawing in *Figure 172* is the official *Diagram A.10,* which shows the class with the curved frames, Standard No. 4 boiler, and top feed, in their final condition before withdrawal.

Figure 173

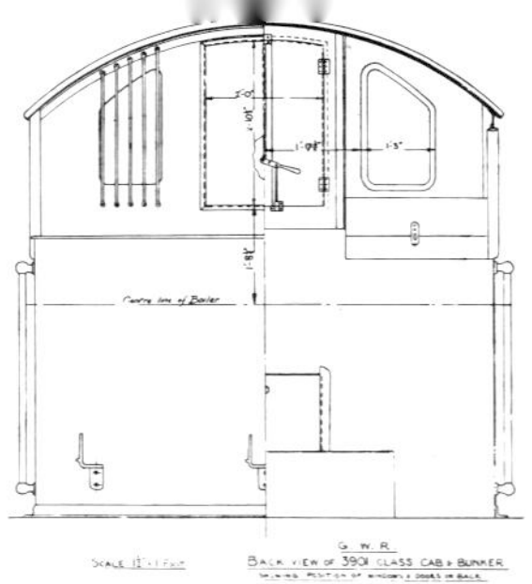

Figure 174

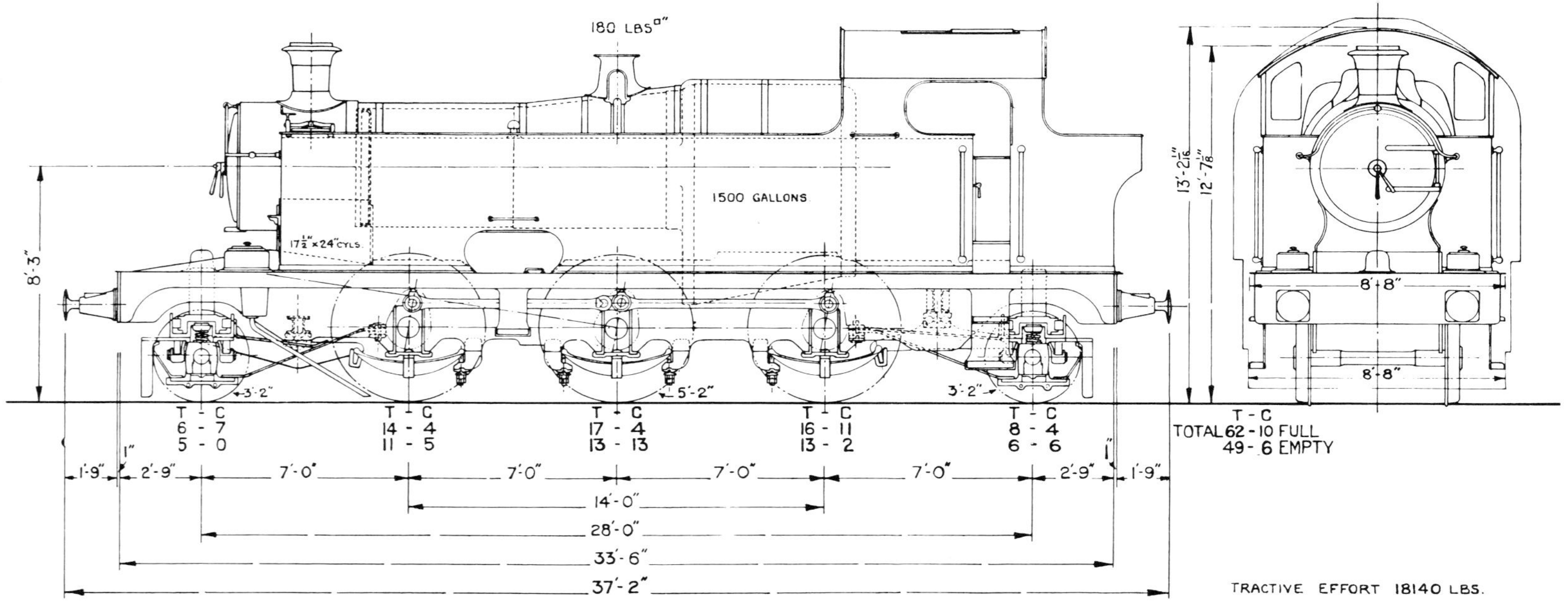

As has already been illustrated, Swindon factory could take a locomotive, and by utilizing the main frames, motion and driving wheels, completely rebuild the engine so as to be scarcely recognisable from the original machine. One such notable example of this practice was the series of twenty Dean goods engines Nos. 2491-2510, which were fitted with a No. 5 standard boiler, side tanks in place of the tender, an enclosed cab, and a pony truck at each end, making a 2-6-2 tank engine, suitable for double-ended running. The need for these engines arose through decline of goods traffic and the increase of the suburban passenger services with the opening of the North Warwick line in 1907. The drawing seen in *Figure 174* is the official Swindon *A.8* diagram, showing the engine as fitted with superheater. The photograph in *Figure 175* is of the class as built, without top feed and with saturated boiler. Numbers were 3901-20 and Lot was No. 167.

Figure 175

There were three diagrams issued for this converted Dean goods, the first drawing showing the new 2-6-2T configuration being the *F* diagram which was of the engine as reconstructed in 1907. *Figure 177* is a 4 m/m reproduction of this official drawing. In *Figure 176 Diagram N* is shown, which shows the engine with the 6/48 superheater.

The final drawing was the *A.8* which is seen on the previous page.

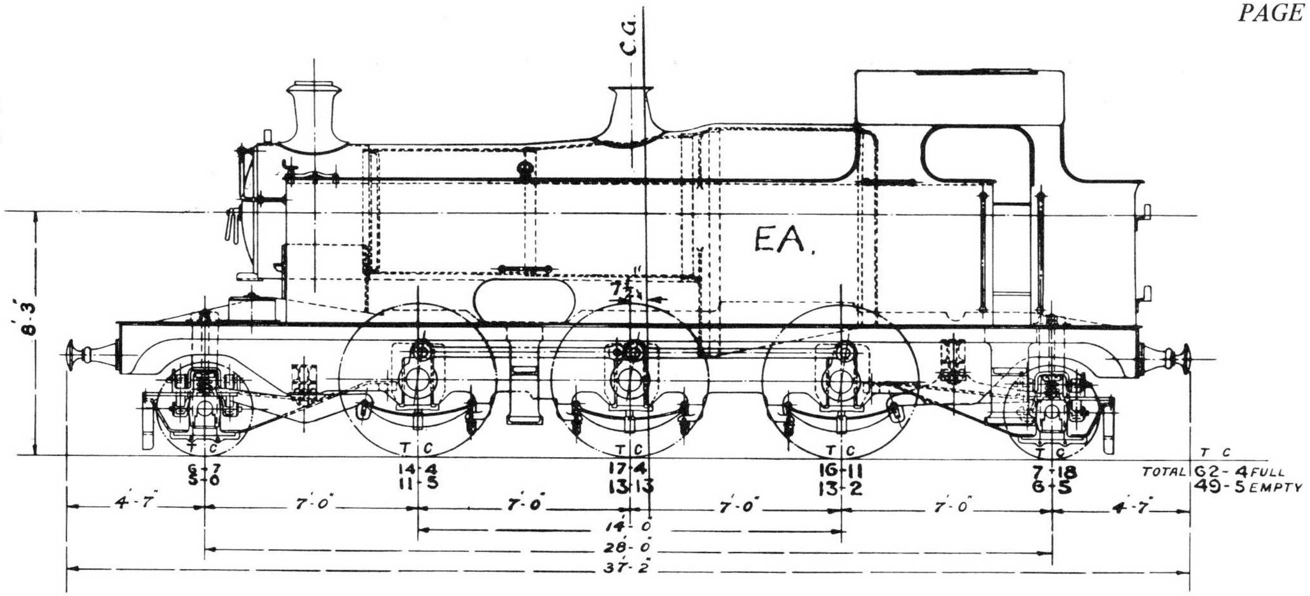

Figure 176

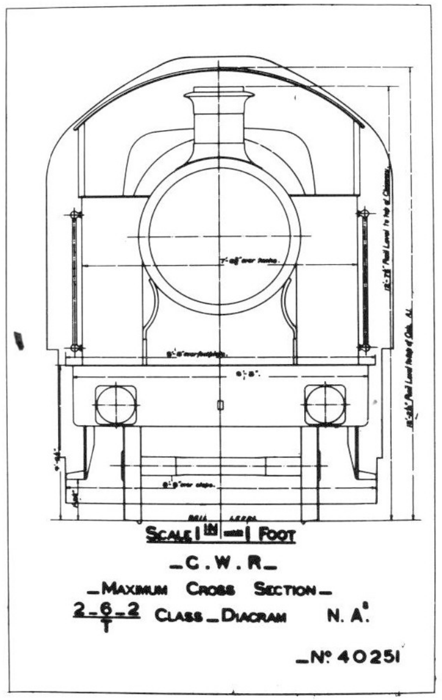

Figure 177

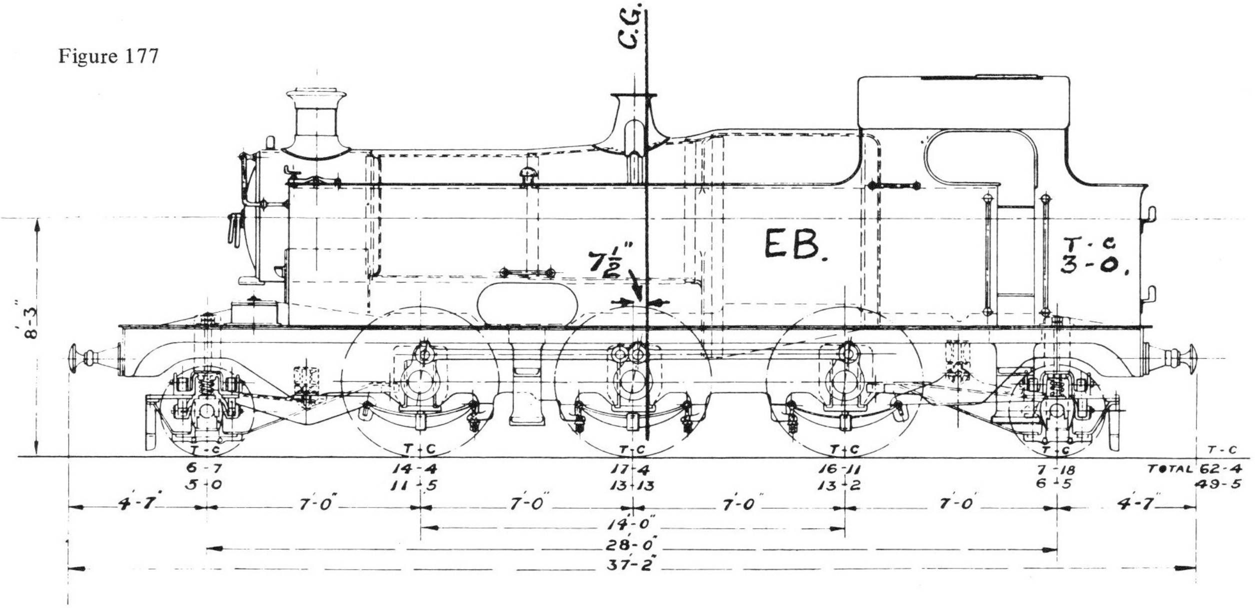

The 3901 class were the only series of 2-6-2 tanks to be built with inside cylinders on the Great Western and to be honest, they were rather ugly machines, although I have been told they did their job well. As previously mentioned, their work was confined to the Birmingham area until 1923, and *Figure 179* shows No. 3916 standing in the middle road at the south end of Snow Hill station in 1909. Compare these with the Dean goods in *Figure 178,* the original engines.

With the long 1,500 gallon side tanks running the full length of the boiler, access to the motion for oiling was achieved by the large hole and footstep above and between the first two pairs of driving wheels. Note that in this photograph the engine is unsuperheated, has no top feed, and is in fact practically as built. As there is space on this page, a list of numbers with the original Dean engines is given.

Figure 178

Figure 179

Dean 0-6-0	2-6-2T	Withdrawn
2491	3901	1934
2498	3902	1932
2501	3903	1932
2504	3904	1933
2499	3905	1930
2492	3906	1932
2508	3907	1934
2497	3908	1930
2507	3909	1930
2500	3910	1931
2509	3911	1932
2510	3912	1931
2503	3913	1931
2506	3914	1931
2493	3915	1932
2494	3916	1934
2505	3917	1932
2495	3918	1932
2496	3919	1934
2502	3920	1931

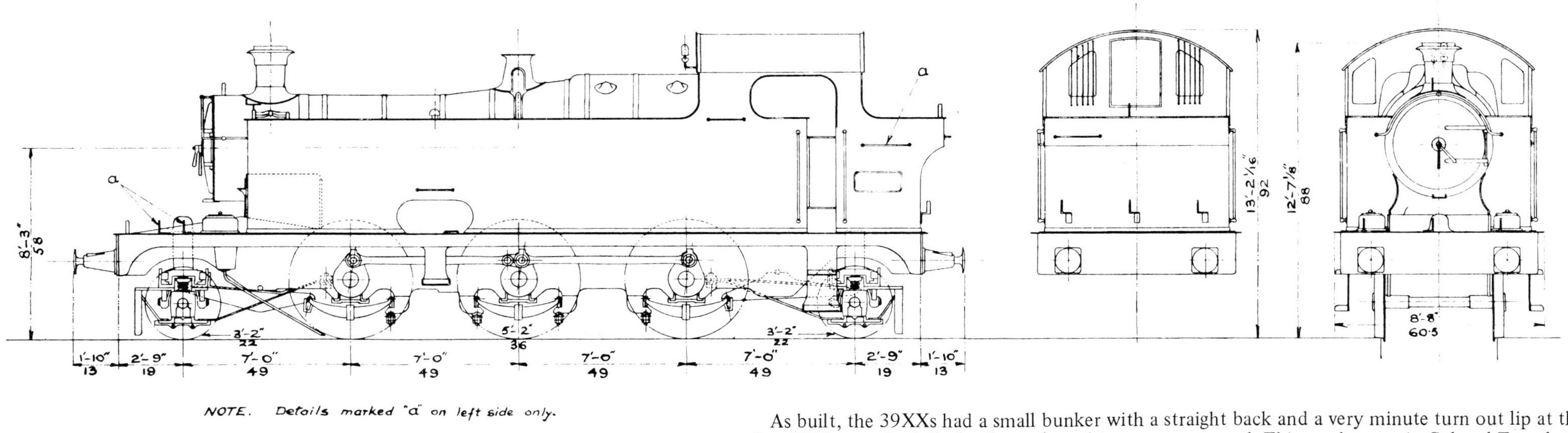

Figure 180

Figure 181

As built, the 39XXs had a small bunker with a straight back and a very minute turn out lip at the top, but after 1920 many had the bunker enlarged to carry more coal. This can be seen in Colonel Templer's drawing in *Figure 180.* Another point about these engines was that compensating beams were used both fore and aft, between pony trucks and drivers. It is not possible to see this feature in the photographs, but they are shown in the drawing. Modellers should also note the smokebox wingplates which were characteristic of the 39XX class. Again warning is given of the profile shown in the drawing of the cast iron chimney, there was no visible step between the base, top and barrel.

Figure 181 shows No. 3920 at Tyseley shed in the late 'twenties, and is interesting not only for the locomotive, but also the close-coupled suburban stock seen in the background.

Several of these engines did eventually see service away from the Midlands; five went to the London division, five to Neath, and one or two the Cardiff area, and Gloucester. Two went West, No. 3909 at Taunton in 1926, and No. 3908 at Westbury in 1924-5. Towards the end of their useful life they were employed on local goods rosters.

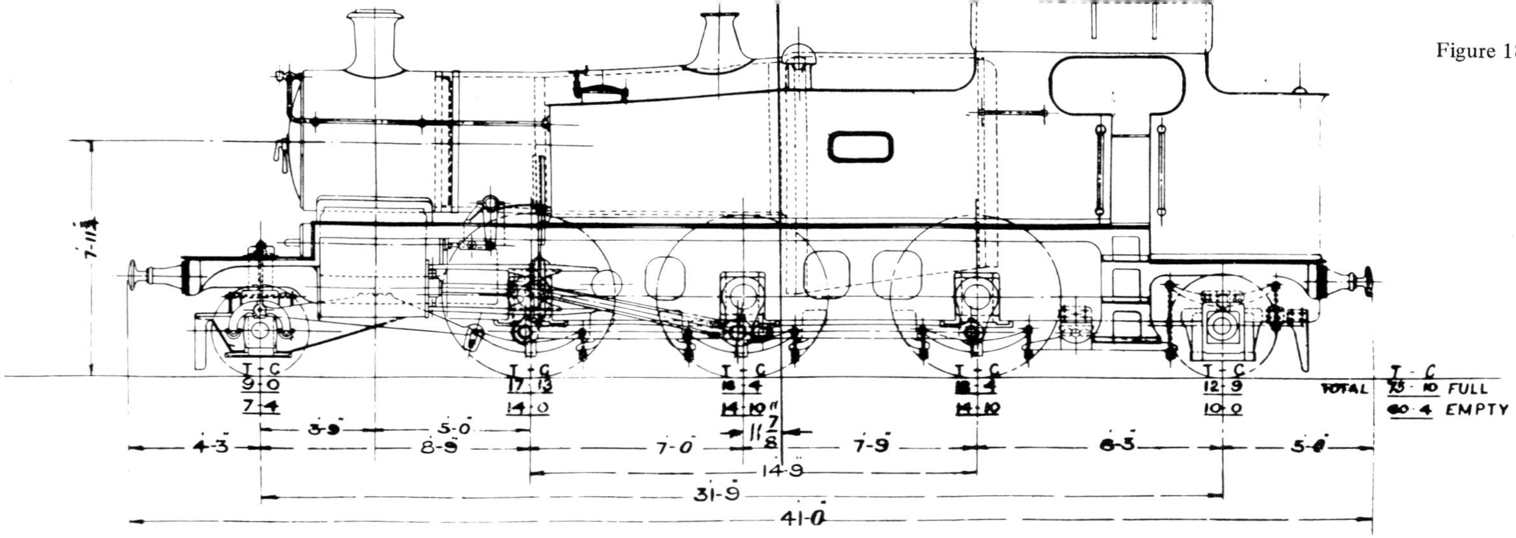

Figure 182

Two stages in the development of the large-wheeled 'Prairie' tanks are illustrated on this page. The '3111' class of 2-6-2T stemmed from the prototype No. 99 of 1903, and the first series of thirty-nine engines built to *Lots 150-152 and 159* during 1905-6 were constructed to *Diagram B* seen in *Figure 182* (Nos. 3111-3149).

As the series were rebuilt with larger bunkers, top feed, and the 6/36 superheater, the diagram issued for this condition was *T,* and this is shown in *Figure 183.*

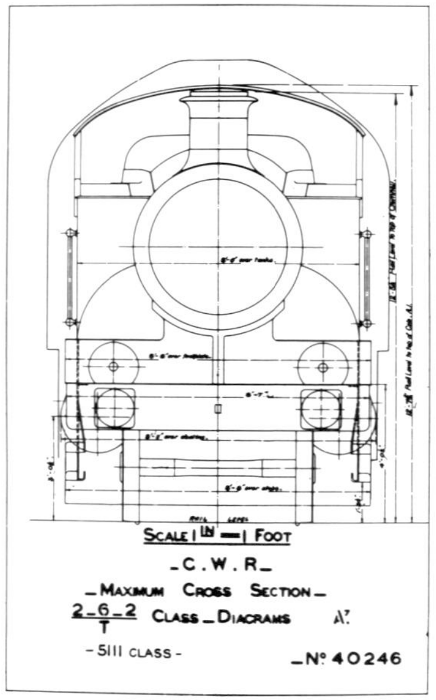

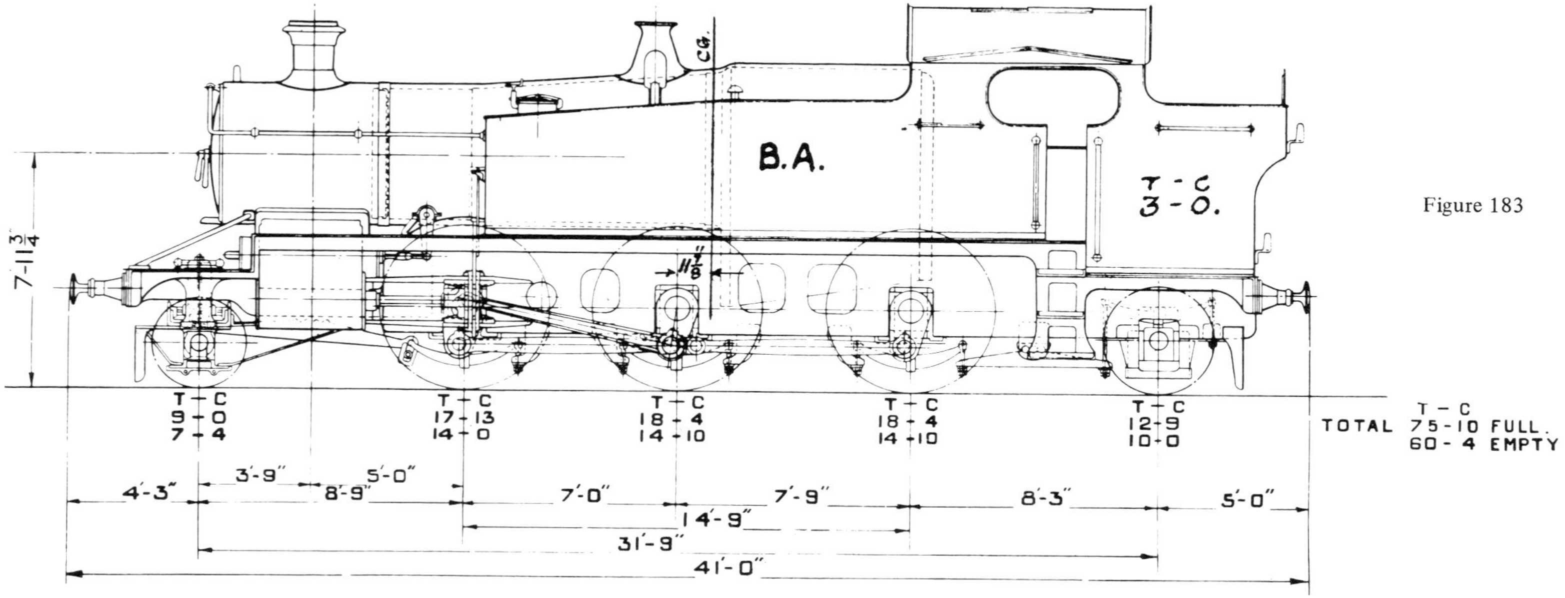

Figure 183

Figure 184

Figure 185

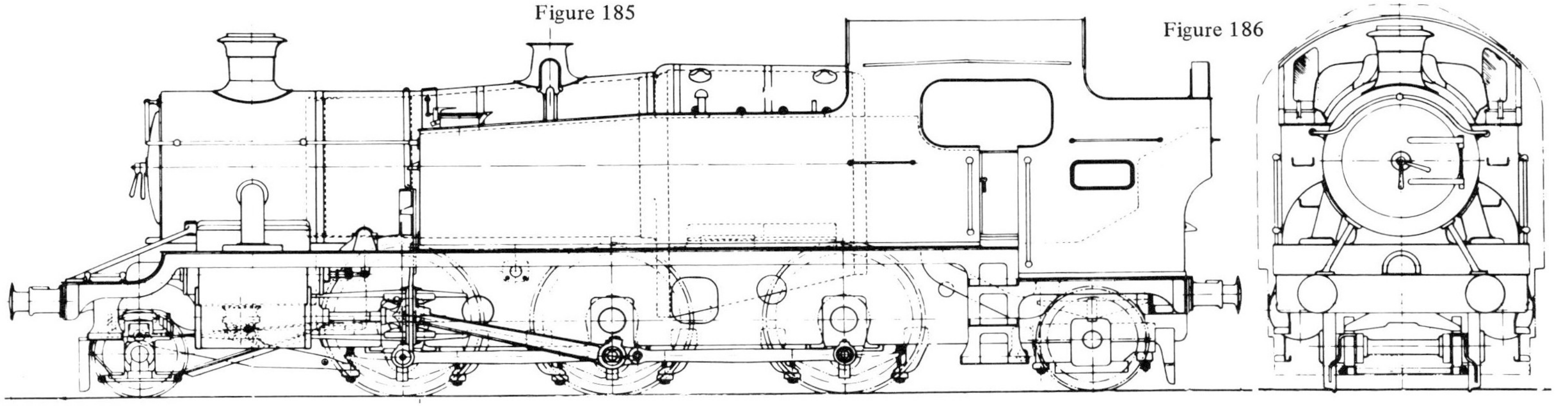

Figure 186

As briefly mentioned on page 39, the 2-6-2T version of the Churchward standard engine policy was No. 99, built in 1903. She was followed in 1905-6 by another thirty-nine sisters, diagrams of which appear on the previous page. An odd point about the prototype engine is that, contrary to the 2221 class, the first engine had the cab sides set in from the tank and bunker plates, whereas the series which followed had the cab sides all flush. The other changes made were in the shape of the tank tops. No. 99 had straight tops, but the '3111' class from 1905 received tanks with sloping tops (see *Diagram B*).

The two photographs illustrate the engines as built with cast iron taper chimney, squared running plates with tool boxes mounted alongside the smokebox, straight-backed bunker, and the number plates fixed to the tank centre. This class of forty engines was not enlarged until 1929, when between then and nationalization a total of 210 locomotives were built to this similar design, superseding the 36XX, 39XX, and 2221 classes completely.

The drawing in *Figure 186* is the Swindon *A.13* of the '3100' class, the last series to be built to this configuration in 1938, and makes a good comparison with the '3111' class (for pictures see page 202).

Figure 187 is included as it shows how the 'two-way' water scoop and ducting was arranged on these 2-6-2T engines.

This 1908 *Diagram G* of the '3150' class is indicative of the last five engines of *Lot 169* (running numbers 3166-70). The equipment was removed after four years use.

Figure 187

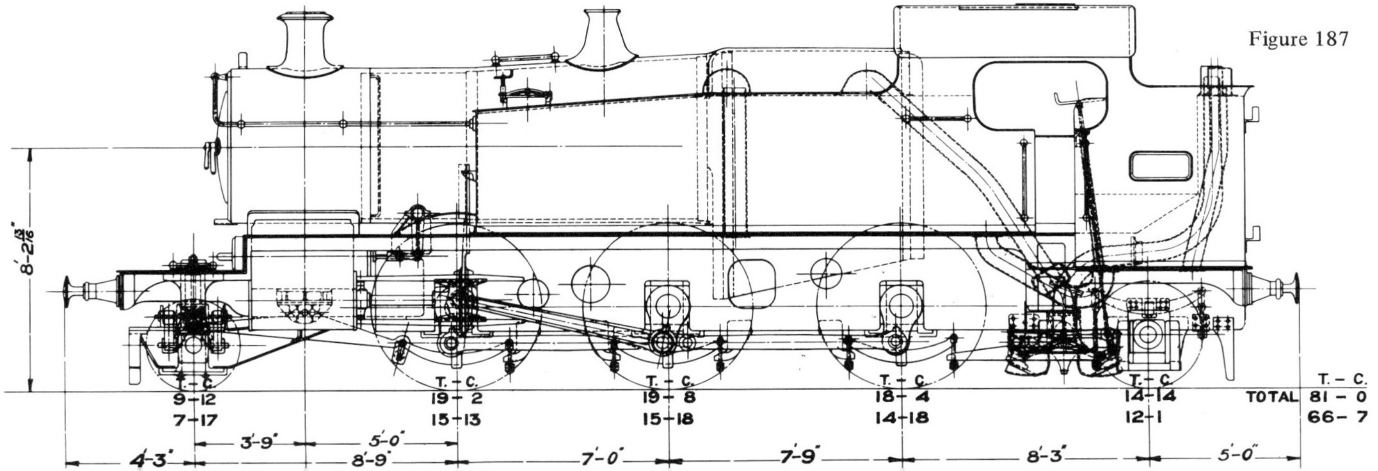

Figure 188

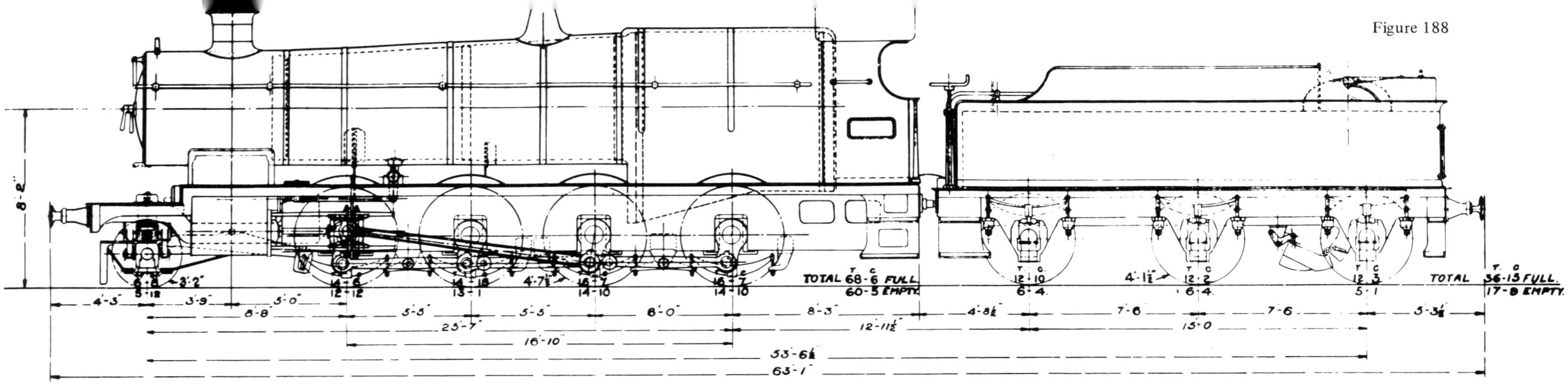

Another 'first' for the Great Western Railway was the production of this the premier 2-8-0 freight engine in the country. One of the original prototypes again, the initial locomotive being No. 97 in the Churchward standardization programme. The design was so successful that engines in the class, with minor differences, were built over the years from 1905 until 1942.

No. 97 (eventually renumbered 2800) was turned out of the factory in 1903 painted black and lined red, but at the first shopping it reverted to the Brunswick Green with black and orange lines. (See *Figure 84* on Page 35.)

The second drawing I have been able to secure shows the subsequent 2801-20 as *Diagram B* (*Figure 190*). At least it is reproduced to 4m/m scale which might give model makers a lead. No. 2803 is shown again on this page to tie up with *Diagram B* and to illustrate the points not clear in the drawing.

The one visible feature in which '97' differed from all her other sisters was that the boiler was at a lower pitch, on a level with the running plate. All subsequent engines were pitched 8½" higher, and clear daylight could be seen underneath the boiler and over the splashers. In 1906 after only three years service the prototype also had her boiler raised to the standard 8′ 2″ and so conformed to the rest of the class. *Figure 188* is the official Swindon *Diagram C* which shows the higher pitch of the boiler on all the series built on *Lots 153-155 and 160*. (See also the photograph on the next page.)

Figure 189

Figure 190

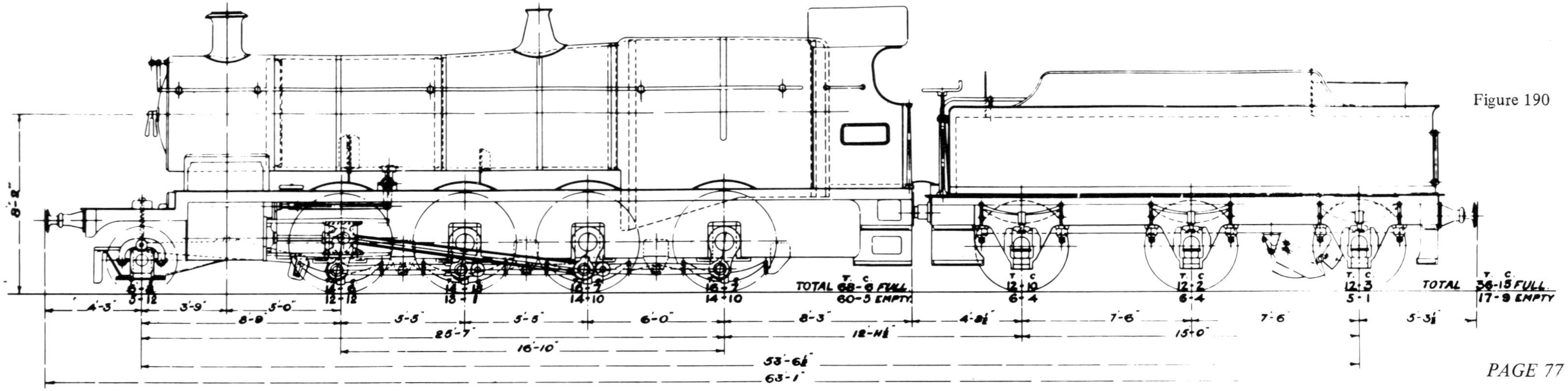

Figure 191

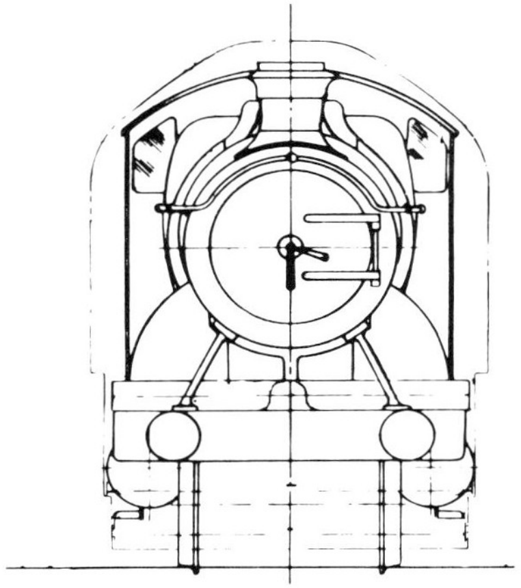

This 1910 photograph is of No. 2811 at Swindon after five years service (*Figure 191*), and fitted with the larger D4 boiler and superheater. It should be noted that at this time the front pair of coupled rods were jointed with a swivel to allow sideways movement. The chimney is now of the larger diameter copper-topped variety, and a small tender is attached. Full lining was still in use, but top feed had not been installed and the framing was still of the square-ended type.

A batch of six, completed in 1911 under *Lot 181,* came out with curved ends to the running plates, and were followed by Nos. 2836-49 in 1912, and 2850-5 in 1913, identical to *Lot 181,* but with top feed already fitted. *Figure 192* shows No. 2840 and illustrates the improvement in appearance to that of *Figure 191.* The drawing (the 2856-83 series) is the official *Diagram I* and is to 4m/m scale for model builders (*Figure 193*).

These engines could and did, work the heaviest freight trains on the Great Western. In February of 1906, although the load for the class was 60 wagons, a test train from Severn Tunnel with No. 2806 started with 54 wagons and dynamometer car behind the engine; at Stoke Gifford the load was increased to 65, and at Swindon was increased again until there were 100 wagons behind the locomotive, which she proceeded to trundle easily all the way to Southall. So was born the ability of the "twenty-eighters" to cope with 100 loaded wagons, and in my time on the Great Western a train left Banbury at 8.10 a.m. every weekday with coal for Southall and loaded to the limit of 100. My father was in charge of this 'Southall' for many years until his death in 1942.

Figure 192

Figure 193

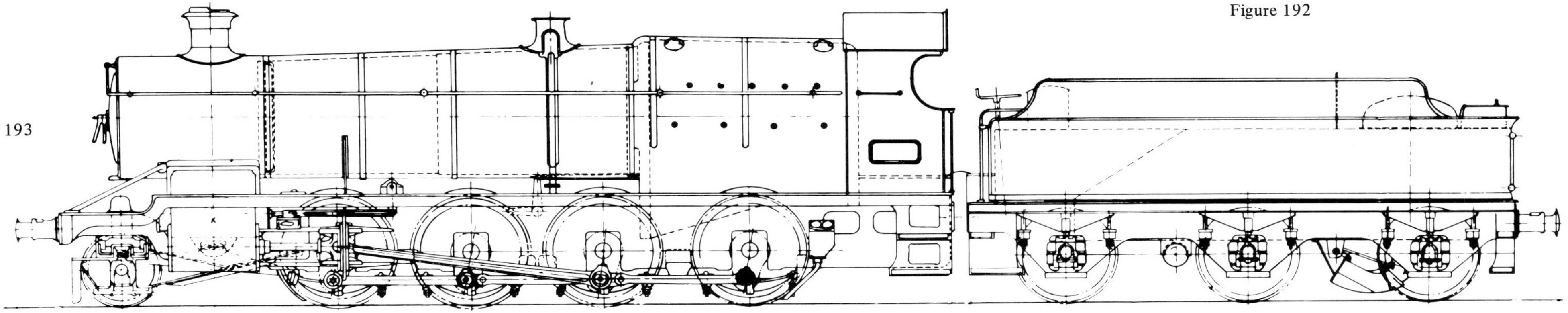

Figure 194

The most famous 'Atlantic' to be built by and run on the Great Western Railway must surely be the first 4-cylinder engine, No. 40, afterwards named *North Star.*

She was constructed in 1906, after Churchward had realized that compounding was not worth while, but the tests with the French engines had proved the advantages of a divided drive with 4 cylinders.

Similar in outline to the 4-6-0 of the 2-cylinder express engines, No. 40 had plate frames with the inside cylinders placed well forward, driving the leading pair of drivers, and the outside cylinders set over the rear pair of bogie wheels, and driving the trailing pair of coupled wheels. This arrangement set the pattern upon which all later 4-cylinder express engines were developed. This not being a text book, but a pictorial record, I have decided to omit technical details and just comment on the photographs, so, in *Figure 195* No. 40 is seen as built in 1906, with no name, and fresh from factory, in *Figure 194* she is seen in Old Oak Common shed with obvious trouble to the big end bearings, and in the lower drawing is seen as first proposed in 4-cylinder layout.

Figure 195

This then was the beginning of a new era in express passenger engines, the '4001' class, and how fitting that the series should commence by being called 'Stars' – these celestial bodies always featuring so largely on the Great Western since the opening of the railway, *North Star* being the first, in 1835, and *Evening Star* the last steam engine to be built at Swindon for British Railways (Western Region) in 1960.

Figure 196

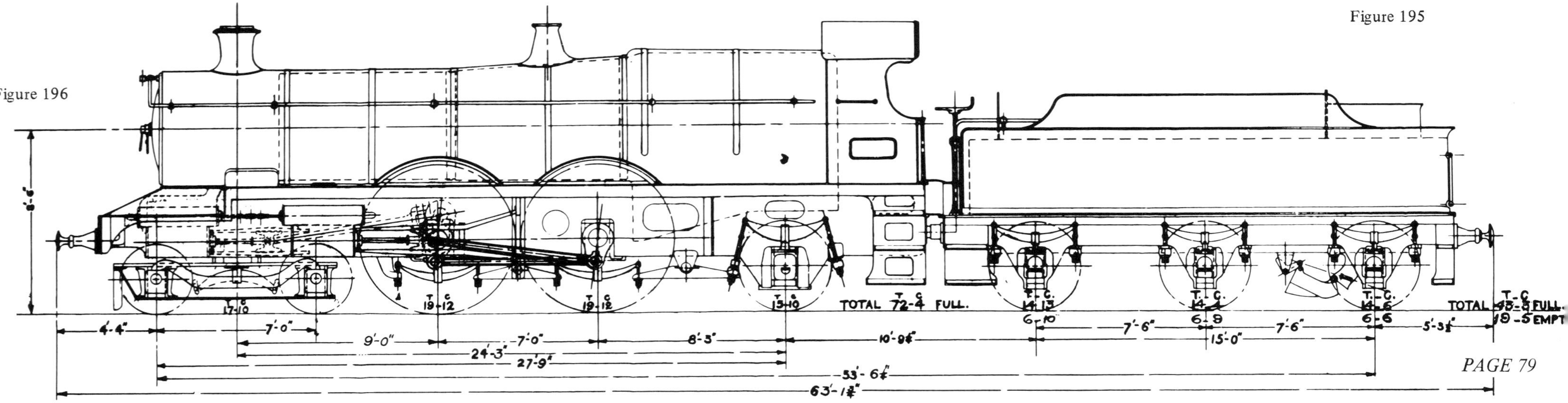

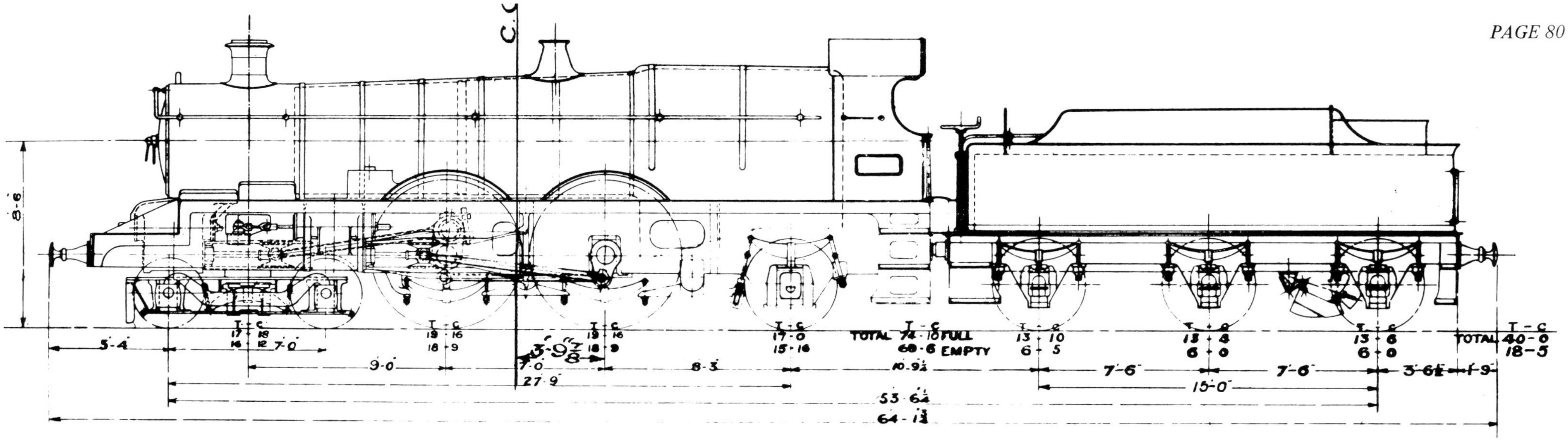

Figure 197

Featured on this page are two more progression drawings, both official Swindon reproductions, and showing the first two stages in the development of the 'Star' class.

In *Figure 197, North Star* is seen as built in 1906, with the 4-4-2 classification and not superheated. In the lower drawing, *Figure 198,* the class is now 4-6-0 and this shows No. 4021 fitted with No. 3 superheater, and curved framing.

Diagrams are *D* and *M* respectively.

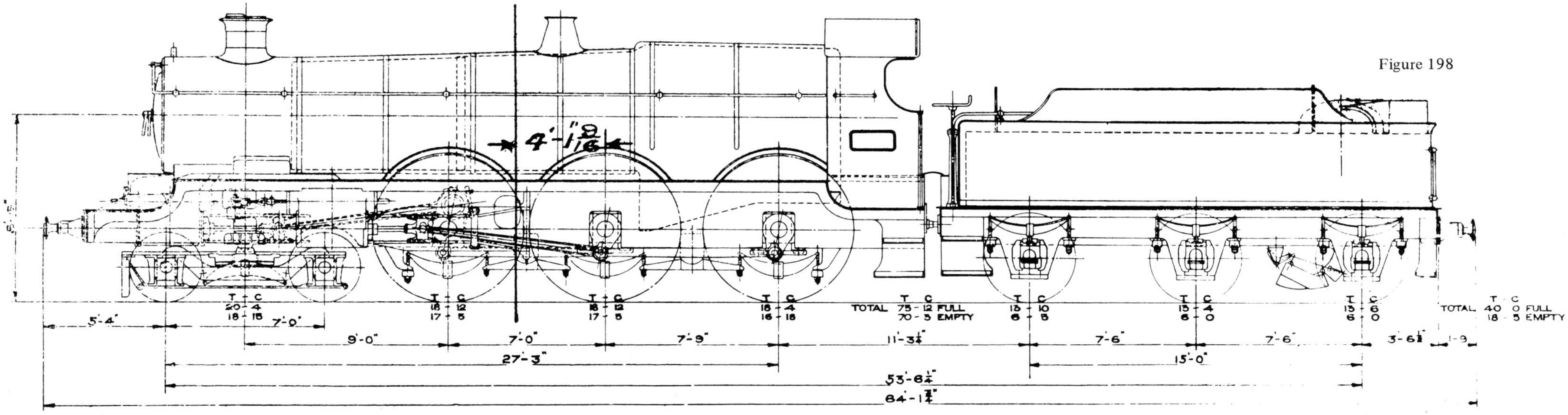

Figure 198

Figure 199

The 'Stars' were ten in number, and were all built in 1907. Handsome engines, they differed from *North Star,* not only in being constructed as 4-6-0's, but the framing was curved harmoniously at both ends, and the sandboxes were fitted underneath the running plate. Also the valve gear was of the ordinary Walschaerts type, and not of the complicated scissors similar to that on No. 40.

Figure 199 is a nice study of *Lode Star* No. 4003, seen at Old Oak Common just prior to backing up to the terminus. Note how clean the engine is, and the polished smokebox door hinges!

The Maskelyne drawing of *Dog Star* shows the class later in their life, after being superheated, fitted with top feed, and the big ejector along the right-hand side of the boiler. Names and numbers, under *Lot 168,* were No. 4001 *Dog Star,* No. 4002 *Evening Star,* No. 4003 *Lode Star,* No. 4004 *Morning Star,* No. 4005 *Polar Star,* No. 4006 *Red Star,* No. 4007 *Rising Star,* No. 4008 *Royal Star,* No. 4010 *Western Star,* and of course *North Star* No. 40, which eventually became No. 4000. *Figure 200* shows her as she first appeared as a 4-6-0 engine.

Figure 200

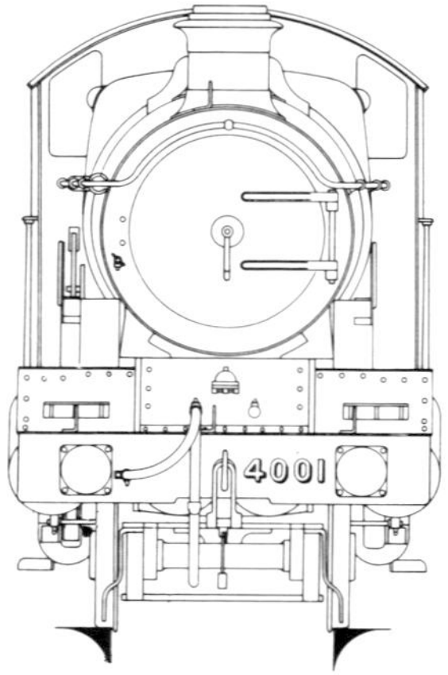

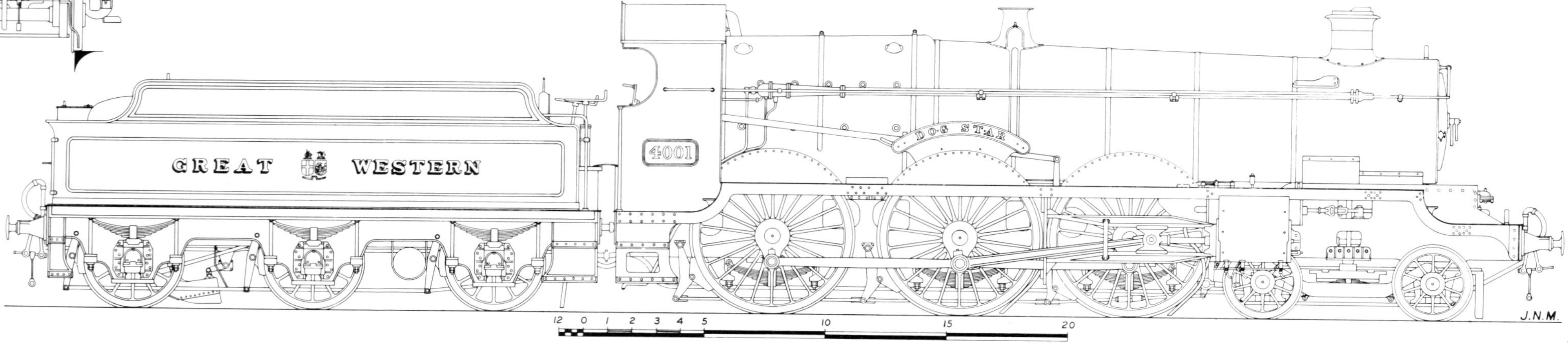

Figure 201

Figure 202

Three early 'Stars' feature here. First in *Figure 202 Rising Star* is seen on the middle road at the old Bristol Temple Meads station and is practically as built. Modellers should note that joggle in the front end of the framing which was to allow the front bogie wheels room to swing. Also it should be noted that as built, these big engines were fitted with bogie brakes.

Figure 203 is the official photograph at Swindon of *Evening Star,* again as built, and *Western Star* is seen at Ranelagh many years later after being fitted with plain chimney and top feed. I would date this picture in the 1915-17 period on account of the plain liver (*Figure 204*).

Figure 203

Figure 204

Figure 206

Figure 207

Figure 208

The next series after the 'Stars' was the '4011-20' class named after Knights and built in 1908. They were followed in 1909 by ten more, named this time after Kings of the realm. In 1910 there appeared ten 'Queens' followed by five 'Princes' in 1913, and in 1914 fifteen 'Princesses' were completed. After this, because of hostilities, there was a gap in construction until 1922-23 when twelve 'Abbeys' completed the series. At the top of this page is seen *Red Star* No. 400 in a photograph dated 1909, whilst in *Figures 206 and 208 King Edward* is illustrated, as fitted with the royal emblems draped in purple for the occasion of the funeral of King Edward, whose funeral train this engine hauled on May 20th 1910 from Paddington to Windsor. On another royal train duty is *Princess Mary* pictured in 1914. Note the improvements in the engine, the top feed and the larger tender, but the works plate has not been fitted to the centre splasher, and the livery is unlined as a wartime measure *(Figure 207).*

Figure 209

Figure 210

A sequence of the 'Star' class locomotive is shown on this and the following page, but at various times in its existence. First in *Figure 209* is a right-hand view of *Western Star* seen in the 'twenties at Old Oak Common shed after bringing a train into Paddington; the fire is obviously being cleaned. The short-lived 'namer' *Knight of the Black Eagle* is seen in *Figure 210* standing at Bristol Temple Meads, built in 1908. War with Germany in 1914 caused this name to be changed to *Knight of Liége* as seen in the 1924 photograph of No. 4017 in *Figure 211.*

Figure 211

An early 'King' No. 4024 as built is shown in *Figure 212* followed by *Queen Mary,* No. 4031, shown in wartime livery in *Figure 213.* The *Prince of Wales* (*Figure 214*) lined out in works grey for the official photograph is shown in full glory, although the picture is dated 1913! *Figure 215,* No. 4049 *Princess Maud,* is seen at Paddington again in wartime austerity, and finally (*Figure 216*) *Reading Abbey* is seen at Old Oak Common shed in plain green and carrying the small tapered cast iron chimney.

Figure 212

Figure 213

Figure 214

Figure 215

Figure 216

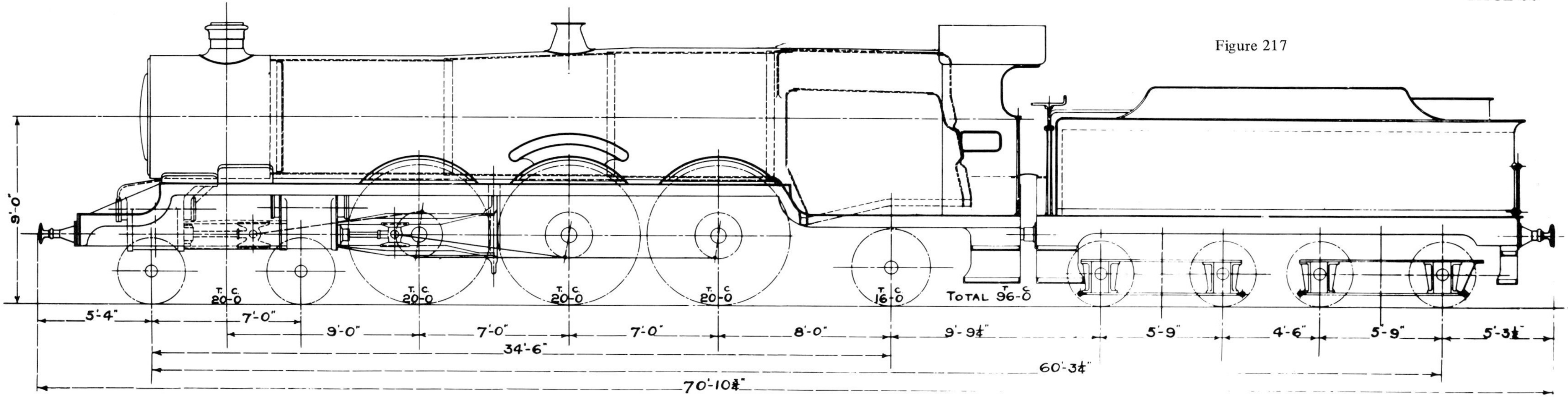

Figure 217

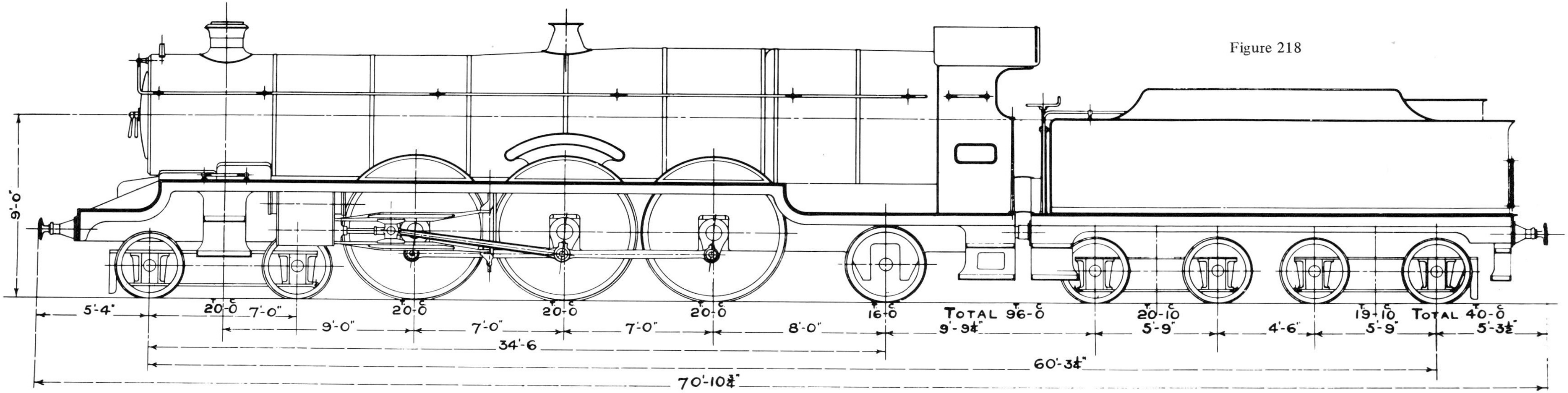

Figure 218

Yet another first for the Great Western Railway was *The Great Bear.* Although many other foreign countries had examples of the 'Pacific' locomotive, this mighty engine was the forerunner of the 4-6-2 type in Great Britain.

It has been quoted many times that No. 111 came into being as a prestige move through pressure on Churchward from the Directors and without doubt this succeeded. By the year 1908 *The Great Bear* was the largest engine to run in the United Kingdom. However, Churchward was never enthusiastic over the project, and No. 111 was simply a machine of large proportions, using standard wheels, motion and cylinders and a huge boiler of plain construction with a wide Belpaire type of firebox which had a sloping backplate. Inside bearings were used on all wheels and those of the trailing truck always proved the 'Achilles heel' of the engine. If outside axle-boxes had been used, similar to the 'Gresley Pacifics', what a different future, engine policy on the Great Western might have been.

The tender was of large proportions to suit the lines of the big engine, and two standard loco bogies with a shortened wheelbase were used to make an eight-wheeled vehicle (see page 84). *Figures 217 and 218* are early sketches to Churchward's orders.

Figure 219

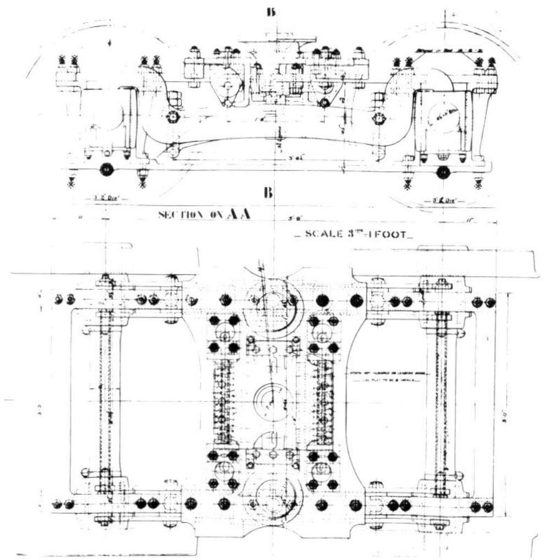

Figure 220

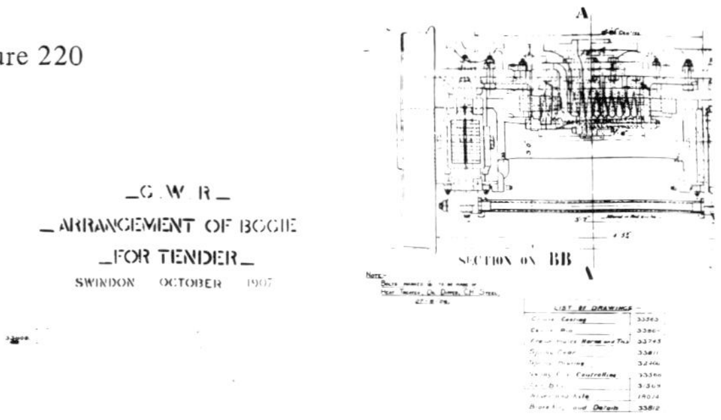

Figure 219 is a little known picture of No. 111 standing at Bathampton, and shows the right-hand side of the loco as built. She is carrying 'B' headlights, and is on the middle road, so one can only surmise trouble! In the lower photograph she is seen at Swindon running shed near the end of her days, as she was withdrawn in 1924, and some of her parts were used for a 'Castle' class engine. Note the cast iron chimney, top feed, and big ejector, and by this time the front steps have now been removed (*Figure 220*). The small inset is a reduction of the works drawing of 111's tender bogie.

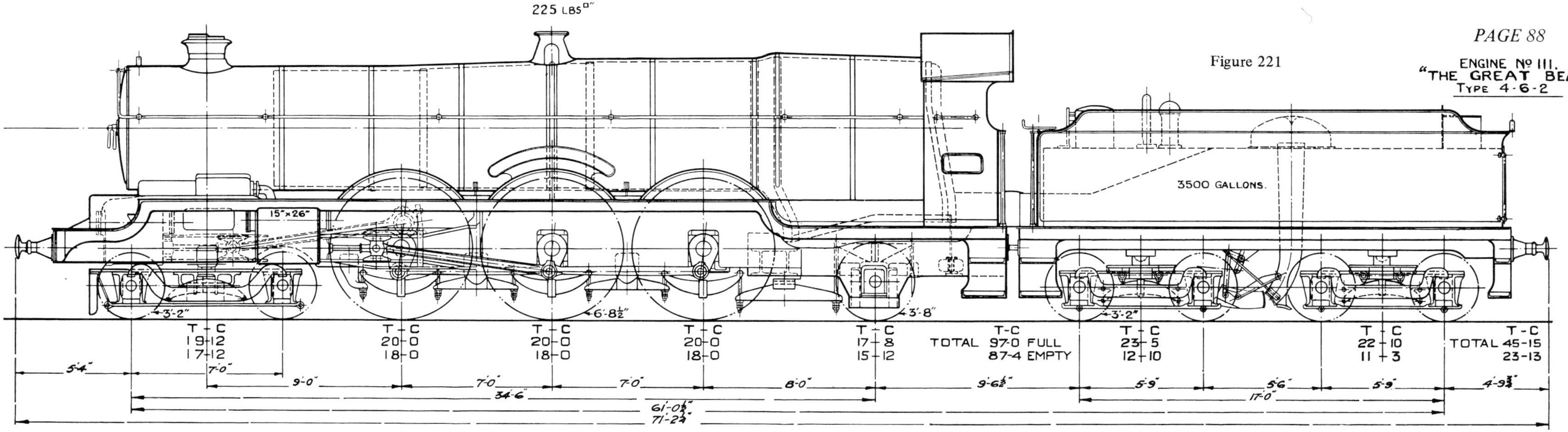

Figure 221

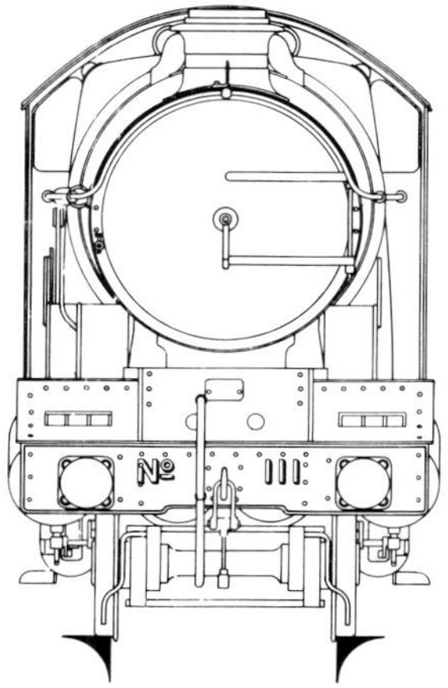

Figure 222

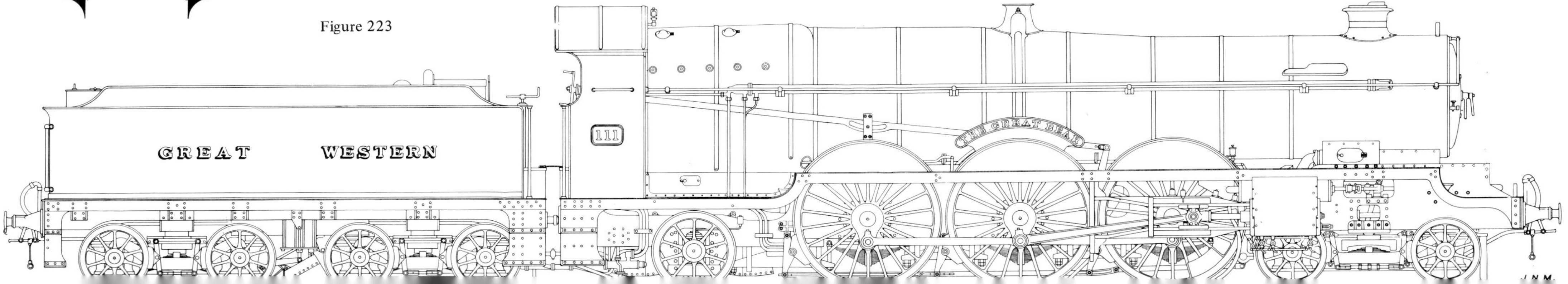

Figure 223

These two drawings should help modellers to obtain the vital statistics of No. 111. *Figure 221* is the official Swindon *Diagram C* and shows her in her last condition before withdrawal and ties up with *Figure 220* on the previous page.

The lovely drawing by J.N. Maskelyne at the foot of the page, is of the engine in the same period but showing the right-hand side, and many details are given which are not on the official diagram.

The interesting photograph of *Figure 222* I found whilst researching at Swindon factory, and it was obviously taken not only to show the terrific disparity of size, but also the odd fact of two engines with the same number!

Figure 224

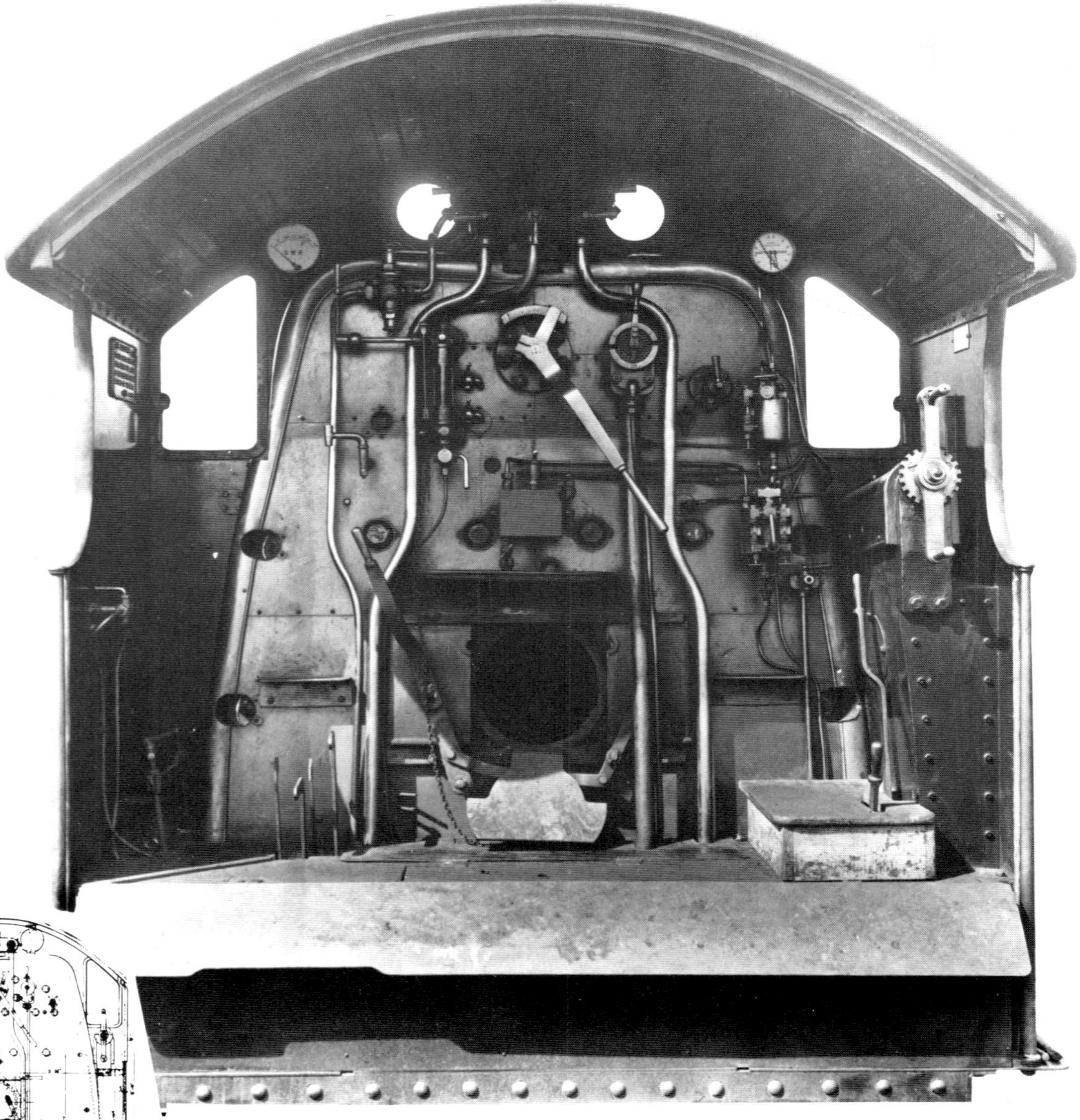

Figure 225

Here are two more helpful photographs to assist model makers, and which will also interest enthusiasts. *Figure 224* shows one of the tender bogies in the shops at Swindon and proves that they were of the standard locomotive bogie pattern. The tender is seen immediately behind, and a small point of interest is that the water content of the tank was calibrated on a gauge (seen at top centre) instead of the more usual float.

The other official picture in *Figure 225* is of the cab and back plate, and with the exception of the huge firebox with sloping sides and back, the fittings are standard. The four cross sections in *Figure 226* give a good indication of '111's' size.

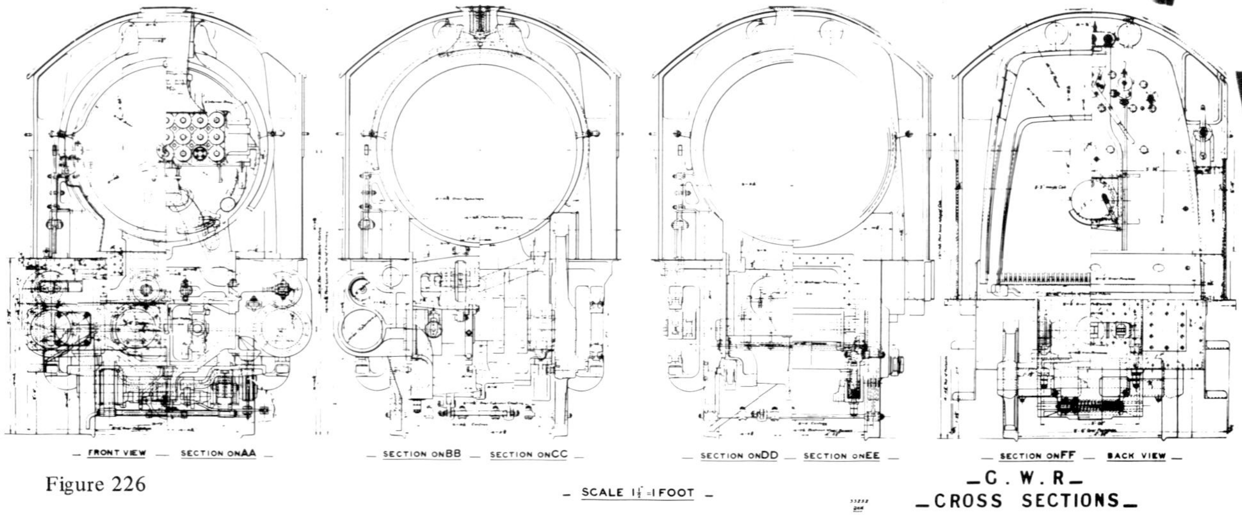

Figure 226

Figure 227

This superb photograph from Paddington archives, illustrates well what a magnificent machine Britain's 'largest engine' really was. That boiler for instance, was made in three rings, the rear one 6′ in diameter and sloping to the front ring of 5′ 6″ diameter. The length was 22′ 7″ between front and firebox tube plates, and the centre line stood 9′ above the rail level! There were 141 tubes of 2½″ diameter, and 21 larger ones of 4¾″ diameter, the superheater had 84 tubes of $1^{3}/8''$ diameter, and there were four $3^{3}/8''$ water tubes fitted in the firebox. (See previous page.)

However, perhaps on account of the extreme length, the *'Bear'* was always a poor steamer, and was confined to the late afternoon Bristol express, returning on a fitted night freight. Her extreme size caused much trouble, No. 1 platform at Paddington was out of bounds for her, and the front steps were always fouling platform edges, so much so that they were quickly removed. Also the cab roof gave firemen trouble, so had to be shortened.

The total weight of the engine in working order was 97 tons and with 45 tons 15 cwt for the massive tender, this made a grand total of 142 tons 15 cwts. No wonder the Civil Engineer restricted her routes and gave the engine many anxious glances!

A superb model of the engine in the same condition as shown in this picture, can be seen at Pendon Museum near Didcot, where a 4m/m miniature made by my friend Guy Williams works regularly on the Vale of the White Horse line, every weekend.

The drawing in *Figure 228* is another by J.N. Maskelyne and was executed in 1914 showing the left-hand side of the engine.

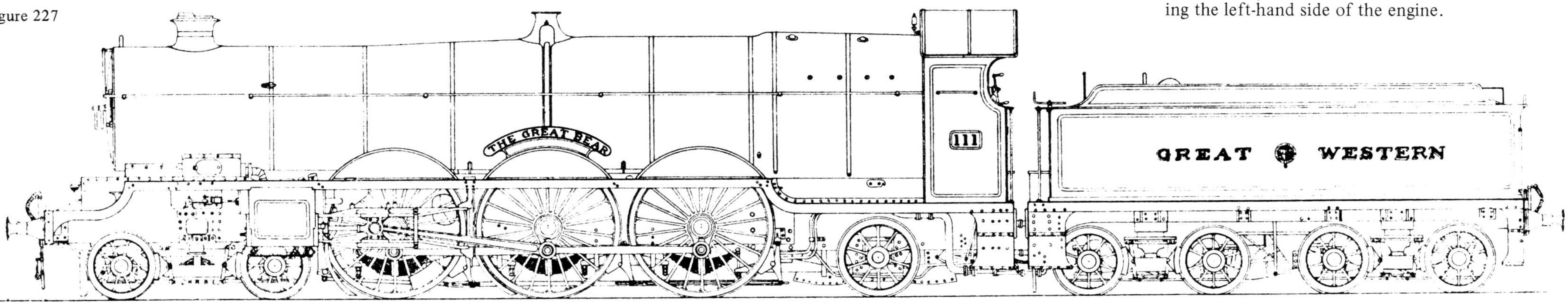

Figure 229

Figure 230

The final study of No. 111 as *The Bear* is shown in *Figure 229.* This was taken at Swindon in 1917, after what was to be her final refit at the factory. When the inner firebox became due for renewal in 1924, the whole engine was scrapped and several pieces were salvaged to emerge again as a new locomotive of the 'Castle' class, namely *Viscount Churchill* as shown in *Figure 230.* (This meant that the 'Saint' class engine carrying this name, No. 2975, had to be renamed, and so from 1924 was fitted with plates *Sir Ernest Palmer,* afterwards shortened to *Lord Palmer* in 1933.) Although *Viscount Churchill* is seen coupled to the large bogie tender, there is speculation as to whether or not this engine ever ran with the *Bear's* water cart. I seem to remember being shown this engine by my father in 1924 and it surely had both the No. 111 and the bogie tender then, as amongst railwaymen of that time *Viscount Churchill* was *The Great Bear* re-incarnated. Finally a few dimensions:- 4 cylinders 15″ diameter, 26″ piston stroke, piston valves 8″ diameter, maximum travel of 7¼″. Walschaerts gear was used, two sets working the inner valves directly, and the outside valves by horizontal rockers. Driving wheels were the standard 6′ 8½″ six coupled, bogies were 3′ 2″ and the trailing truck 3′ 8″. Wheelbase was 34′ 6″, 7′ + 5′ 6″ + 7′ + 7′ + 8′. The overhanging measurements were 6′ at the rear, and 3′ 6″ at the front end. The running plate was 8′ 8″ wide in front and 9′ at the cab end. The firebox was 8′ long and 6′ 6″ wide with a grate area of 41.79 sq. ft. Wheelbase of engine and tender was 61′ 0½″ and over buffers the full length came out at 71′ 2¼″, almost the same as a 'Dreadnought' coach.

We come now to the year 1910, and in this year not only was the 'New Line' London-Birmingham via Bicester opened, but also the '4201' class was introduced. This was another new design by Churchward, developed again from standard parts used in the engine programme, and this time from the '28XX' class freight engine.

The new series was of the 2-8-0T pattern, and was the first in the country to use this wheel plan. Principal usage for this class of locomotive was the haulage of heavy mineral trains in South Wales, and due to the sharp curves encountered, it was necessary to allow side play in the trailing driving wheels. This in turn meant jointed coupling rods, with sideways as well as up and down movement. Therefore the trailing coupling rods were fitted with spherical joints to allow just such movement in any direction.

Figure 232 is the official photograph of the first engine in the series, No. 4201, and although superheated, she was not at this time fitted with top feed. Like so many new designs at this time, she ran alone for fourteen months before proving a success. The second batch was built in 1912 under *Lot 187.* No. 4201 differed from her sisters in having a small flat-topped bunker, and this was not enlarged until 1919. The lower drawing is the official *Diagram D* which shows the engines at a later date when fitted with cast iron chimneys and top feed etc. *Figure 231* shows the first diagram issued for the class, namely *'A'* to *Lot 182* which is as No. 4201 was built.

Figure 231

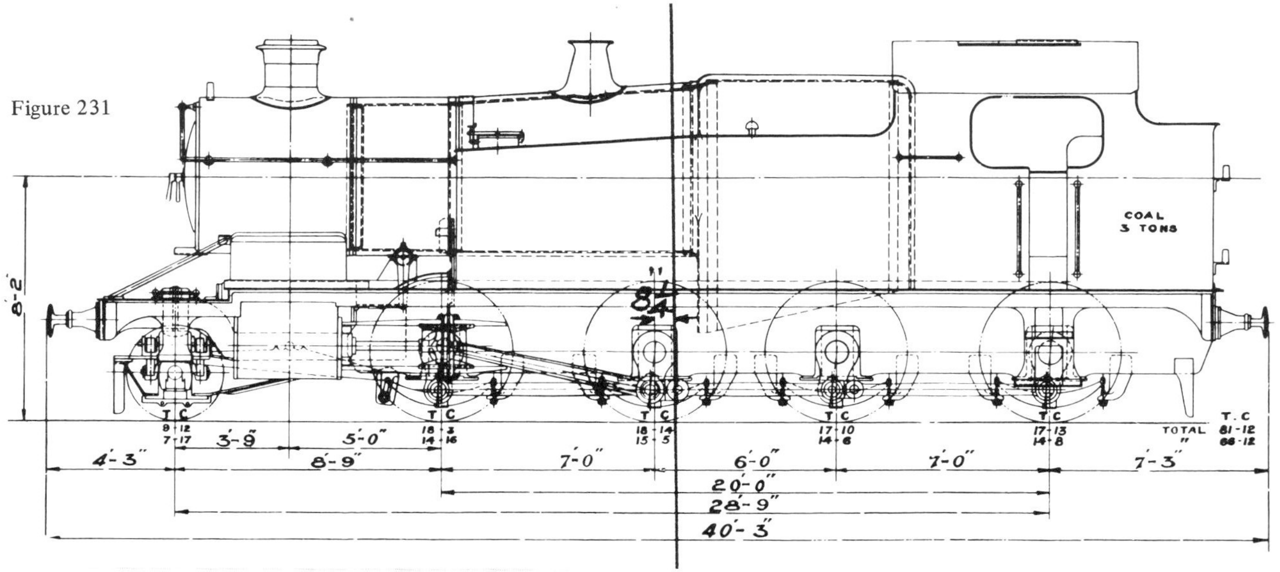

Figure 232

Figure 233

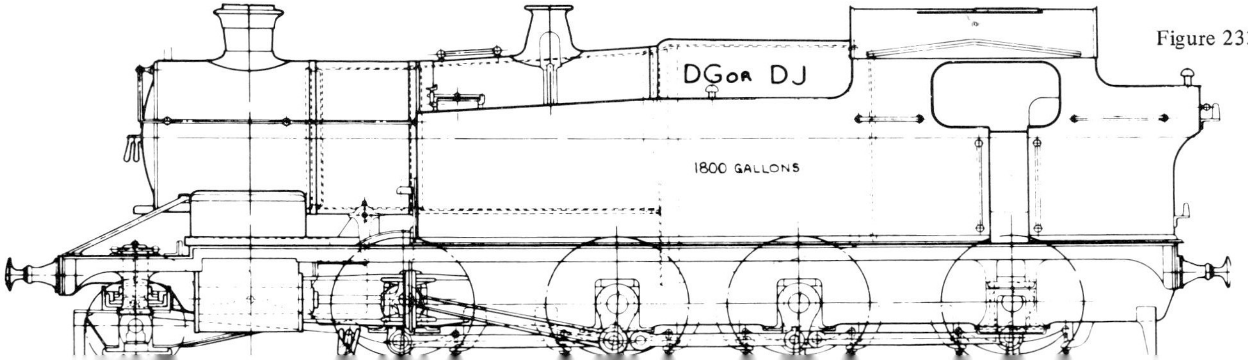

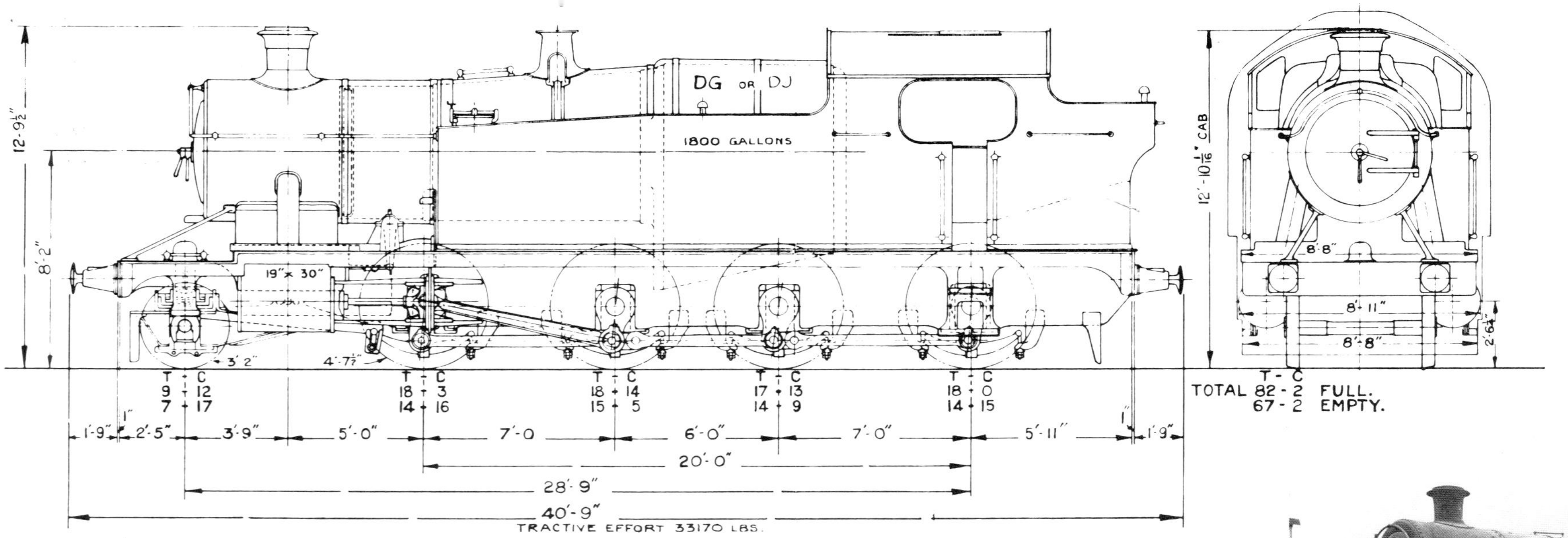

Figure 234

No. 4202 was the first of the 1912 batch to be built, and is illustrated in *Figure 236.* One can see at once the larger bunker with the extended top, and the top feed fitted to the series from here on. These powerful tank engines proved very satisfactory in service, and building carried on over the years, up until 1940, when a total of 165 engines had been built. In 1923 outside steam pipes to the cylinders were fitted and this can be seen both in *Figure 235* of No. 5211 and also in the *Diagram E* (*Figure 234*). In 1919 the batch of 2-8-0T's completed under *Lot 213* were turned out with cast iron taper chimneys, and gradually the whole series were fitted with this pattern in place of the copper-topped built-up type which adorned the first five lots. Also in this year, as the engines passed through the shops, the bunkers were lengthened by 6" to accommodate more coal in order to extend their range.

Figure 235

Figure 236

Modellers should note that the wheelbase on these engines does not conform to that on the 28XX class, the driving wheel centres being 7' + 6' + 7' against those of the 2-8-0 tender engines which were 5' 5" + 5' 5" + 6' 0". Note also the injector overflow pipe passes under the trailing coupling rod, and outlets behind the cab steps.

No. 4200 shown in *Figure 237* at Plymouth North Road in 1928, was not the prototype engine. It was the custom of the authorities at Swindon to start a series with 'XX01' and later if necessary bring in the 'XX00' of the class, and so it was in this case. No. 4200 was built as late as 1923 under *Lot 223* together with the 5205-14 batch. It should be noted that at this period the tall safety valve bonnet was still being used, but taper chimneys were fitted and the bunker was extended.

In *Figure 238* more of Colonel Templer's excellent drawings figure, and illustrate both the early short series with the square dropped framing and the later curved frame of the 5275-94 series. These drawings are to 4m/m scale, and notes are added from Colonel Templer's own pen.

Figure 237

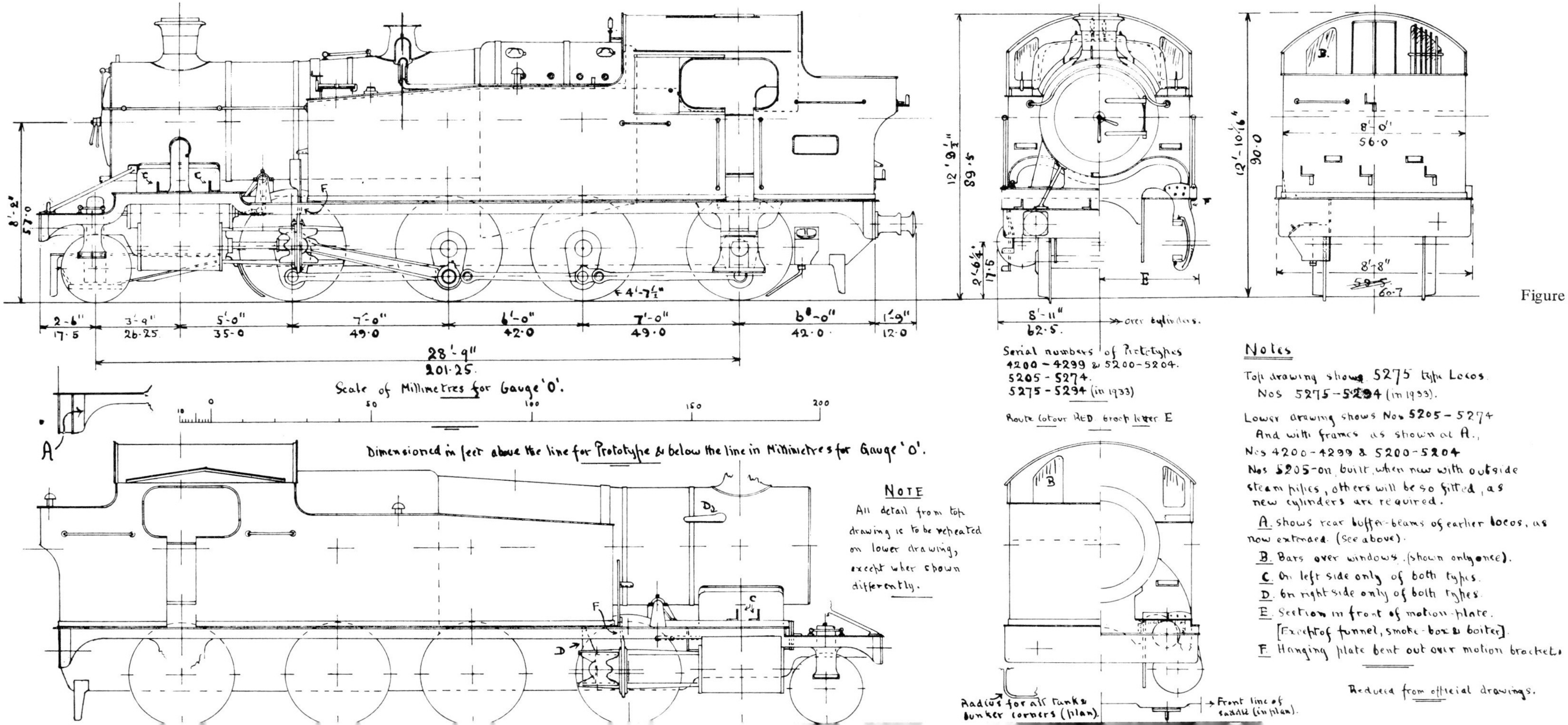

Figure 238

Figure 239

Figure 240

A page of '42XX's photographed in the 1940's. *Figures 239 and 240* show No. 4250 in far West Wales on a freight from Neyland to Carmarthen. Note how the framing over the cylinders goes up over and down again, whereas in No. 4221 (shown in *Figure 241* at Swindon) outside steam pipes were fitted in 1945, but the framing was left straight. The official picture in *Figure 242* was taken in 1946 and shows No. 4231 without curved frames or outside steam pipes, and destined for Cardiff shed. In these pictures both the tall and the short safety valve bonnets are shown and also the sliding shutters which were fitted to the cab sides. In service these engines were always reckoned even stronger than the 28XX class, as all the weight of the water was available for adhesion. I never saw one of these 2-8-0T's slip!

Figure 241

Figure 242

Figure 243

It is not generally known that long before the streamlined Diesel cars, the Great Western had experimented with a small rail-bus vehicle. In 1911 the Company purchased a Petrol-Electric railcar which was designed by British Thompson-Houston & Co. It consisted of a four-wheeled car, driven by a 40 HP Maudsley petrol engine which drove a dynamo for supplying current to two electric motors on the axles.

The car which could seat 46, had a capable mileage of 250, and could reach a speed of 35 mph.

However, after a short life, spent mostly on the Windsor branch, it was withdrawn in 1919 due to overheating trouble with the valves, and was eventually sold to Lever Bros. of Port Sunlight.

Figure 243 is the official picture of the car which was given the number 100 after this photograph was taken. The livery was crimson lake with gold lining and white roof.

Figure 244

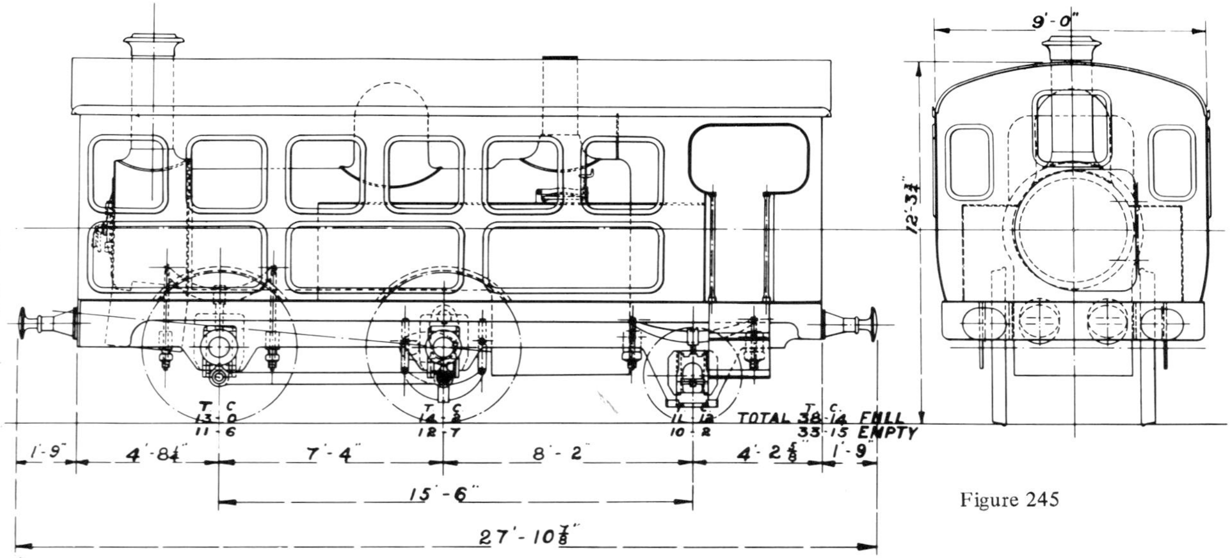

Figure 245

Figure 246

The popularity of the autocar working system for branch lines brought about an unusual engine transformation in 1906. In an effort to harmonise the locomotive with the passenger carriages, one of the '2021' class of 0-6-0 Wolverhampton saddle tanks was refitted with a short square tank, new boiler fittings and was completely clothed in a shell, which, from the outside looked like a coach body, complete with the windows and fully lined out in the carriage livery.

The idea was that, sandwiched in between a set of four trailer cars, the whole train would present a more pleasing aspect to the travelling public than the more practical engine outline.

Two windows were provided in the front end over the smokebox, and three in the rear, over the bunker. However in service the enclosed cabin proved much too hot for the enginemen and the experiment was abandoned in 1911.

As well as No. 2120, another engine of the same class was dealt with similarly at Newton Abbot; this was No. 2140, and also two of the '517' class 0-4-2T's were fitted with this dummy coach shell; these were Nos. 533 and 833.

Figure 246 illustrates No. 2120 as turned out at Swindon in 1906 dressed as a coach, and the dummy panelling can be clearly seen. The tall boxes with handle in the entrance to the cab were the sandboxes for the trailing wheels.

In *Figure 244* we see No. 2120 running as a normal pannier tank in 1920, but before this, she had been turned out of Newton Abbot with the square tank, spark arresting chimney and a deep bunker, which eventually became the pattern used at Swindon from 1924. (Note the high firebox.) *Figure 245* is a 4m/m reproduction of the official diagram and shows the appearance of the 0-4-2T transformation.

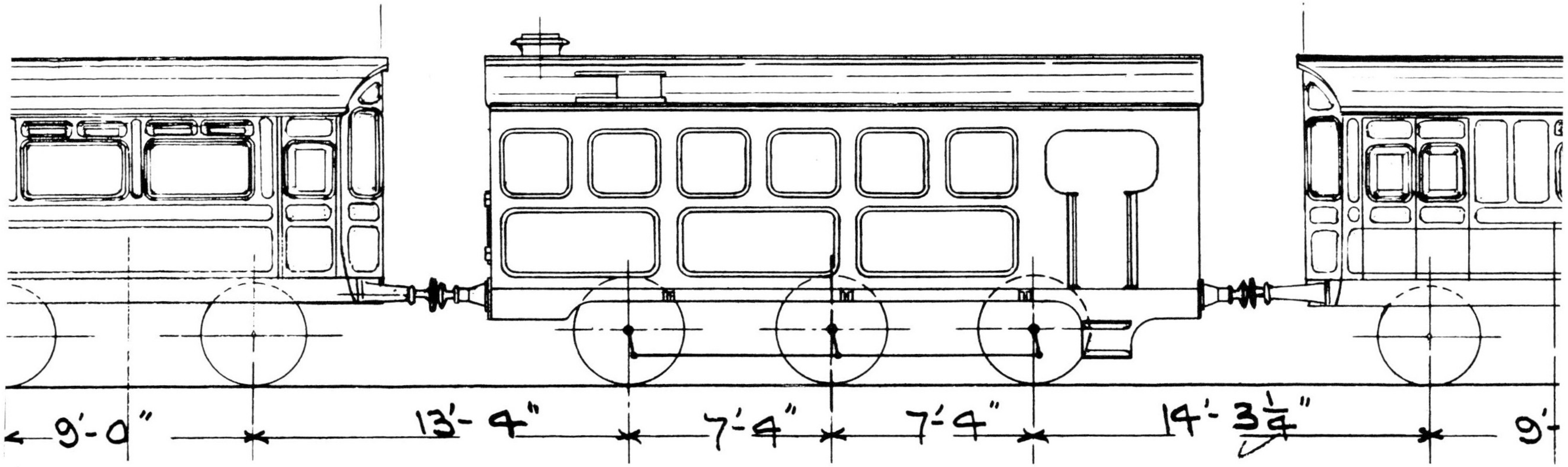

Figure 247

Figure 247 is reduced from an official blueprint to 4m/m scale, and shows how these clothed engines appeared sandwiched between the trailer cars, whilst *Figure 248* is the official diagram of the 0-6-0T so treated.

Figure 248

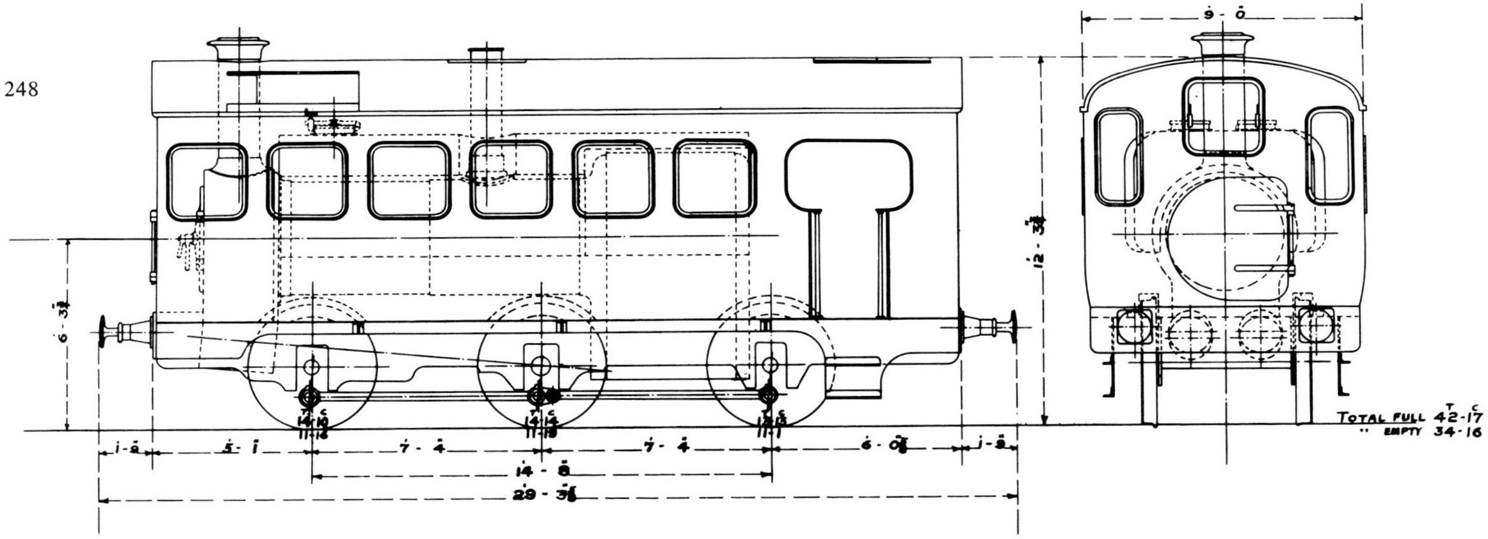

Figure 249

This picture shows No. 2140 after being stripped of her coach body, and before being converted back to a normal pannier tank in 1916. The picture is most useful to modellers, as it shows what was under the coach clothing. One can see the square tank, tall chimney and safety valve (no dome) and also the tank filler lids, which when fitted with the coach shell, were filled through a sliding shutter in the roof. Note the whistles are mounted horizontally and big headed buffers are fitted. Modellers should also note the non-standard hand rails and cab windows.

The history of this engine is thus interesting, she was originally built with saddle tanks in January 1904, converted to the dummy coach form with square tanks in 1908, stripped of the shell in 1911 to the condition seen in *Figure 249,* rebuilt at Newton Abbot in 1915 with open cab, deep bunker, but still carrying the square tank, and spark arrester, had pannier tanks fitted in 1916, and continued in service right up until May 1952.

Figure 250 is the official *Diagram A.58* and shows No. 2120 with the square tanks and tall chimney like the photograph of No. 2140, but stripped of the large cab.

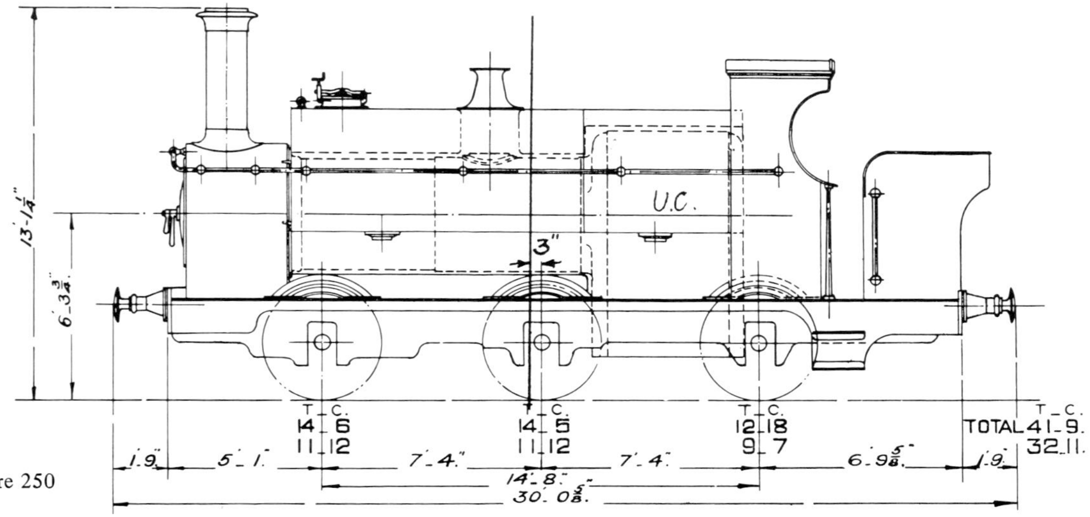

Figure 250

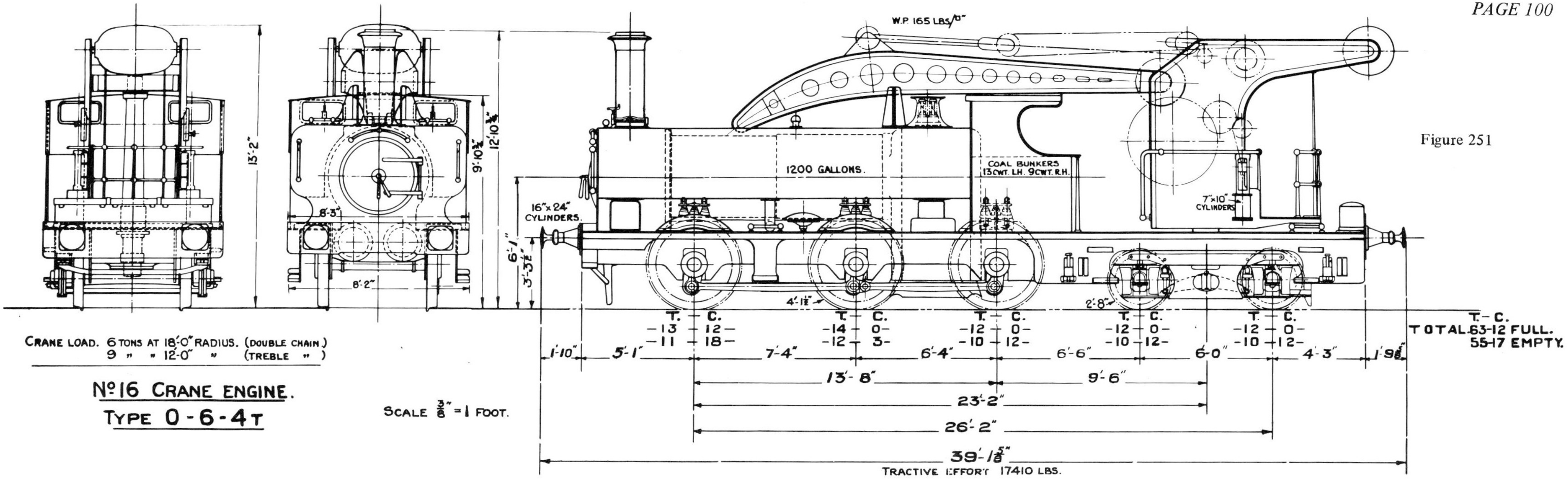

Figure 251

– DESCRIPTION –

CYLINDERS	DIAR. 16" STROKE 24". STEAM PORTS 14"X 1⅜" EXHAUST 14"X 3½".
BOILER	BARREL 10'-0". DIAR. OUTS. 3'-10" & 3'-9⅝".
FIREBOX	OUTS. 4'-0" X 4'-0". INS. 3'-3$\frac{13}{16}$" X 3'-4". HEIGHT 5'-5½".

In the year 1901, two unusual machines were built at Swindon under *Lot 121.* They were the crane engines Nos. 17 and 18 named respectively *Cyclops* and *Steropes.* Basically they consisted of an engine of the '850' class with frame extended backward to accommodate a steam crane, taking its power supply from the main engine boiler, but being operated from the swivelling turntable on the crane itself. This rear end was supported on a four-wheeled bogie of 6' wheelbase. Apart from one other engine, No. 1490, this was the first use of pannier tanks on Swindon locomotives.

As can be seen in both the drawing at *Figure 251* and in the official 1901 photograph, the boilers were domeless, with a short safety valve bonnet, in order to allow the swivelling jib to lay along the boiler top when travelling. A low cab profile had also to be used, to clear both the jib and the counterbalance weight when the crane was at work. The official drawing in *Figure 251* gives many relevant measurements and even shows the position and sizes of the gear train on the crane itself. Note that the engine springs are of the volute type, whilst those of the crane bogie are the long transverse leaf style. This *Diagram* is *C* for No. 16 only.

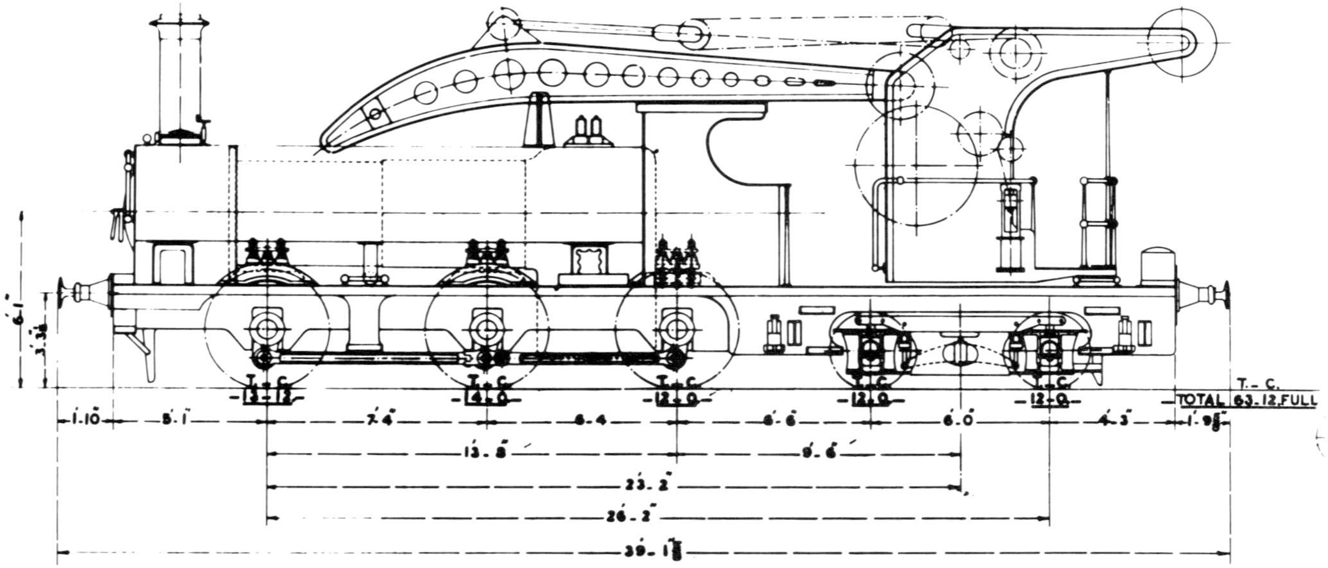

Figure 253

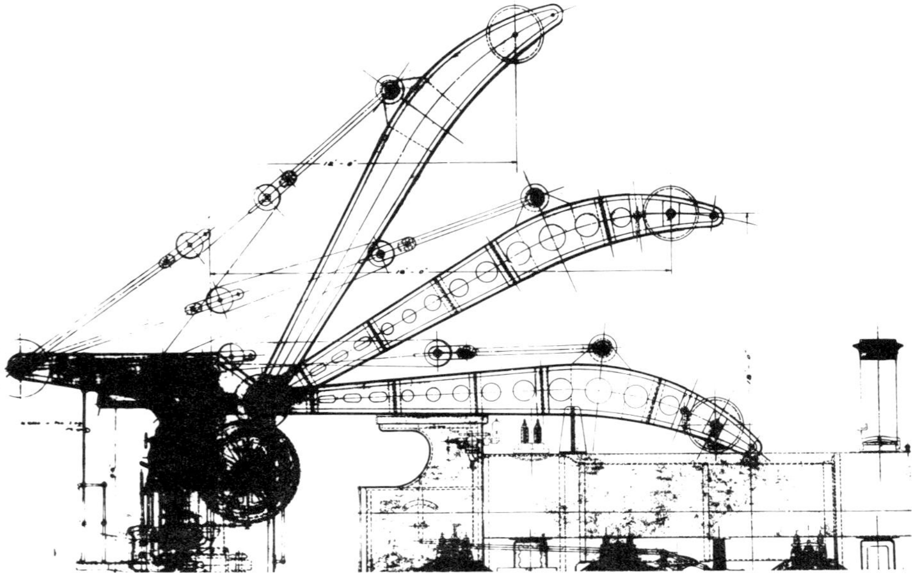

Figure 254 shows No. 16 *Hercules,* which was the third and last crane engine to be built, and twenty years after the first two! The photograph shows the machine in the travelling position, and *Figure 252* illustrates No. 17 with the jib extended into the working attitude at almost full radius. The drawing is *Diagram A* which applied to numbers 17 and 18. These two were fitted with the old round top boiler RO whilst No. 16 had a Belpaire firebox and boiler. Inset shows three positions of jib.

Figure 254

Figure 255

Figure 257

Figure 256

The driving platform of No. 17 *Cyclops* is shown in close detail in *Figure 256* and it is possible to identify the regulator in the centre, with the levers for raising and lowering the jib, lifting and slewing, all grouped to the left of the platform. The main crankshaft can be seen passing right across the superstructure, and the main steam supply pipes emerging from the centre tower pivot. The large counter-weight can also be seen at the top of the picture which helped to balance the weight of the jib and chains. Later in service the rear of the driving platform was sheeted in, as can be seen in *Figure 255* which shows No. 18 *Steropes* on one of her last duties, namely the renewal of the platform faces at Paddington in 1933. Note the old wooden arrival signal box still in place although the electric box was erected close by.

Figure 257 shows a right-hand view of No. 18 at Swindon just before withdrawal in 1936. I would add that I knew these little engines well, and was always fascinated by their square cab windows and very wide cab, which had a coal bunker on each side behind the number plate (see *Figure 255*).

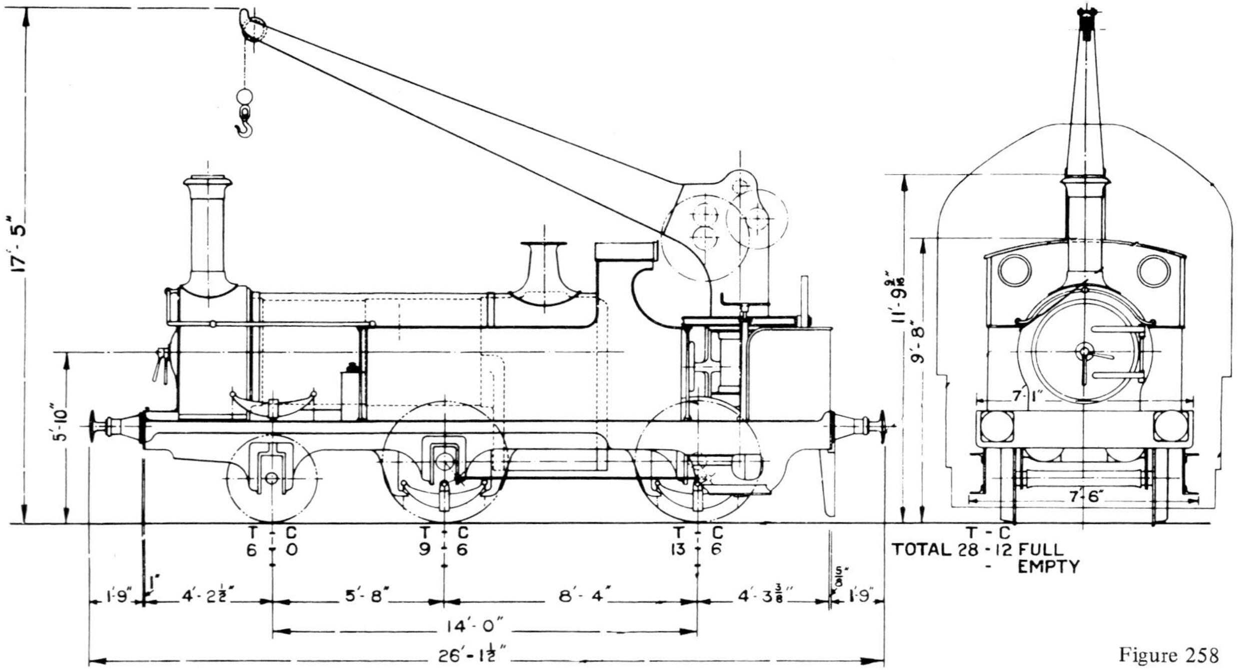

Figure 258

Figure 259

One other odd little crane engine was No. 1299 seen in these next four illustrations at Swindon in 1928, but a locomotive with a very long history indeed. She was being built at Newton Abbot by the South Devon Railway at the time of that Company being amalgamated with the Great Western, and was finished at Swindon in 1878 as a 2-4-0 side tank along with two sister engines Nos. 1298 and 1300. In 1881 No. 1299 was fitted with a hand crane, capable of lifting 1½ tons at a fixed radius of 16′ 6″, and went to the Engineering Department at Reading until 1893. She then went into stock until 1925, when a new boiler was fitted and this is the condition as shown in the photographs. Finally she went back into Departmental stock in 1929 until 1936, and was cut up in 1938. *Figure 258* is the official diagram for No. 1299.

For any would-be modellers I have managed to get these illustrations to show front, back and both sides, and as a bonus, *Figure 262* includes the front view of *Steropes.* Driving wheels were 4′ 1½″ with leading wheels of 3′ diameter, wheelbase was 5′ 8″ + 6′ 4″. What is so puzzling is how this engine negotiated any bridges or structures, as the jib seems to be fixed, standing 17′ 5″ above rail level!

Figure 262

Figure 261

One of the most versatile of the Great Western locomotives to be built, was the 43XX class. This handy engine was the traffic department's delight, as it could handle anything from the local stopping goods to the mainline express, and frequently did. The design came about in 1910 by Churchward realizing the need for a mixed traffic engine, asking H. Holcroft, one of his principal assistants in the Swindon drawing office, to sketch out "a 2-6-0 tender engine with 5′ 8″ driving wheels, outside cylinders and using the No. 4 boiler" (in fact all standard parts).

Mr. Holcroft, having noted the use of the 'Mogul' type of engine during his tour of America and Canada, set to and produced the 43XX design, by welding together many standard parts, including the 'Saint' cab, which became so successful, that over the years,

Figure 260

no less than 342 were built, only to be superseded by the advent of the 'Hall' class.

The engine part of the 43XXs followed closely on the design of the '3150' class 2-6-2 tank and was virtually a tender version of this series, although it appeared four years after the building of the tank class. The first twenty appeared in 1911 under *Lot 183* and were numbered 4301-20. They were all fitted immediately with top feed and started life with handsome copper-topped chimneys, as witness the two official pictures of Nos. 4301 and

4302. Incidentally, the first ten to be built, were the last engines to carry the Swindon works plate under the smokebox.

Figure 263 is the official *Diagram G* which pertained to the initial series '4301-20' of 1911, and the photograph is the Swindon picture of the first engine No. 4301. Note the elongated centre splasher, right hand side only.

Figure 263

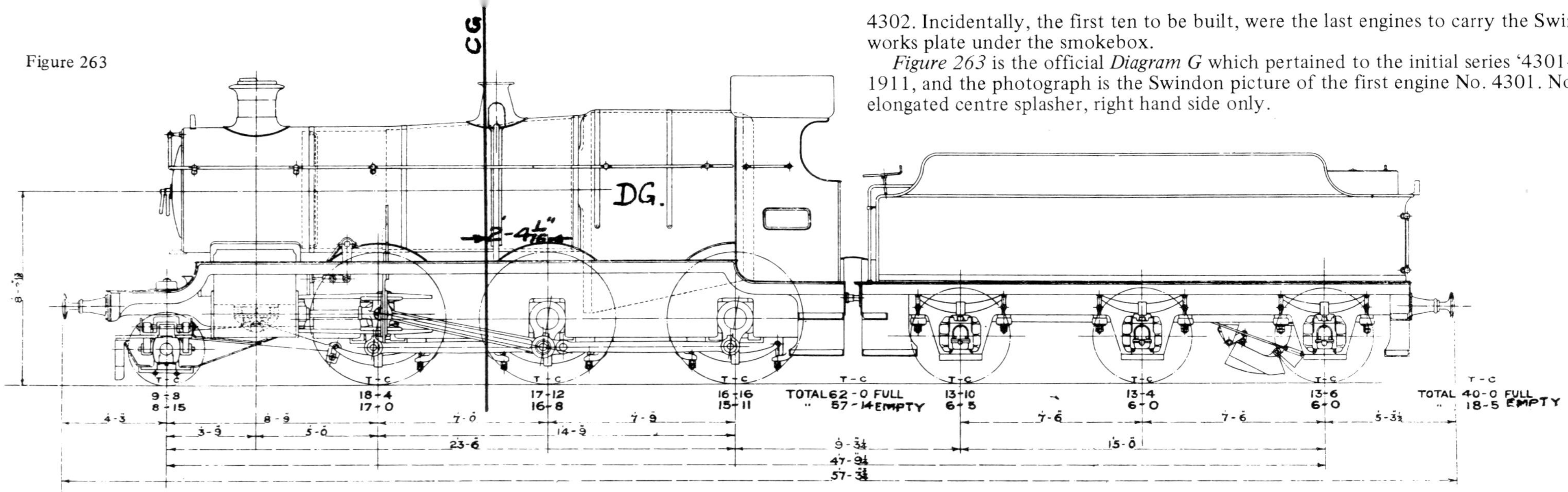

Figure 264

Figure 265

Figure 265 is the official 'works grey' photograph of No. 4302, the second 'Mogul' to be constructed, and shows the left hand side of the engine. Note the tall safety valve bonnet. When some of the series were eventually fitted with Group 87 boilers, they had short valve bonnets and appeared as per *Diagram V* shown in *Figure 266.*

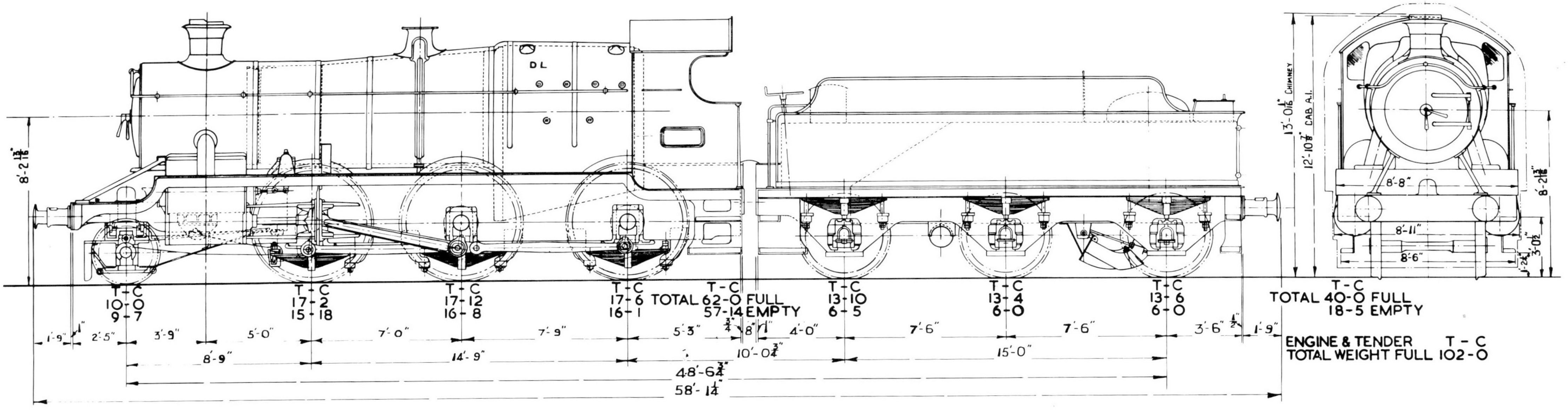

Figure 266

Figure 267

Figure 267 shows the prototype engine No. 4301 pictured at Swindon in June 1911 just before being handed over to the running shed. What a workmanlike little machine she was. She was small, so much so, that all subsequent engines of the series, after the initial twenty, had their frames lengthened 9" under the cab to give more room and access to the plumbing. This can be clearly seen on this page, by comparing the two figures. *Figure 268* shows No. 4341 taking water; note the difference in size of cab side and cab steps. Notice also, that the early engines had brass beading both on wheel splashers and cab front edges, and one important feature, that extra long centre driving splasher on the right-hand side which covered not only the driving wheel but also the air pump. (This does not apply to 63XXs, 73XX and 93XX series.)

Figure 268

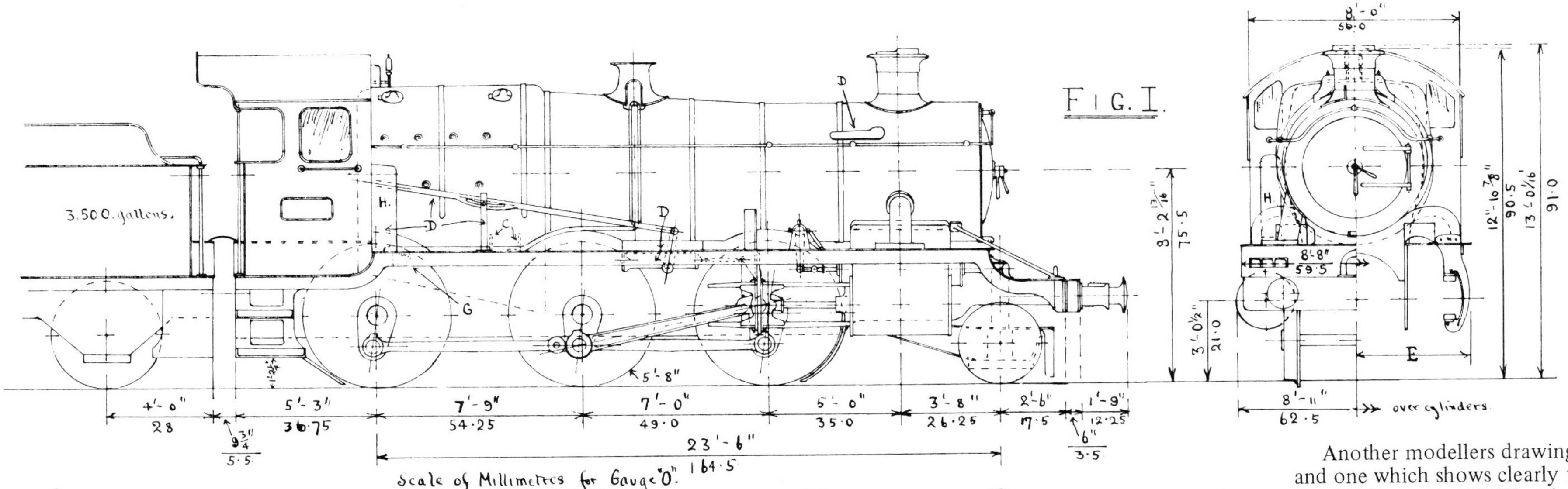

Figure 269

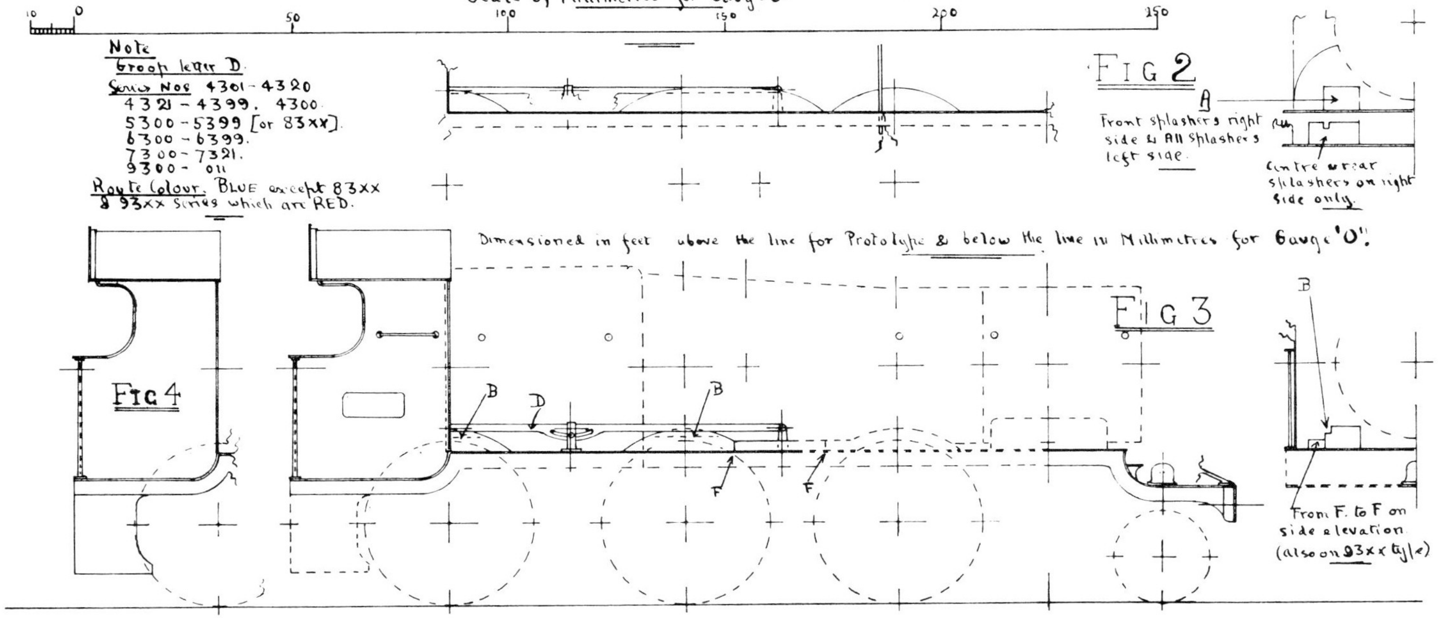

Another modellers drawing from Colonel Templer's pen, and one which shows clearly the variations in the series from the 43XXs to the 93XXs. The notes are as follows:– 'A' *Figure 2.* End section also for all splashers on left side and of all splashers. 'B' splashers cut away on 63XX and 73XX types. *Figure 3.* 'C' on left side only, all types. 'D' on right side only all types. 'E' end section in front of motion plate except of funnel, smokebox and boiler, 'G' Frame narrows under cab to same width as tender. 'H' on 93XX series only.
Figure 1 shows 93XX type.
Figure 2 shows 43XX, 53XX where they differ from 63XX and 73XX.
Figure 3 shows 63XX and 73XX types in solid lines where these differ from 93XX series, all other detail as per *Figure 1* (except H).
Figure 4 shows cab for 4301-20 series. Nos. 4300, 4321-99, 5300-99 have cab roof as *Figure 4,* but frames like *Figure 3.*

All types have splashers on left side, plain arcs of a circle with end sections as in *Figure 2* letter 'A'. The majority of the 53XX class had extended buffer beams as in *Figure 1* added, making the route colour 'RED' and those so altered have been renumbered 93XX, keeping their last two numerals.

Figure 270 shows No. 5321 hauling the 'Limited' empty stock up to Paddington with three 'Centenary' coaches leading. Picture dated December 1936.

Figure 270

Figure 271

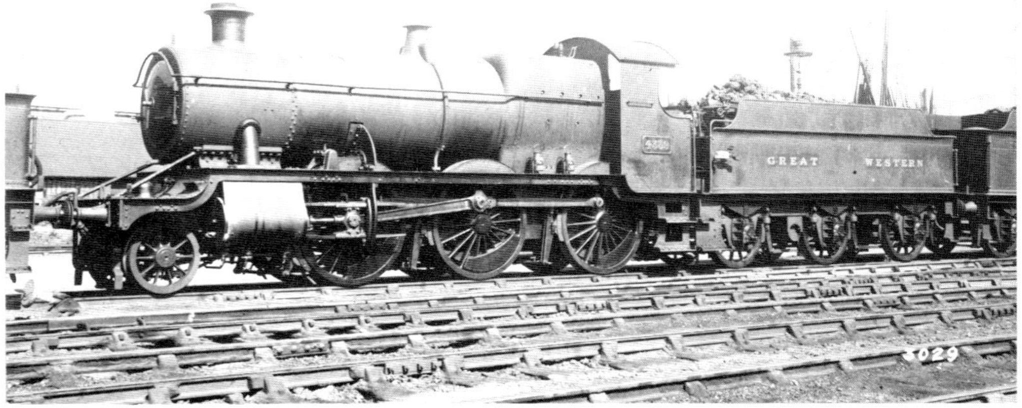

Figure 272

Here are five photographs showing the variants in the 2-6-0 tender engine class. The first two *Figures 271 and 272* depict the 43XX series, and those which were built in 1913-14. The engine with the right-hand view is No. 4356 with the built-up chimney, and No. 4339 is seen at Swindon showing the left-hand side (note the staff-catcher on the tender side). *Figure 273* is of No. 5352, and No. 6336 is seen in *Figure 275,* in B.R. days at Swindon with cast iron chimney and short safety valve bonnet. Note that the motion bracket has on it a flange. In the lower illustration, No. 9306 is seen at Swindon and one can see immediately the large windowed cab, the screw reversing gear, outside steam pipes, extended front buffer beam and the cut-away centre splasher (right-hand side only). *Figure 274.*

Figure 273

Figure 274

Figure 275

Figure 276

Figure 277

In 1928 sixty-five engines of the 53XX series were slightly altered, to give the pony truck more weight, in order to relieve the leading driver flanges on the sharp curves in the West Country. The initial experiment of moving the front buffer beam forward one foot and loading it with a heavy casting was tried out first on Nos. 4351/86/95/85, and having proved successful, these four reverted to normal and the chosen 53XXs became 83XXs. No. 8326 is seen in South Wales in *Figure 276.* In 1921 Robert Stephenson built thirty-five engines of this class for the Great Western, numbered 6370-99 and 7300-04, and *Figure 277* shows No. 6378, one of this batch. They could be identified by the small works plate affixed to the centre splasher.

Two 73XXs are shown in *Figures 278 and 279* but these two had a different history. No. 7325 started life in 1932 as No. 9303 and was altered to the 73XX style in 1958. (Note the windowed cab.) No. 7307, on the other hand is shown as built in 1921, but with the addition of outside steam pipes in 1954.

Figure 279

Figure 278

The drawing is the official Swindon *Diagram M* of 1925 which is for the 6342-69, 7320-1 series with outside steam pipes.

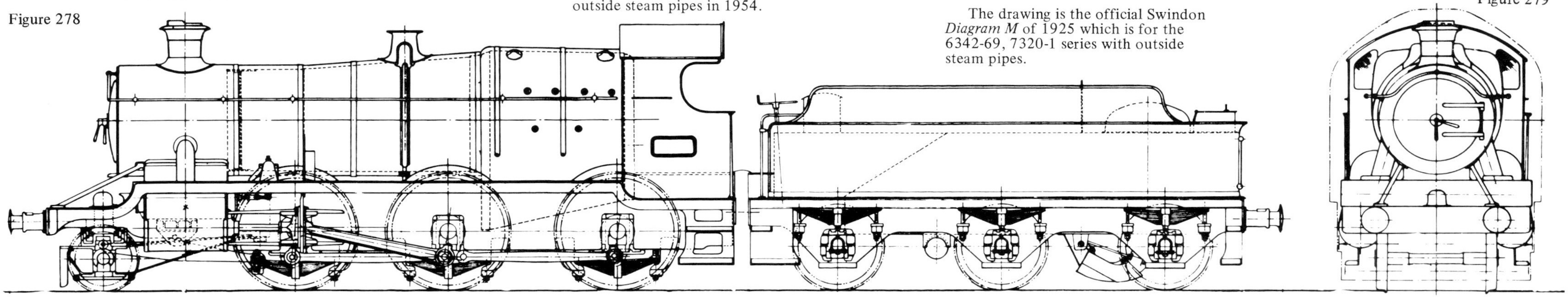

Figure 280

Figure 281

Figure 282

Figure 283

This 'Mogul' drawing to *Diagram W* shows the 93XX series as modified in British Rail days and renumbered 7322-41, and this ties up with the photograph in *Figure 278.* No. 7304, seen at Dulverton (*Figure 282*), also in British Rail ownership, is another example of the batch built by Stephensons. The two pictures of No. 7320 (*Figures 283 and 284*) are of the small batch of two (7321-22) built in 1925 together with Nos. 6362-69 all to *Lot 230.* The two views of this engine link up with *Diagram M* in *Figure 280.*

Figure 284

Figure 285 Figure 286

Figure 287

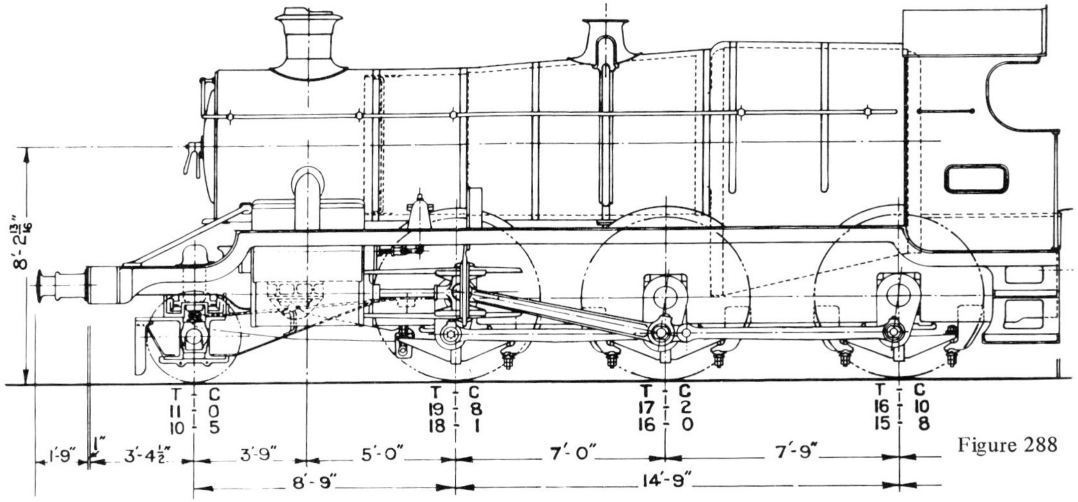

Figure 288

The pictures on this page are devoted to the converted 53XXs at the time when they were running with the heavy front end, and renumbered 83XXs. Top left is No. 8313 which started as No. 5313 in 1917, was altered to No. 8313 in 1928, reverted to No. 5313 in 1944, acquired the outside steam pipes in 1944, and was withdrawn in 1958. *Figure 286* is of No. 8388 which was No. 5388 of 1920, converted in 1928, and reverted in 1944, scrapped in 1959. *Figure 287* is of No. 8386, originally No. 5386 also of 1920, altered in 1928, and back again in 1944, being withdrawn in 1958.

These pictures show the large extension piece well, and coupled with the official *Diagram P* in *Figure 288* modellers should have little difficulty in making a good model.

Figure 289

Finally, for those modellers who feel tempted to have a go at the 93XX series of the 2-6-0 tender engines, here is a left-hand official photograph at Swindon of No. 9313 taken in 1932 (which eventually reverted to No. 7335 in 1958), and close-up of detail of No. 9301 taken in 1935 to show cab and reversing gear detail clearly. Perhaps it should be mentioned here that 88 of the 43XX series, and 12 of the 83XXs were withdrawn between 1936 and 1939, and their wheels and motion used in the 'Grange' and 'Manor' classes.

Figure 290

Figure 291

Figure 292

Figure 293

The history of the 2-8-0 R.O.D. engines on the Great Western is rather complicated, but as briefly as possible the situation was thus. During the First World War, the Government ordered a large quantity of these Robinson designed engines from The North British Locomotive Co., Nasmyth, Wilson & Co., and Robert Stephenson and Company, and between 1917 and 1919, 521 locomotives had been built to this design, many more than were needed of course, and the majority of those constructed after 1918 remained in this country. After hostilities had ceased in 1919, the Great Western purchased twenty of these engines, which became Nos. 3000-19, this batch being almost new. They hired a further eighty which had seen service and consequently were not so good as those purchased outright. In 1921-2, all these 80 locos were returned to the Government, who finally disposed of them to any buyer for £1,500 apiece. So in 1925 the Great Western purchased a further eighty, of which some were good and some bad! Thirty were shopped properly and turned out with numbers 3020-49, the other fifty were "cobbled up" and put into service with numbering 3050-99 and had all been scrapped by 1930, except No. 3093 which lasted until 1931. So the best ones were the 3000-19 batch, followed by the 3029-49 series, the rest were best forgotten as any who drove them will tell you. *Figure 292* shows No. 3007 of the series with the Great Central Railway type chimney. *Figure 294* illustrates '3006' just as she was received from the War Department complete with jacks on the buffer beam and Rosspop valves. *Figure 293* shows No. 3048 in British Rail days with '47XX' class chimney and tall valve bonnet. The drawing of the design as built by the Great Central Railway is of course by J.N. Maskelyne.

Figure 294

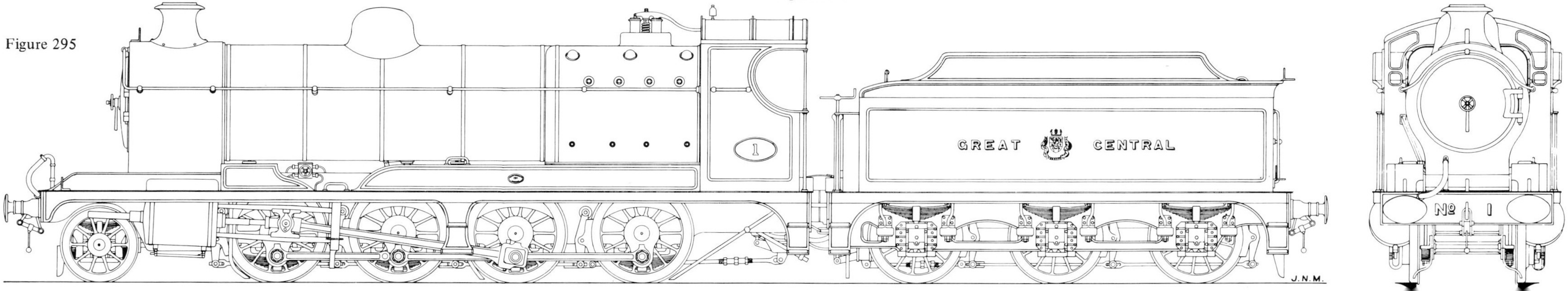

Figure 295

Originally these locomotives were given the diagram *G*, but when fitted with Swindon superheaters, MB boilers and copper firebox, plus the Great Western safety valves, they were issued on a *K* diagram, which is shown in *Figure 297*. Note that they kept the original tender, and these latter in fact, after being parted from their parent engines, were used again coupled to many of the 26XX class.

The official picture of No. 3016 seen at Swindon just after overhaul illustrates the Robinson chimney and Western valve bonnet, and in fact links up well with the diagram in *Figure 297*.

Figure 296

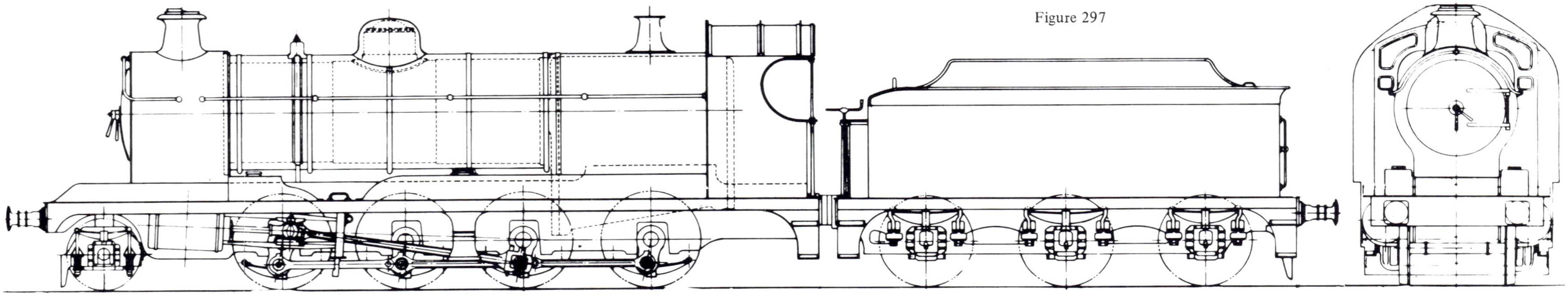

Figure 297

A very small attractive little tank engine was the '1361' series. This, the last saddle tank locomotive class to be constructed at Swindon was the design of Mr. Holcroft. One can read in his *Outline of Great Western Locomotive Practice* how, in 1909, a roll of old drawings emanating from the '1392' early Cornwall Railway locomotive had been dropped on to his desk, with instructions to design an 0-6-0 tank similar, which could traverse curves of 2 chains radius but using up-to-date practices. So was the '1361' class born.

There were only five engines built to this *Lot No. 179,* and the numbers were 1361-5. As can be seen from the official photograph and *A.13 diagram,* the boilers had high round-topped fireboxes and carried domes on the front ring, the dome cover perching on top of the saddle tank. The modern cab had large windows in front and rear, and the bunker with the straight sloping back had a capacity of 2 tons.

Wheels were 3′ 8″ in diameter with wheelbases 5′ + 6′, a total of 11′ 0″. Over the years the only alteration was the fitting of a taller chimney, and I am glad to report that one of these little engines is in preservation.

Figure 298

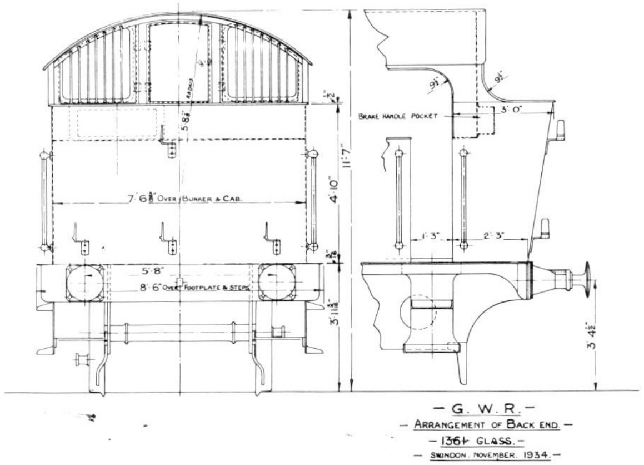

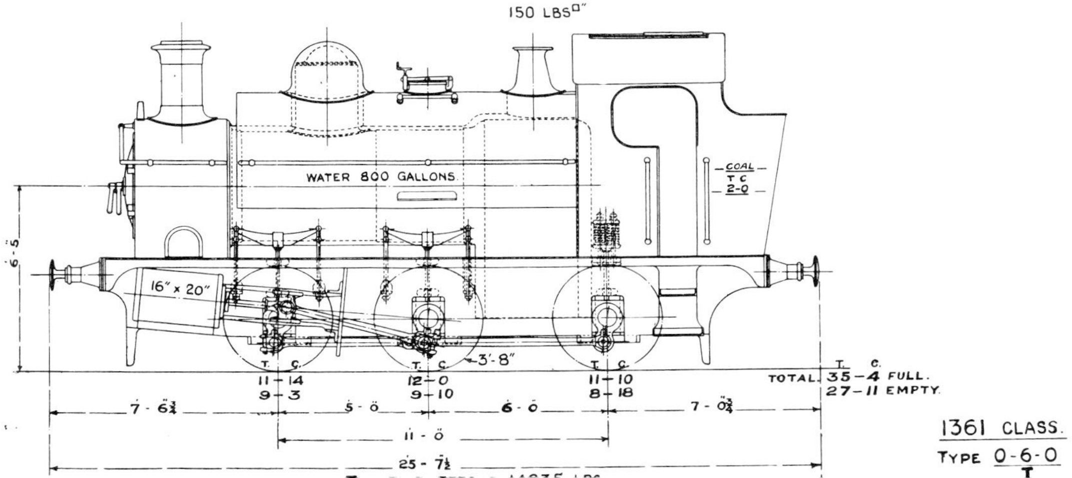

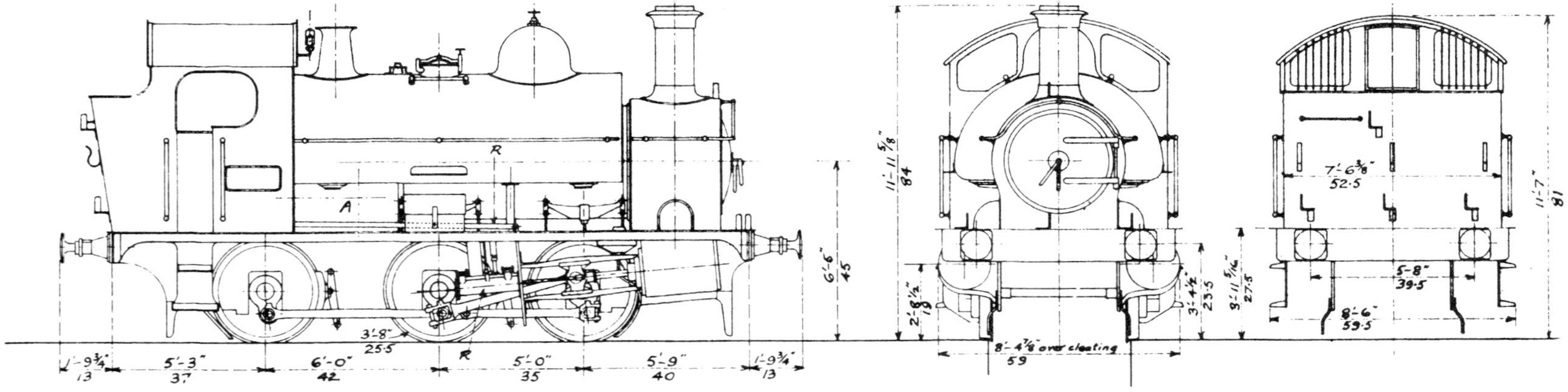

Figure 300

For position of tool-box on left side, and details at 'A', see fig 1.

NOTES. Details marked "R" on right side only; those marked "L" on left side only. Wheel treads and flanges drawn to scale; allowances must be made for out-of-scale wheels. Dimensions in feet (full size), and in millimetres to the nearest half millimetre for Gauge "O".

Diagram A.13 on the previous page shows the '1361' class on the left-hand side. Colonel Templer's 4m/m drawing on this page in *Figure 300* illustrates the right-hand view and also adds a front elevation. This, together with the three-quarter view of '1361' in *Figure 301,* gives a good idea of the front cab windows for modelling purposes.

During their working lives on the Great Western, these engines saw service mostly at Plymouth and Weymouth Docks, but have also been reported at Newton Abbot, St. Blazey and Taunton for Bridgwater docks. Their moment of fame occurred when one of these engines replaced the very old Beattie 2-4-0 on the ex-S.R. Wadebridge branch in British Rail days.

Figure 301

Figure 302

Figure 303

One of the smallest engines on my own model railway is No. 1364, and so that I could construct my miniature with a reasonable degree of accuracy, I took many pictures of the class at Swindon in 1950 and three are reproduced on this page.

Figure 302 shows the rear end in general, and the bunker details in particular of No. 1365, and *Figure 303* illustrates the opposite side of the same locomotive showing the tool box on the right-hand side running plate. In *Figure 306* the tool box on No. 1362 is seen on the left-hand side, and note the tall chimney. The small picture in *Figure 305* is of a Sharp Stewart locomotive, No. 1395, which started life on the Cornwall Mineral Railway as No. 4, in 1873, was given a saddle tank in 1883 and reboilered at Swindon in 1901, finally being withdrawn in 1934. This was the class from which the Swindon-built '1361's stemmed and it is plain to see the similarity of the designs. The drawing in *Figure 304* comes from the Swindon *Small Engine Diagrams* book.

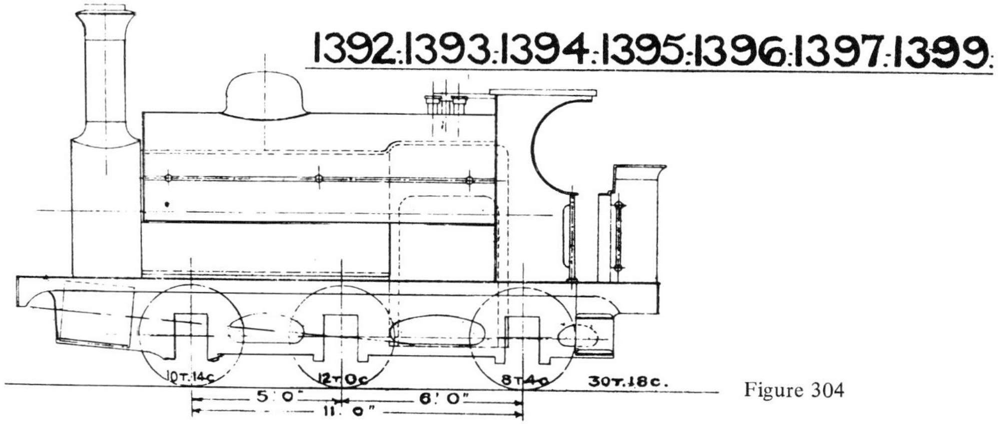

Figure 304

Figure 305

At the end of the First World War, there was a need for a large freight engine to handle the increasing night vacuum-fitted goods services, and to meet this need, Mr. Churchward designed the 47XX class of 2-8-0 tender engines.

It was in effect an enlarged 43XX class, having an extra pair of driving wheels still at 5′ 8″ diameter, and carrying the No. 1 boiler in the place of the 43XX's No. 4. The result, as can be seen in *Figure 307,* was a truly magnificent machine, and one which the Great Western men came to respect. They were always complete masters of any service upon which they were put. We knew them well here in Banbury, as many fast fitted freights ('the vacuums') were formed in the marshalling yards and dispatched with a 47XX at the head, usually in the small hours of the night.

The original prototype No. 4700, being fitted with the standard No. 1 boiler as mentioned, had to have an extraordinarily 8′ long smokebox in order to reach the saddle, and more daylight was visible underneath this boiler than with the rest of the class. It was found, however, that the engine required a larger boiler than the No. 1, and so in 1921 the big 2-8-0 was fitted with the Swindon No. 7 with outside steam pipes and snifting valves on the steam chests. The other eight engines, Nos. 4701-8 built in 1922-3, were built with these details already in place. *Figure 307* is the official 1919 picture of No. 4700 at Swindon factory and *Figure 308* is of the same engine in 1922 with the new boiler.

The *Diagram L* shows the class with the 4,000 gall. tender and extended cab roof, the last diagram issued.

Figure 307

Figure 308

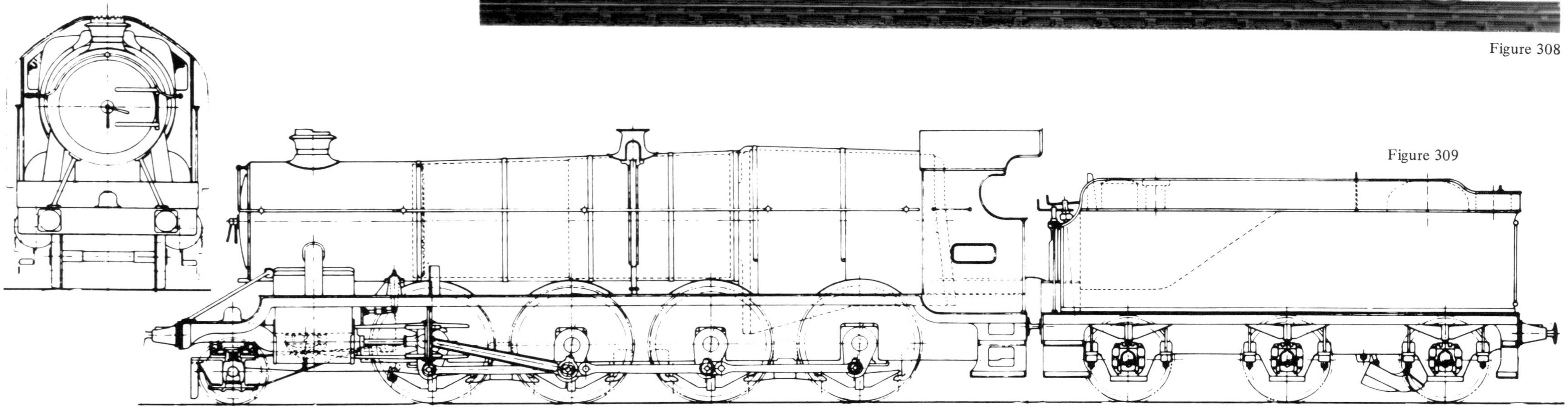

Figure 309

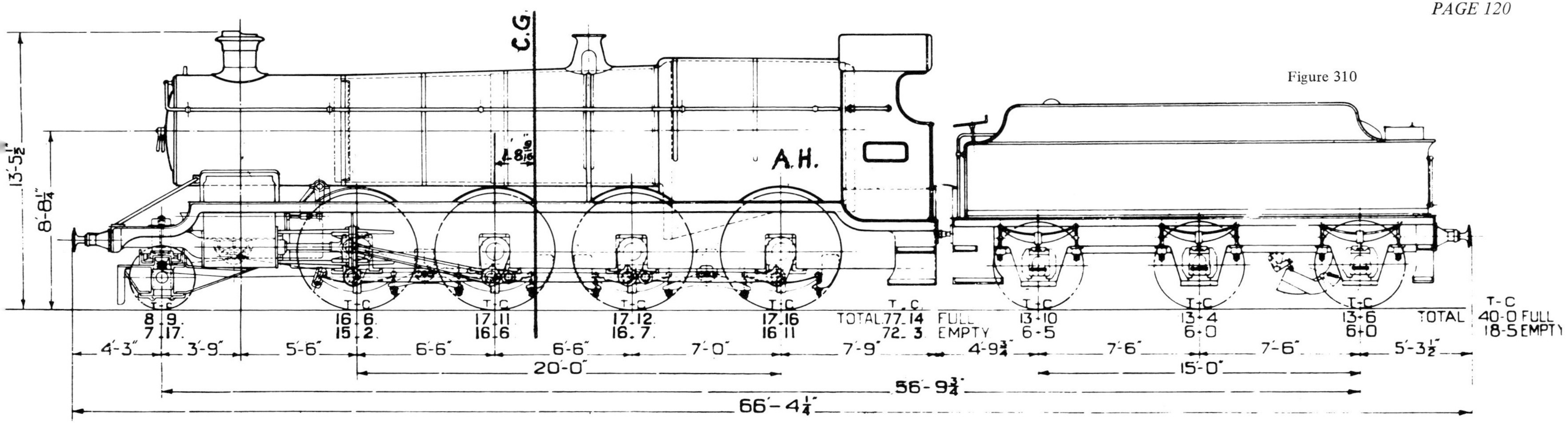

Figure 310

Again, access to the Swindon Engine Diagram book has given the opportunity to reproduce the two earlier drawings of the 4700 class, which enables the points made on the previous page to be illustrated. *Figure 310* is a copy of *Diagram F,* which shows the prototype engine only, No. 4700, as built with the Standard No. 1 boiler and the small tender. Note the standard boiler fittings which the smaller boiler allowed. This drawing links with the photograph *307* on the previous page.

Figure 311 is of *Diagram J* of the same class, and shows the larger boiler in place, slightly larger tender (but not the final 4,000 gallon shown in *Diagram L*) and the special chimney and safety valve bonnets, which these engines had to carry to be within the loading gauge.

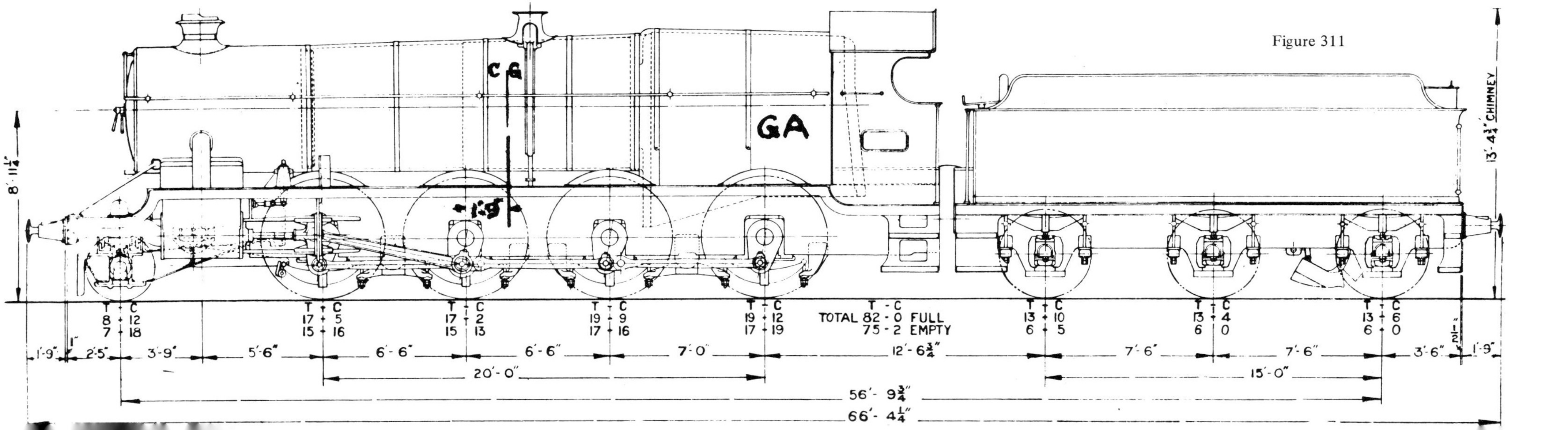

Figure 311

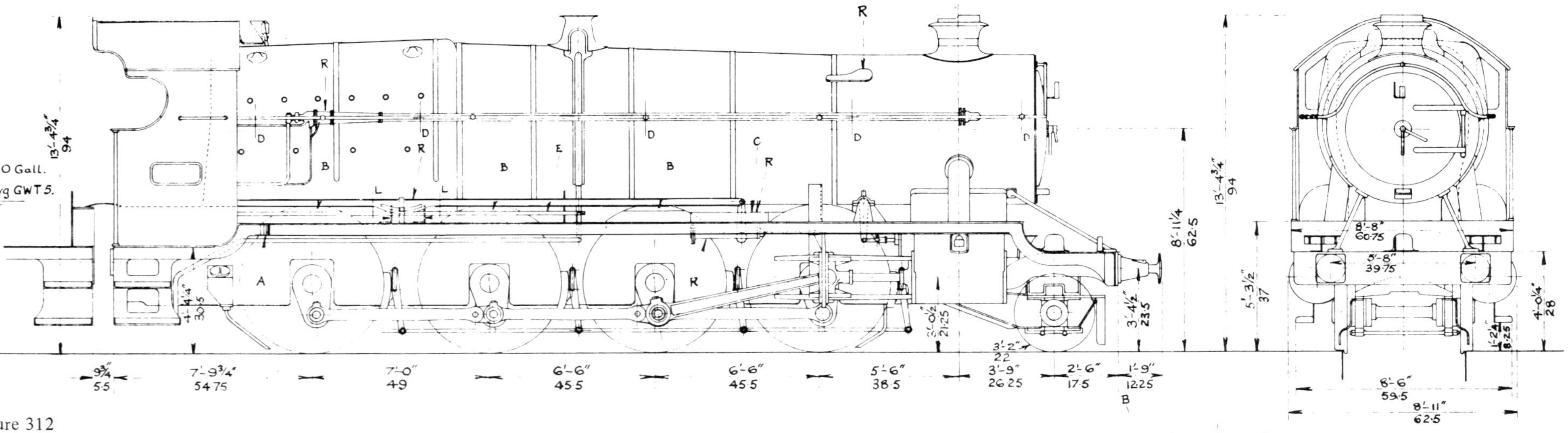

Figure 312

NOTES.

A. Running-plate angle narrows to rear here from 8'-0" to 7'-2" between.
B. Top portion of driving, inter., & trailing splashers on right side relieved to give clearance for reverse rod. Leading splasher on right side and all on left side are plain. See scrap end view.
C. Air pump cover.
D. Centre lines marking position of hand-rail stunchions on left side.
E. Sand gear rod.

DIMENSIONS IN FEET (FULL SIZE), AND IN M.M FOR GAUGE 'O'. SCALE 4 M.M=1 FT. REDUCED FROM OFFICIAL DRAWINGS.

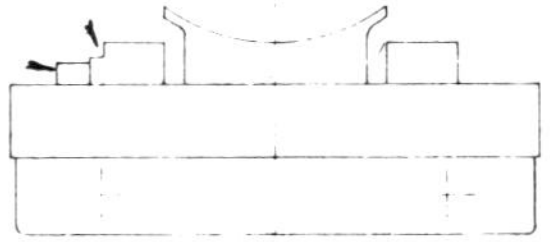

Scrap end view, showing profile of splashers, air pump cover & smoke-box saddle. See Notes.

G.W.R. | **4700 CLASS.**

Again it is possible to show both sides of a locomotive class as the Swindon diagram gives the left-hand side, and Colonel Templer's drawing the right-hand view. Note that all the items marked with an 'R' appeared only on the right-hand side of the engines and were not on the left-side.

Figure 313 is a fine study of No. 4702 standing in Old Oak Common round house in the 1924 period. Note that she is still coupled to the small tender as the large 4,000 gallon variety were not brought into use until 1932-3. One point not generally known, is that these big 2-8-0's, in common with the other 8 coupled classes of the Great Western, had thinner flanges on the two inner pairs of driving wheels, and also, to allow a slight modicum of side play, the coupling rods had spherical seatings at the joints in the rods.

Figure 313

Figure 314

Figure 315

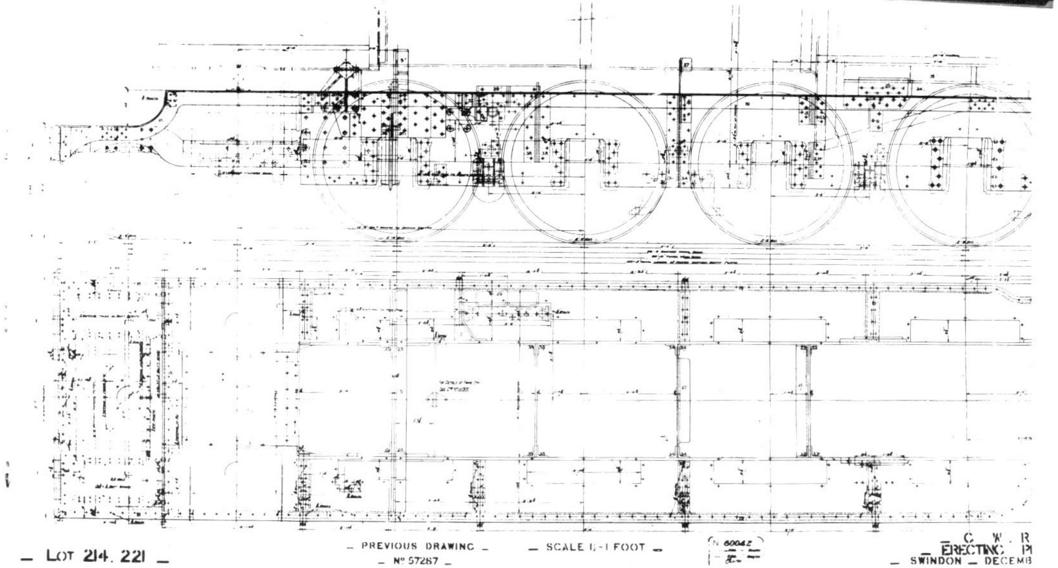

Two more pictures of the 47XX class from the archives which serve to show what really big engines the 2-8-0's were. *Figure 314* is of No. 4701 at Old Oak Common shed and gives the right-hand details well. Note the 'pole' reversing gear with the rod running close alongside the small wheel-splashers, also at this date (1925 era), the front pony truck pivot did not have the bell-like cover which appeared later. No. 4704 shown almost head-on in *Figure 315* again emphasises the majestic lines of the class. This engine has 'A' headlights, obviously prior to hauling an express service out of the terminus, a task they performed with ease on many busy holiday Saturdays. Inset is a small copy of the 'Erecting Plan'.

Figure 317

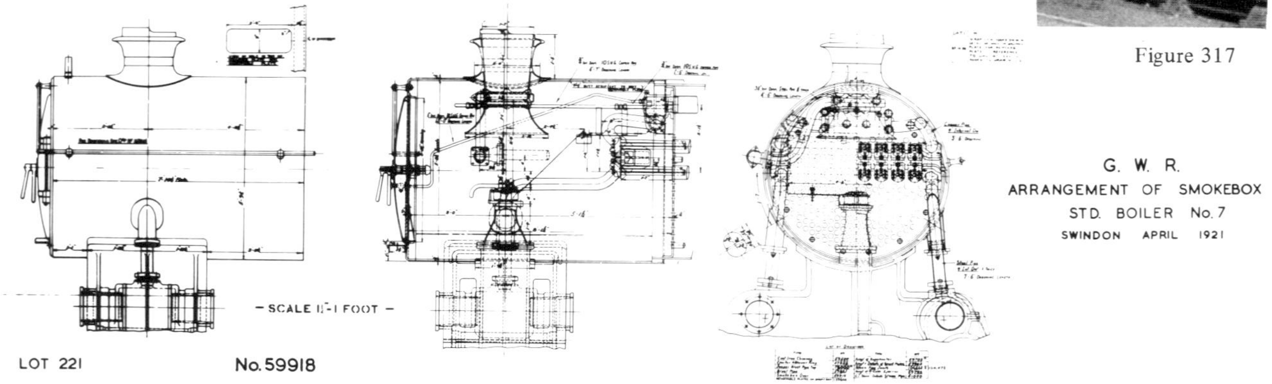

Two further studies of the 'Night Vacuum' engines. These show No. 4705 at Swindon yard in 1935 and coupled to the large 4,000 gallon tender. Other points of difference are that the pony pivot cover is now bell-shaped, and the vacuum pipe is of the low fitted variety. Previously this front pipe had stood up much higher, but was found to get in the way of the tube cleaning gang.

It is not generally known that the prototype engine, No. 4700, was fully lined in passenger livery in 1925 for the purpose of attending the Railway Centenary gathering at Darlington. When in service on the Great Western they were painted unrelieved green and black. At the nationalization they were turned out all black, except No. 4702 which had red, grey and cream lining, and then in 1957 they all had the green restored, and in addition were fully lined out!

Alas, now they are no more, and it is a pity that one was not preserved.

Figure 316

Under the Railways Act of 1921, many small constituent companies were amalgamated into the Great Western, and amongst them was the Midland & South Western Joint Railway, which ran from Andoversford Junction to Andover on its own metals and had running powers over the Great Western to Cheltenham and over the London South Western Railway to Southampton. Upon being absorbed into the parent Great Western Railway, the locomotive stock eventually came to Swindon for major overhaul, and many consequently lost their original identity, and became 'Swindonised' oddities. Two such were Nos. 17 and 18, which were tank engines of unusual wheel arrangement 4-4-4. Built in 1897 by Sharp Stewart, they came to Great Western stock in 1923, see *Figure 318* for the Midland and South Western Junction diagram.

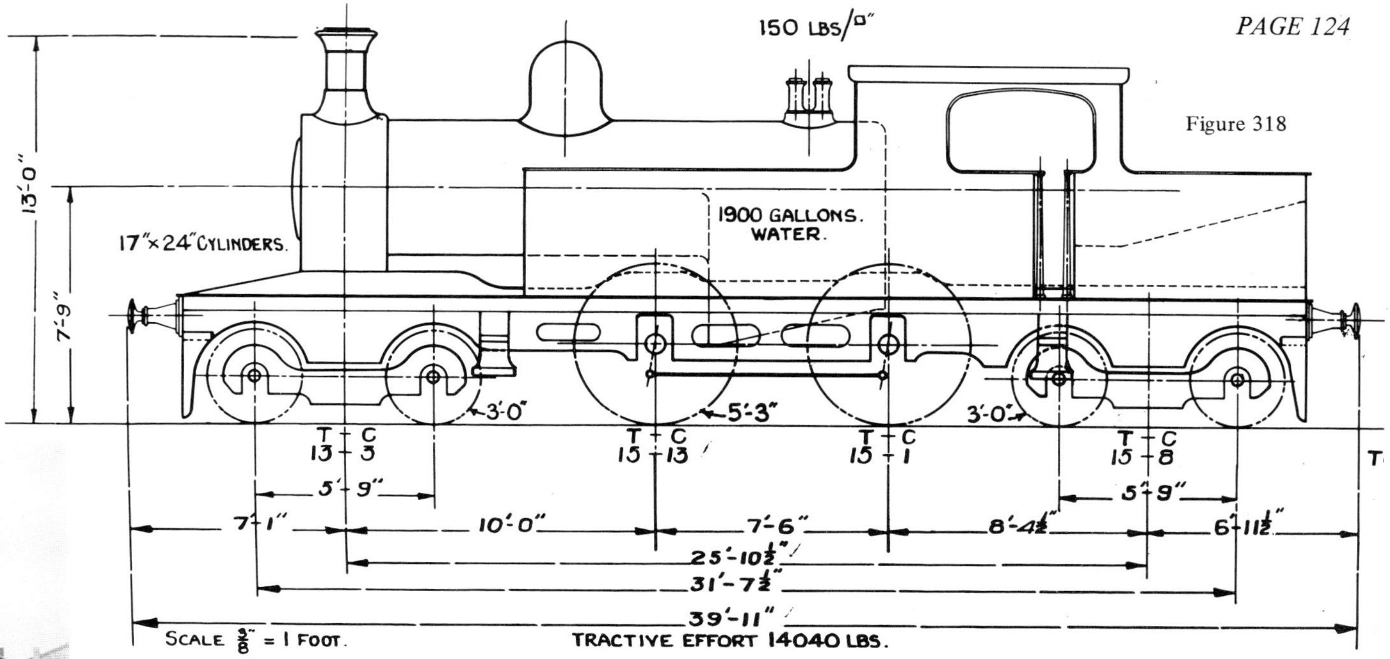

Figure 318

Figure 319

No. 17 became Great Western No. 25, and was not greatly changed, except for an extended smokebox and 'Western' boiler fittings. In this form she can be seen at Swindon station, where she worked the shuttle service between Swindon Town and Swindon Junction stations until 1927 (*Figure 319*). No. 18, on the other hand, suffered a complete transformation, and was turned out of the factory in 1925, with a No. 10 superheated taper boiler, Belpaire firebox, new cab and boiler fittings, making an attractive 4-4-4 tank with a Great Western outline, as per *Figure 320.*

Figure 320

Figure 321

Personally I have always been interested in these 'one-off jobs'. I rather like oddities, as I have mentioned before, and I would like a model of No. 27. To this end I have managed to get both 'before' and 'after' diagrams of this 4-4-4T from the Swindon book, and have reproduced them to 4m/m scale (*Figure 322*). *Figure 321* illustrates the engine in full broadside shot which links well with the sketch.

The wheel sizes were 5′ 3″ for the drivers, bogies being 3′ in diameter, wheelbases being 5′ 9″ + 7′ 1½″ + 7′ 6″ + 5′ 6″ + 5′ 9″, a total of 31′ 7½″.

From 1925 until withdrawal in 1929, No. 27 was used in the Kidderminster district mostly on local suburban services.

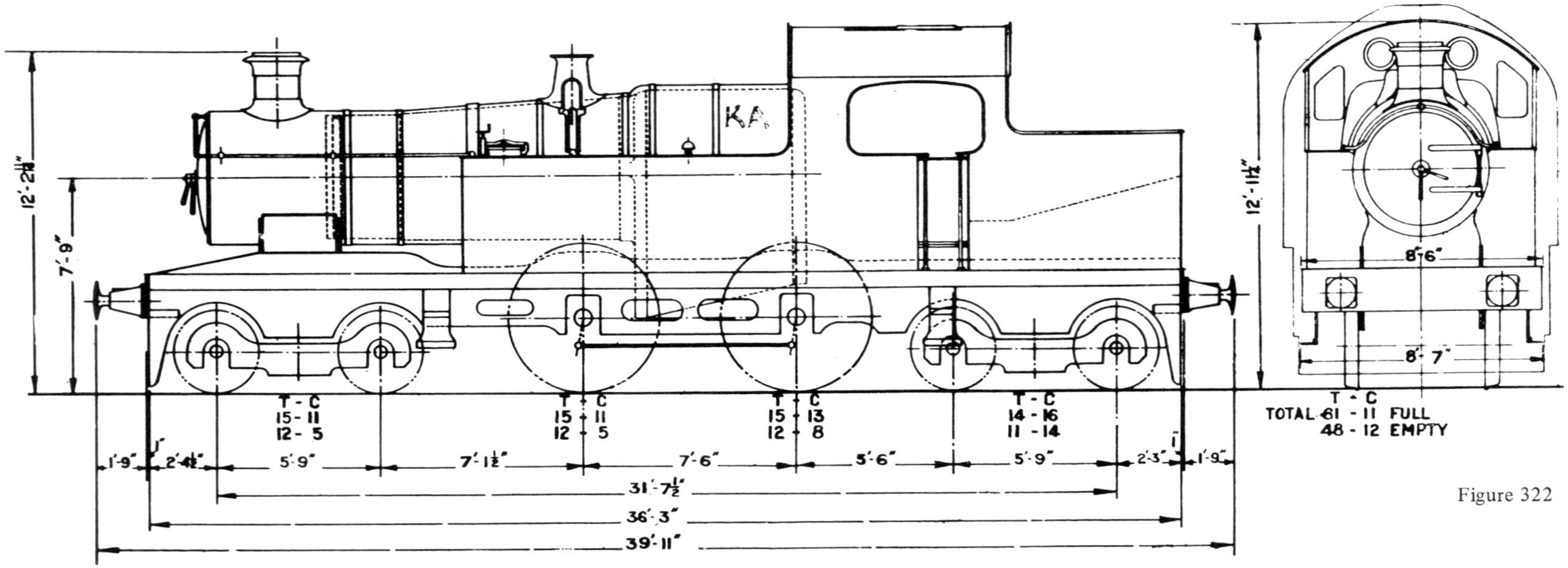

Figure 322

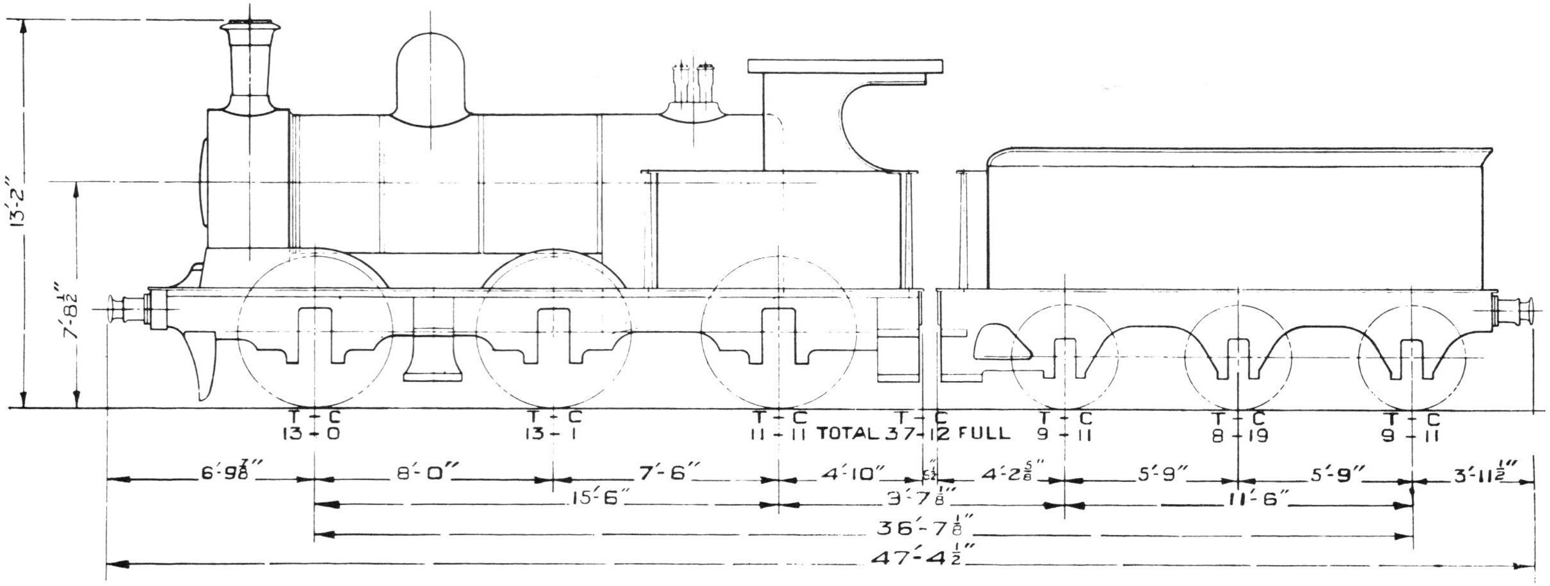

Figure 323

Another 'before' and 'after' pair of drawings, and of one particular class of absorbed engines. These little 0-6-0 tender engines were constructed by Beyer-Peacock in the years 1899-1902 for the Midland and South Western Junction Railway.

Their original numbers were 19-28, and some of the first design had square panels to the cab sides rather like the London North Western Railway style.

The diagram in *Figure 323* is as built, and in *Figure 324* after the 'Swindon' treatment, diagram Nos. being *A.19* and *A.24* respectively.

Rails were at first fitted to the tenders, but eventually were replaced by side plates.

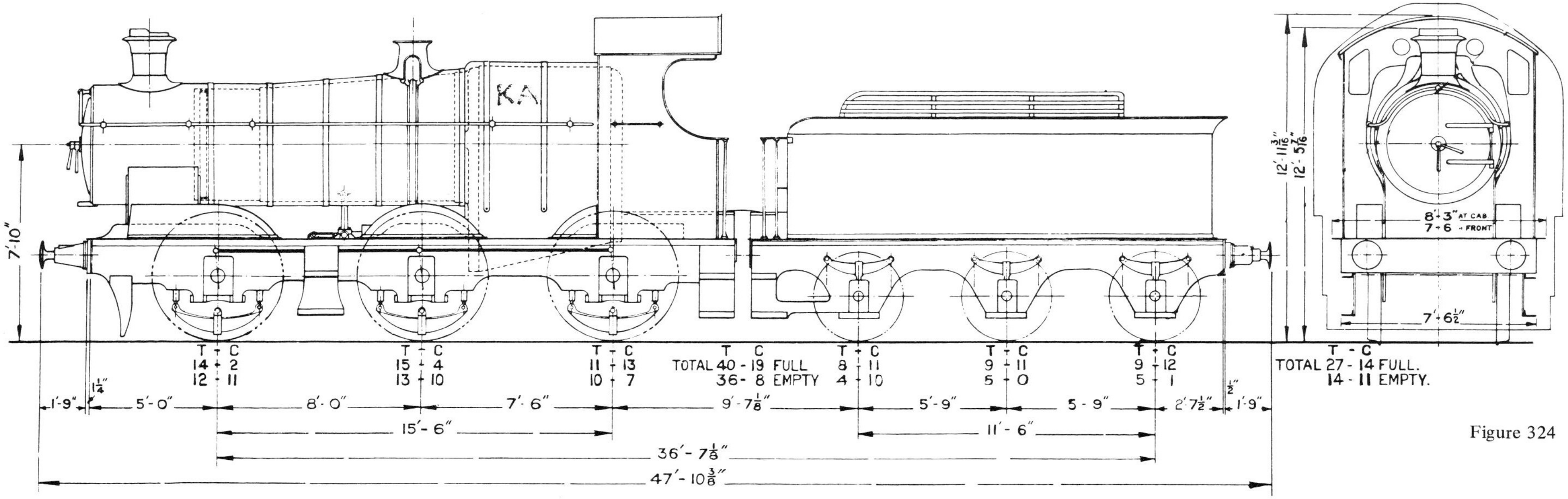

Figure 324

Figure 326

Figure 325

Figure 327

Three photographs of these little 0-6-0s follow, one at rest, one in action and the other on show.

At Swindon they were fitted with the Standard No. 10 boiler, Great Western cabs and solid plates fitted in place of the coal rails on the tenders, and numbered 1003-11/13.

In appearance these ten engines resembled closely the Collett '2251' class which did not appear until 1930, but close inspection would always reveal the slender chimney, and sand-box-cum-splasher over the front driver.

In the illustrations, No. 1008 is seen at Swindon running shed (*Figure 325*), whilst *Figure 326* shows one of the series actually on the ex-Midland and South Western Junction Railway line with a local passenger service, and *Figure 327* is the official Swindon photograph of the class, No. 1005 outside the Works in 1925.

Figure 328

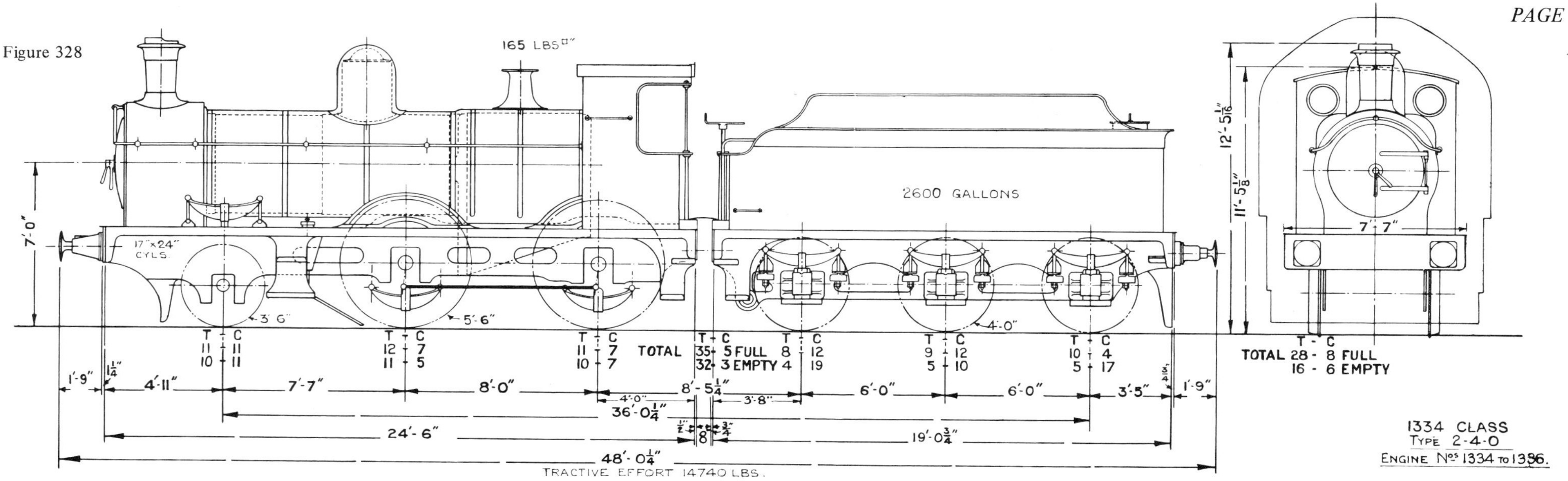

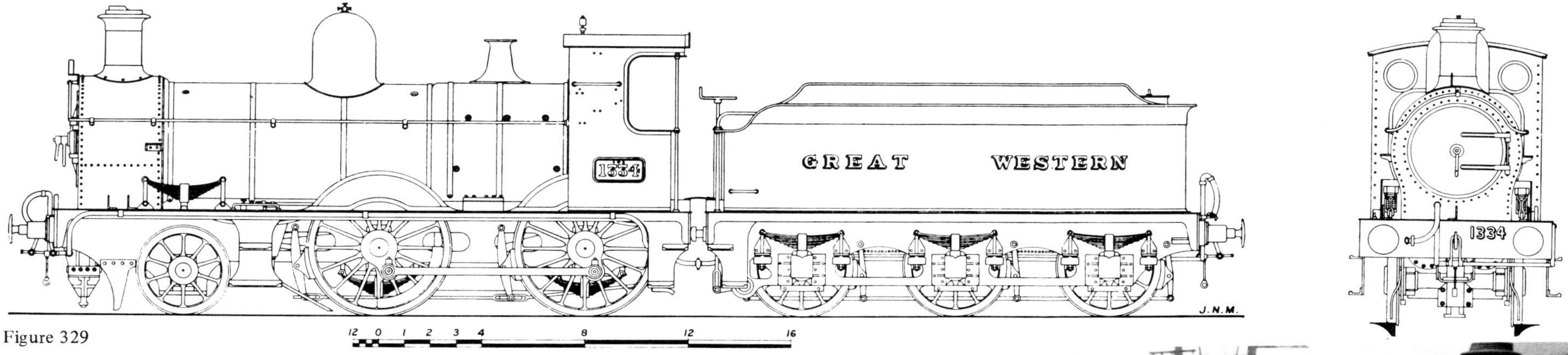

Figure 329

Figure 330

Three more tender engines taken over with the Midland and South Western Junction Railway, were the 2-4-0's built by Dubbs & Co., in 1894 and originally numbered 10-12. These three eventually became Great Western Nos. 1334-36, being rebuilt with the Swindon No. 11 boiler with a dome similar to the 'Dean' Goods. They spent most of their 'Western' life on the Lambourn branch, and could often be found either at Didcot or Reading sheds.

The top drawing is the official *Diagram A.9* and that in *Figure 329* is of course from the pen of J.N. Maskelyne. Note the two different patterns of chimneys.

The small illustration is of No. 1336 on a special excursion trip for the Gloucestershire Railway Society seen here at Gloucester (*Figure 315*).

Figure 331

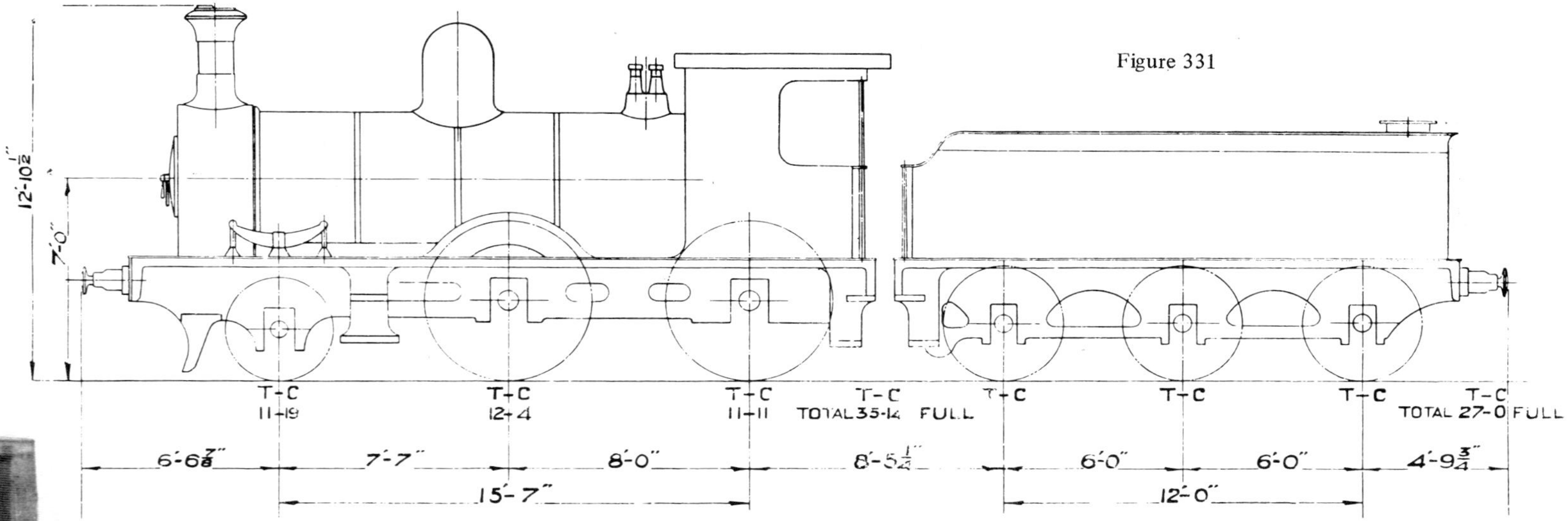

These two illustrations show the subtle difference in the two chimneys fitted on this small class of 2-4-0 Midland and South Western Junction Railway engines. *Figure 332* is a delightful picture of No. 1335 taken by that master, Maurice Earley. The engine is standing outside Reading shed and the 'RDG' can be seen clearly on the front buffer beam.

The drawing in *Figure 331* shows the engine as built in 1894 and one can see the waisted chimney as compared with the parallel-sided Dean chimney. The most unusual feature of these three engines was the original cab which they always retained, very square and angular with an almost flat roof. They also kept their tenders, but with the addition of coal side plates. Swindon gave them *Diagram A.7* for their original 'as built' condition.

Figure 332

Figure 333

Figure 334

The engine featured on this page is the outside cylindered 2-6-0 known to railwaymen as 'Galloping Gertie'. She started life with one other similar locomotive as No. 16. The two engines were built by Beyer Peacock & Co., for a South American Railway but the transaction, like so many at that time, came to nothing, and they passed into the stock of the Midland and South Western Junction Railway, one in 1895 and No. 16 in 1896.

The earliest engine No. 14 did not pass into Great Western hands but went to various collieries, ending its days in 1943. No. 16 however received the Swindon treatment in 1925 and was turned out in the condition shown in these two studies, as No. 24. Fitted with a Standard No. 9 boiler, with Belpaire firebox and dome on the second ring, she was coupled to a 2,500 gallon Great Western tender and looked very workmanlike indeed. She was used for local freight pick-up duties between Stoke Gifford and Swindon, and had her moment of glory, when a 'King' failed on an Up Bristol express; she was called upon to deputize and hauled the express as far as Swindon!

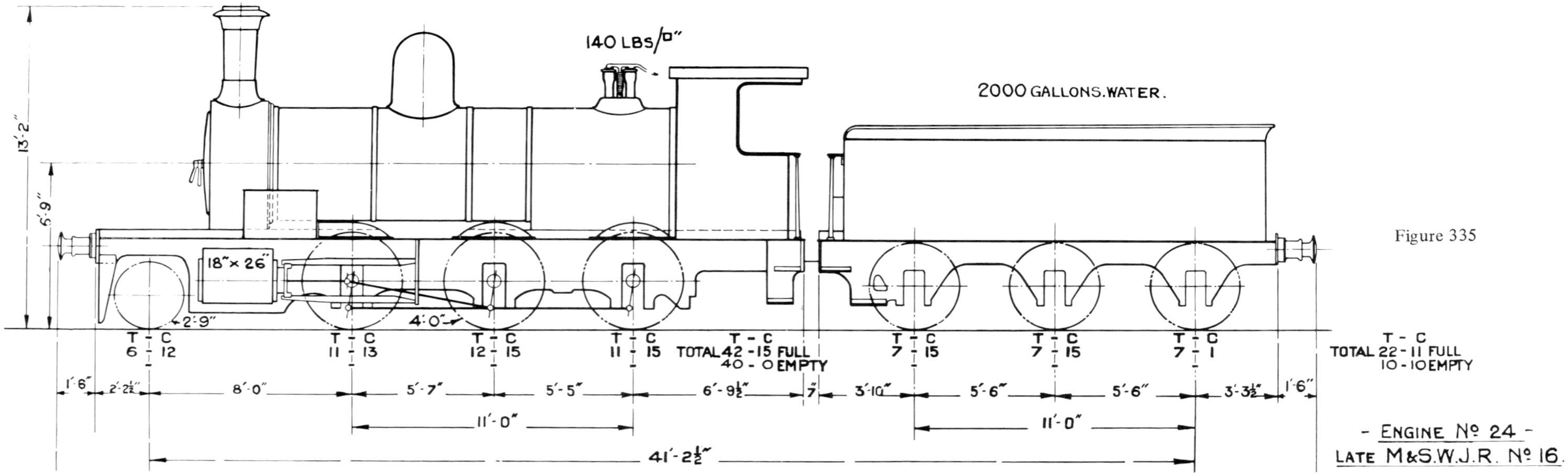

Figure 335

On this page are the official drawings of 'Galloping Gertie', which I know will be of interest to some modellers, as my friends at Pendon have expressed a wish to construct a model of this 2-6-0 oddity. They hope eventually to run this on the miniature 'Vale of the White Horse' layout.

The upper drawing is as the engine was originally built in 1895, and is recorded as *Diagram N.* The *Diagram O*, however, in *Figure 336* is reproduced as near as possible to the 1/64 scale, and shows the engine as she ran on the Great Western metals.

Note the different boiler, firebox, cab, chimney and fittings and also the Midland and South Western Junction tender (*Figure 335*).

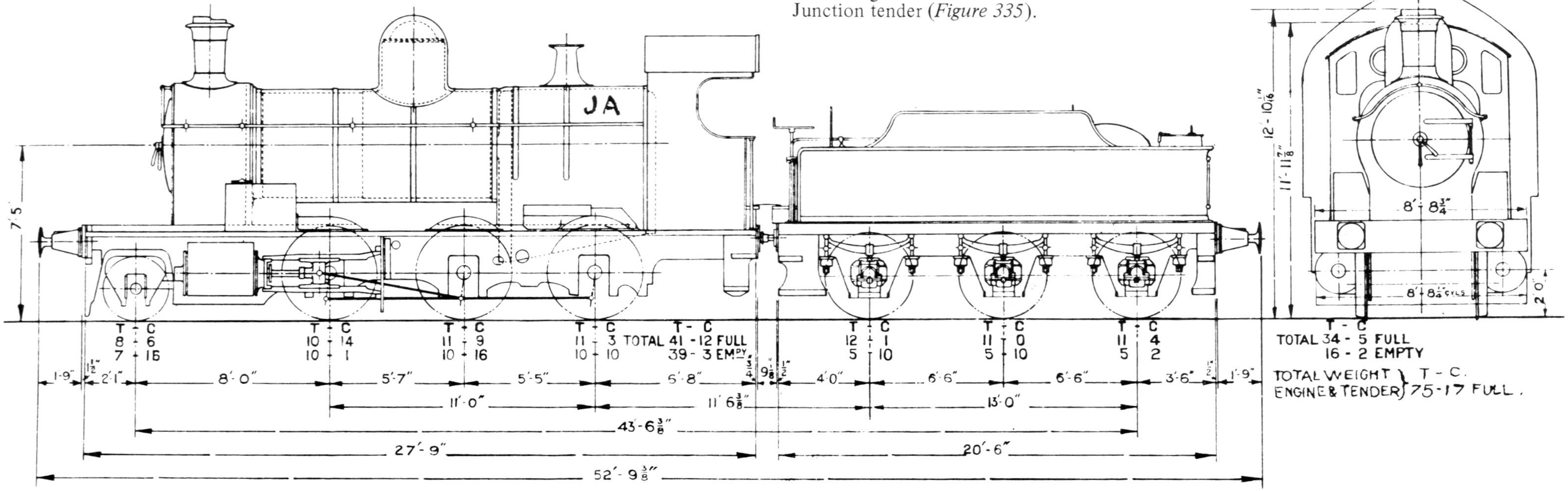

Figure 336

Another Beyer-Peacock built engine which came over from the Midland and South Western Junction Railway after the grouping, was No. 15. Built in 1895, she had inside frames, bearings, and cylinders, an overall cab, and a flush topped boiler.

Wheels were 5′ 2″ coupled, and 3′ trailing to the 4-4-0T configuration, as can be seen in *Figure 337,* the original *Diagram F* of the class.

She passed through the factory in 1925, and emerged, with a standard No. 11 boiler with the dome on the back ring, a Belpaire casing and a boiler pressure of 140 lbs. Although keeping the cab, she was refitted with a Great Western pattern bunker. Her duties were sharing the shuttle service between the two Swindon stations, with No. 25. Her number became Great Western 23 as can be seen in *Figure 338.*

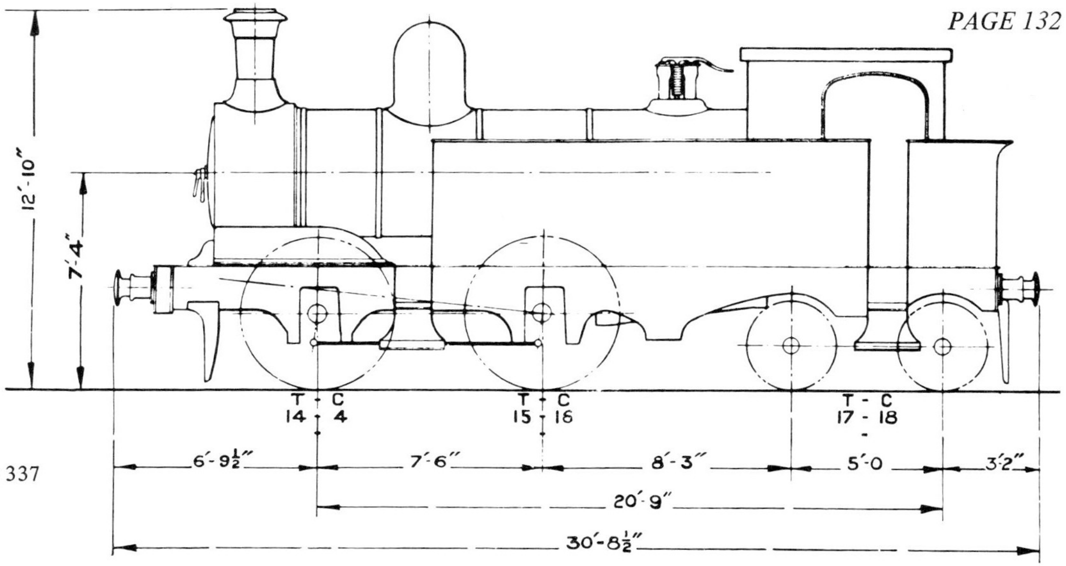

Figure 337

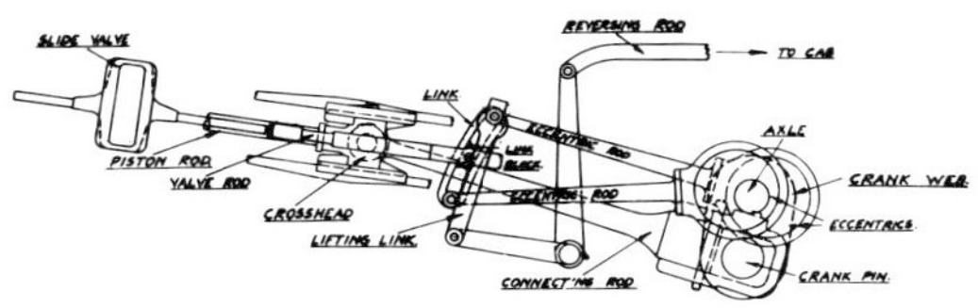

DIAGRAM OF "STEPHENSON" VALVE GEAR
SLIDE VALVE _ INSIDE CYLINDERS

Figure 338

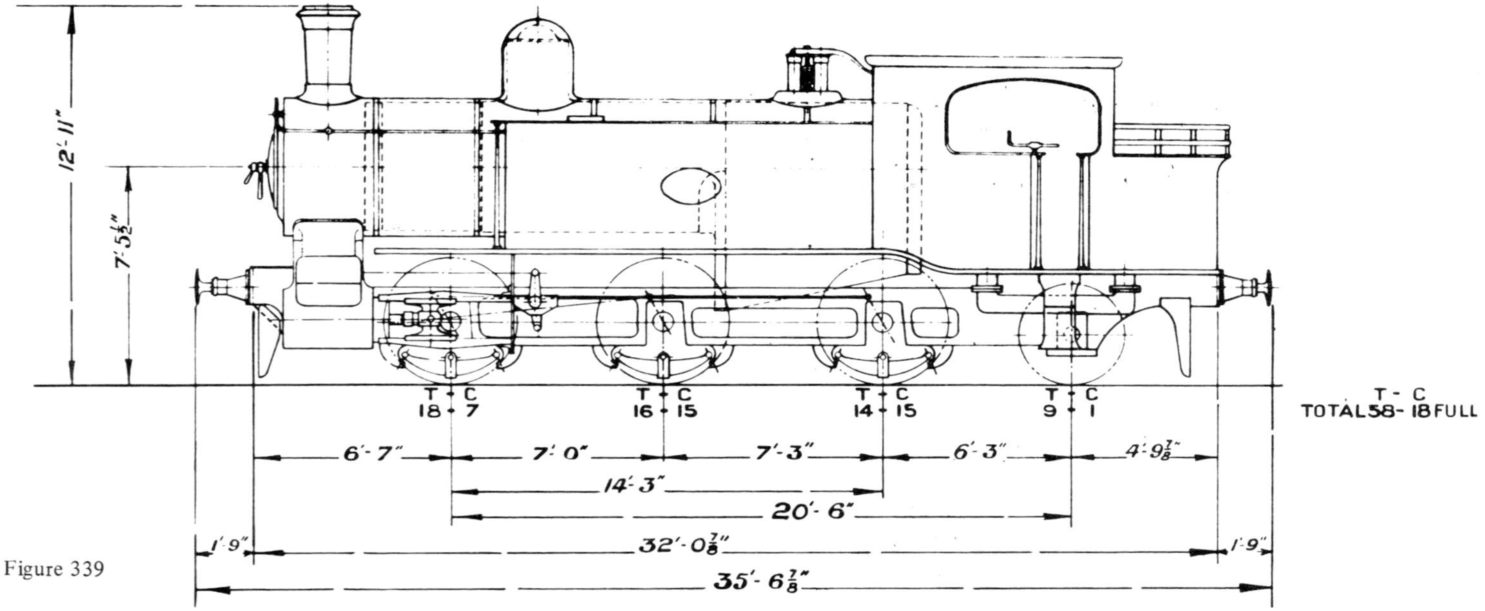

Figure 339

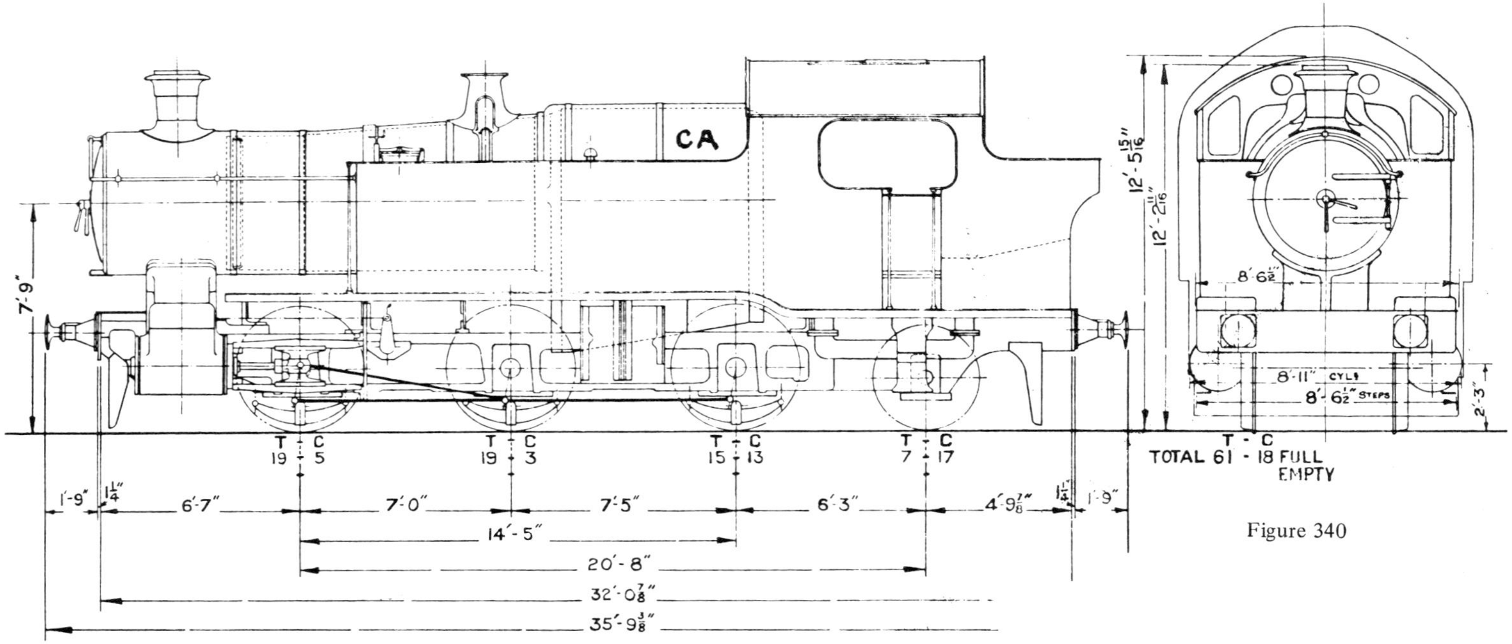

Figure 340

Two drawings of the 0-6-2T class of American engines, which were shipped over for a Welsh railway, namely the Barry Railway, but eventually absorbed into the Great Western. The diagrams show (*Figure 339*) them as purchased, *Diagram Y* numbered 117-21 and in *Figure 340 Diagram A.31* in Great Western days, as numbers 193-197.

Figure 341

One of the five Barry Railway 0-6-2T engines from the American Cooke Company of 1899, No. 196 is illustrated in *Figure 341* after receiving the Swindon rebuilding treatment in 1923. Their original numbers on the Barry list were 117-21, and they became Great Western Nos. 193-7. It is interesting to see their American ancestry in the wheels, motion and framing, married to the standard Great Western outline above the running plate.

Figure 342 shows another unusual class of engine which was used on the Barry Railway and eventually absorbed into the Great Western. This was originally No. 141, one of the series of ten engines which were designed by Mr. Auld and built by Hawthorn Leslie in 1914. Nos. 139-148 became Great Western 1347-1355/7 in 1923 when they were Swindonized as shown in the official photograph.

Figure 342

Two more official diagrams to illustrate the rebuilding of the 0-6-4T described on the previous page. The Hawthorn Leslie design is seen in *Figure 343* as built for the Barry Railway. This is Swindon *Diagram B,* and directly below is the rebuilt version as shown in the photograph on page 134. This was *Diagram C* in the official book (*Figure 344*).

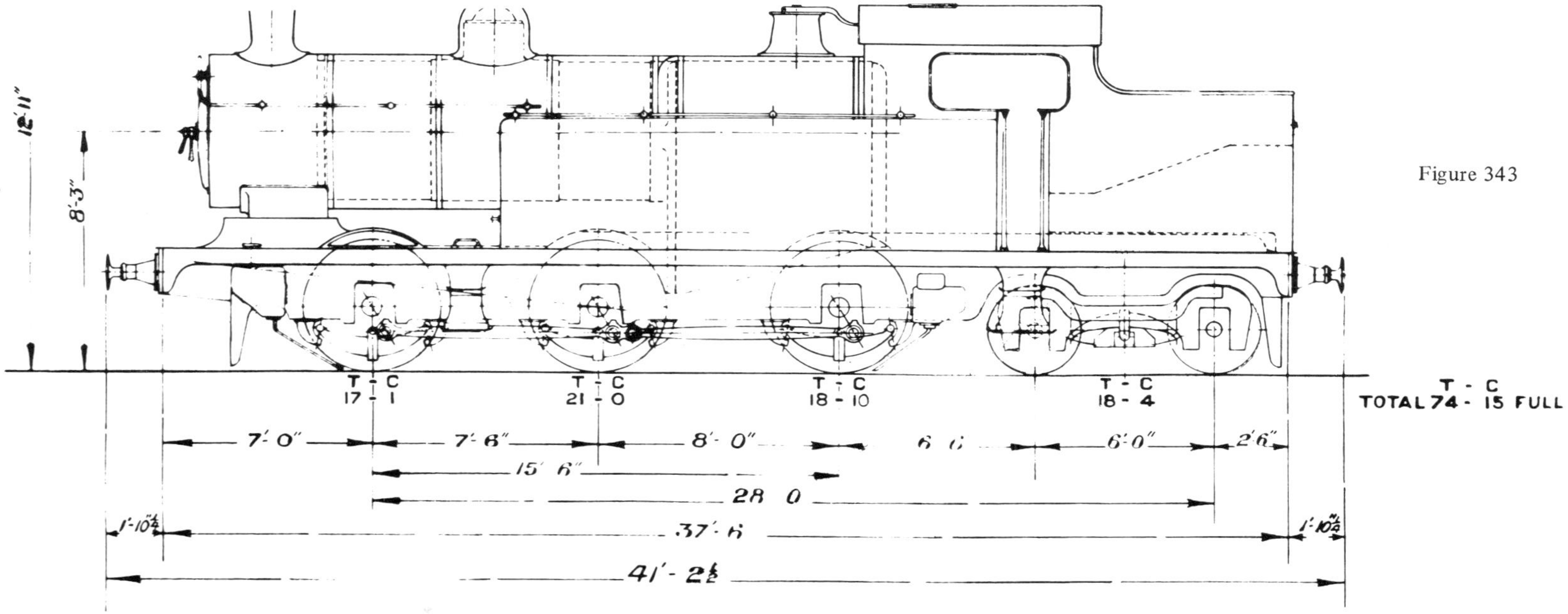

Figure 343

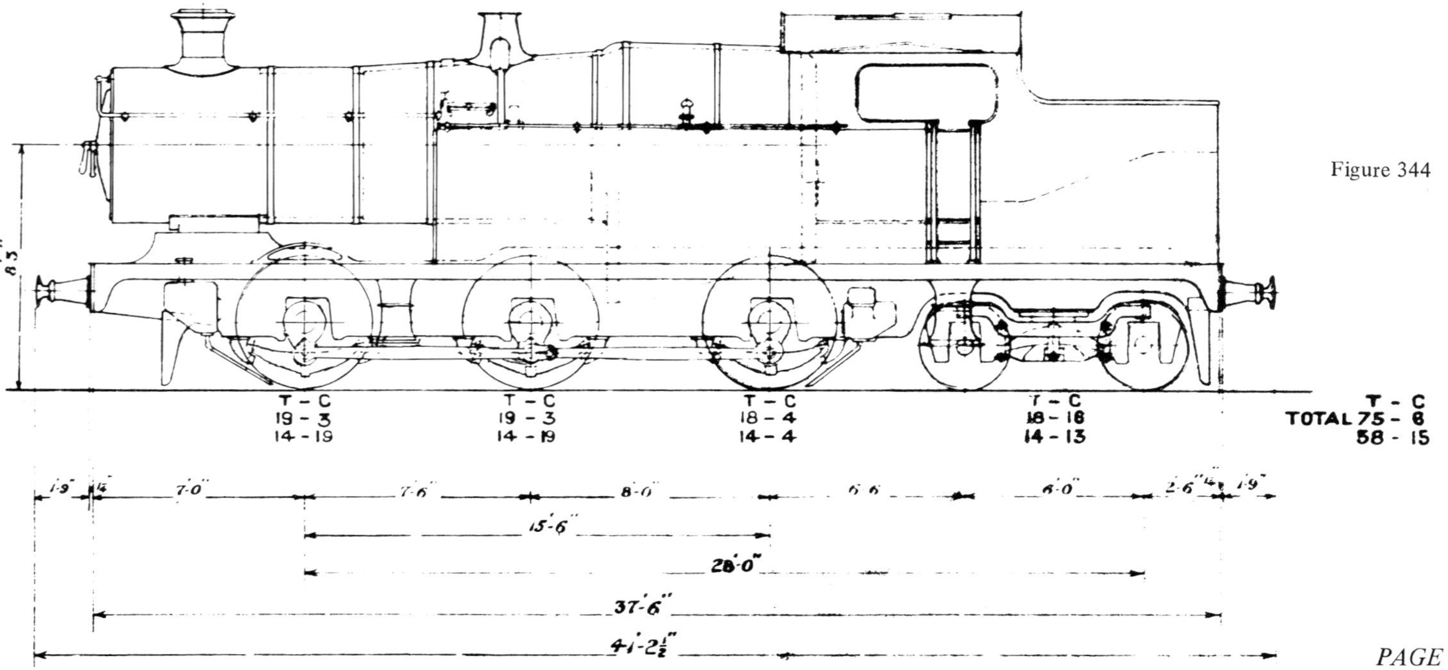

Figure 344

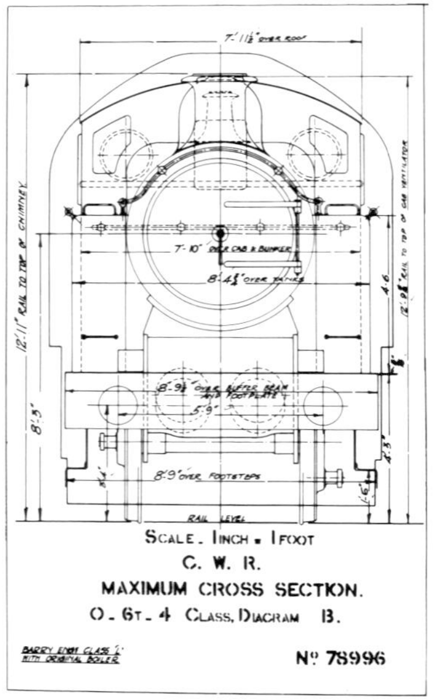

Figure 345

Figure 346

Two other adopted engines, which lasted for many years on the Great Western Railway, were the pair of 2-6-2T engines, built for the Alexander Dock Railway by Hawthorn Leslie in 1920. They were actually the last engines to be constructed for the Alexander Dock Railway and were altered very little when owned by the Great Western Railway as can be seen from the original *Diagram W* in *Figure 347,* and the two photographs I took of the class at Hereford in 1951.

Alexander Dock Railway numbers were 36 and 37 and the Great Western numbers were 1205 and 1206. No. 1205 lasted until 1956.

These then are just a tiny sample of the grand total of 925 engines which came on to the stock list of the Great Western Railway at the Grouping, the subject of absorbed engines is so vast as to fill several volumes by itself alone, but perhaps these few samples have shown how Swindon could take 'foreign' locomotives and by one or two deft changes, breathe a 'Western' character over the most 'way-out' design. A book on the absorbed engines is in preparation at this time.

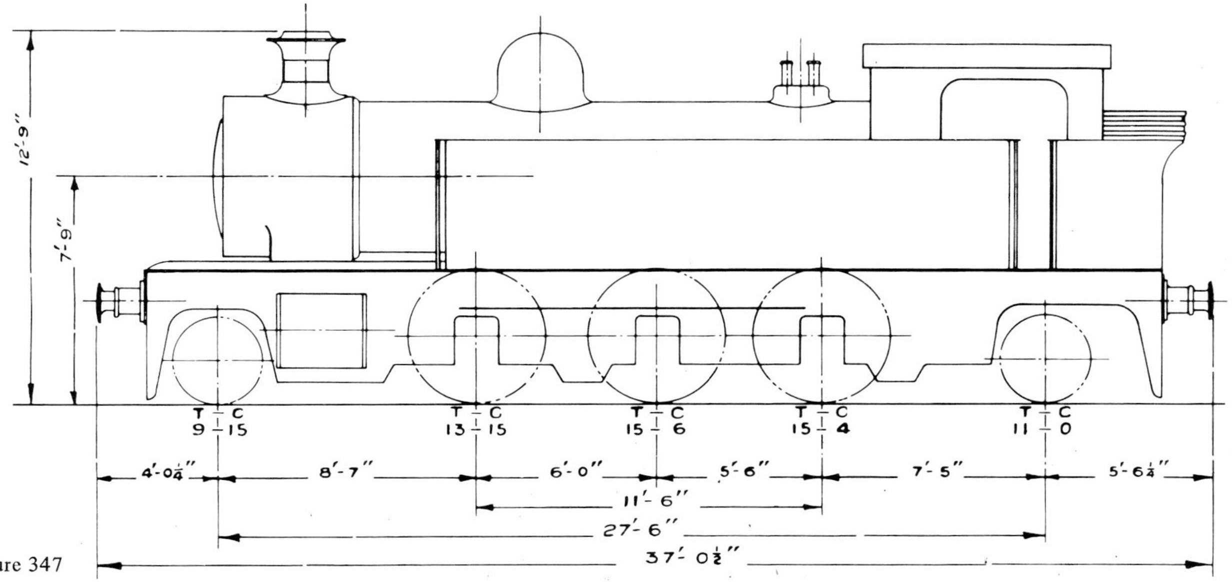

Figure 347

Figure 348

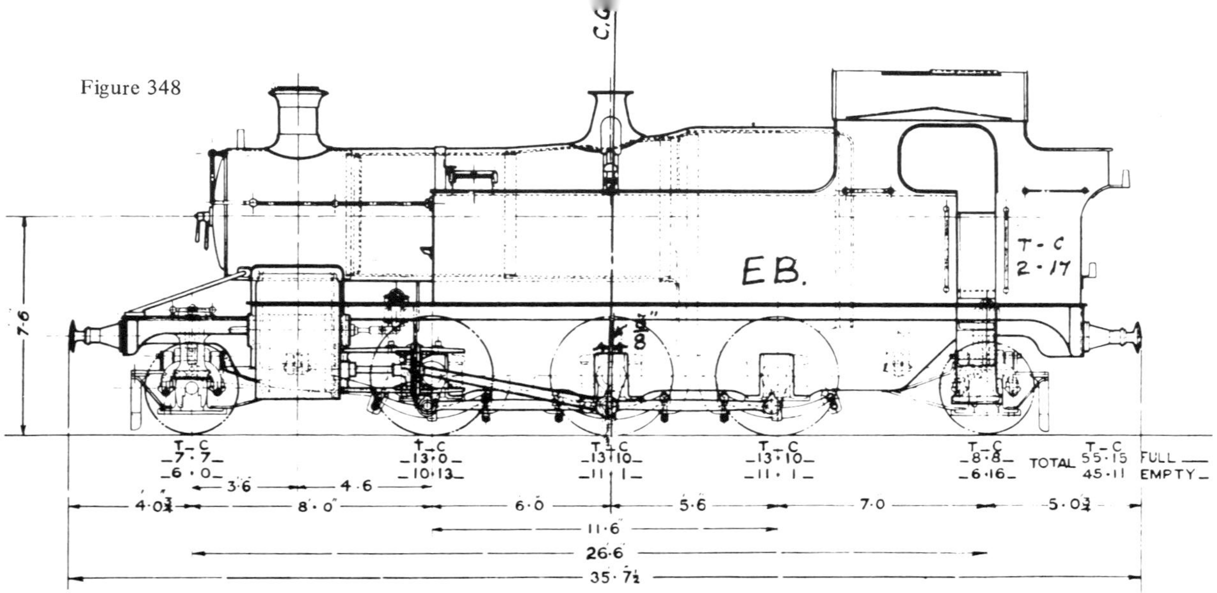

As already mentioned on page 35, Churchward introduced a small-wheeled 2-6-2 tank in 1904 in the form of No. 115. This little engine was a scaled-down version of the big 'Prairie' No. 99 and was such an immediate success by virtue of its powers, of acceleration and general handiness, that ten others were ordered in 1905-6. The prototype was built at Swindon on *Lot 144,* and, although the remainder were scheduled to follow suit, they were, in fact constructed at Wolverhampton. At first allotted Nos. 3101-10, they became 4401-10 at the renumbering and the prototype No. 115, was given the initial '4400'. When built they had small bunkers, short smokeboxes and cast iron chimneys, but gradually superheaters were fitted and the bunkers extended to accommodate more coal. In *Figure 348* (the Swindon *Diagram O*), it is possible to see the extent of the bunker enlargement, from the original *Diagram C* seen on page 35; note also that top feed has been fitted. Copper-topped chimneys were used in 1910-11 but were replaced eventually by the taper cast variety once more. The two illustrations in *Figure 349* and *350* show No. 4407 and No. 4409 carrying the built-up type of chimney.

Figure 349

Figure 350

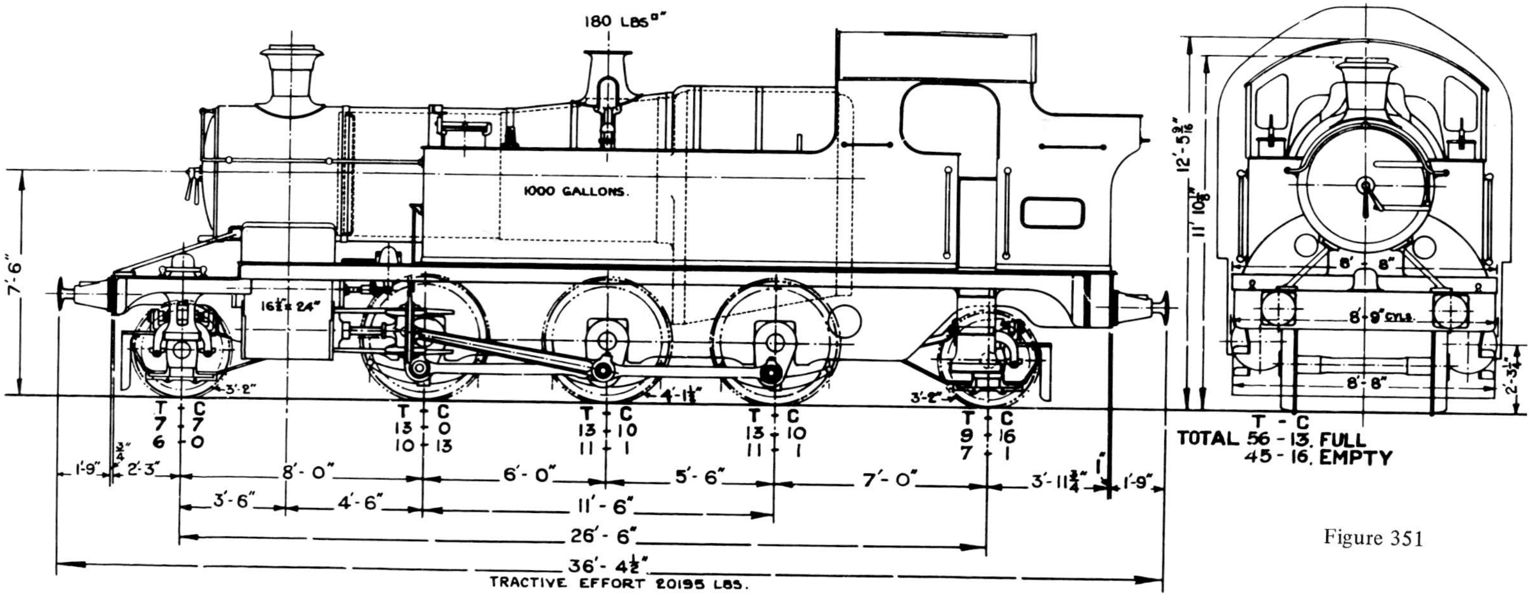

Figure 351

These little 44XX's are very popular amongst modellers and there is an excellent kit available. I am showing two full pages of detail shots which I hope will prove helpful to modellers. *Figure 351* shows the final *Diagram A.4* to 4m/m scale and gives useful measurements. No. 4402 shows the front end, whilst taking water at Kingsbridge in *Figure 352,* and in *Figure 353* the top of the boiler, cab and firebox are seen of No. 4406. Let the pictures on the next two pages speak for themselves. All are details of the 44XX class.

Figure 352

Figure 353

Figure 354

Figure 355

Figure 356

Figure 357

Figure 358 Figure 359

Figure 360

Figure 361

Figure 362

Figure 363

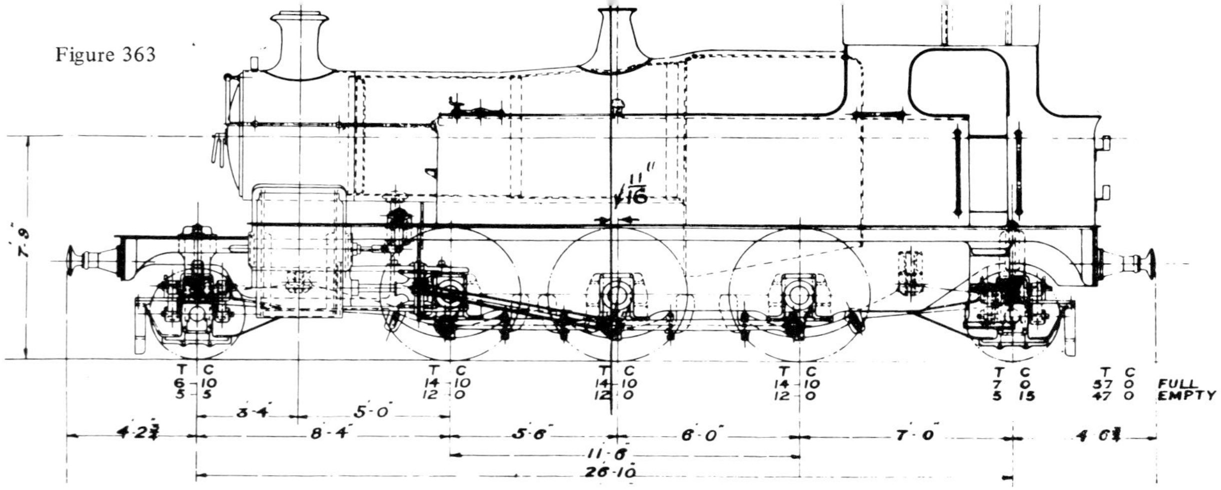

The 44XX class had six driving wheels of 4′ 1½″ diameter, which was rather small for any fast running and so limited their use to the twisty hilly branches in the West Country, with one or two exceptions in South Wales at one period. Therefore when more similar engines were needed, it was thought wiser to increase the wheel diameter to 4′ 7½″ as so it was that the famous 45XX series evolved.

The first batch of 20 was built at Wolverhampton in 1906-8 to *Lot N.3* and originally numbered 2161-80, but the next ten, 2181-90, and indeed the whole of the series, apart from the first twenty, were constructed at Swindon factory between 1909 and 1929. The first thirty engines of the class had the square drop ends, but from 4530 onward the curved running plate was adopted. When first built, many had the copper topped chimney, but later this was replaced by the taper cast type which became standard.

Figure 364

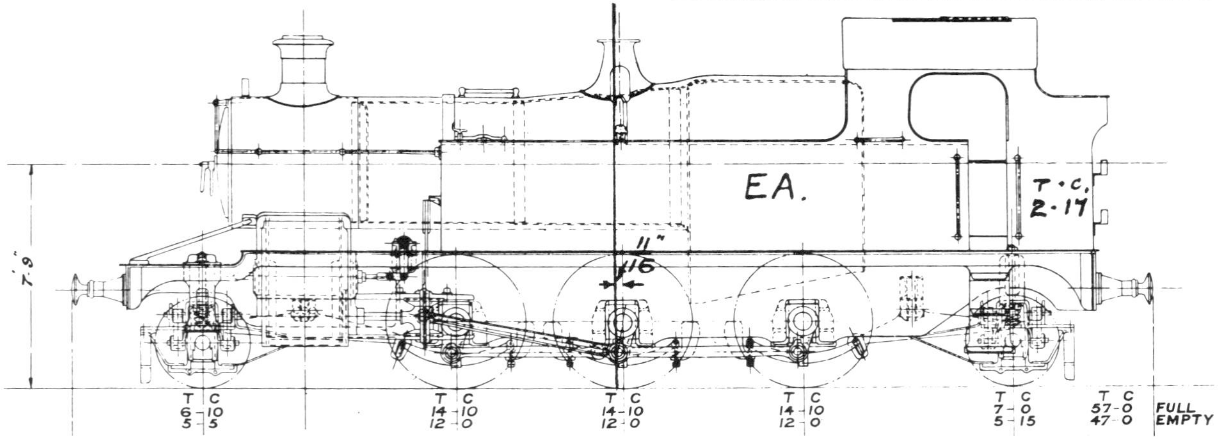

The series can be divided into two varieties, Nos. 4500 to 4574, which all had the flat-topped tank, and from '4575' onward they were fitted with a sloping tank top. Like their sisters the 44XXs, the 45XXs had their bunkers enlarged, and many were fitted with front struts and later outside steam pipes. On this page we see No. 4567 in *Figure 362* at Gloucester in 1949, and No. 4540 at Swindon in 1914. The 4m/m drawings are the official diagrams. *Figure 363* is *Diagram D* as built (4500-39) with small bunker and taper chimney etc. *Figure 365* is *Diagram M* which shows the class with extended bunker, top feed, but not superheated.

Figure 365

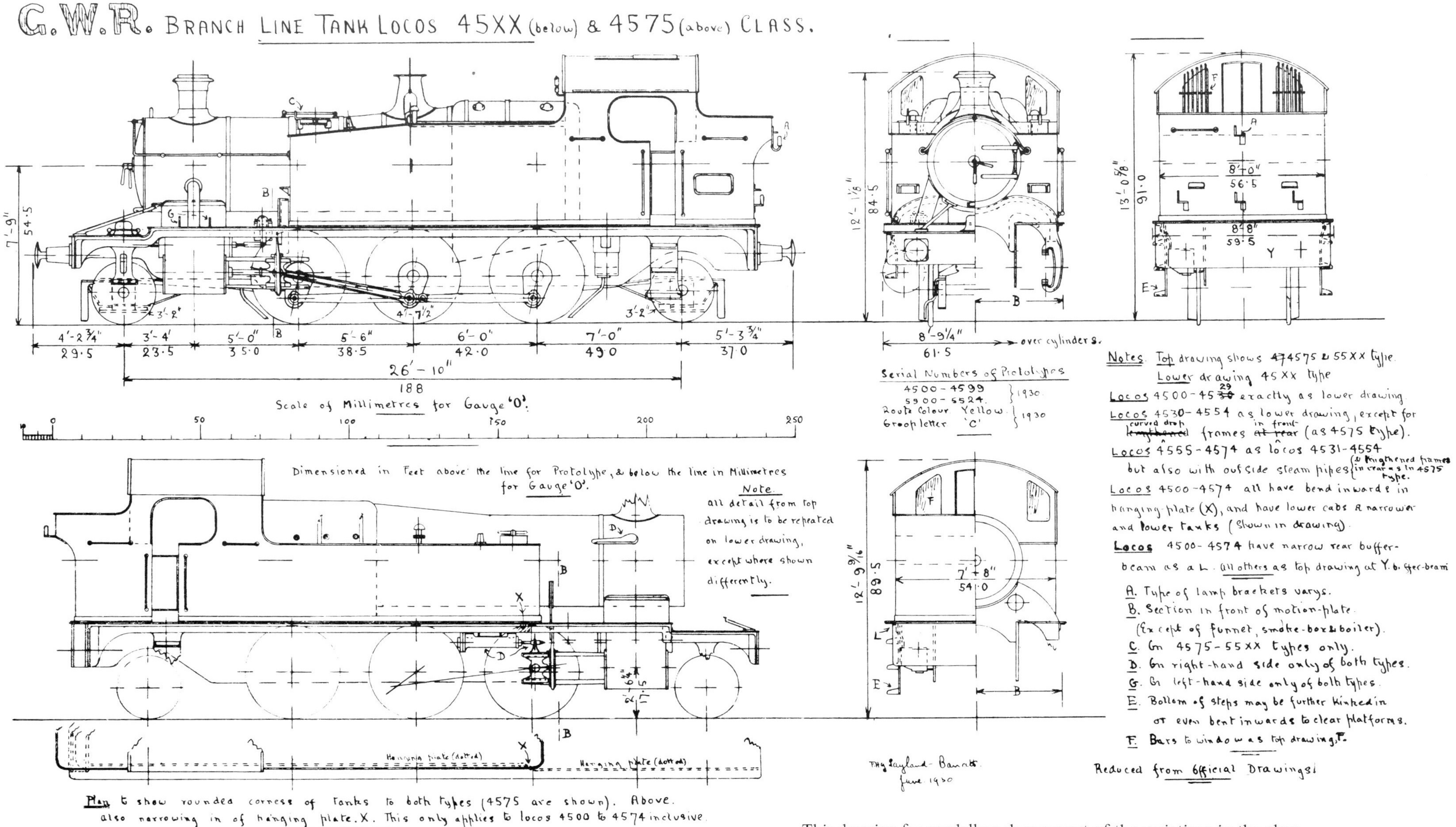

Figure 366

This drawing for modellers shows most of the variations in the class, not only both sides, but front and end elevations as well. The notes at the side speak for themselves. This is one of several excellent drawings from the skilled pen of Capt. Layland-Barratt in 1930 (*Figure 366*).

Figure 367

Figure 368

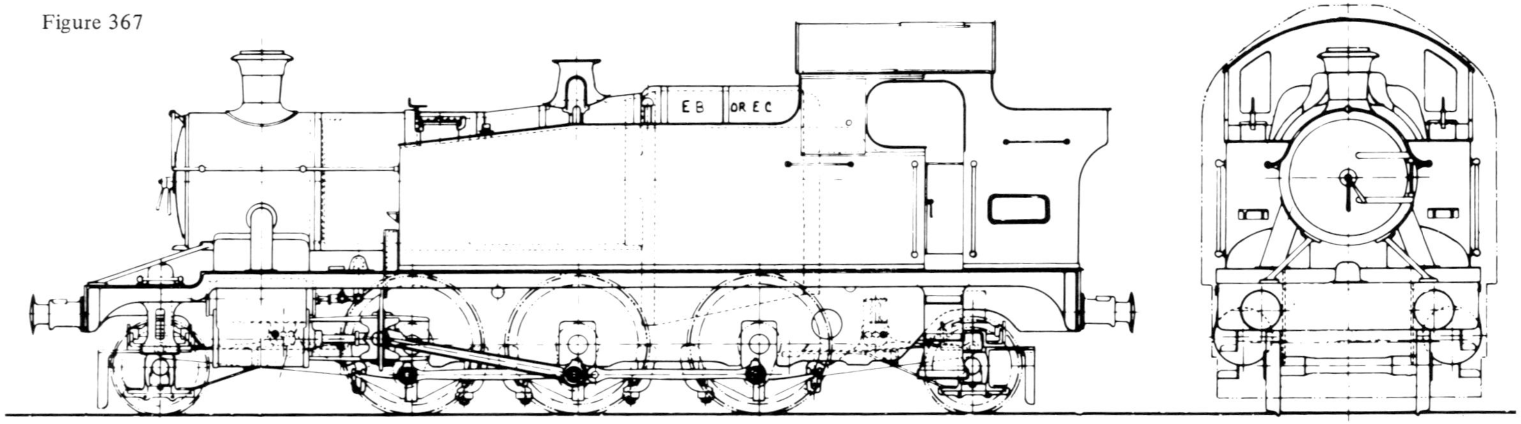

Figure 369

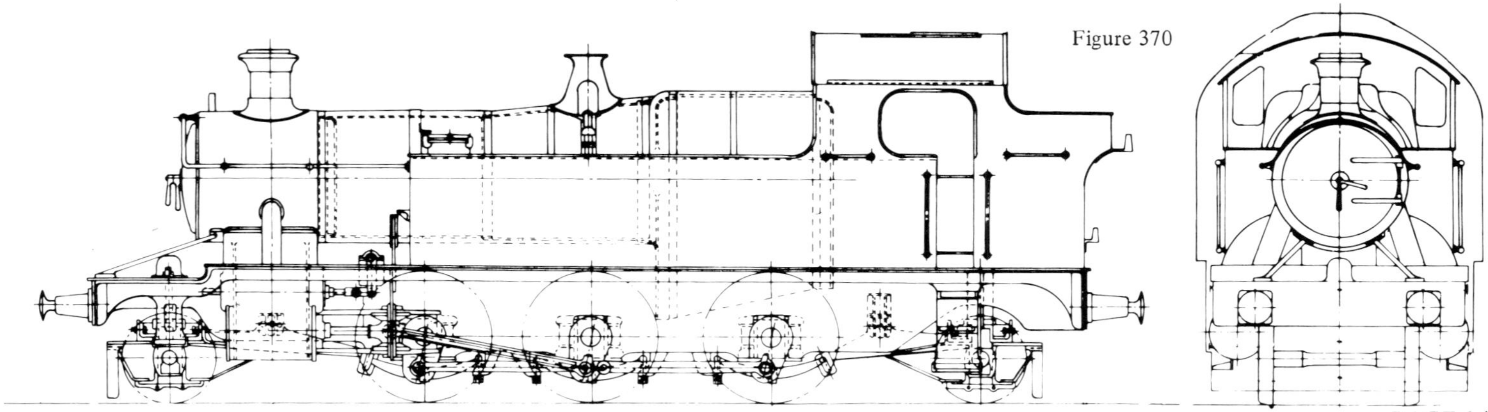

Figure 370

Two of the '55XX's are shown here. In *Figure 367* we see '5525' condemned at Swindon in 1962 and in *Figure 368* No. 5572 is illustrated from a high view point, showing the boiler top and fittings.

The drawings are the official diagrams of the '4575' class, which pertains to the engines in the photographs in *Figure 373*, (*Diagram A.5*) and *Figure 370* (*Diagram A.2*) which showed the '4500' class with superheater, and the 1000 gallon side tanks. The enlarged tanks of the '4575' class had a capacity of 1300 gallons (*see page 145*).

Figure 371

Figure 371 is a Swindon portrait in the nineteen-forties of No. 5531 just out of shops. Note the unusual place for the yellow classification disc. No. 4599 is seen on a local suburban train at Paddington approaches in *Figure 372* (date 1929) and in *Figure 373* No. 4584 has just been weighed on the Swindon weighbridge after a major overhaul in 1935.

Figure 372

Figure 373

Figure 374

Figure 375

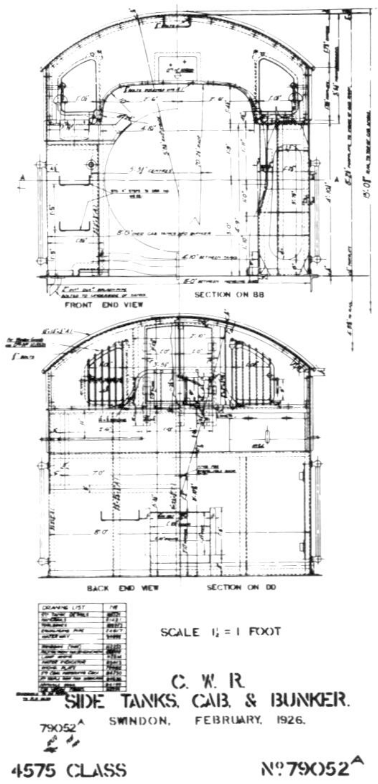

Figure 378

Figure 376

Figure 377

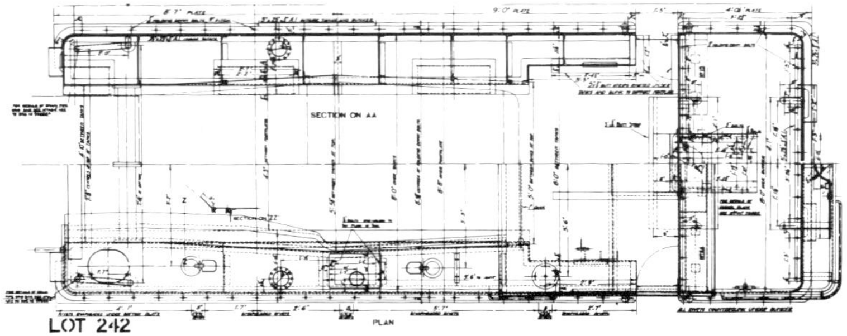

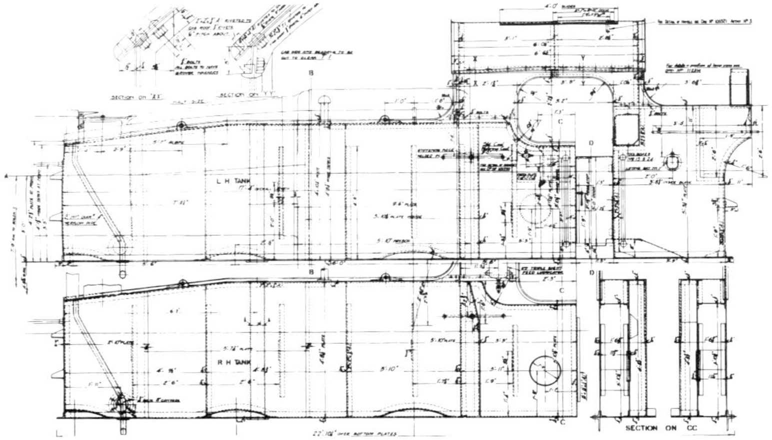

The two small photographs on the left were taken in the late 'forties and are of interest as they show minor differences between engines of the same series. In *Figure 374* we see No. 4527 at Bridport with a plain bunker back, and in *Figure 375* No. 4507 is shown on a local train at Totnes, but fitted with a coal guard around the top lamp bracket, and outside steam pipes. This should stress the point so often made that modellers should select one particular locomotive in any series, if authenticity is to be obtained.

An example of this maxim can be seen in *Figure 377.* Believe it or not this is an 'O' gauge model of No. 4523, made by that expert, the late Mike Longridge and shows what can be achieved with patience, and by modelling one particular engine.

The other illustration is one from Maurice Earley's collection and shows No. 4568 at Barnstaple in 1925, at the head of a Taunton stopping passenger train (*Figure 376*).

The works drawing (in 4m/m scale) show the enlarged tanks etc., of the '4575' class (*Figure 378*).

Figure 379

Figure 380

Figure 381

Three final 45XX pictures. In *Figures 379 and 380* are the rear and front ends of No. 4549 as she stands at the head of a 'F' headlight freight in Taunton yard way back in 1930. This engine was never fitted with outside steam pipes, and lasted until December 1961. One of the last batch of the series to be built in 1928-29 is shown in *Figure 381* from the direct front, which gives a good view of both the smokebox struts and the outside steam pipes.

The 'Dukes' have been mentioned earlier in this work, but as they were constantly being altered and rebuilt to keep them up to date, another two pages are devoted to these changes here.

In *Figure 382,* No. 3267 *Cornishman* is seen in Swindon works grey and the date on the photograph is 1924. This would have been the time when the engine was fitted with a Belpaire boiler and top feed, also an extra wide and higher cab was installed. Note how the back edge of the cab side sheets is flared out to help the slipstream away from the footplate gap. When built this engine was No. 3274.

In *Figure 383* we have a Swindon drawing to 4m/m scale of *Diagram A.39* similar to *Cornishman* but with a wide cab, which fitted outside the trailing springs. The old number of 3267 as built in 1896 was 3274, and the little engine carried on in service right up to December 1936.

The small inset shows the variation in the class fitted with the narrow cab and round windows.

Figure 382

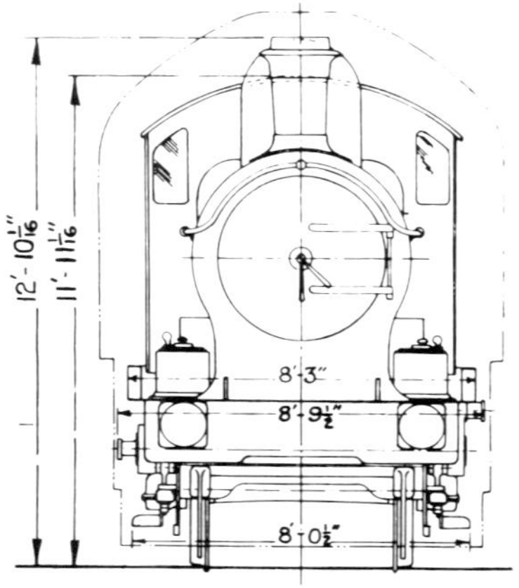

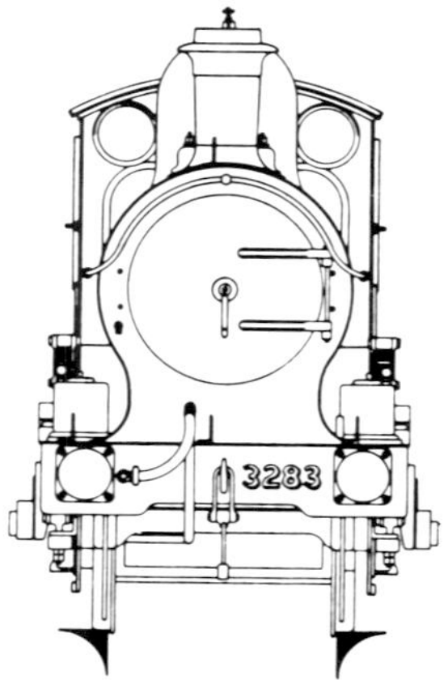

Figure 383

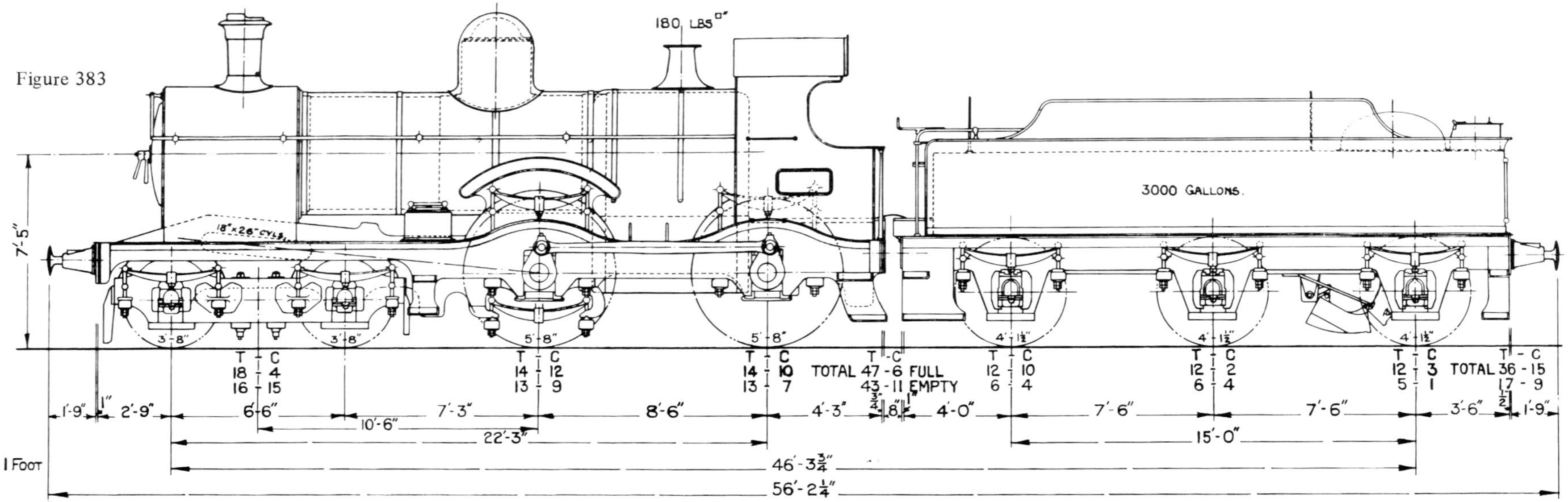

In 1929 one of the 'Duke' class, No. 3265, was withdrawn together with a 'Bulldog' No. 3365. Parts from these two engines, plus a spare 'Duke' boiler, were assembled to make what was a prototype for a new class, the 'Earls' which were to number from 3200-19 and later a further nine 3220-28.

Apart from the reconstituted No. 3265, *Tre Pol & Pen,* the first engine to be turned out was No. 3201 named *St. Michael* as it was intended to perpetuate the old 'Duke' names, and this engine is shown in *Figure 384.* However, she only carried this name for a short while, as the class were named after 'Earls', but, as the real owners of the titles were not flattered by the small engines, the names were removed and found a better place on the 'Castle' class. The drawing is the official *A.43 diagram,* which applied to these rebuilds (*Figure 385*).

Figure 384

Figure 385

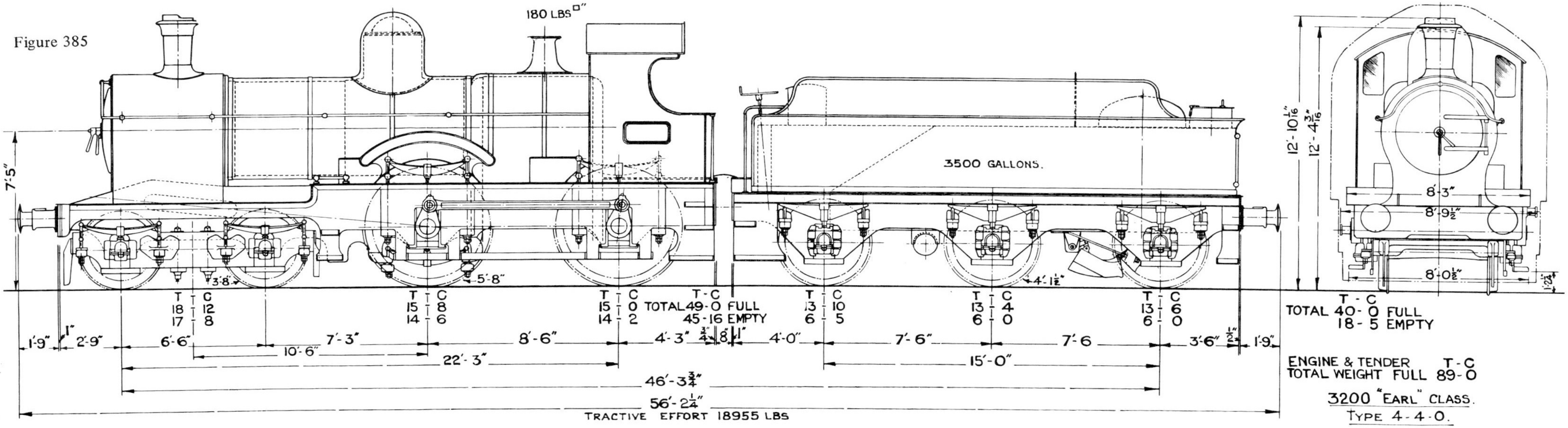

In 1922 Mr. Collett took over at Swindon from Mr. Churchward, and one of the first major designs to be produced by the new Chief was the 'Castle' class. Initially it was intended to enlarge the 'Star' class by fitting a large No. 7 boiler but this was frowned upon by the Civil Engineer as being too heavy, and therefore a new slightly smaller boiler (No. 8) was produced.

The photograph on this page by my friend Maurice Earley, shows the last 'Star' to be built, namely No. 4072 *Tresco Abbey* in 1926 at Twyford. This was the final condition of these magnificent engines before they were eclipsed by the more powerful 'Castles'. Between 1937 and 1940 the last ten, 4063-72, were withdrawn and many pieces of them were used in rebuilds into the 'Castle' class and renumbered 5082-93.

The detailed drawing by Colonel Templer, shows the many variations in the rebuilding of the 'Star' class and the notes will give most of the necessary information (*Figure 387*). As a note of interest, I recently saw the nameplates of *Tresco Abbey* affixed to a trailer behind a Fordson tractor on the quay at Crow Point, Isles of Scilly!

Figure 386

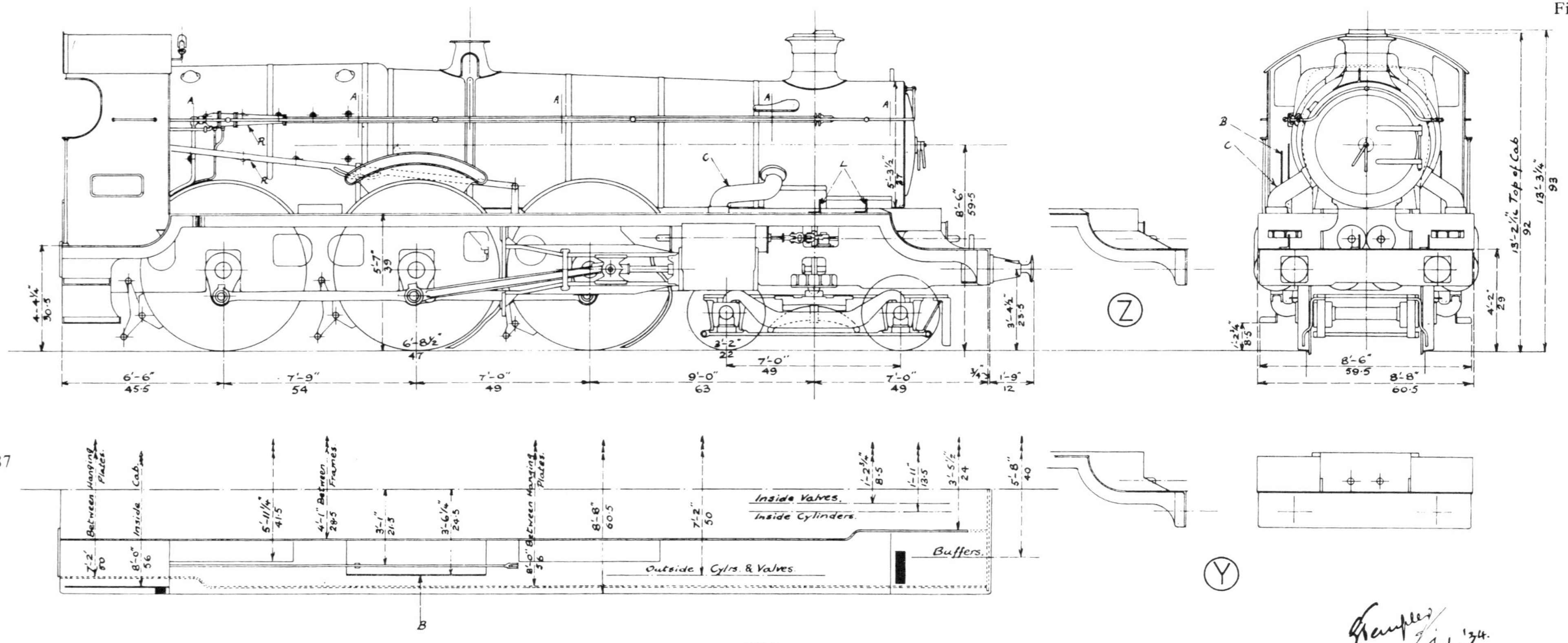

Figure 387

NOTES.

Diagram Y: Inside Valve Covers Nos 4001-8, 4010-5 & 4017-20. Diagram Y: Inside Valve Covers Nos 4021-30. Hand-rail knobs on left side given by centre lines A. Centre splasher B on right side set out to clear reverse rod: splashers on left side in line. External steam pipes C only fitted with new cylinders. Details marked L on left side only: those marked R on right side only. Wheel treads and flanges drawn to scale: allowances must be made for out-of-scale wheels. Dimensions in feet (full size) and in millimetres to the nearest half-m'metre for Gauge "0".

Figure 388

Figure 389

So much has been written about *Caerphilly Castle* and of the class generally, that I consider it sufficient to illustrate the prototype engine, several of her sisters which are of particular interest, and to supply a good drawing giving the leading dimensions.

In *Figure 388* we see No. 4073 just as turned out of the factory in 1923, with small tender and diagonal rain strips on the cab roof. Compare her with No. 5022 *Wigmore Castle* which was built in 1932, but is shown in the 1948 condition with short chimney and Hawksworth tender. It is very pleasant to report that No. 4073 has been preserved and can still be seen in Great Western livery in the Science Museum, Kensington. (Note the unlagged outside steam pipes on '4073'!)

The official diagram of the prototype No. 4073 appears on page 154 in *Figure 401*.

Colonel Templer's drawing of the 'Castle' class with all the usual notations at the side explaining the variations.

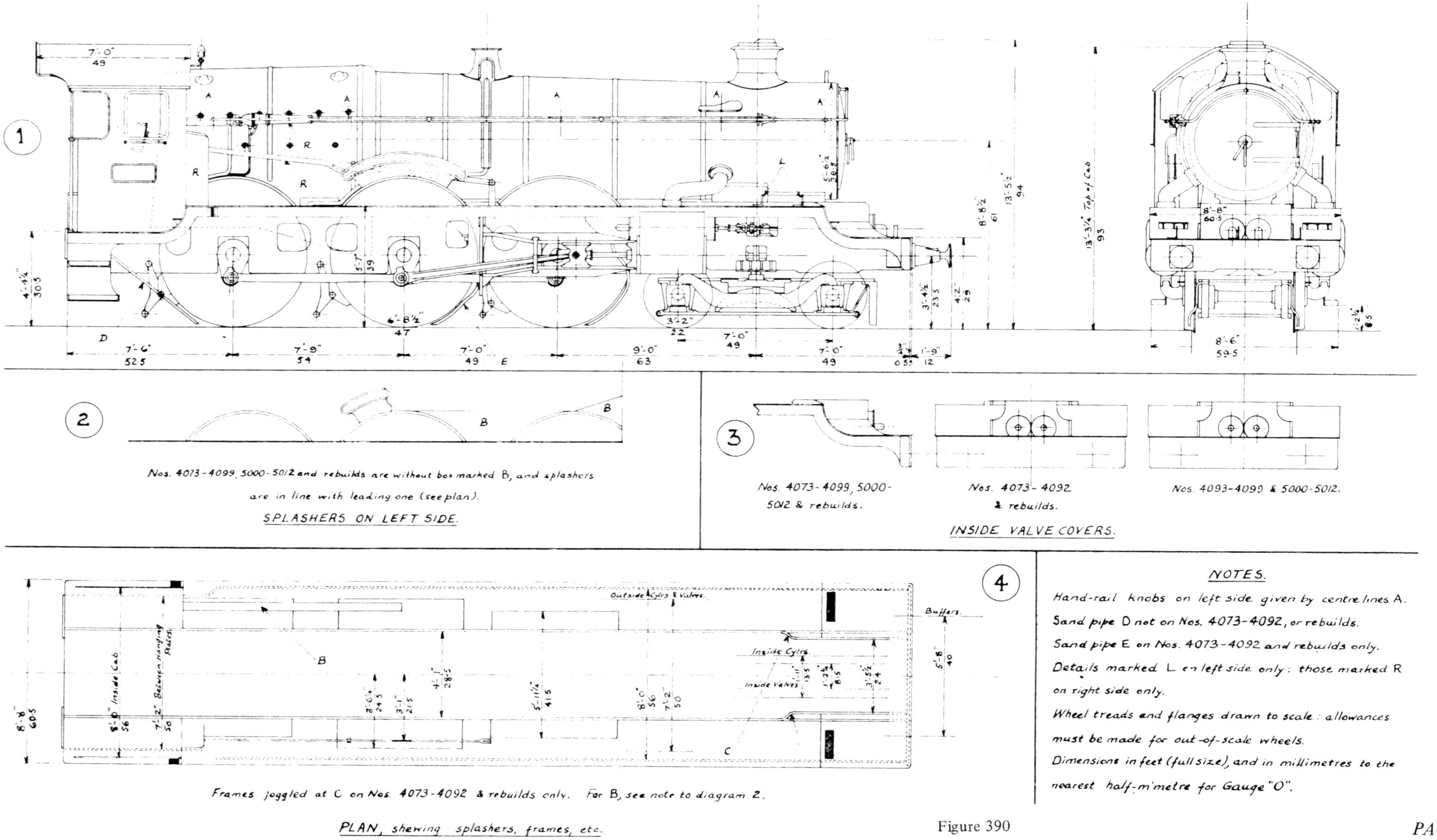

Figure 390

Figure 391

Figure 392

Four famous 'Castles' in the mid-twenties when the 3500 gallon tenders were still in use. *Figure 391* shows No. 5006 *Tregenna Castle* at Old Oak Common shed, which was her home depot for many years. No. 4076 *Carmarthen Castle* was also stabled at Old Oak when first in service and was one of the initial ten to be constructed in 1923-4. She is seen in *Figure 392* at Plymouth. Another early one was No. 4081.

Warwick Castle seen in *Figure 393* again at Old Oak shed, and I had the pleasure of driving this engine at Oxford in 1950! The late King George V was also interested enough to drive one of these early 'Castles', and *Figure 394* illustrates the actual locomotive used, *Windsor Castle;* she carried two commemorative plaques to that effect on her cab sides for many years, which can be seen just above the number plate.

Figure 393

Figure 394

Figure 395

Figure 396

Figure 395 Windsor Castle again in British Railway ownership awaiting her last overhaul at Swindon before withdrawal.

Figure 397 No. 5025 *Chirk Castle* in Sonning Cutting in 1952 showing the mechanical lubricator on running plate.

Figure 398 No. 7013 *Bristol Castle* in the experimental light green livery. This is the engine who donned *Windsor Castle's* nameplate for hauling the funeral train of the late King George VI in 1952, as the real 4082 was unavailable.

Figure 396 shows No. 7007, the last engine to be built at Swindon under the Great Western, appropriately named *Great Western.*

Figure 397

Figure 398

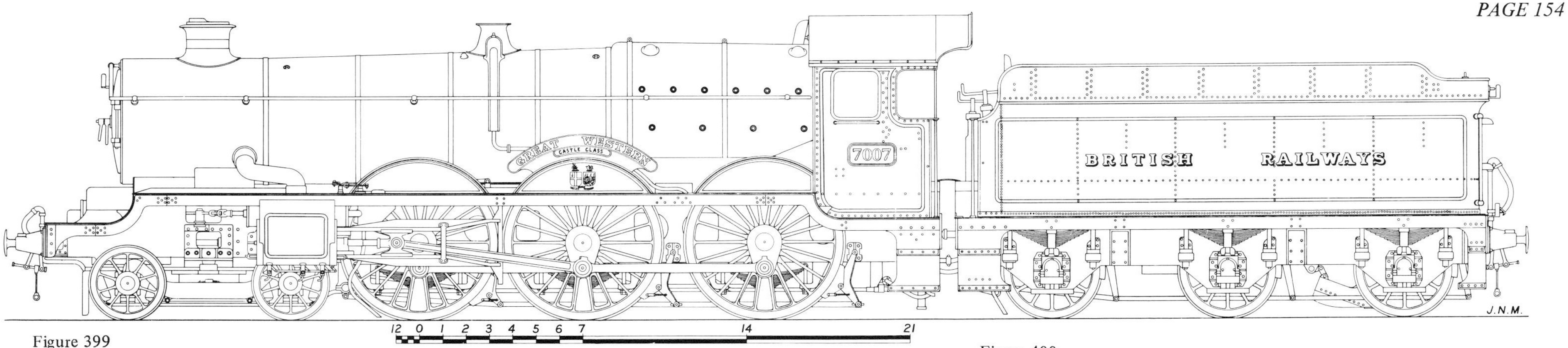

Figure 399

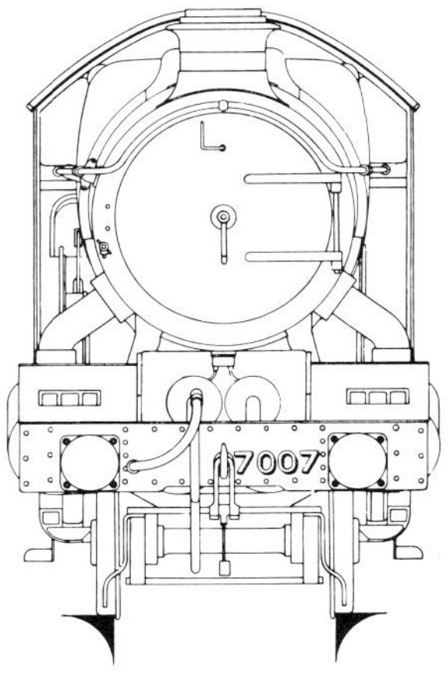

Figure 400

To round off this brief reference to the 4-6-0 'Castle' class, what better than to illustrate the first and last of the series. *Figure 400* shows No. 4000 *North Star,* which was the first 4-cylinder express engine to be built at Swindon, admittedly as an 'Atlantic', but after her rebuilds she is seen in the photograph practically as a 'Castle', and this is the condition in which she was finally withdrawn. Compare her with the lovely drawing of *Great Western* the last to be built by the Company as such at Swindon in 1941. Originally named *Ogmore Castle,* the name was changed in January 1948 with the coat of arms on the centre splasher (*Figure 399*).

It is still possible to see in this year of 1975, three 'Castles' which are still in preservation, namely *Caerphilly, Clun,* and *Pendennis.*

Figure 401 shows the prototype 'Castle' No. 4073 built in 1923.

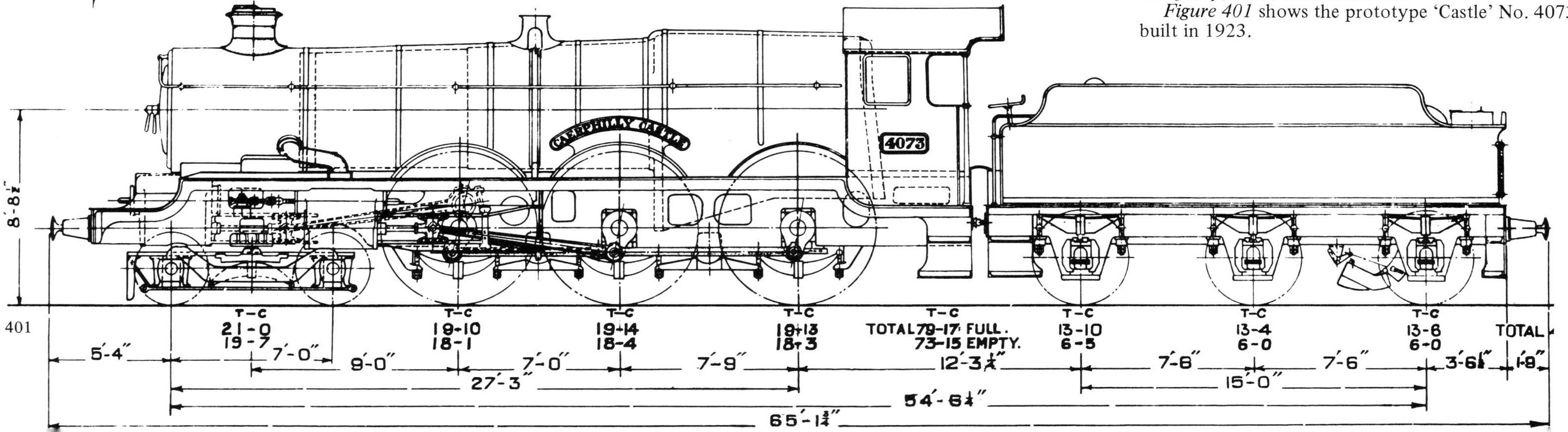

Figure 401

Figure 402

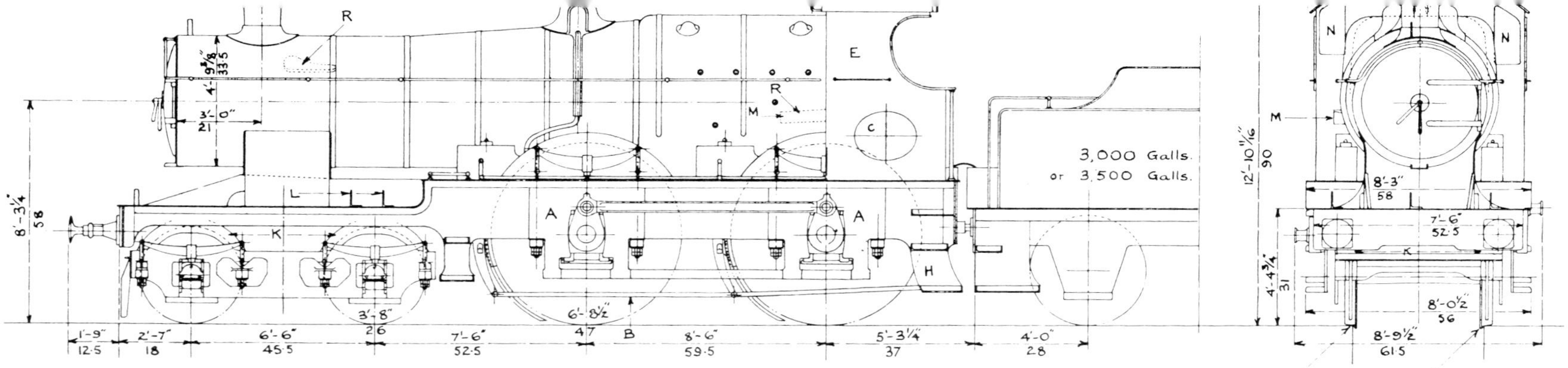

1. "ATBARA" SERIES.

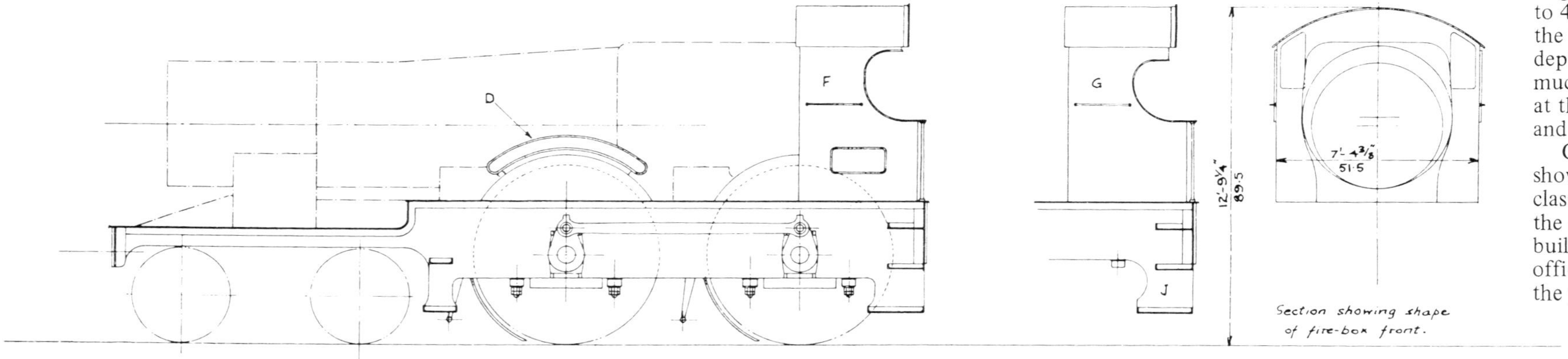

2. "FLOWER" SERIES.

Bogie, and all details above running-plate not shown in full, are exactly as in upper drawing.

Templer, March '31.

NOTES. A. Strengthening plates. B. Brake rigging outside wheels. C. Combined name & number plates; Nos. 4120-4138 only, except Nos. 4121 & 4122. D. Name plates thus on Nos. 4121, 4122 & 4139-4168. E. Cabs thus on Nos. 4120-4128 only; height dimension not available. F. Cabs thus on Nos 4139-4168 only. G. Cabs thus on Nos. 4129-4138 only. H. Footsteps thus on Nos. 4120-4138 only. J. Footsteps thus on Nos. 4139-4148 only. K. Bogie splashers approximately flush with frame. L. On left side only. M. Reverse rod cover; on certain Atbaras only. N. Windows of either height used on type E cabs. R. On right side only. W. Wheel treads & flanges drawn to scale: allowance must be made for out-of-scale wheels. Dimensions in feet (full size), and in millimetres to the nearest half m'metre for Gauge "O".

G. W. R. 4100 CLASS. "ATBARA" Series, Nos. 4120-4148. "FLOWER" Series, Nos. 4149-4168.

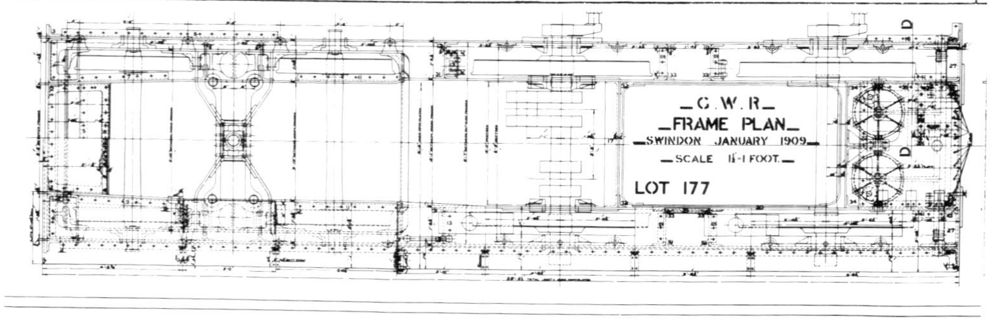

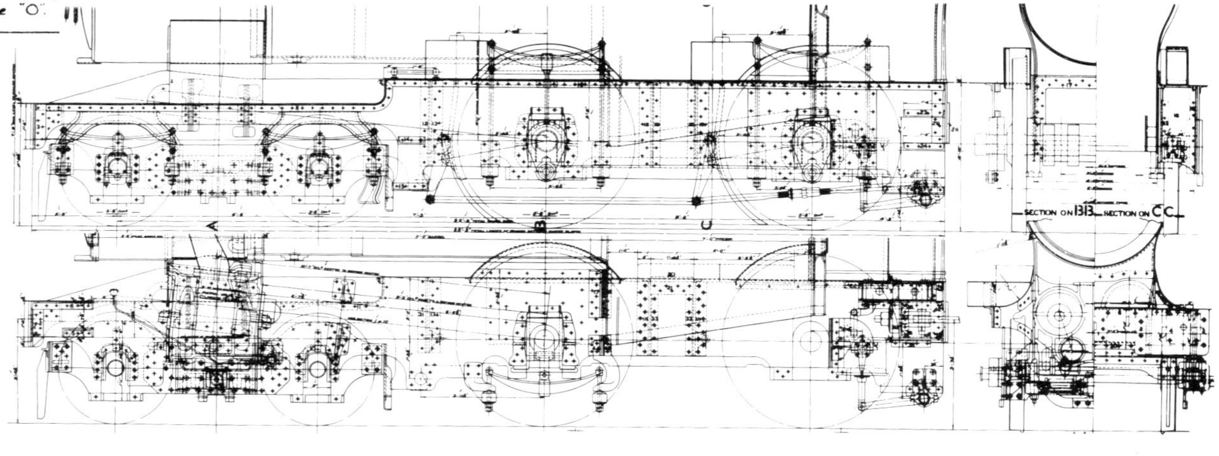

It is necessary here to revert back in years, in order to cover the development of the 'Bird' class which were still being shopped in 1946. The 'Atbara' class has already been mentioned earlier, but in the 1908 period the engines were still performing excellent work on the short cross-country services, so much so, that it was decided to build a further twenty similar engines. These were known as the 'Flowers' and numbered originally 4101-4120 and renumbered later to 4149-68. The main difference between the 'Flowers' and the 'Atbaras' was in the depth of the frames, the 'Flowers' being much deeper. Also these engines were fitted at the outset with vacuum brake cylinders and copper-topped chimneys.

Colonel Templer's drawing in *Figure 402* shows the small differences between the two classes well, but modellers should note that the chimneys on the 4149-68 series were the built-up type. A 4m/m scale reduction of the official frame plan is shown at the bottom of the page.

Figure 403

In *Figure 403,* at the top of the page, is shown one of the first of the 'Atbara' class, namely *Powerful,* as originally built in 1900. This picture is inserted as a comparison of this class over a period of twenty years.

Two studies by Maurice Earley of the 'Atbara' class which are of great interest as they show the oval name-plates. In *Figure 404* we see No. 4138 standing at Reading station in 1922. Notice particularly the Westinghouse pump which was fitted to the right-hand side of this locomotive.

Figure 404

Figure 405

In *Figure 405* is another 'Atbara' on milk train duties. This is No. 4126 *Kitchener* passing Tilehurst box in 1926. The variety of stock is intriguing, with many different types of Siphons as well as a couple of Pythons!

Figure 406

The three types of inside framed 4-4-0 passenger engines are illustrated on this page for comparisons. In *Figure 406* one of the 'Bulldogs' No. 3341 is seen carrying the oval nameplate *Blasius*, in 1935. No. 3466 *Barbados* (later 3404) is seen in *Figure 407* practically as built in 1904 with no top feed and coal rails on the tender. Then we come to the 'Flower' class in *Figure 408;* this is No. 4160 *Carnation,* as she was in 1924 at the factory. It is very apparent from these pictures that the 'Flower' and 'Atbara' class had the large 6′ 8½″ express driving wheels whereas the 'Bulldogs' only sported the 5′ 8″ type.

Figure 408

Following the 'Flowers' in 1909-10 came the 'Bird' class. These were of the small-wheeled inside framed design, similar in all respects to the 'Bulldog' class of which they were part, except that they had the deep framing like the 'Flowers'. Screw reverse was fitted, and they also had enlarged sandboxes for both leading and trailing drivers. *Figure 410* shows *Peacock* in 1924, and *Pelican* is shown at Swindon in 1946, with the large tender *Figure 409.* There were fifteen in this series numbering 3441-55 (originally 3731-45). The last diagram issued was the *A.46* covering Nos. 3440-55 (*Figure 411*).

Figure 409

Figure 410

Figure 411

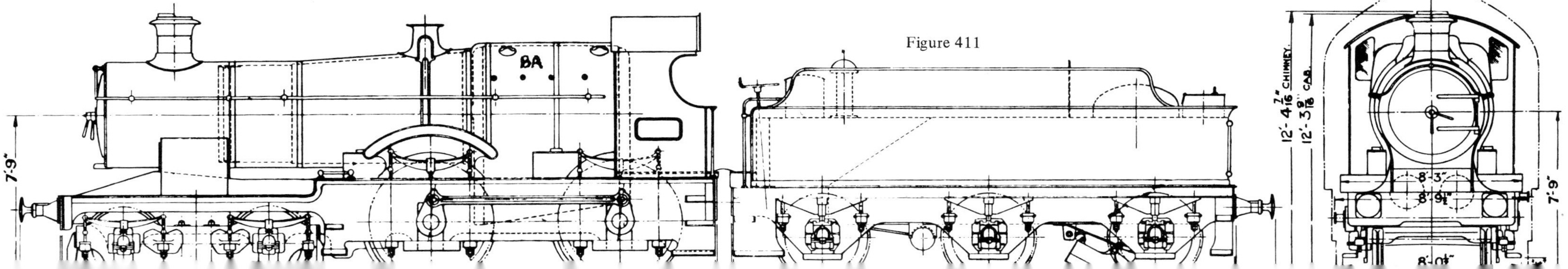

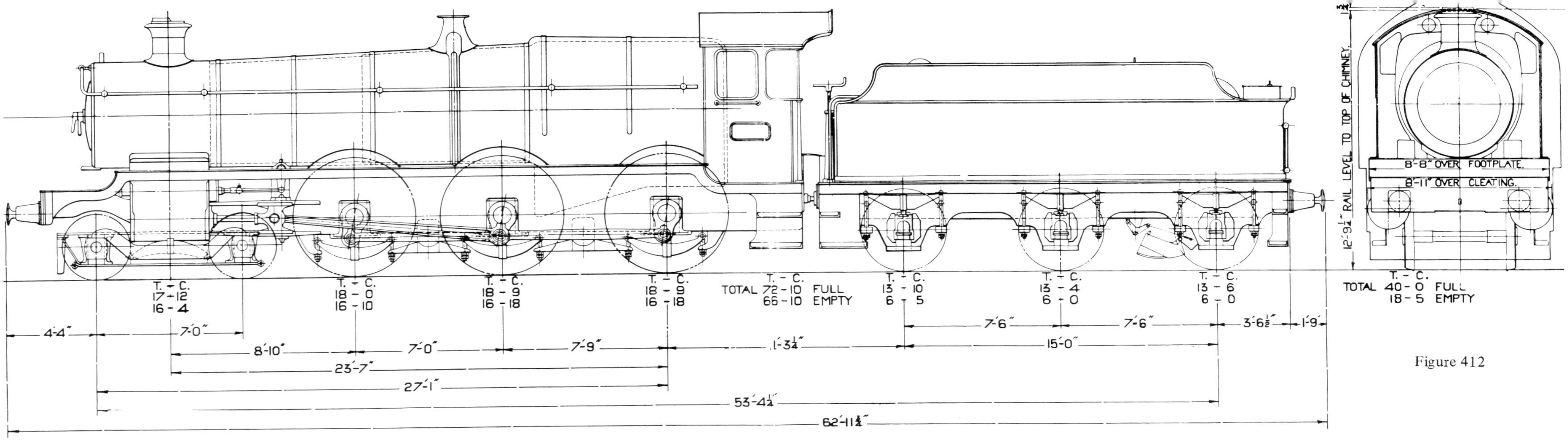

Figure 412

Figure 413

In the search for an improved '43XX' class, Mr. Collett in 1924 took one of the 'Saint' class locomotives, No. 2925 *Saint Martin,* and refitted it with 6′ 0″ diameter driving wheels instead of the normal 6′ 8½″, and in place of the Churchward cab, installed a 'Castle' type, with side windows, seats and extended roof. This engine ran trials for four years and proved not only a success, but became so popular with the running department that more than 300 were constructed over the years, the last being built in November 1950.

The drawing in *Figure 412* is the official Swindon *Diagram X* which was concerned only with No. 2925 *Saint Martin* which was the 'guinea pig'.

Figure 413 shows the engine as turned out of Swindon in 1924 still carrying the 'Saint' numbering and in *Figure 414* (next page) she is seen with the new number '4900' which was bestowed on the engine in January 1929. The outside steam pipes were not added to No. 4900 until December 1948.

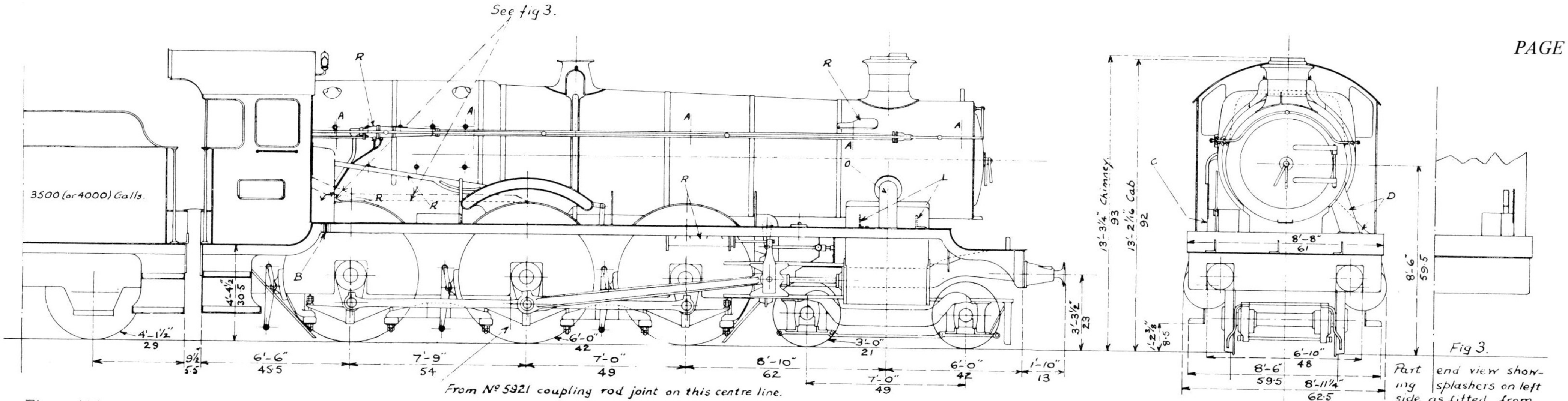

Figure 414

Fig. 1. 4901 (Hall) Class.

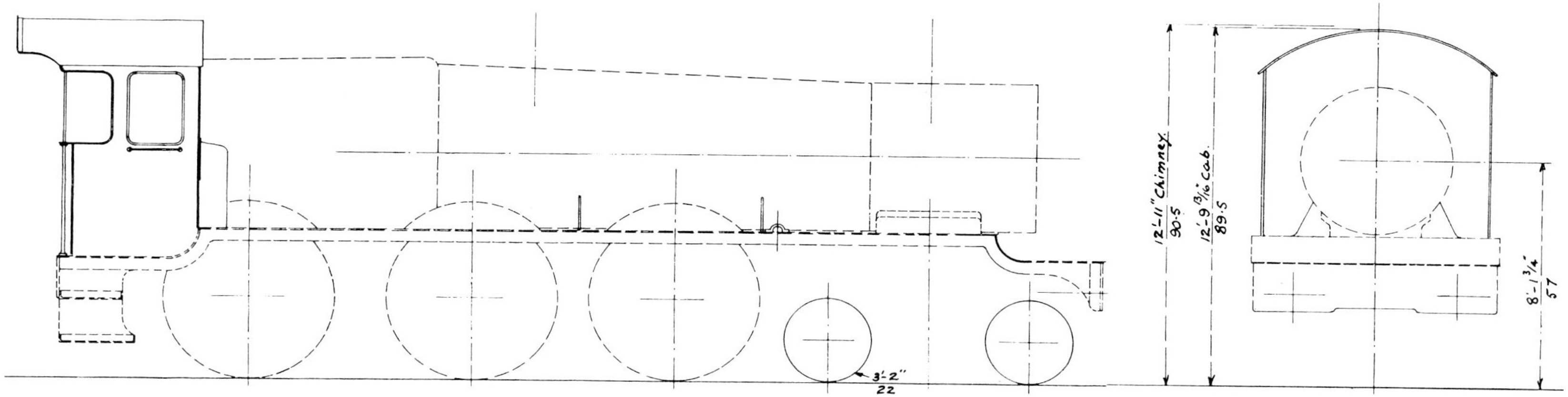

1. 4901 (Hall) Class.
2. No 4900 (Saint Martin).

Notes. Centre lines A give positions of hand-rail knobs on left side. Hanging Plate narrows at B to same width as tender. C – Centre splasher on right side set out to clear reverse rod. D – Frame Stay and Steam Pipe omitted from end view on other side so as to show splashers and reverse rod. Details marked L on left side only: those marked R on right side only. Wheel treads and flanges drawn to scale; allowance must be made for out-of-scale wheels. Dimensions in feet (full size), and in millimetres to the nearest half m'metre for Gauge "O".

Fig. 2. No 4900 (Saint Martin). As rebuilt from No 2925. Omit details marked O in fig 1.

Other details same as fig 1 except those shown in full lines. Dimensions as in fig 1, except where shown different.

The first *Lot* ordered of 'Hall' class engines in 1928 was for eighty, which is some indication of the popularity of the design. They numbered from 4901-80, although it was intended to start at 4900 (in fact No. 4901 carried No. 4900 plates whilst building). Eventually 4900 was the number given to the prototype *Saint Martin* as mentioned.

The differences between *Saint Martin* and the 'Halls' proper, lay in the boiler being raised 4½" in height, modified frames and smaller bogie wheels, 3' instead of 3' 2" as on 2925.

This drawing by Colonel Templer illustrates the variations well, and the notes give the details.

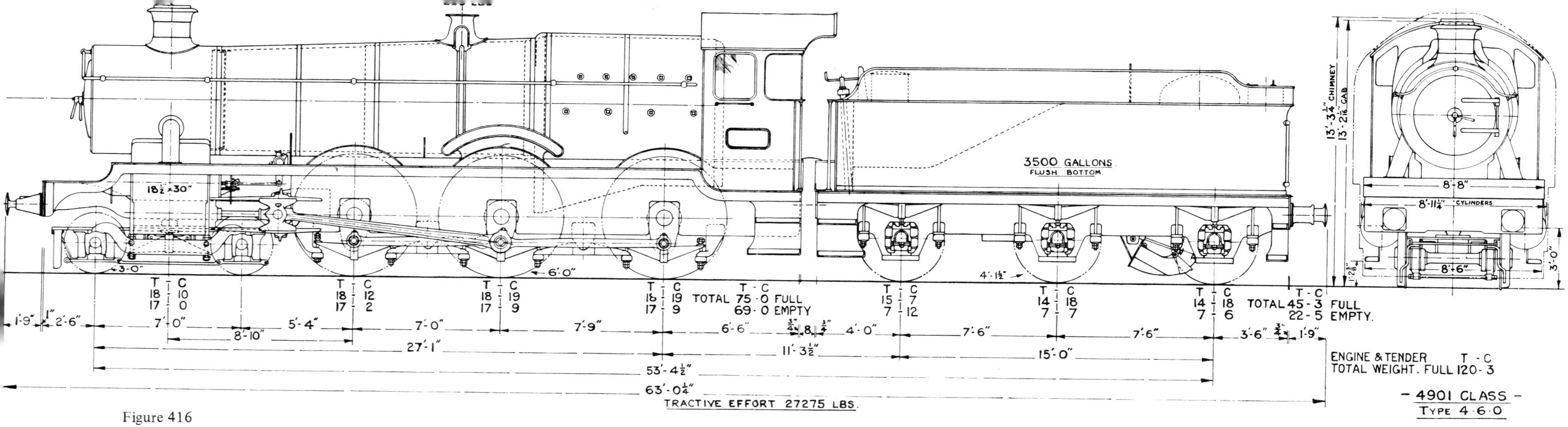

Figure 416

The first 'Hall' to be built, apart from the guinea-pig *Saint Martin,* was *Adderley Hall* No. 4901. The series kept to the old traditional method of alphabetical order in names, until No. 4980, then started again with *Lot 268* from No. 4981 *Abberley Hall* up to No. 5920 *Wycliffe Hall.* After this the barrel had to be scraped for new names, and things went out off course a little, although efforts were made to stick to the system. *Figure 417* shows No. 4901 as built in 1928, with the small tender of the Churchward design. In the *Diagram A.2* seen in *Figure 416,* the class is shown equipped with the larger Collett 3500 gallon flush bottom tender.

Figure 417

Figure 418

In the 1920's the coal traffic in South Wales was still booming, and as most of the locomotives used for hauling this traffic were of the 0-6-2 tank versions Rhymney, Taff and Barry Railways having used this class for years – when new engines were decided upon for these services, it was decided to stick to the 0-6-2T wheel arrangement. So Mr. Collett in 1924 designed the '56XX' class.

What better picture to introduce the class than the one on page 162 which shows two loaded coal trains descending and one empty going up at Taffs Well with Walnut Tree Viaduct behind. One engine is No. 6662 and the other No. 6676. (Note the somersault signals under the viaduct.)

Figure 419 illustrates the first engine of the series which was completed at Swindon in 1924. Still in the undercoat works livery, the transfers have been affixed for photographs only and immediately afterwards the engine would return to the paint shop for the finishing coats of paint. Nevertheless, this flat grey finish does show the detail well. A few interesting notes, inside cylinders, 18″ by 26″ stroke, worked by piston valves above at an angle, operated indirectly by Stephenson's gear. Driving wheels were the standard freight 4′ 7½″ diameter and the trailing, 3′ 8″ diameter. The wheelbases can be clearly seen on the official *Diagram A.30* in *Figure 420.*

In 1934 recesses were fitted into the bunker back of these engines as they passed through the shops, and detail of this can be seen in the small drawing.

Figure 419

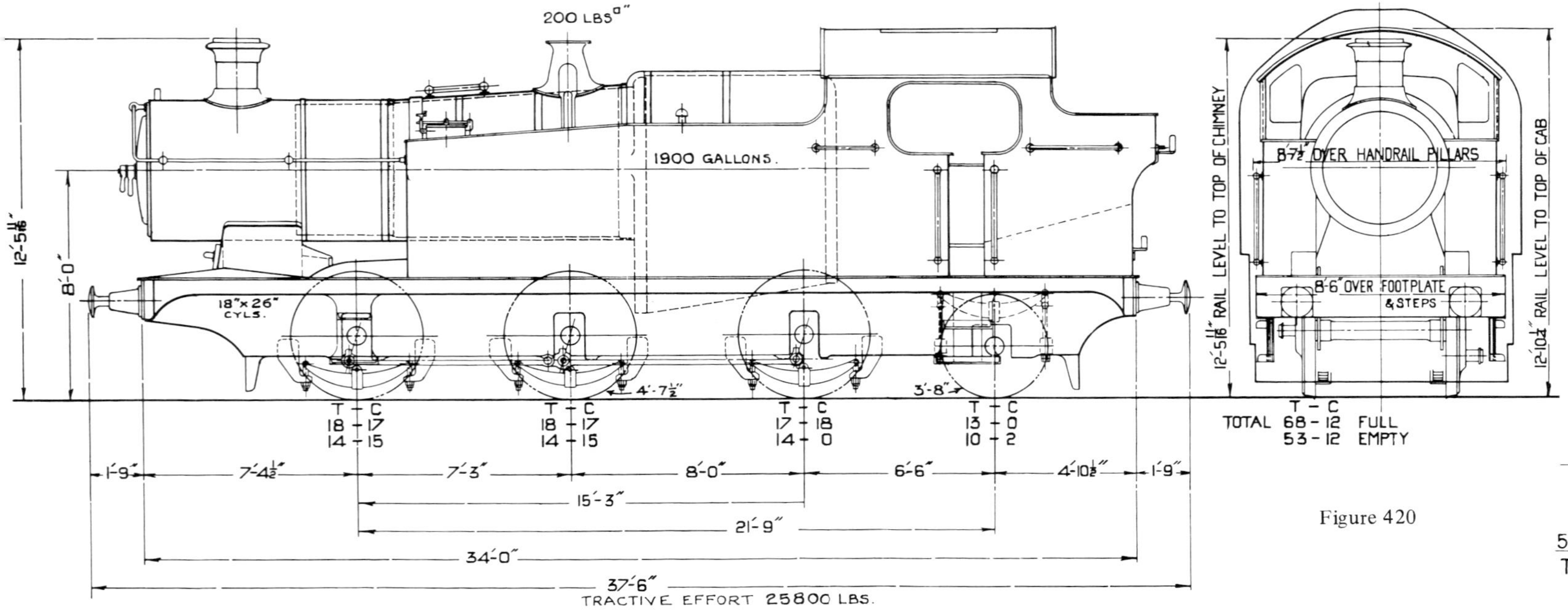

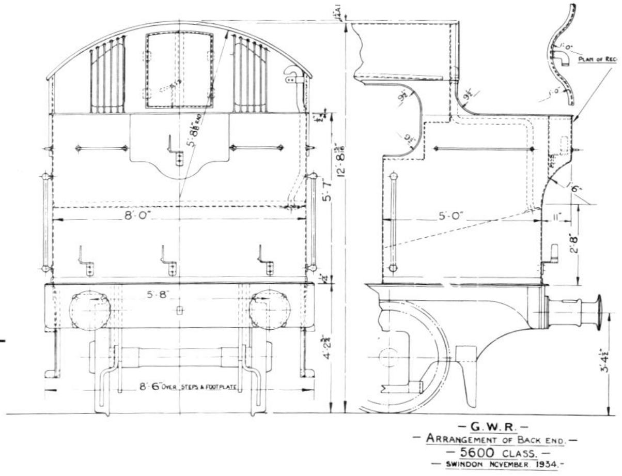

Figure 420

Figure 421

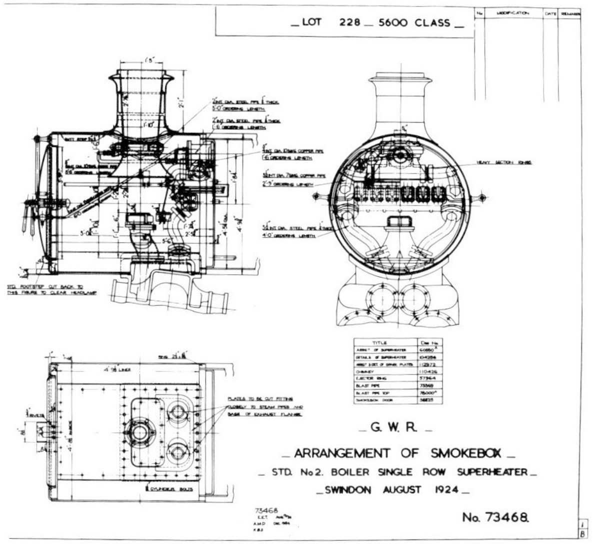

These two pictures are almost thirty years apart! The full broadside (not up to Swindon's standard) is of the prototype No. 5600 as built in 1926, and in *Figure 422* No. 5697 originally constructed in January 1927 is seen on Reading shed in 1955, pictured by Maurice Earley. Note the slight differences; parallel buffers have been fitted, sliding shutters to the cab side sheets, A.T.C. control under the front buffer beam, and one other detail not to be missed by modellers, the front motion step has been set back directly over the front driving wheel. Also note the heavy balance weights which were later found necessary.

Figure 422

Figure 423

Figure 424

Figure 425

No. 6631 features on this page, in three photographs taken in 1930. It can be seen at once that this engine still has the plain bunker back with single hand rail, she has however been fitted with the cab sliding shutters. Modellers should note that to capture the atmosphere of the 56XX class, the chimney was of a particular shape. It was short and fat with no capuchon (only No. 6699 had this feature). The official drawing, and Colonel Templer's, give a wrong impression, although copper-topped, the join between top, middle and top could not be distinguished. Get this feature right, and you are halfway to creating an accurate model.

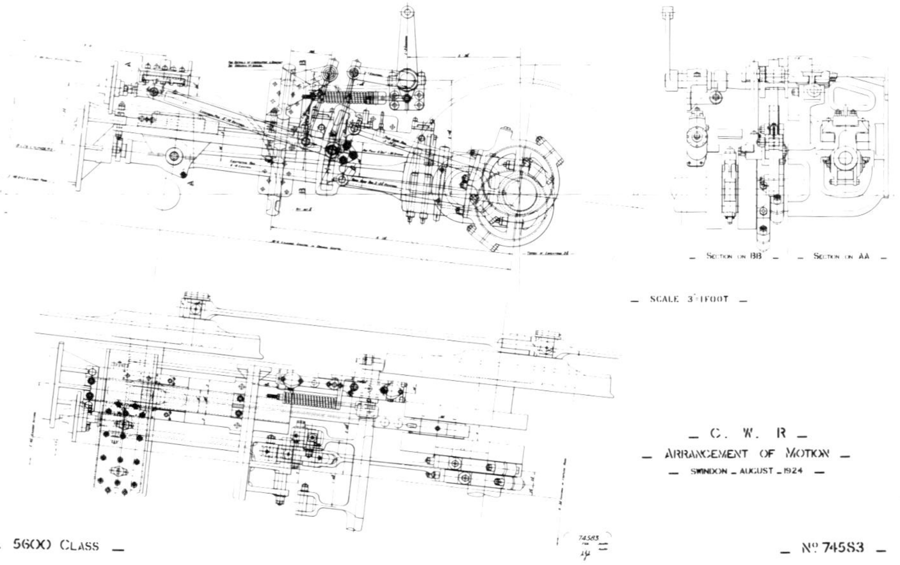

Figure 426

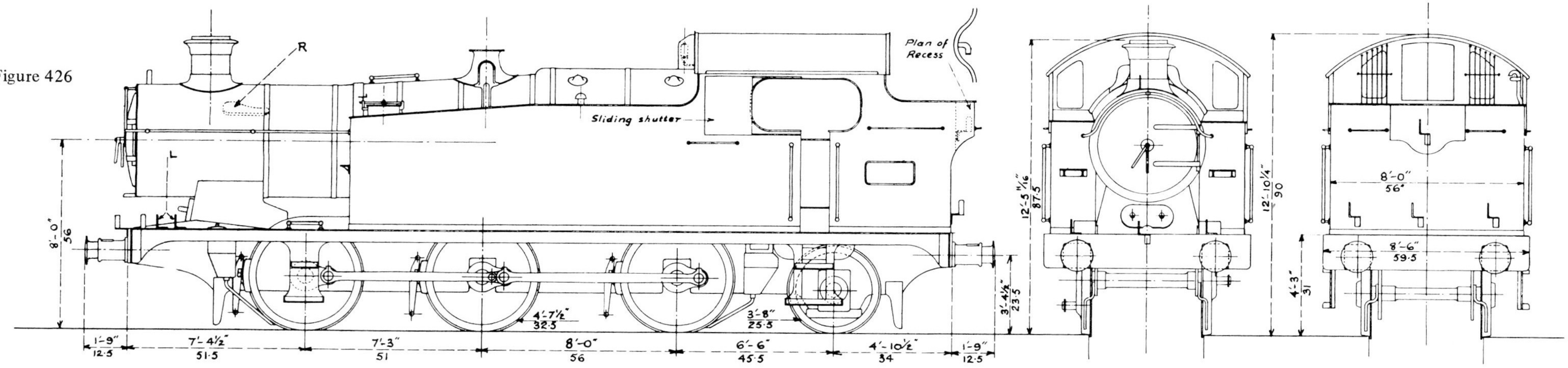

NOTES. Details marked L on left side only: those marked R on right side only. Wheel treads and flanges drawn to scale: allowances must be made for out-of-scale wheels. Dimensions in feet (full size), and in millimetres to nearest half mimetre for Gauge O.

C. W. R.	5600 Class. Type 0-6-2/T.	Scale 4 m/m = 1 foot Reduced from official drawings.

Figure 427

PAGE 166

On this page is the drawing by Colonel Templer, to 4m/m scale, showing the class after 1934 and in *Figure 427* a higher view of No. 6631 to show the boiler top more clearly. In contrast *Figure 428* shows No. 5636 in fairly clean condition in 1928, still with the taper buffers and small round windows in the spectacle plate. No. A.T.C. or sliding shutters have been fitted, and steam and vacuum pipes do not run along the valance, but along the frame inside. One hundred and fifty of these engines were built at Swindon, numbering from 5600-6649, and a further 50 were constructed to the same design by Messrs. Armstrong Whitworth & Co., in 1928. These were built to *Lot 255* and were numbered 6650-6699.

I have cause to remember this last batch, as No. 6696 was shedded at Banbury in the mid-thirties and was on shunting duties in the Northend yard. Every time the brakes were applied, terrible grinding noises were heard, so much so, that complaints were received from lineside householders, and the engine and indeed most of this Armstrong batch had to go to Swindon for modification.

PAGE 167

An odd fact about the Great Western steam history, is that throughout the standard gauge history, only one 0-4-0 tank engine was designed and built at Swindon or Wolverhampton Works! Nevertheless, the Company eventually possessed many such small dock engines, but all were either absorbed, or in one small series, ordered from an outside locomotive builder.

This was the '1101' class, six powerful tanks ordered from Avonside Engine Co., of Bristol in 1926. The reason for this order was to replace the much older 0-4-0 tanks which had been taken over from the Swansea Harbour Trust, and the six new engines spent most of their working lives in this area, shedded at Danygraig.

Numbers of the engines were 1101-1106 to *Lot 246*. The large picture shows No. 1104 when fitted with the rounded cornered cab, but before receiving the Great Western safety valve bonnet.

The small picture shows first No. 1143, one of the Swansea Harbour Trust engines, which the '1101' class was to supersede, and the Avonside designed No. 1104 is seen behind.

The diagram for the '1101' class is seen in *Figure 431* and was letter *T* as built. The tanks had squared cabs, but owing to clearance difficulties in the docks, the corners were eventually rounded off as seen in this picture.

Figure 429

Figure 430

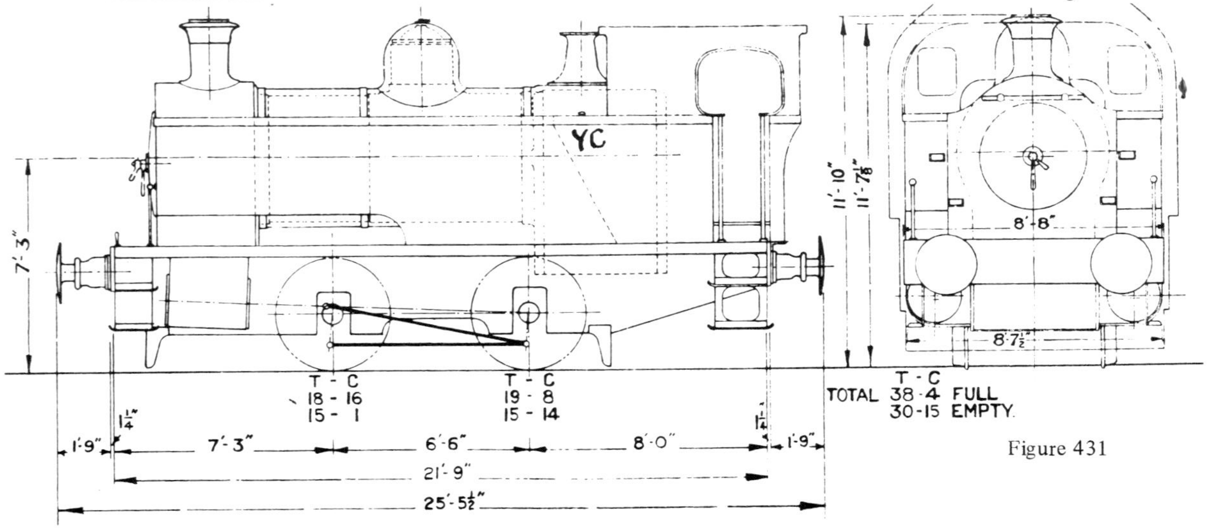

Figure 431

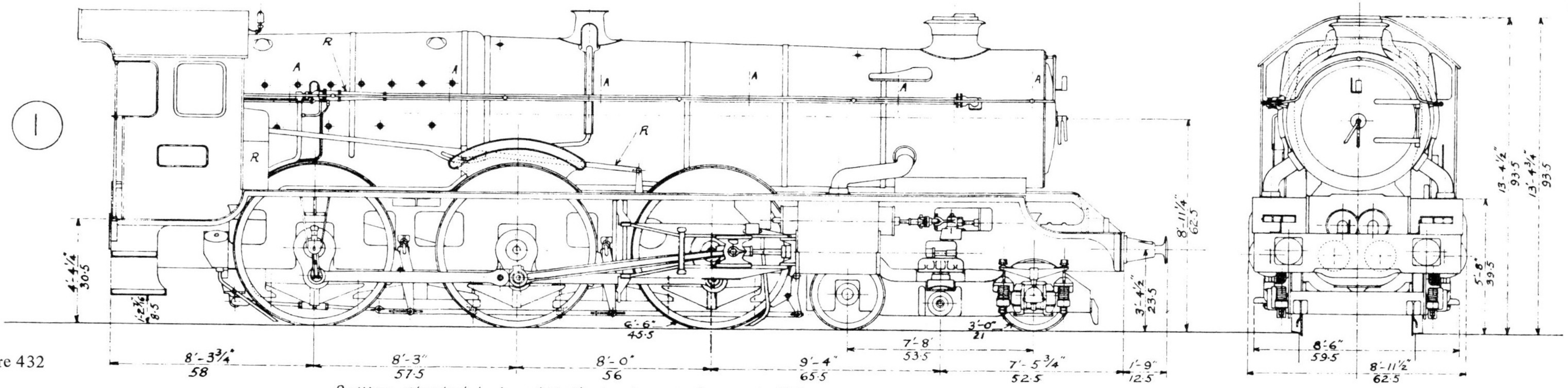

Figure 432

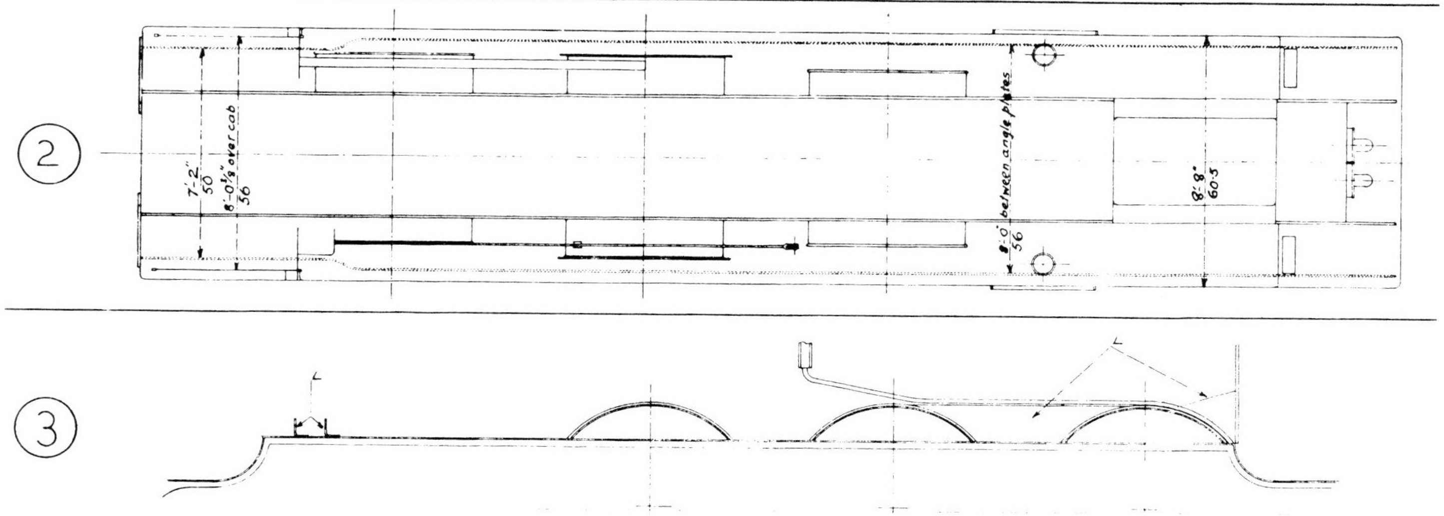

The 'Kings' were the ultimate in Great Western engine design, and the axle loading was right up to the limit allowed by the Civil Engineer, namely 22½ tons per axle. Designed by Mr. Collett in 1927 as a logical advancement of the 'Castles', they not only handled the heaviest of the Great Western expresses, but also, and most important from the Board's prestige viewpoint, became known as the most powerful locomotives in the United Kingdom.

As with the 'Castles', much has been written extolling their virtues and I do not intend to add to this, and only insert two drawings and a few interesting pictures to keep the record straight. *Note:* There are two excellent volumes entitled *G.W.R. Kings, Castles and Stars,* Part I & II published by David and Charles, by O.S. Nock.

Figure 432 is Colonel Templer's excellent drawing in which the cab window is recorded accurately; even on the Swindon diagram on the next page, it is drawn as oblong, when in fact, if one looks at the photographs, one can see it is almost square.

The photograph in *Figure 433* is an interesting one, in that on Swindon's register, this picture was banned in red ink for many years, as it shows No. 6029 named *King Edward VIII,* a case of 'jumping the gun' because, as history proved, the Prince of Wales abdicated, did not have a coronation, and instead became the Duke of Windsor. Nevertheless, this engine, the last 'King' to be built, and which at first was christened *King Stephen,* still kept the 'Edward VIII' plates until the end.

NOTES.

Fig 2 shows splashers, reverse rod, etc. in plan. Fig 3 shows arrangement of splashers and top feed pipe on left side. Details marked "L" on left side only, those marked "R" on right side only. Wheel treads and flanges drawn to scale; allowances must be made for out-of-scale wheels. Dimensions in feet (full size), and in millimetres to nearest half m'metre for Gauge "O"

6000 Class. Type 4-6-0.

Figure 433

is the special 'mock-up' that was prepared at the drawing office for Mr. Collett to get some idea of the appearance of an enlarged 'Castle'. It can be seen that the 'Castle' class driving wheels are shown, which, in the prototype No. 6000, were reduced to 6′ 6″, the 6′ 8½″ not giving (on paper) the necessary tractive effort to beat the Southern Railway's *Lord Nelson* class.

The cylinders were enlarged fractionally to 16¼″, the stroke lengthened to 28″ and the steam pressure went up to 250 lbs. *Figure 435* shows No. 6000 fitted with Westinghouse brake, just prior to sailing to America to take part in the Baltimore & Ohio's Centenary in 1927. *Figure 436* illustrates No. 6027 in the factory in 1951, fitted with the double chimney.

The drawing is the official Swindon *Diagram Z* of the class as built. As mentioned previously, that cab window is suspect, again an example of the fallibility of a drawn line! *Figure 437*.

Figure 435

Figure 436

Figure 437

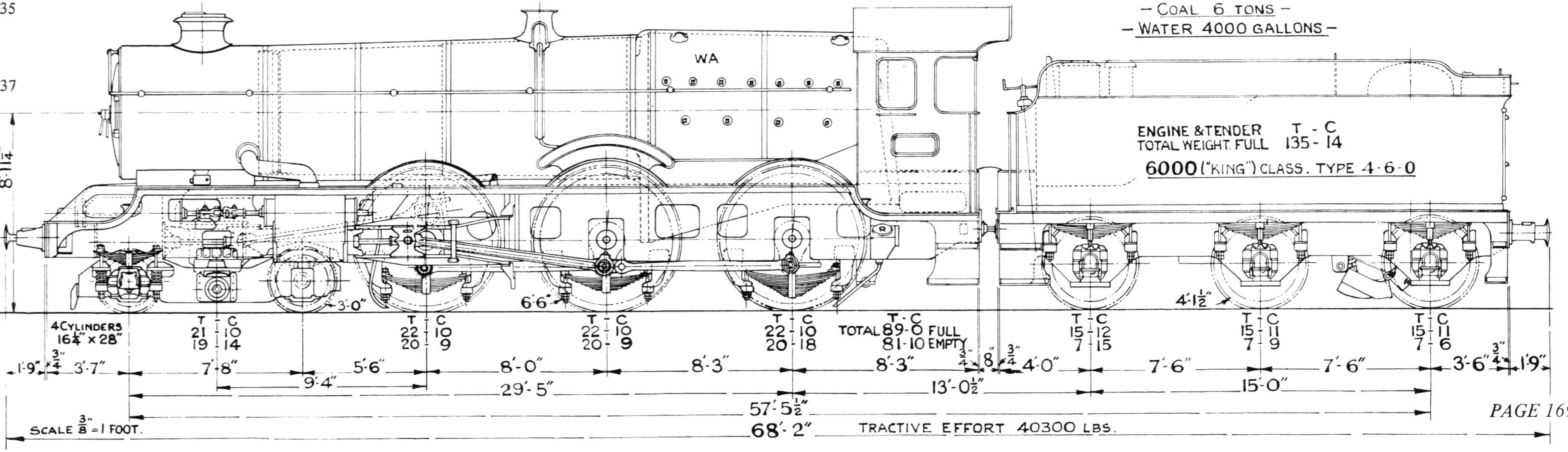

Figure 438

Figure 439

To prove once and for all that the 'King' class cab windows were nearly square, here on this page are two close-up shots I took myself showing the right-hand side of 6011 at Paddington in 1949 (*Figure 438*). The left-hand side of 6027 is seen in *Figure 439* at Swindon in 1951. The official drawing in *Figure 440* was prepared at Swindon drawing office in 1937 for publicity purposes, and this shows the cab window correctly!

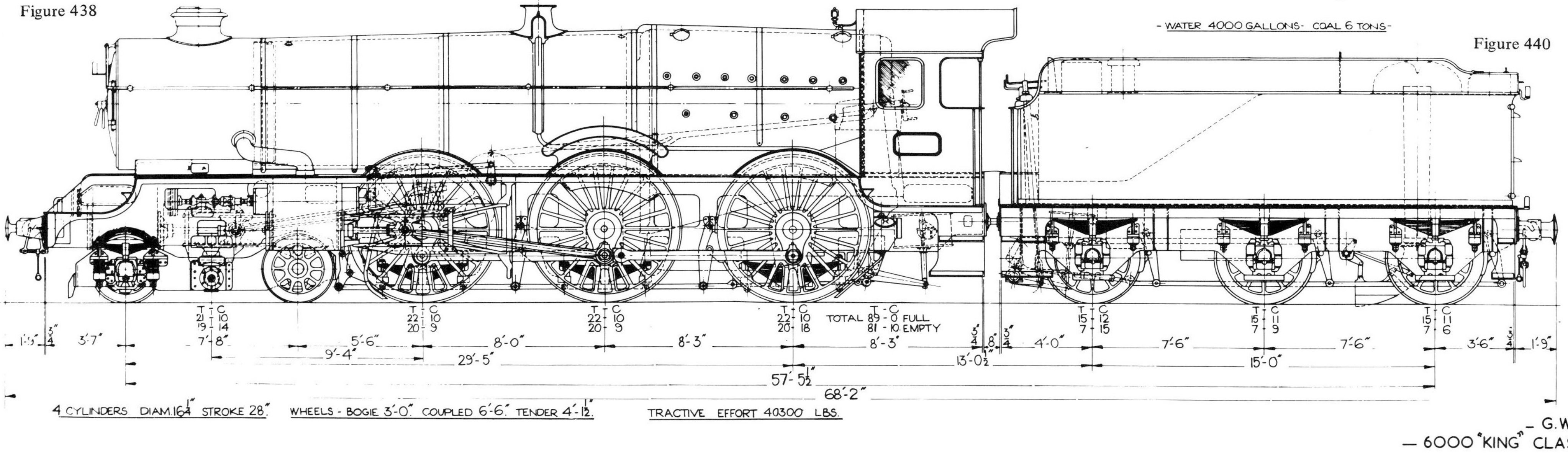

Figure 440

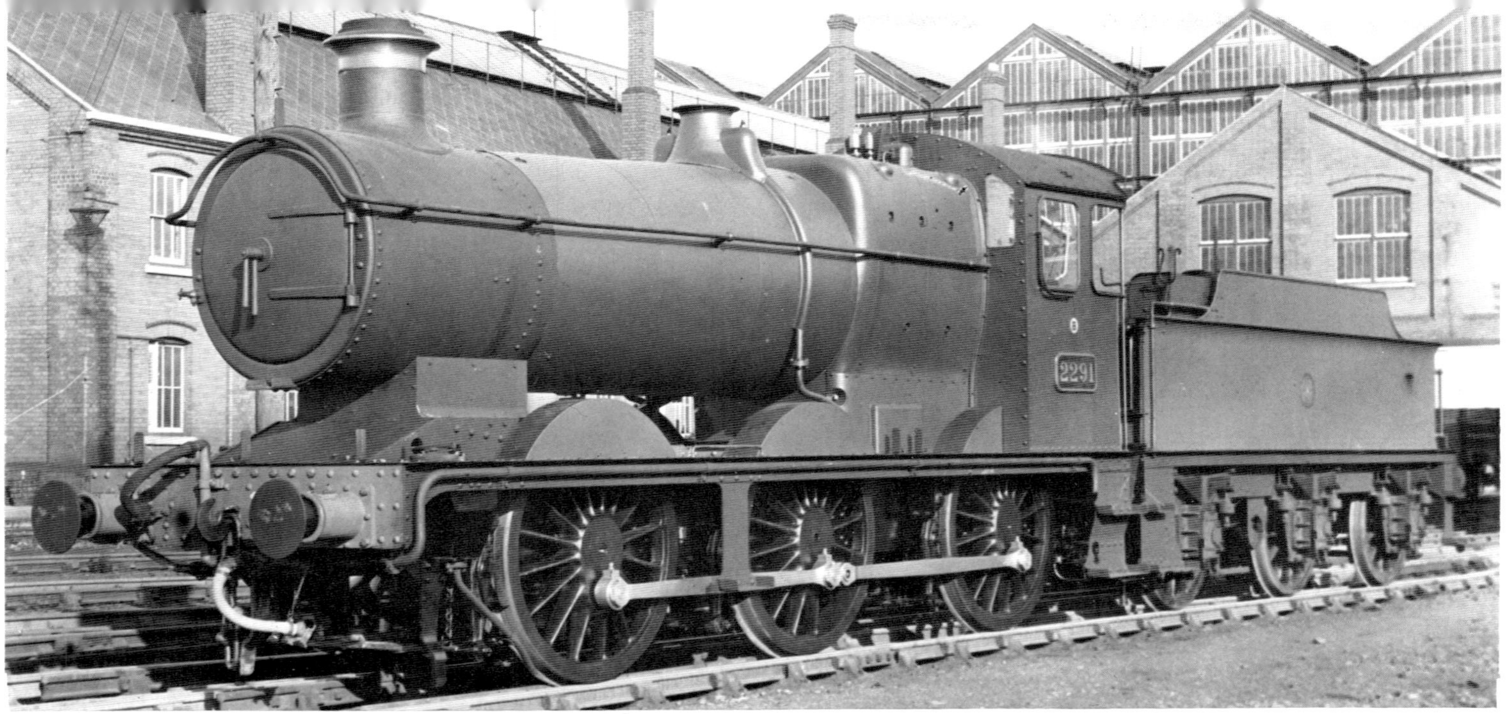

Figure 441

The year 1930 saw the introduction of the '2251' class. This was a light 0-6-0 tender engine, designed to replace the 'Armstrong' and 'Dean' goods engines which were carrying the brunt of the work over the light absorbed lines in Central Wales. Very similar to the Dean goods in the framing, wheels, and motion, the engines were fitted with a Standard No. 10 boiler, copper-topped chimney and a large wide cab. The building of these engines was spread over 18 years. The first five batches had side windows in the cab, but the twenty constructed in 1940 to *Lot 337* had windowless cabs, like No. 2211 in *Figure 442*.

These two photographs show No. 2291 as at 1938 with the small tender, and No. 2211 in exactly the same place in 1940 with the large Collett tender.

Figure 442

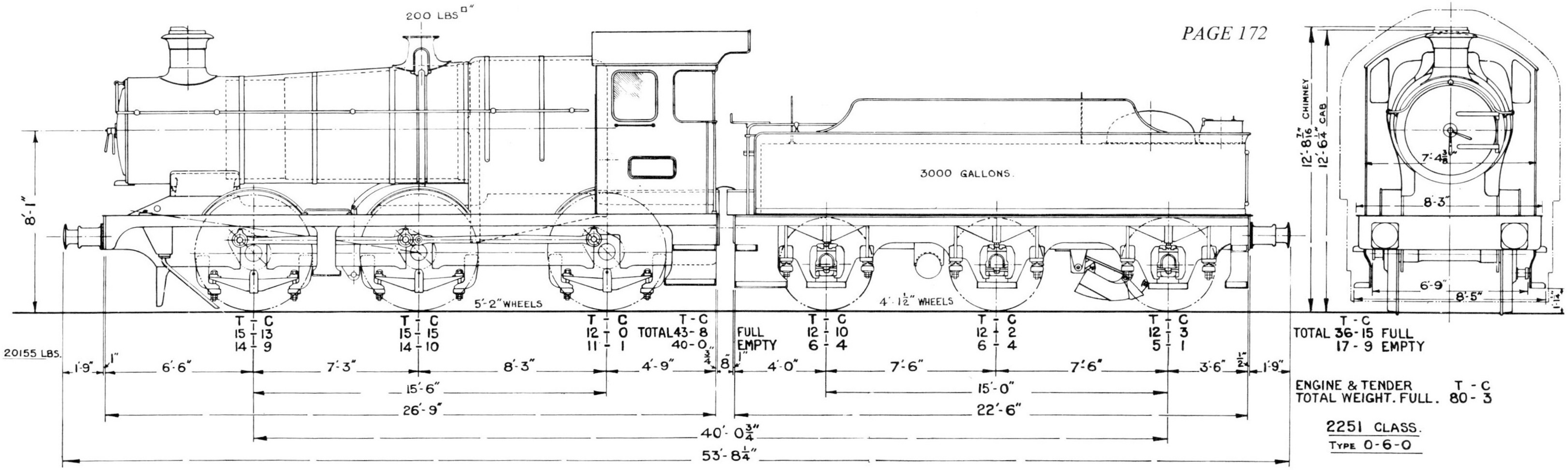

Figure 443

Figure 444

Figure 446

Figure 445

In service these 22XX's proved very versatile little machines, and although intended to displace the 'Dean' goods, they in fact took over many of the short haul main line trains and stopping passenger work. It was found their weight on the driving axle (15 tons) put them in the yellow route colour, whereas the 'Deans' were still under 14 tons (uncoloured).

The drawing in *Figure 443* is the official *Diagram A.27. Figure 444* shows No. 2251 outside the Works, being the first of the class to be built. No. 2244 in *Figure 446* on the other hand was not constructed until 1944 and No. 3206 in *Figure 445* was one of the last batch built to *Lot 360* in 1946-8. The reason for the complication is that 2251-2299 and 2200 were built first, in 1930-38 and 2201-2250, 3200-3219 came afterwards between 1939 and 1948.

Although the Diesel Railcars of 1933 have been described in the companion volume *A Pictorial Record of Great Western Coaches Part II* these vehicles did come under the care and service of the Locomotive Department. It is right therefore that the mechanics of these cars should receive a place in this work on Great Western engines.

The complete car looked from the outside like No. 2 which is featured in *Figure 449* on this page. The chassis, which was built by A.E.C. Ltd., of Slough can be seen in detail in *Figures 447 and 448.*

Initially, there was only one engine which drove one bogie, but this was controlled from either driving end. After No. 1, the subsequent cars were powered with two engines of 121 BHP, each driving a separate bogie.

Figure 447

Figure 448

Figure 449

PAGE 174 and 175

This copy of the engine diagram gives all the details of the frame and mechanical assembly of the No. 1 car. Because of the limitations of space, it has had to be shown in half with a section on each of two pages, otherwise the small text would have been unreadable.

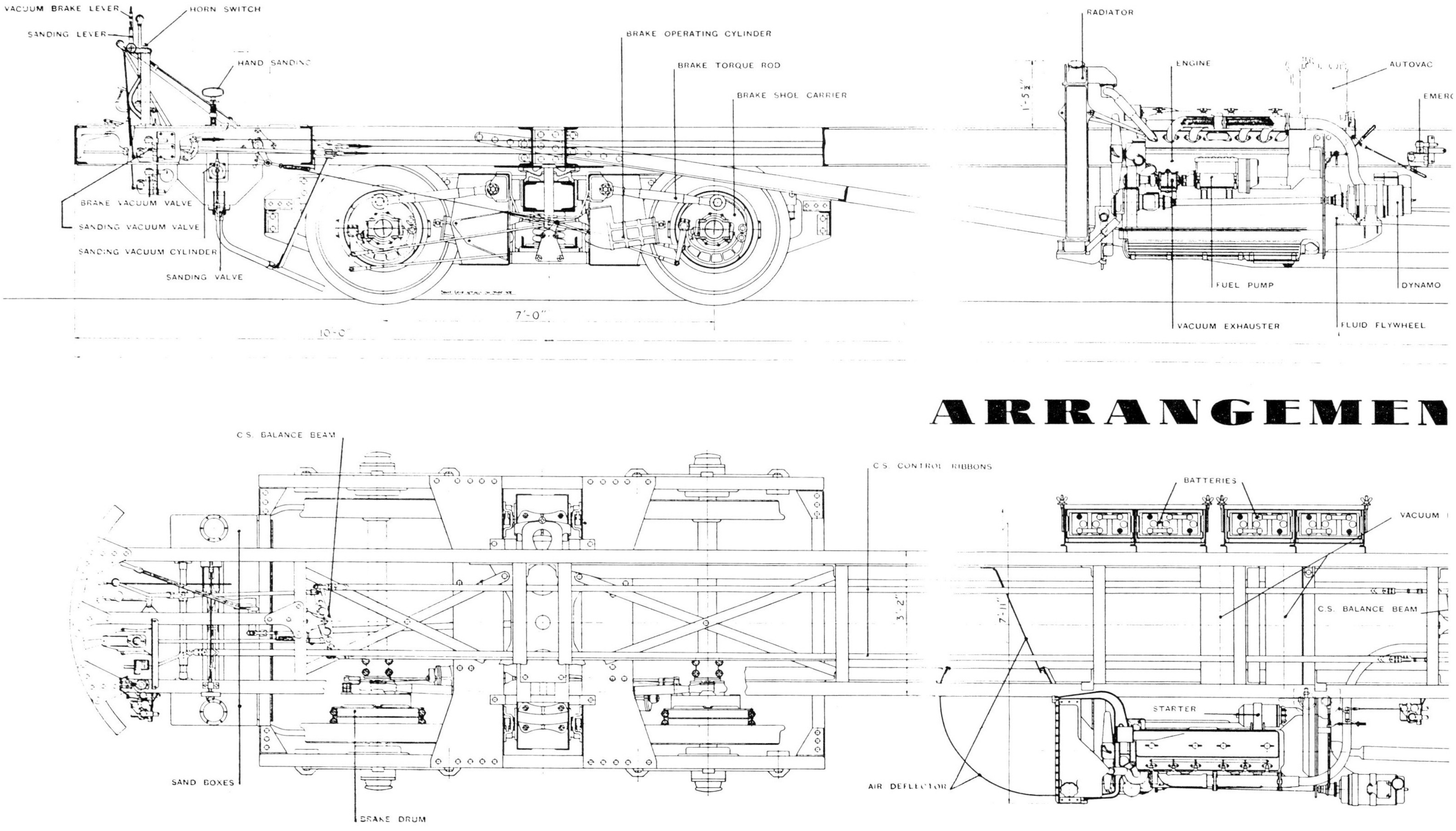

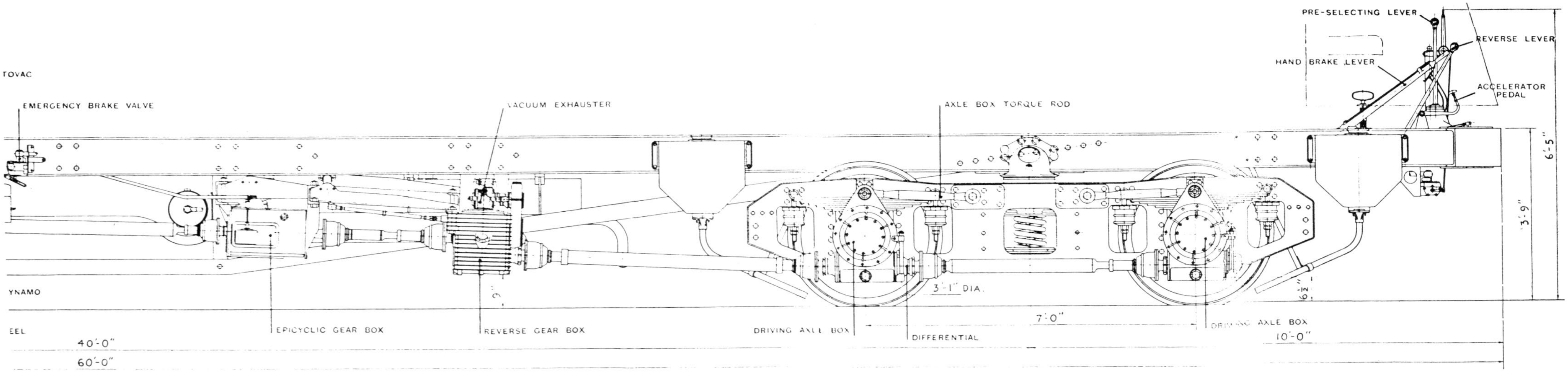

NT OF CHASSIS

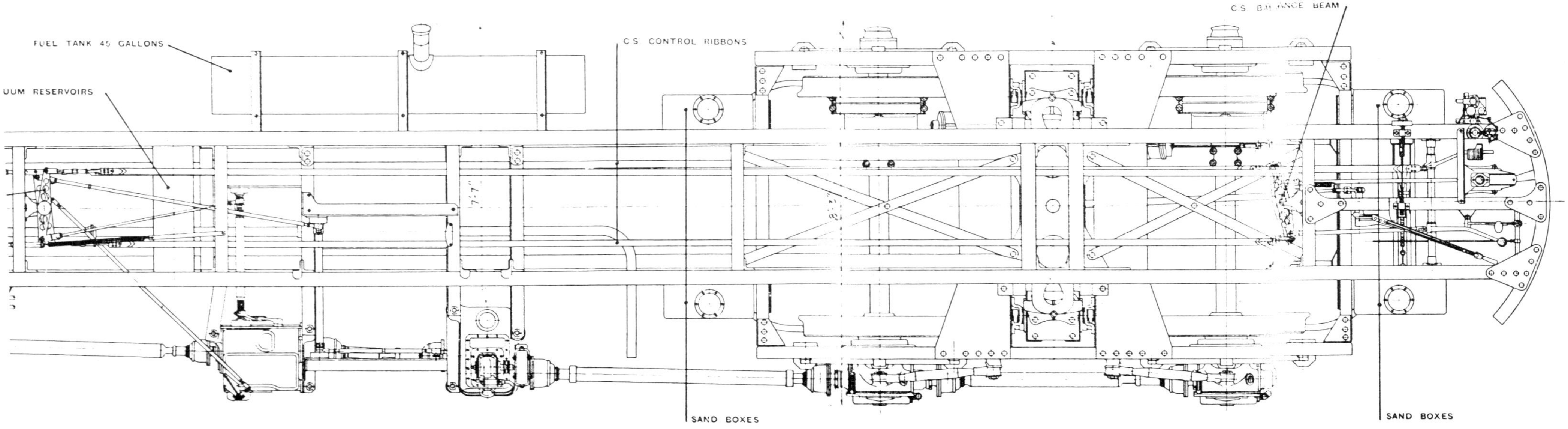

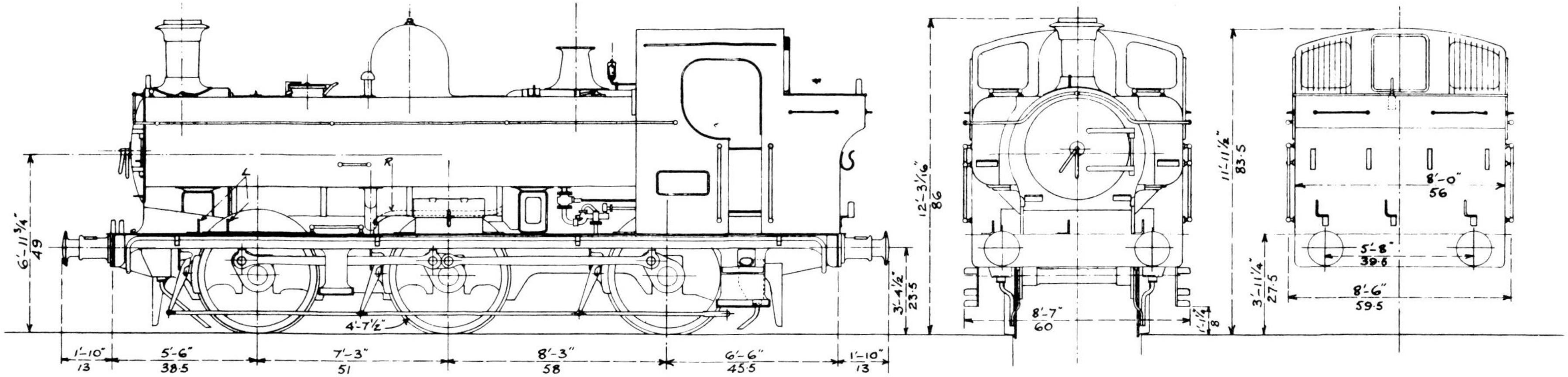

In 1929 a start was made on replacements for the ubiquitous 0-6-0 saddle and pannier tanks, of the '27XX', '1854', '1813', and similar classes, many of which dated back to the 1880's.

The first batch to be constructed was of one hundred engines, fifty at Swindon factory and fifty by the North British Locomotive Co. The latter were numbered 5700-49, and those built by the Company 5750-99. In due course, 863 of this design were made, 200 by various companies including Bagnalls, Kerr Stuarts, Yorkshire Engine Co., Armstrong Whitworths, and Beyer Peacock & Co. The remainder from 1933 to 1950 were constructed at Swindon. Total class numbered were 5700-99, 6700-6779, 7700-7799, 8700-8799, 9701-9799, 3600-3699, 3700-3799, 4600-4699, 9600-9682.

These new 0-6-0 tanks were identical to the earlier '2721' series, with the exception of having Belpaire boilers, closed cabs, a greater pressure of 200 lbs instead of 180, and a larger extended bunker.

Colonel Templer's drawing shows some of the variations amongst the class (*Figure 451*).

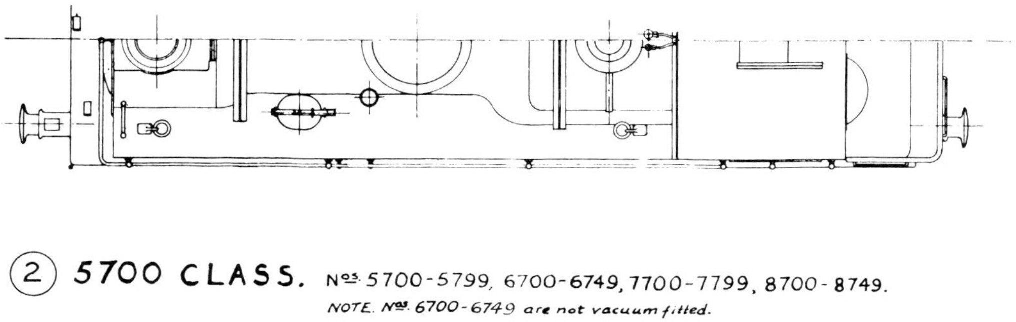

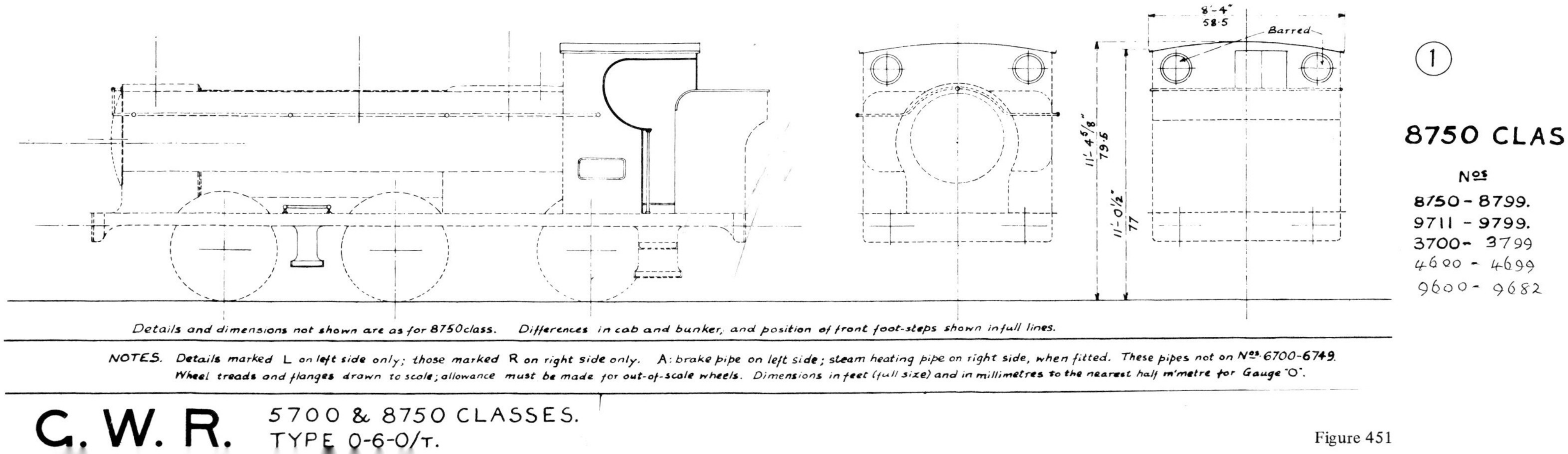

Figure 451

Figure 452

Figure 453

Four examples are shown here of the '5700' class tanks. *Figure 452* shows No. 6752 at Swindon after a general overhaul in 1947. *Figure 453* illustrates No. 3670 in Swindon yard in 1950. No. 4609 is seen as station pilot in the down bay at Reading in 1952. In direct contrast is No. 7713, (*Figure 454*), one of the series built by Kerr Stuarts in 1930. Note the old type cab and polished safety valve. Note also that the two engines on the left are fitted with top feed.

Figure 454

Figure 455

Figure 456

Figure 457

For comparison, here are three 1930 pictures of the '1813' class, the particular engine being No. 1819. She is shown from the side, front and top, and if compared with the '5700' class, the only obvious differences are in the parallel chimney, and the thickness of the running plate valance, fore and aft.

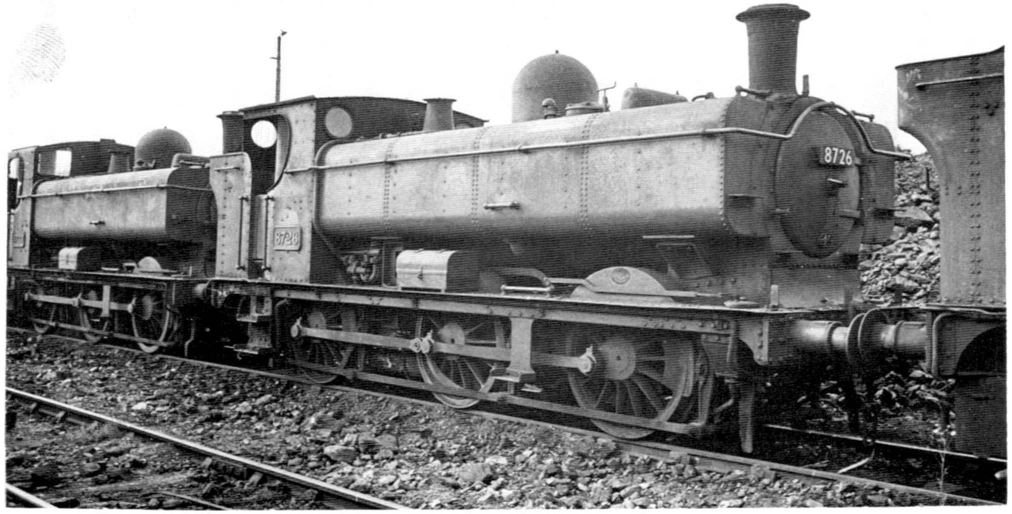

Figure 459

Figure 460

I make no excuse for showing more '5700' Class pannier tanks; the four here are at different dates and locations. *Figure 459* shows No. 8726, one of the Bagnall engines, at Swindon dump in 1962. No. 8763 (*Figure 460*) is at Paddington 'arrival' in British Railway days, and shows the tank painted black and fully lined out in red and light grey. No. 8752 is seen in *Figure 461* during 1937 outside Paddington 'departure', proudly carrying the full Great Western insignia. Then in *Figure 462* we see No. 4672 at Waterloo on train movement duties in 1959.

Figure 461

Figure 462

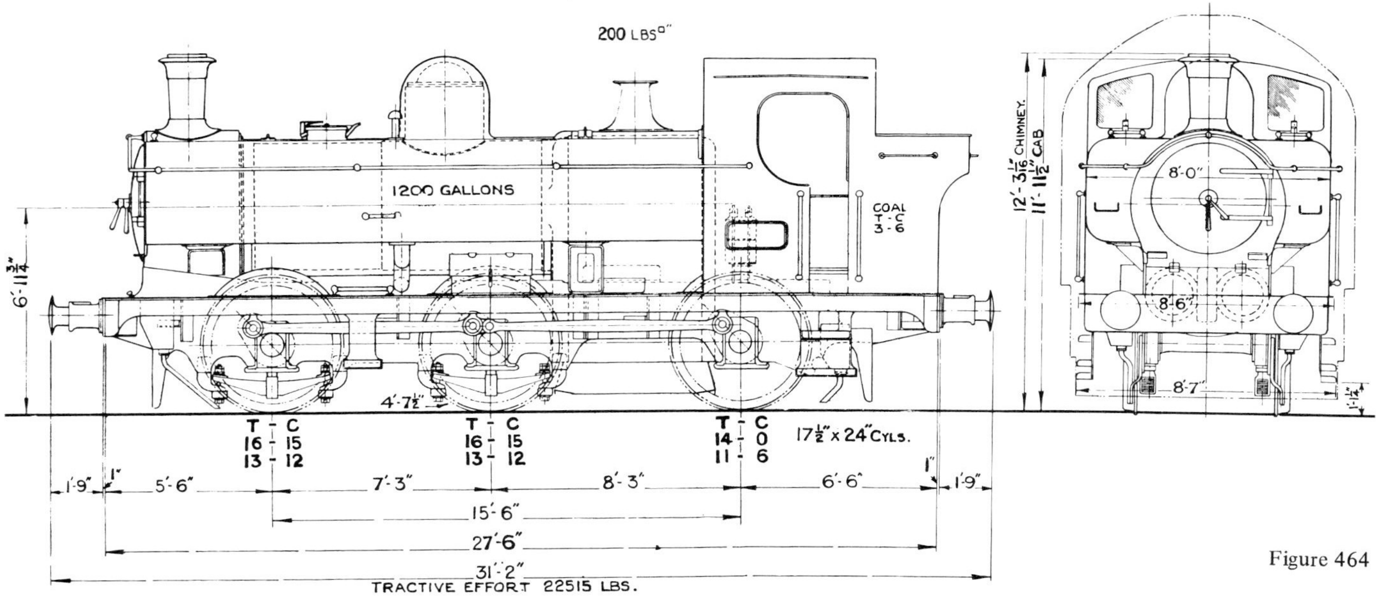

Figure 463

Figure 464

A final page of the '8700' class. *Figure 463* gives the official *Diagram B.70. Figure 466* shows No. 9732, carrying the G.W.R. roundel in 1935. The last two pictures are of No. 8757 at Paddington with the Breakdown Vans, dealing with a derailment at No. 10 platform, in 1955.

Figure 465

Figure 466

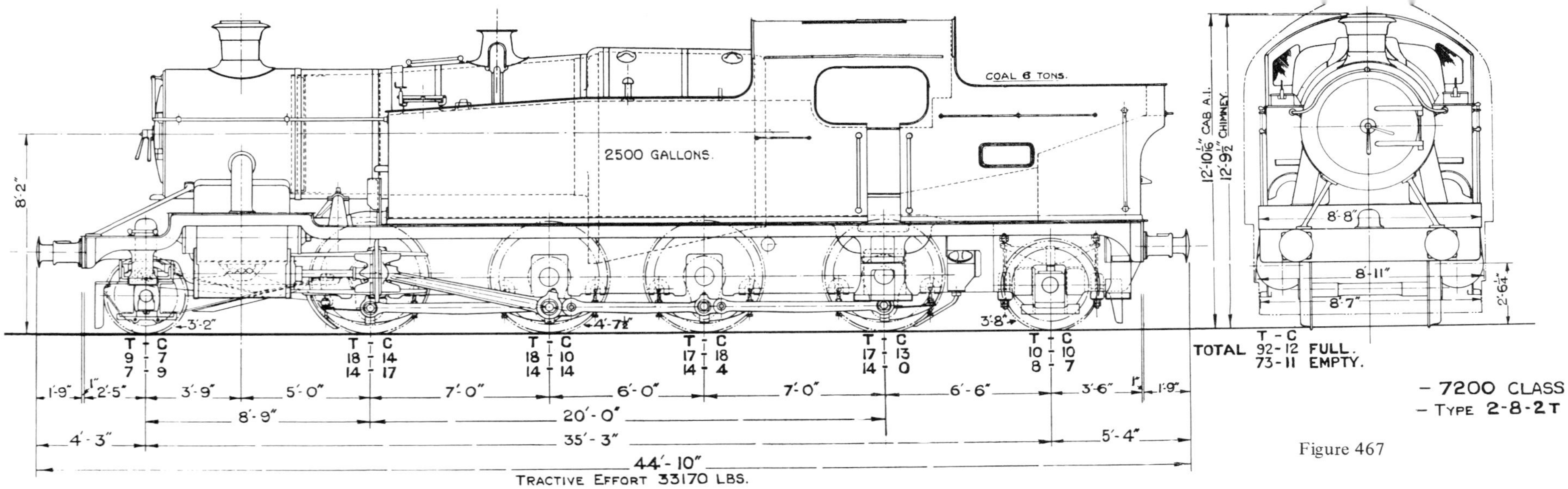

Figure 467

Figure 468

Having jumped ahead to British Railways ownership in order to illustrate the pannier tanks in their final phase, to keep to a form of continuity, we must return to the nineteen thirties, and 1934 in particular.

This was a period of depression, and with the South Wales coal traffic falling off, the large series of 2-8-0T's locomotives, 42XX's and 52XX's were more than enough for the dwindling colliery trade. Therefore it was decided to enlarge their coal and water capacity to give them a wider field of activity.

Nos. 5275-94 were the first twenty to be so rebuilt, the frames being lengthened at the rear by bolting on a 4′ 1″ extension to accommodate a trailing pony truck. The bunker and back water tank were both extended to give the engine an extra 700 gallons of water and two tons of coal.

The drawing in *Figure 467* is the official *Diagram A* of the 7200 class, as built. *Diagrams B* and *C* were for 7220-39 and 7240-53 respectively (note the slight difference at the front ends).

The prototype of the class is seen in the official photograph in *Figure 468* on the usual site used at Swindon for engine pictures.

Figure 469

Figure 470

Four pictures of the large 2-8-2 tanks are included here. *Figure 469* shows No. 7240 at Swindon Shops in 1947 with the initials on the tank sides. *Figure 470* is of No. 7218 at Banbury Junction *en route* to the Ironstone Sidings, for a South Wales ore train. No. 7241 is seen in *Figure 471* outside 'A' erecting shop at Swindon, and No. 7209 in *Figure 472* is shown at Oxford in 1955 having her tubes cleaned. In service, these engines were always curve shy; they were so often being derailed in Banbury Yard that many sidings were put out of bounds for them.

Figure 471

Figure 472

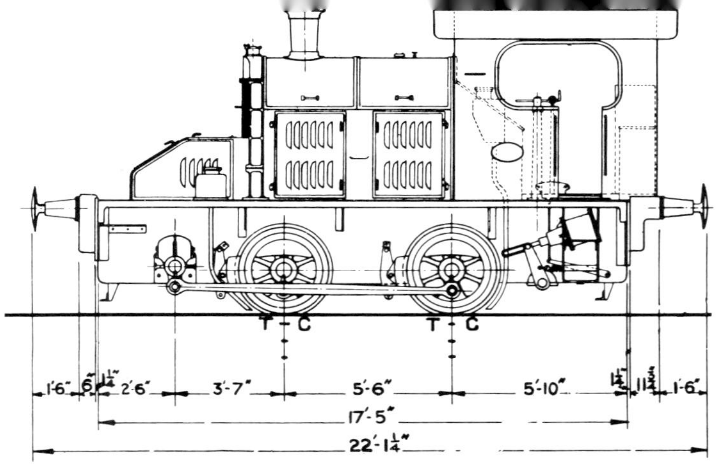

Figure 473

Figure 474

Figure 475

The Great Western was essentially a steam powered railway, but always open to try new forms of motive traction. Over the years the Company experimented firstly with a Petrol-Electric railcar in 1911, and later in 1933 with the Diesel Railcars (see *A Pictorial Record of Great Western Coaches (2)*. Petrol shunting engines were tried in the form of Nos. 15, 23-27 built by Simplex Works of Bedford and used in departmental sidings, and a Diesel Electric shunter was used at Swansea for many years from 1936, being No. 2 in the stock book.

No. 1, however, (illustrated on this page) was the interesting little machine, built by Fowlers of Leeds, the famous traction engine and road roller manufacturer. This was a six cylinder four-wheeled Diesel mechanical shunter with an ancillary petrol engine mounted on the side for starting purposes.

When at work, this locomotive had Westinghouse brake equipment, but this must have been on the engine only, as the official photographs shown on this page do not show any brake hoses.

The engine was of 70 BHP and the wheels were of 3′ diameter with a wheelbase of 5′ 6″.

The exhaust gases were emitted through that strange little brass capped chimney and a whistle was fitted, operated by compressed air. The little shunter was painted and lined out in Great Western colours and would, I feel, make an attractive model.

She was sold in 1940 to George Cohen, Sons & Co., of Leeds, who passed her on to the Ministry of Supply. *Figure 473* is the official *Diagram B* which is reproduced to 4m/m scale.

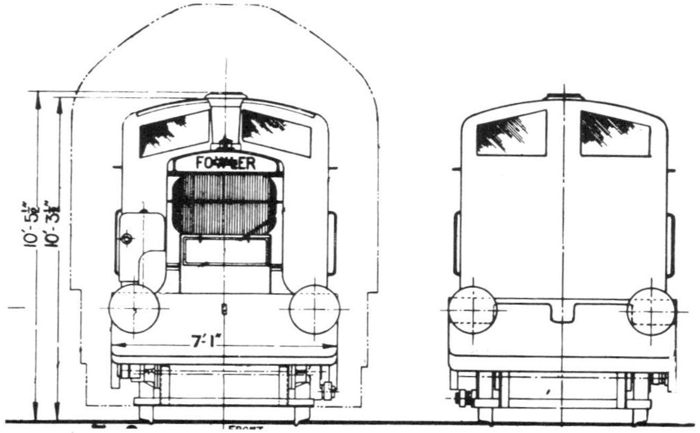

Also in 1934, several more small dock tanks were required to replace the very old '1392' class which were by now worn out, and so, six more of the outside cylindered six-coupled dock tanks were built to the same basic design as the '1361' class. These had pannier tanks, a modern cab, Belpaire fireboxes and boilers in one piece. This was known as the '1366' class as the numbers ran from 1366-71, the *Lot* number being *286. Figure 476* illustrates the prototype No. 1366 lined up for its portrait at Swindon; this was quite a nice spot for photographs, as the morning sun lit both side and front well, and the coupling rods are down in the recognised 'proper' position.

Figure 476

Swindon again of course, but as these engines were built primarily for work in the Wagon shops, this is understandable. *Figure 477* shows No. 1367 in full right-hand side view, and with the sun shining all the details can be seen nicely. This picture was of the leading engine in a row of three, which I thought most unusual, and *Figure 478* depicts these three in line at the running shed entrance. The Numbers are 1367, 1369 and 1368.

The official drawing is the only one issued, namely *Diagram B.68,* and for more detail see Colonel Templer's illustration on the following page.

Figure 477

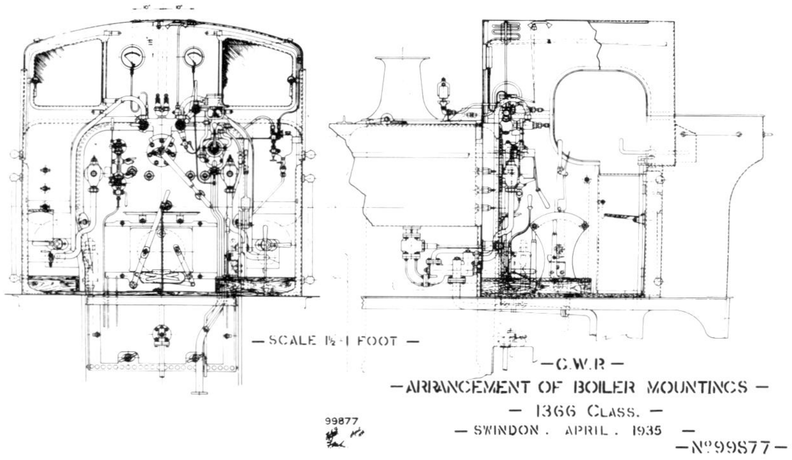

Figure 478

Figure 479

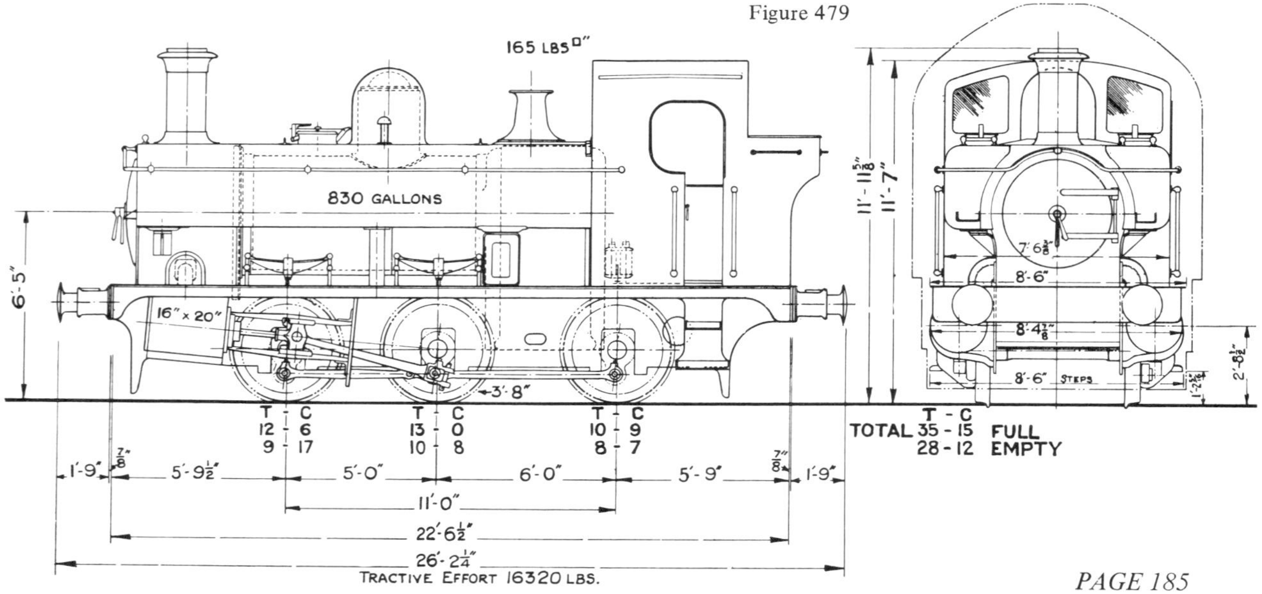

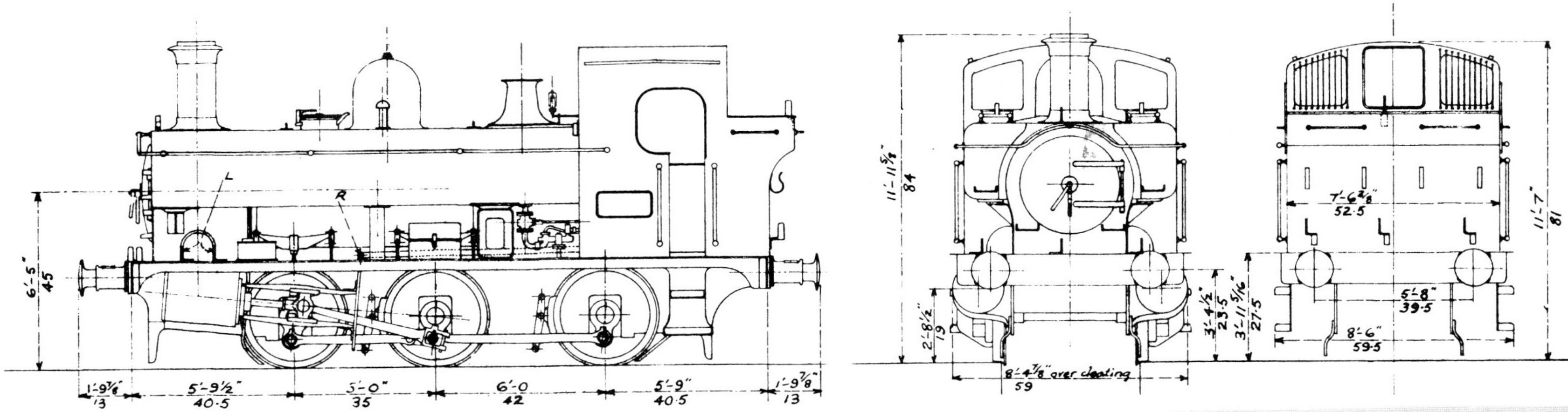

Figure 480

For arrangement of vacuum pump, and position of tool-box on right side, see fig 2.

Figure 481

Figure 483

This drawing by Colonel Templer is one of two, and shows the left-hand side of the '1366' class plus front and rear elevations, and its fellow on page 117 shows the right-hand side of the '1361' class. This is very useful, as the framing, motion and wheels of the two classes were identical.

Figure 481 depicts No. 1368 hauling the Channel Islands Boat Express through Weymouth streets in 1946. Note the train guard is on the footplate. A point about this working, all coaches used 3 link couplings for this short journey through the streets, because of the severe curvature of the track, and warning bells were used on some of the engines.

Also at Weymouth, we see the same engine in the goods yard coupled to a box van. I rather like this photo as it shows how small the locos were.

Finally No. 1366 is seen awaiting withdrawal at Swindon in 1961. Fortunately the Dart Valley railway has one of these tanks preserved beautifully on their line in Devon.

Figure 484

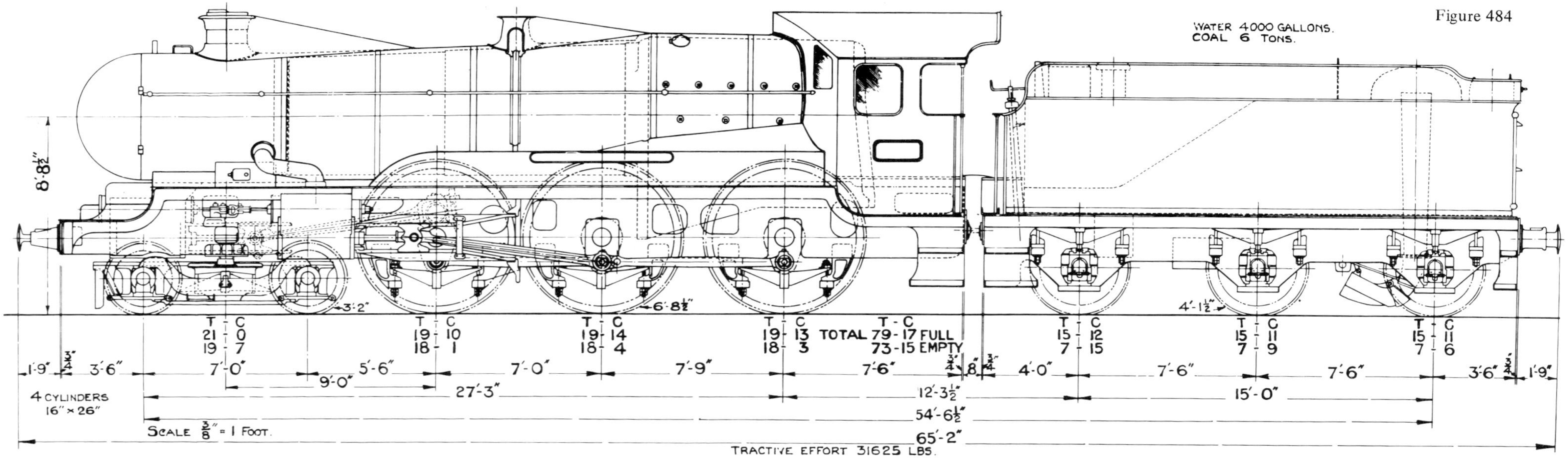

A 7

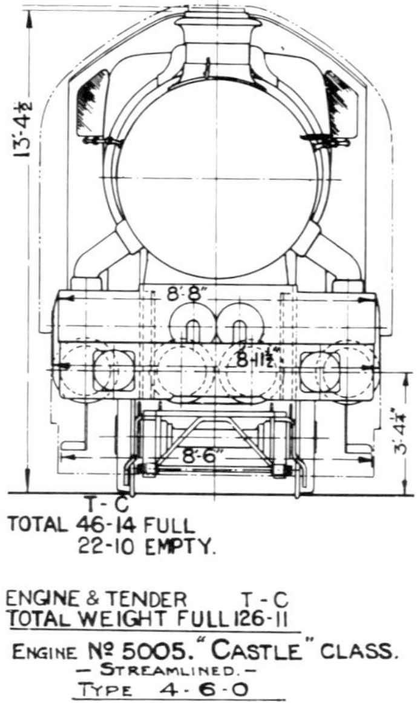

In 1935 it was the done thing to streamline locomotives. The London North Eastern Railway and the London Midland and Scottish Railway covering the whole engine in a highly decorated casing which was supposed to help in the air flow around the engine at speed. It certainly caught the travelling public's eye, but the effect on speed or fuel consumption was unnoticeable, and eventually all streamlining was dispensed with.

However, before this, the Great Western Board, always publicity conscious, decided that the Swindon express locomotives should 'keep up with the Jones's' and required a 'Castle' and a 'King' class to be partially streamed-off in the 'modern' manner. The result is seen in this drawing and photograph of *Manorbier Castle.* I think the picture speaks for itself, suffice it to say the practice was not furthered, and gradually the extra 'bits' were removed.

By 1937 the fairings over the cylinders, steam pipes and tender had gone, the bullnose went in 1939, the chunks behind the chimney and valve hung on until 1943, and by 1947 the cab front and long splashers vanished, bringing the engine back to a normal outline.

The *Diagram A. 7* seen in *Figure 484* is to 4m/m scale.

Figure 485

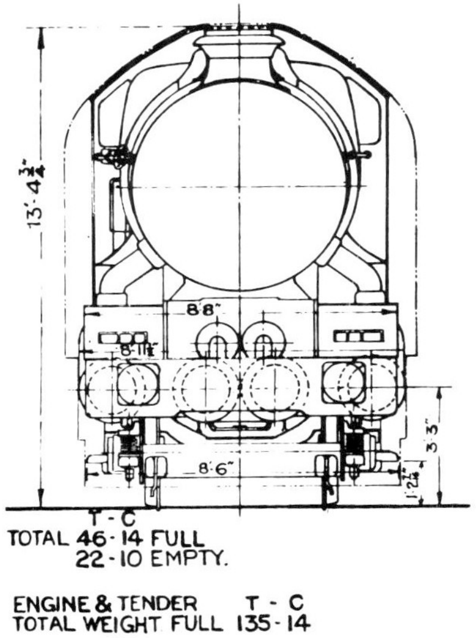

Figure 486 is an interesting picture, showing No. 6014 being turned on the table at Kingswear, preparatory to returning to London with the up 'Torbay' Express. The date would be about 1937, as the fairings over the front framing, steam pipes and tender have already been removed. Notice particularly the special fairing to merge the taper boiler into the shoulders of the Belpaire firebox. This engine kept the wedge-shaped cab until 1953, but all the rest of the streamlining was removed many years before.

Figure 487 is the official *Diagram A.6* giving dimensions of the streamlining, in case any reader should be tempted to have a try at a model, and this is to 4m/m scale.

Figure 486

Figure 487

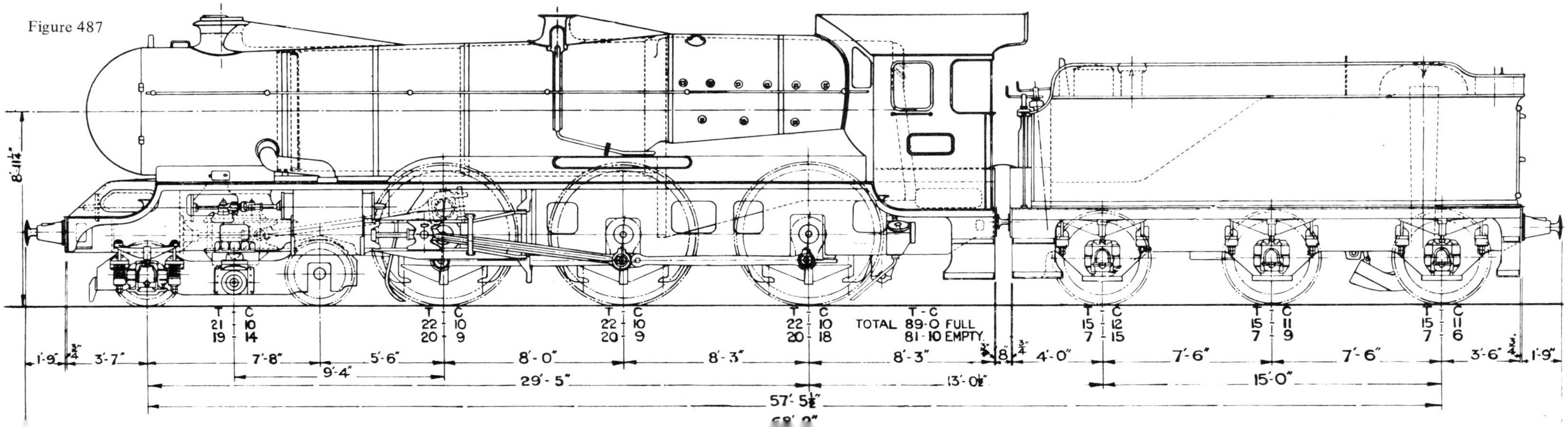

Figure 488

Figure 489

The official portrait of *King Henry VII* in the full streamlining is shown in *Figure 488.* In it one can see the fairing over the front buffer beam, and the tender. It would appear that the usual good taste which one expected from the C.M.E.'s office at Swindon seemed to be totally lacking here. Was it perhaps another case of *The Great Bear* all over again – Board versus Engineer?

However, to my prejudiced eye, *King Edward VIII* seen in *Figure 489* looks far more business-like than the bulbous affair in *Figure 488.* This picture was one of a series, posed for the publicity department and entitled 'Getting ready for the road'. Actually the driver is putting his own trimmings in, and oiling the cross-head slides.

As already mentioned, the practice of rebuilding the old 'Duke' class with parts of both 'Duke' and 'Bulldog' led eventually to a new class, and the first engine to be experimented with in this way was No. 3265. In 1929 the frames of 'Bulldog' No. 3365 received a spare 'Duke' boiler, plus numerous bits of No. 3265, and was turned out as *Diagram A.40* seen in *Figure 492.*

More withdrawals of both 'Dukes' and 'Bulldogs' in 1936, resulted in twenty-nine hybrids being produced, as per the illustrated No. 3216 in *Figure 490.* The class eventually became the '9000' class and is seen in the last phase in *Figure 491* which is *Diagram A.45.* Note the larger tender and shorter boiler mountings.

Figure 490

Figure 491

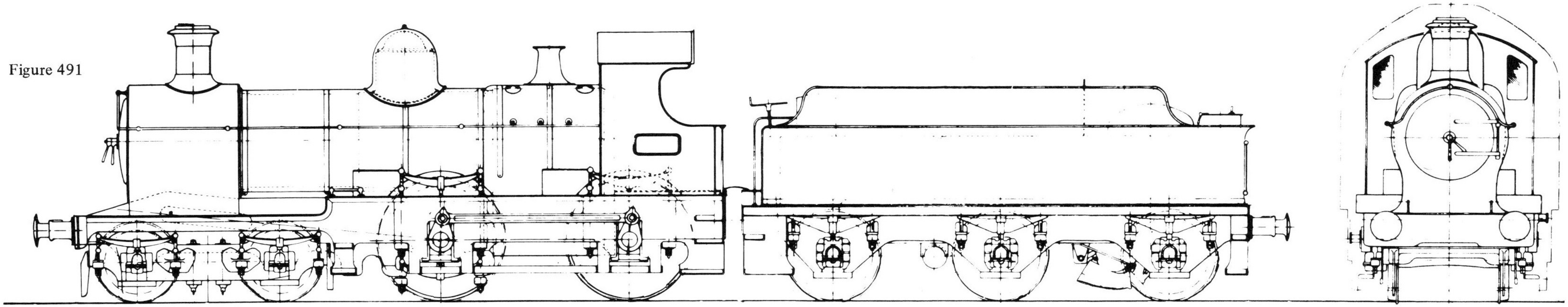

Figure 492

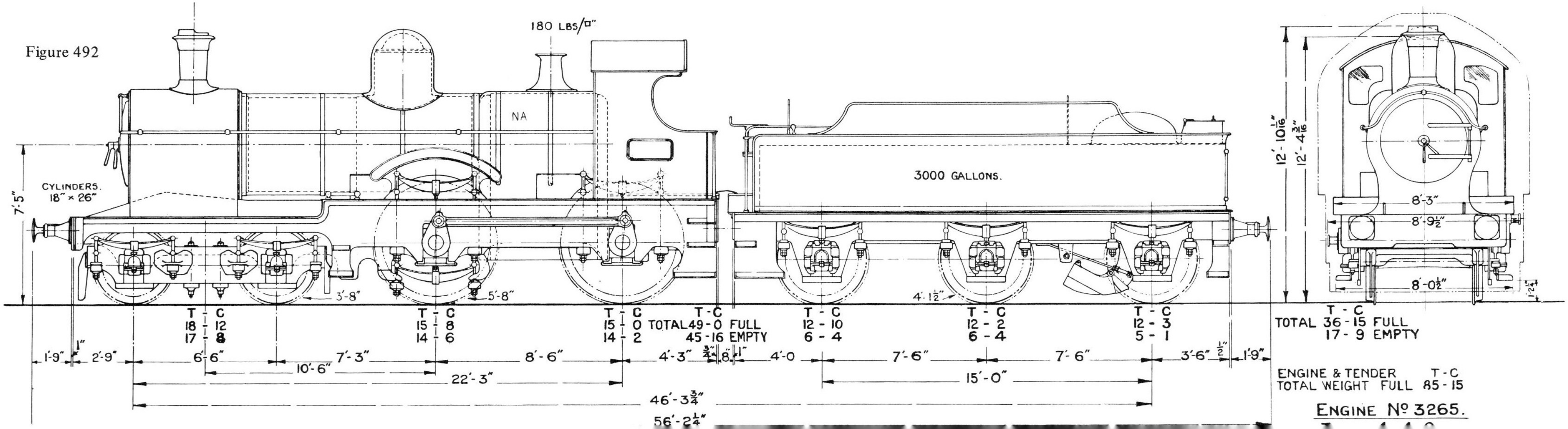

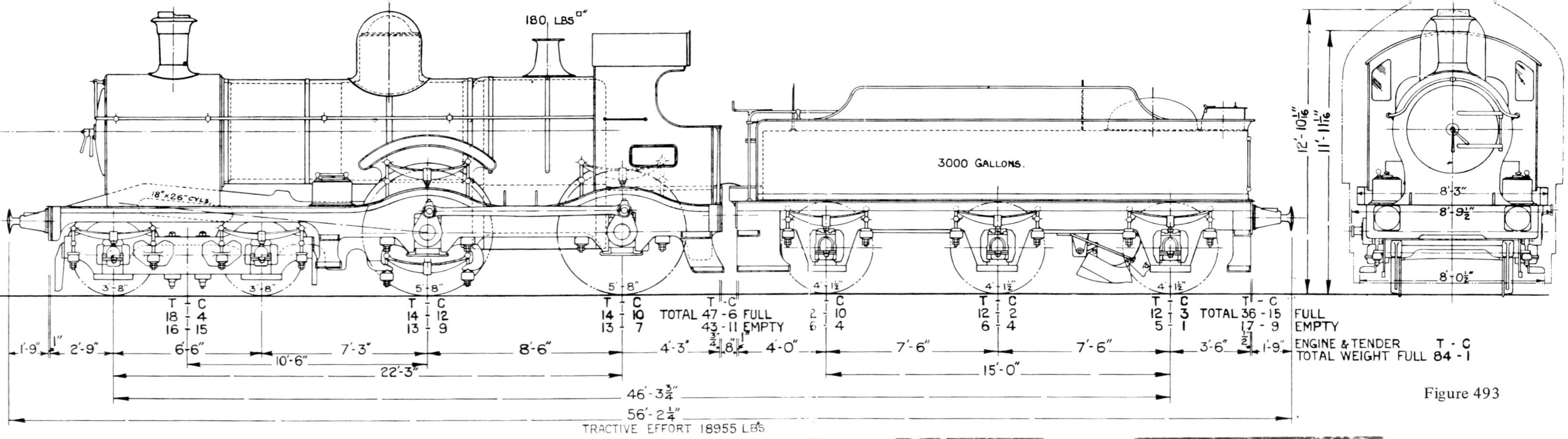

Figure 493

Figure 494

Figure 495

Figure 496

Even some of the old 'Dukes' were received into the '9000' class, and this page shows some of the 'old stagers' at the end of their long life. The drawing in *Figure 493* is Swindon's *Diagram A.39* and shows the curved frame and flush Belpaire boiler.

Figure 494 is of No. 9076 at Banbury in 1947.

Figure 495 illustrates No. 9073 at Moreton Cutting and *Figure 496* is of No. 9019 with the tiny tender at Banbury Loco shed in 1946.

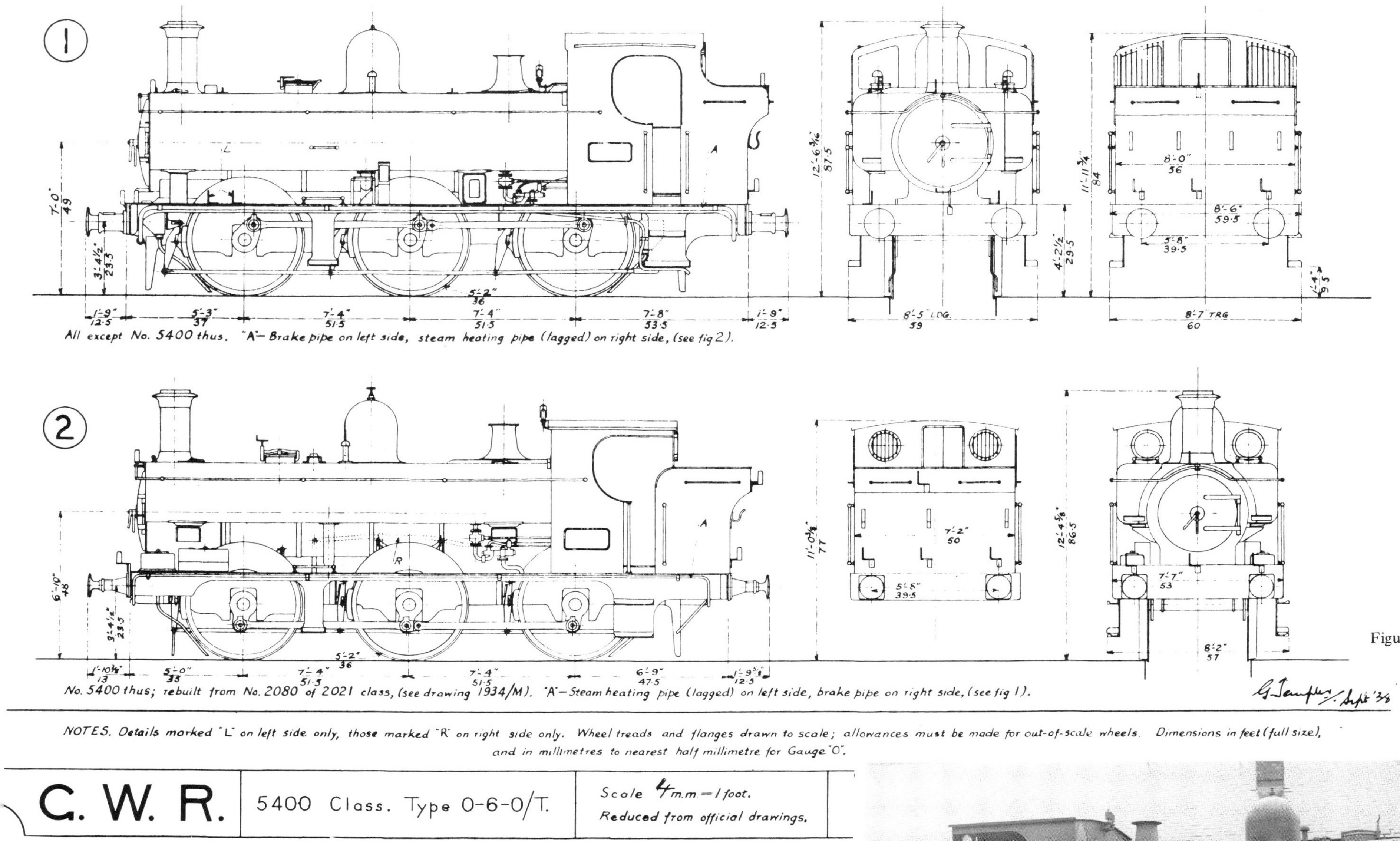

Figure 497

Figure 498

In 1930 there was a desperate need to replace all the elderly 0-6-0 pannier tanks, which had been fitted with auto-gear, and pressed into passenger service on branch line work.

As was usual at Swindon, a guinea pig was required to try out the idea of fitting larger wheels to a pannier 0-6-0 tank. No. 2080 was selected for the experiment and can be seen in *Figure 498* fitted with 5′ 2″ wheels and big splashers. The trials proved successful and a new class of large wheeled 0-6-0 tanks were built in 1931-32 and numbered 5400-19, and five more in 1935, Nos. 5420-4. No. 2080 was eventually numbered 5400, but in 1932 was scrapped and a new '5400' built in its place.

Colonel Templer's drawings make the situation clear, and shows both experimental and standard engines (*Figure 497*).

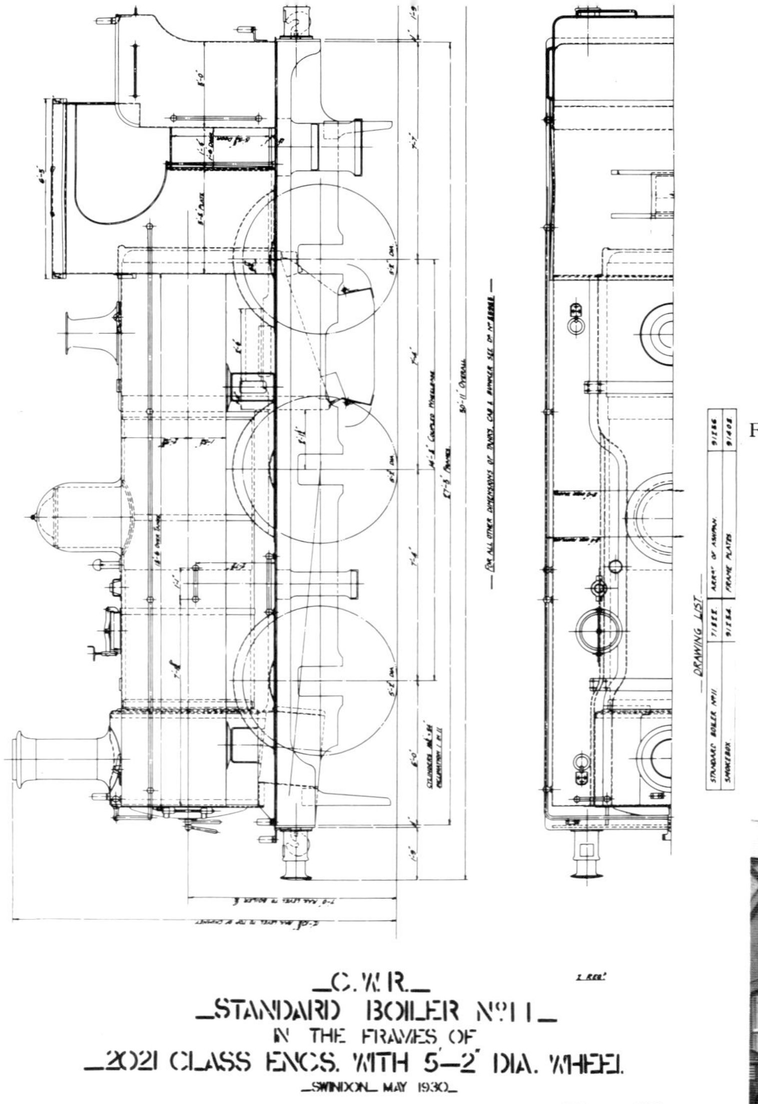

Figure 499A

Figure 500

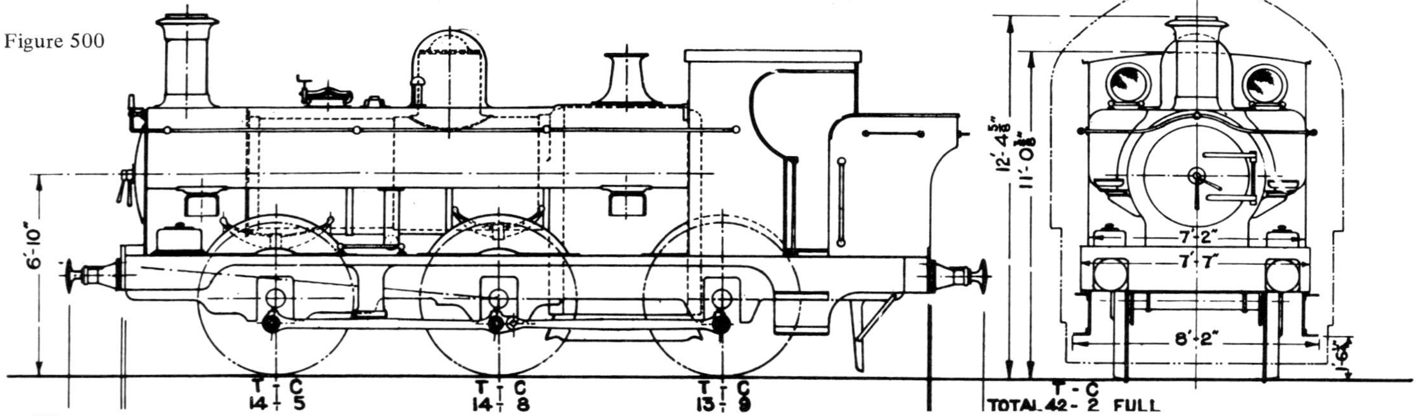

Figure 499

This picture illustrates the reconstituted No. 2080 in 1930 at Swindon and renumbered '5400'. Note the auto-gear on the front buffer beam, and the 5′ 2″ driving wheels. The drawing is the official *Diagram B.53,* issued for this conversion, plus the Swindon drawing (*Figure 499A*) showing the standard boiler No. 11 fitted to this class.

The new series of '5401' class were handy fast little engines, the side tanks were slightly smaller than the prototype, and the rounded roofed cab was fitted with the large windows.

Figure 501 shows the left-hand broadside view of No. 5403 which was built in 1931. Their route colour was yellow, and power letter 'A'.

The drawing is Swindon *Diagram B.61* which shows the boiler class FA standard No. 21.

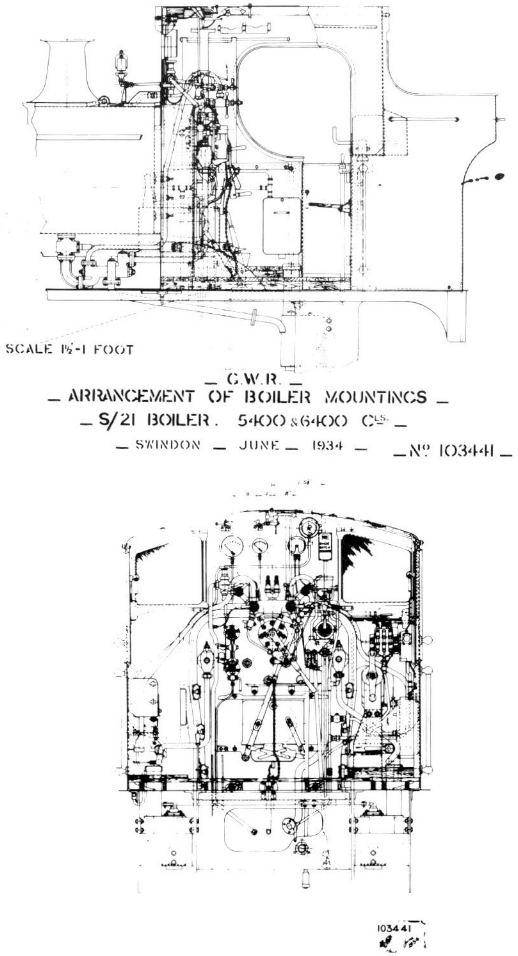

Figure 501

Figure 502

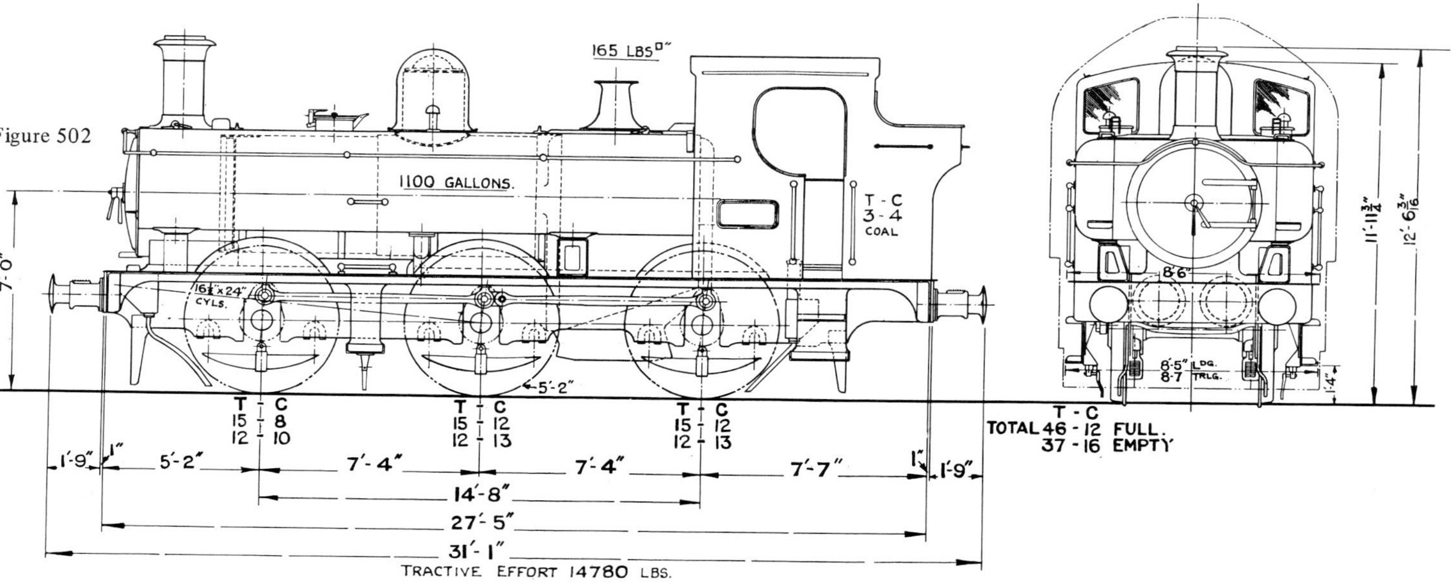

igure 503

igure 504

Figure 505

For a long time three of these '54XX' class were shedded at Banbury, and were used on the auto-car services between Banbury and Princes Risborough. In *Figure 503* we see No. 5401 just running on to the Aynho water troughs, in the up direction with the 1.55 p.m. ex-Banbury. *Figures 504* and *505* illustrate No. 5414 on Banbury shed in 1946, she had just been returned from a major overhaul at the factory. Notice the top feed behind the chimney and the A.T.C. battery box behind the cab steps.

Figure 506

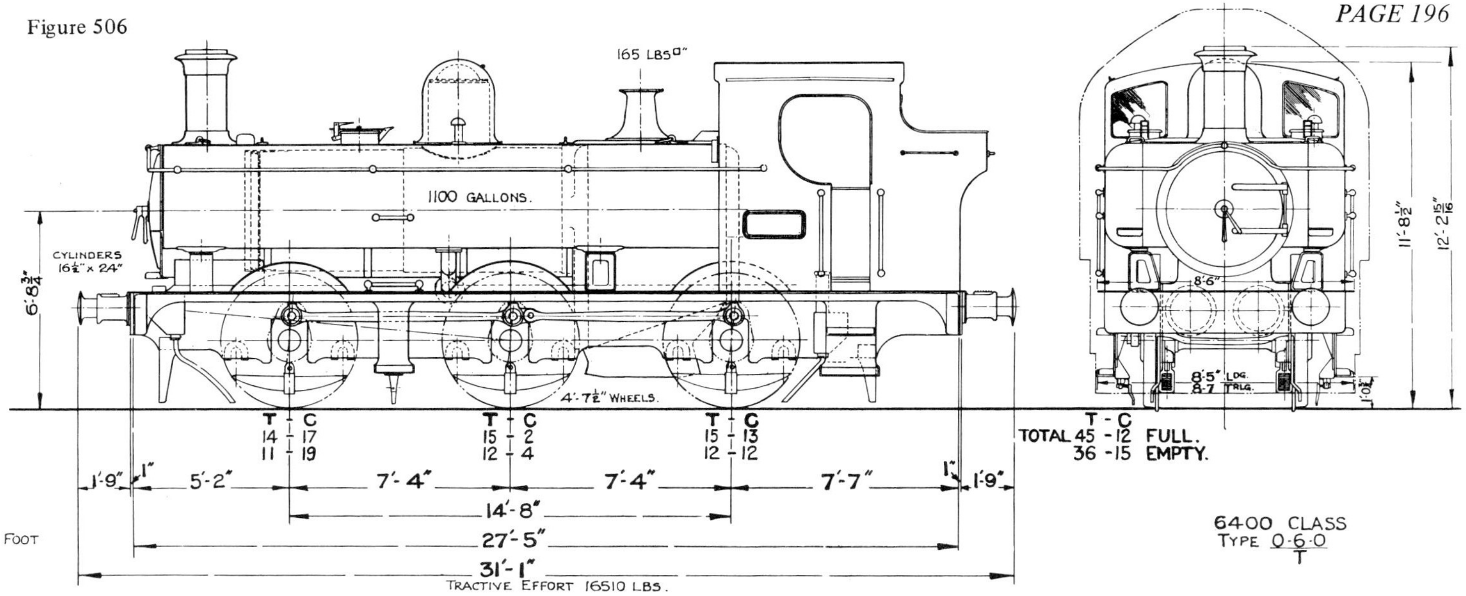

The '54XX' class proved so successful, that in 1932 a further series of similar locomotives was produced but fitted with smaller driving wheels, after some experimentation on a guinea pig engine No. 2062. The new series were numbered 6400-39 to distinguish them from their sisters with the 5′ 2″ wheels, and were built in four lots, No. 277 of 1932, No. 294 of 1934, No. 300 of 1935 and No. 305 of 1937. These two pictures show, in *Figure 507,* engine No. 6403 and in *Figure 508* No. 6438 and the diagram is *B.62.* This auto-fitted smaller-wheeled 0-6-0T class, found most of their work in the hilly South Wales Valleys, although a few were allocated to both Laira and Kidderminster sheds.

Figure 507

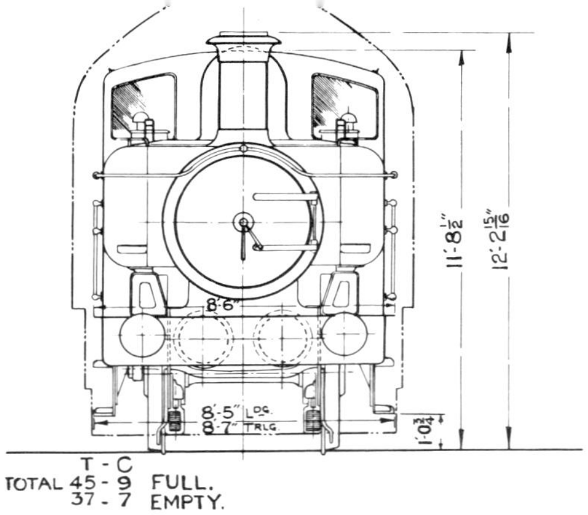

7400 Class.

Type 0-6-0T

A further series of 'modern' 0-6-0T panniers was built in 1936-7 and additions to the class continued after the War. These were the 74XX series, and although to outward appearances identical to the 64XX series, in fact they were considerably stronger, having a pressure of 180 lbs against the 165 lbs of the previous design. They were not fitted for auto-working, and the driving wheels were 4' 7½" as on the 64XX's. One small feature could always identify them from both the 54XX's and 64XX's and this was the join of the bunker to the cab back plate. On these engines the join was square, whereas on the sister series, it was formed into an arc. *Figure 510* illustrates No. 7406 and *Figure 509* No. 7400 both before they received the top feed which was generally applied to these engines after the War. Building dates, lot numbers and serials were as follows:–

7400-29 of 1936-7 to *Lot 307*
7430-9 of 1948 to *Lot 371*
7440-9 of 1950 to *Lot 380*

The diagram is the official *B.72. Figure 511.* Note the steps on the fireman's side of the bunker only, on all these latter series.

Figure 509

Figure 510

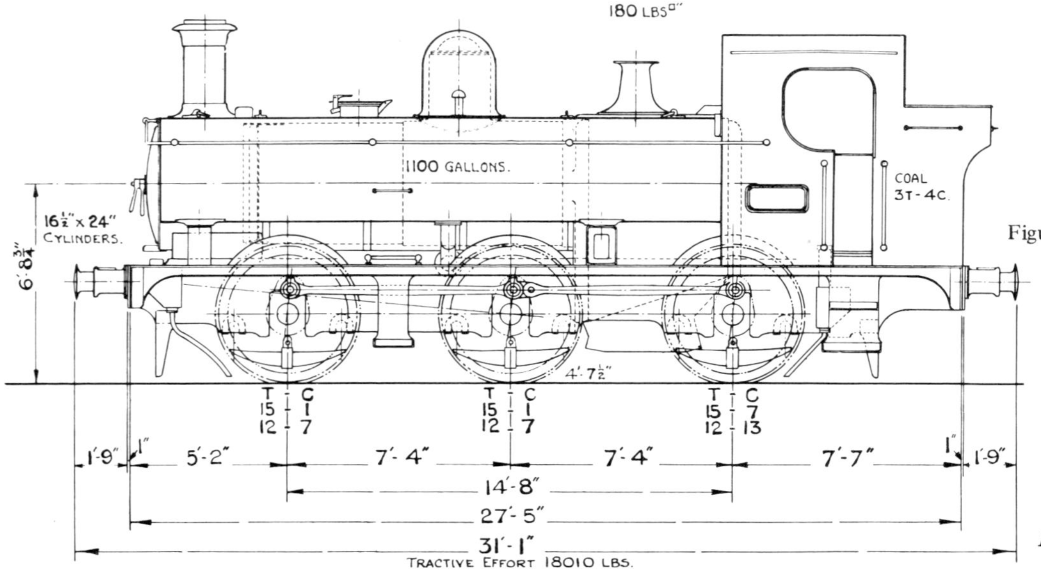

Figure 511

Figure 512

Figure 513

The history of the large 2-6-2 tanks is not only long, but rather complicated. However, to summarise:—

The class started with the prototype No. 99 in 1903 (*seen on page 35*) which was later numbered '3100', and was followed by a series of thirty-nine engines in 1905-6 numbering 3111-49, and forty-one similar in 1906-8 but with larger boilers and numbered 3150-90. Numbers 3100 to 3149 were later renumbered 5100, 5111-5149 when their axle loading was reduced in 1927.

Then in 1929-30 the gaps in the numbering were filled in and supplemented when the 5101-10, 5150-9, series were constructed. Being highly successful, the class was enlarged until 5199 was built in 1934, and ten more numbered 6160-9 were constructed in 1935. Numbers for the class having run out, further additions were built between 1935 and 1948 and had to be numbered 4100-4180.

A very similar series, but with boiler pressures raised to 225 lbs against the previous 200 lbs, were produced between 1931 and 1935, and these were numbered 6100-6169.

Figure 512 illustrates the prototype engine No. 5100 at Swindon in 1929 (previously No. 99) and *Figures 513 and 514* show the front and rear of 6154 built fifty years after the start of the class. Apart from curved frame and outside steam pipes there is not much outward change.

Figure 515

Figure 516

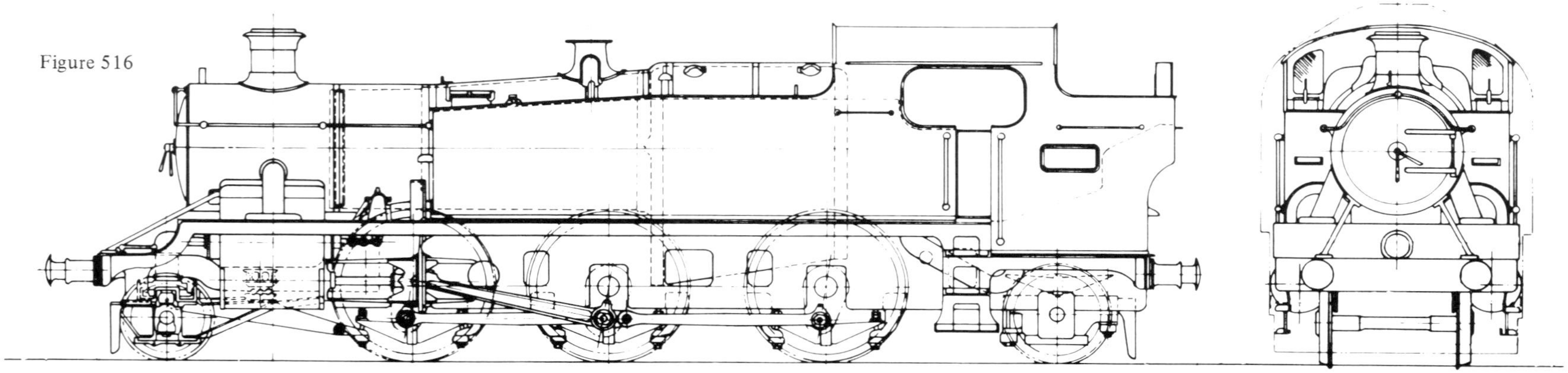

This large picture illustrates the '61xx' class of 2-6-2T locomotive as built at Swindon in 1931. This particular engine was the first of the series to be fitted with the sliding shutters to the cab sides, and this was the reason for the photograph. The drawing is the official *Diagram A.10* which shows the class as built before the addition of the sliding shutters.

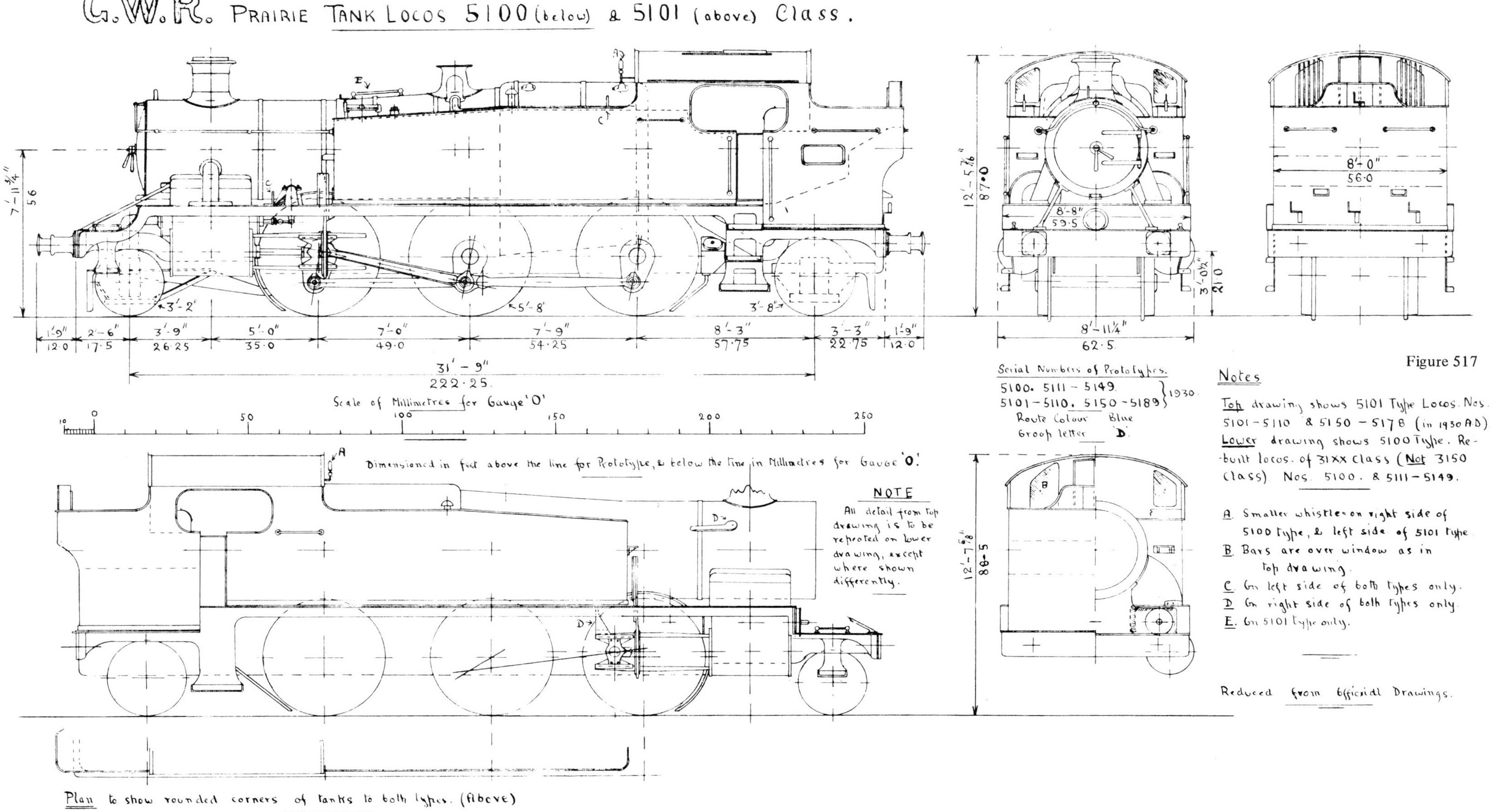

Figure 517

Sir Layland-Barratt's detailed drawings of the 5100 and 5101 series are shown here to give the variations in the two series. Again the notes speak for themselves, so no comment is necessary (*Figure 517*).

In 1938 it was intended to take the old '3100' and '3150' class into the factory and rebuild them with a higher boiler pressure, curved framing and the smaller 5′ 3″ driving wheels, as their ultimate duty would be for banking purposes at places like Hatton, Dainton, Whiteball, etc. However, the Second War being imminent, put a stop to this scheme, after only five engines had been so treated in 1938-9. These were the old frames of Nos. 3155, 3156, 3173, 3179 and 3183, which became Nos. 3103, 3101, 3100, 3104 and 3102 respectively. All the engines previously carrying these numbers having been withdrawn.

Figure 518 shows this new rebuild as at 1938, in the official photograph and this is supported by *Diagram A.13.* In *Figure 520* is shown one of the old series No. 3131 to compare the larger wheels and square framing, etc.

Figure 518

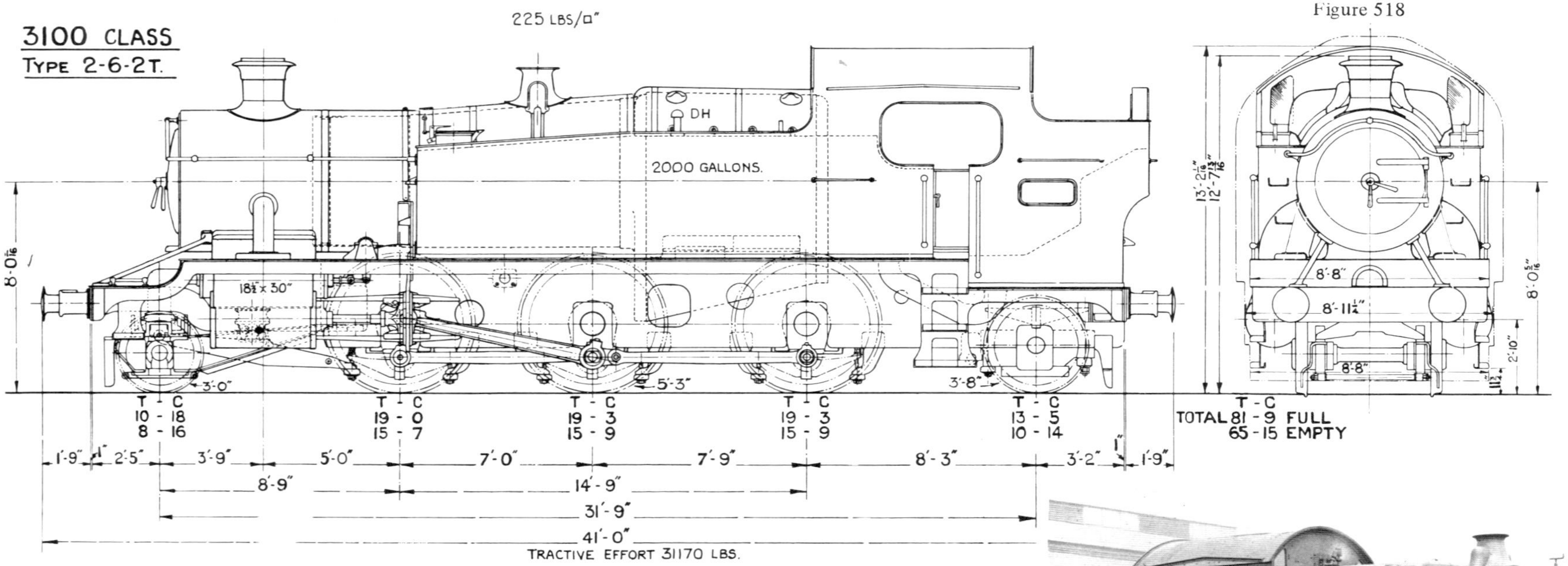

Figure 519

Figure 520

Figure 521

Another page of comparisons. *Figure 521* illustrates one of the '3150' class, No. 3177 as built with the large wheels, but with superheater and taper chimney of the late 'twenties. In *Figure 522* is one of the '3100' class, No. 3128 in 1927 at Reading, before being converted to No. 5128 in December of 1928. In *Figure 523* the 'newer' '3100' class rebuild of 1938 is seen after overhaul at Swindon in 1946, with the 5′ 3″ wheels.

Figure 522

Figure 523

These little 0-4-2Ts, originally the 48XX and 58XX class, must surely be as well known to Great Western enthusiasts as the 'Castles' and 'Halls'. They were designed in 1932 by Mr. Collett to take the place of the old '517' class, many of which by this time were getting way past their best.

Although to outward appearances very much like their forerunners, the rebuilds of the '517's, there the similarity ended. The boiler was of the Group 7 SS type, still carrying a dome, and with a pressure of 165 lbs. A large enclosed cab was fitted with large windows fore and aft, and the motion included a new form of crosshead having three slide bars, 5′ 2″ drivers were fitted with trailing wheels at 3′ 8″ and all those from 4800-4874 had both A.T.C. and auto-car gear fitted. *Figure 524* is of the prototype engine at Swindon factory in 1932, and what a pretty picture she makes!

Figure 524

Figure 525

Figure 526

Figure 527

Figure 527A

Figure 528

Figure 529

PAGE 204

The 58XX series, which only consisted of twenty engines, Nos. 5800-5819, were all built in 1933 and differed from the sister 48XX's only in that originally they were not fitted with either auto-gear or A.T.C., although several were later fitted with the A.T.C. *Figure 525* shows the front end of No. 5805 and in particular the rod crossing over the buffer beam which is the link rod for operating the front sandboxes.

In 1946 the Great Western started trials with oil burning engines, and amongst those so fitted were some of the 2-8-0 freight engines. As these oil burners were distinguished by being renumbered into a 48XX series, this meant that these small Collett 0-4-2T's also had to be changed, and therefore all those 4800-4874 were renumbered 1400-1474. These little tanks had an axle load of under 14 tons, were uncoloured on the route system and could go anywhere and handle any light jobs. My pictures show bottom left, No. 1405 at Wallingford shed in 1947, top right No. 1406 bringing two trailers into Cheltenham from Kingham, No. 1451 in far West Wales on local branch duty, and at the bottom No. 1402 also handling a local train in Mid-Wales in 1955.

Figure 530

Figure 531

PAGE 205

As the branch lines were closed, so these little tanks lost their jobs, and at first were put into store, but then sadly found their way to that long siding at the far West of Swindon Works, from which there was no return.

The top two pictures are of No. 1419 awaiting the torch, in good order, but just redundant, and also amongst the wild flowers on the left, is No. 1474. The drawing is one of Colonel Templer's which shows the Collett 0-4-2T's side, front and rear elevations (*Figure 532*).

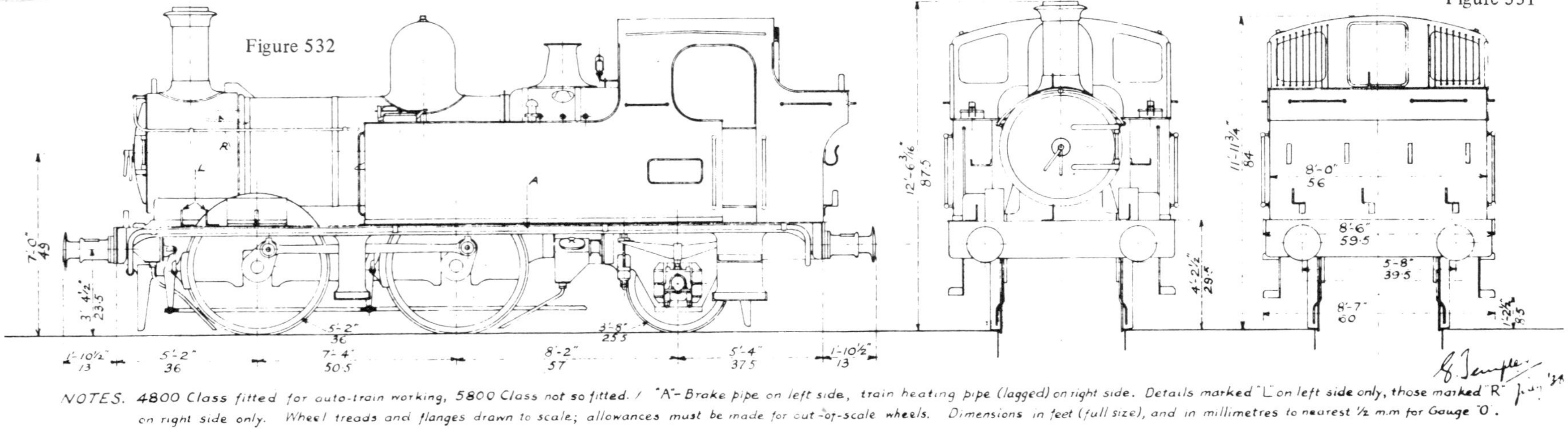

Figure 532

Figure 533

Figure 534

Two more of the 14XX class awaiting the scrap heap in 1960 at Swindon. On the left, No. 1403 has already lost its number plates, as has No. 1434 on the right, but No. 1433, pictured on the triangle at Swindon yard, still had a few more duties to perform. Note the inner cab window slides with which these engines were fitted. The drawing is the official *Diagram M* of the class. Again, it is pleasant to report that examples can still be seen on the Dart Valley line.

Figure 535

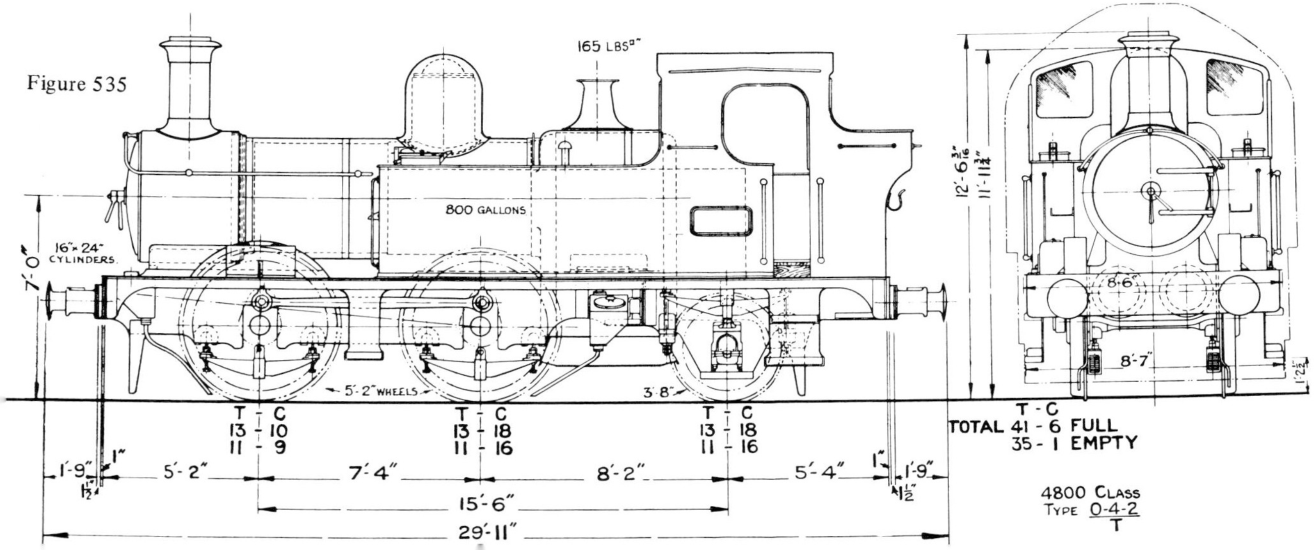

Figure 536

Figure 537

The meat traffic which was worked over the Metropolitan lines to Smithfield, had been handled for years by engines of the 'Metro' 2-4-0T's and the '633' class, which were fitted with condensing apparatus especially for this work. This special gear was needed for steam engines working in underground tunnels, which normally filled the bores with steam vapour and smoke. This apparatus conveys the exhaust steam by means of branch pipes from the smoke-box into the side water tanks, which have vents to allow the cooled steam to escape after being through the water. One big snag of passing the exhaust through the water tanks, is that this water supply is warmed by contact with the exhaust gases, and it is well known that steam injectors for boiler feed will not work with hot or warm water. Therefore to overcome this problem a 'Weir' water pump had to be installed.

In 1932 there was a need for a replacement locomotive series to take over from the older '633's and 'Metro's, so No. 8700, one of the pannier tank engines built by Beyer-Peacock in 1931, was used as a prototype.

As can be seen in *Figure 537* the tanks were cut back at the smokebox end to allow the 'Weir' pump to be fitted on the right-hand platform and all the necessary condensing gear was fitted together with the vacuum trip gear which was in use on the electrified lines (just under the motion step). *Figure 538* shows a close-up view of the feed water pump. The official drawing in *Figure 539* is *Diagram B.63* which was prepared for the conversion of No. 8700 only.

(*End elevation on page 208*)

Figure 539

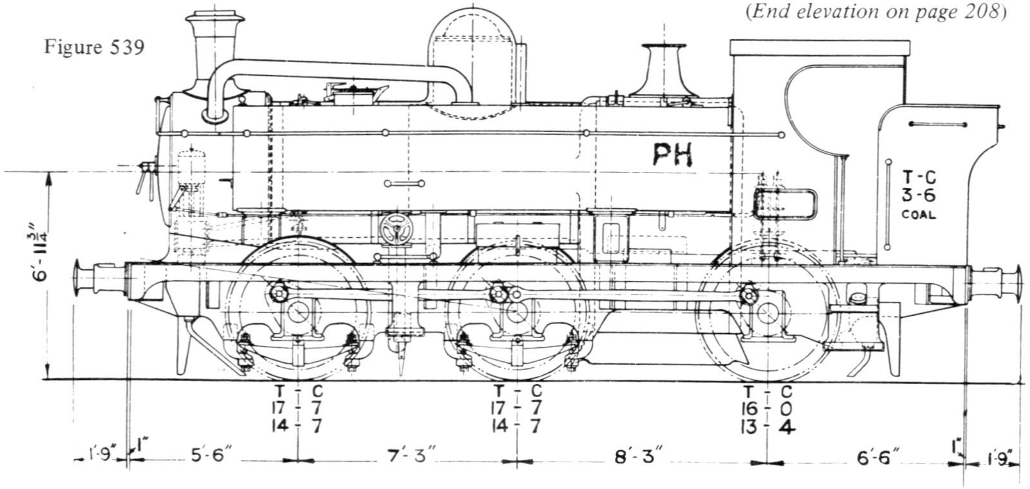

Figure 538

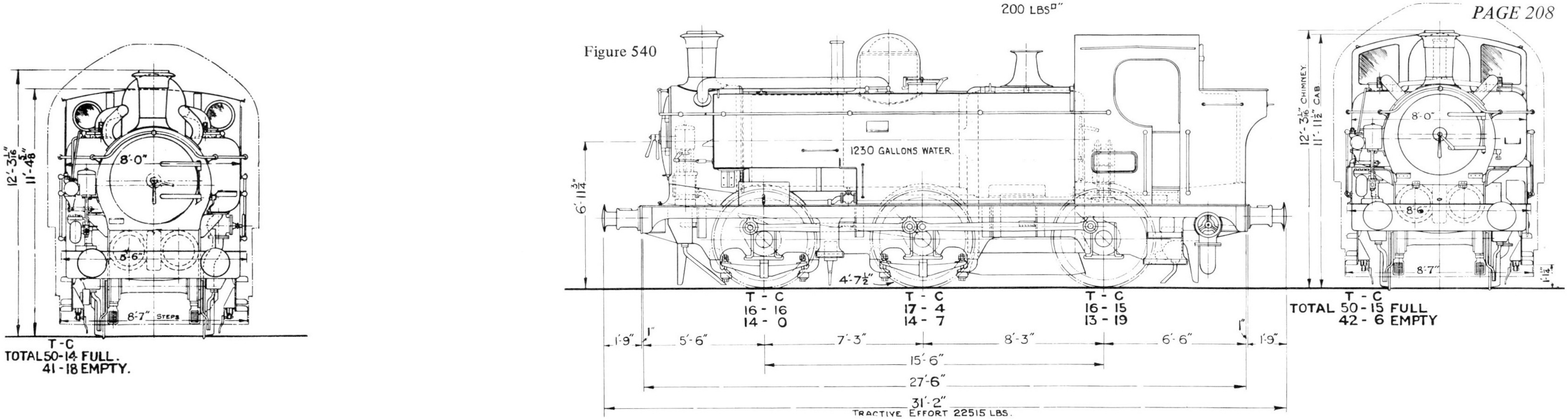

Figure 540

No. 8700 went on a year's trial, and proved successful in every way, except that the lack of water due to cutting back the tank was sorely felt, and so when the '9701' series was designed in 1933, allowance was made to increase the water capacity to 1230 gallons by extending the back half of the pannier tanks down to the running plate, which always gave the series their unique character.

Ten engines were built to *Lot 282* and numbered 9701-10. The prototype No. 8700 was brought into line in 1934 and renumbered 9700 in traditional Great Western fashion.

Figure 541 shows No. 9701 at Swindon as built, together with the official *Diagram B.69.* One other small point of interest about these engines is that they were equipped with special A.T.C. gear, which automatically clipped up on entering electrified lines to avoid the third centre rail and was released when rejoining Great Western metals.

Figure 541

PAGE 209

These two pictures show No. 9704 actually at work, bringing the empty train off the Metropolitan lines at Paddington in 1947, and finally awaiting scrapping at Swindon in 1962. The hand wheel under the bunker was for supplying water to the 'Weir' pump. It might be of interest to record that experiments were tried to use these engines as fire pumps during the London Blitz, but it was found that their water supply was soon exhausted.

Figure 542

Figure 543

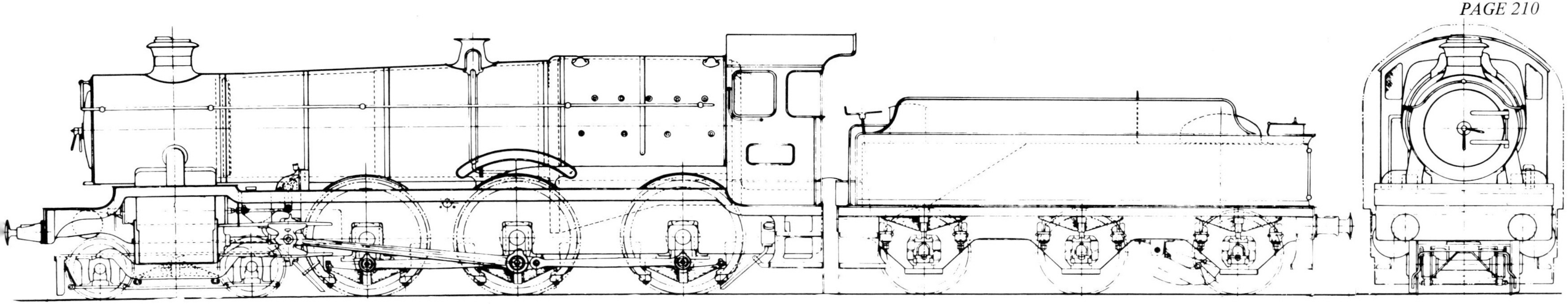

Figure 544

The first 'Grange' class locomotive was built in 1936, and although the scheme was to replace all the 43XX class with these and the 'Manors', the Second World War broke out after only eighty had been constructed, and their building was not continued after hostilities ceased.

This '6800' series was a modern light passenger engine of 4-6-0 classification, and made use of the displaced 43XX wheels, and motion, the drivers being 5′ 8″ of course, and a bogie between the cylinders had four 3′ diameter wheels.

Being so much lower in height with their 6′ 0″ wheels than the 'Hall' class, the framing had a raised part over the outside cylinders, a characteristic also shared by the 'Manors'.

Notice that the initial engines had a cast iron chimney which was also fitted to No. 6801-3, but later 'Granges' had the slightly waisted copper-topped type seen on Page 224. As they had 18 tons 8 cwts on each driving axle, the grouping was red and classification 'D' so their range was not so wide as the 43XX's they replaced! The drawing in *Figure 544* is the official *Diagram A.8* of the class.

Figure 546

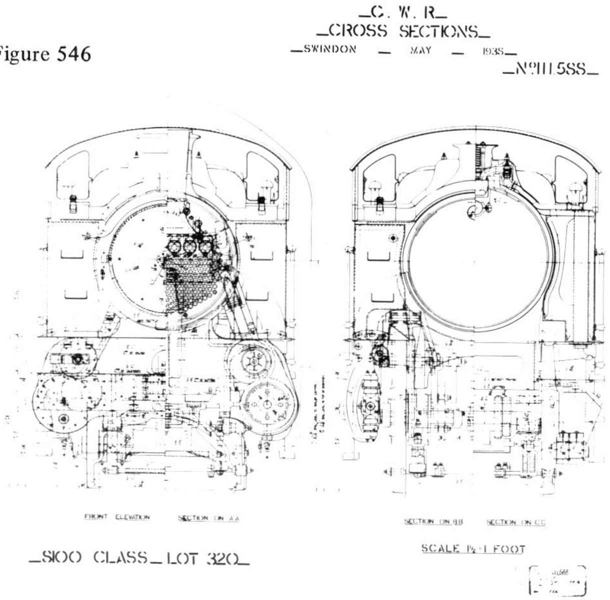

The '8100' series of 2-6-2 big 'Prairie' tanks were the last of the type built by the Great Western. They were intended as replacements, or rather rebuilds of the withdrawn '51XX' class. The frames of the old '51XX's' were used, and higher pressured boilers of 225 lbs were fitted. Slightly smaller driving wheels of 5′ 6″ were utilized which altogether produced a very fast powerful machine with excellent acceleration, for use on the London suburban services. Only ten had been built when War was declared, and like so many programmes, this Lot which was for fifty engines, never went further than the ten 8100-8109.

Figures 546 and 547 show Nos. 8102 and 8103 with different chimneys.

Figure 547

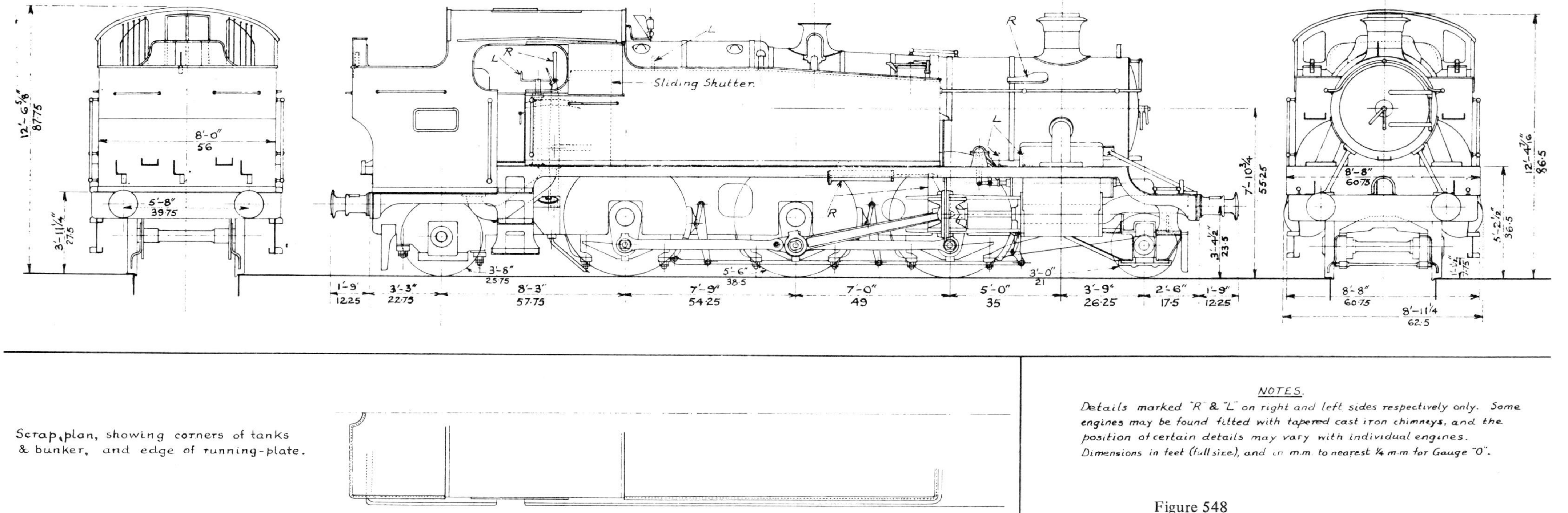

NOTES.

Details marked "R" & "L" on right and left sides respectively only. Some engines may be found fitted with tapered cast iron chimneys, and the position of certain details may vary with individual engines. Dimensions in feet (full size), and in m.m. to nearest ¼ m.m for Gauge "0".

Figure 548

G. W. R. 8100 CLASS. TYPE 2-6-2/T.

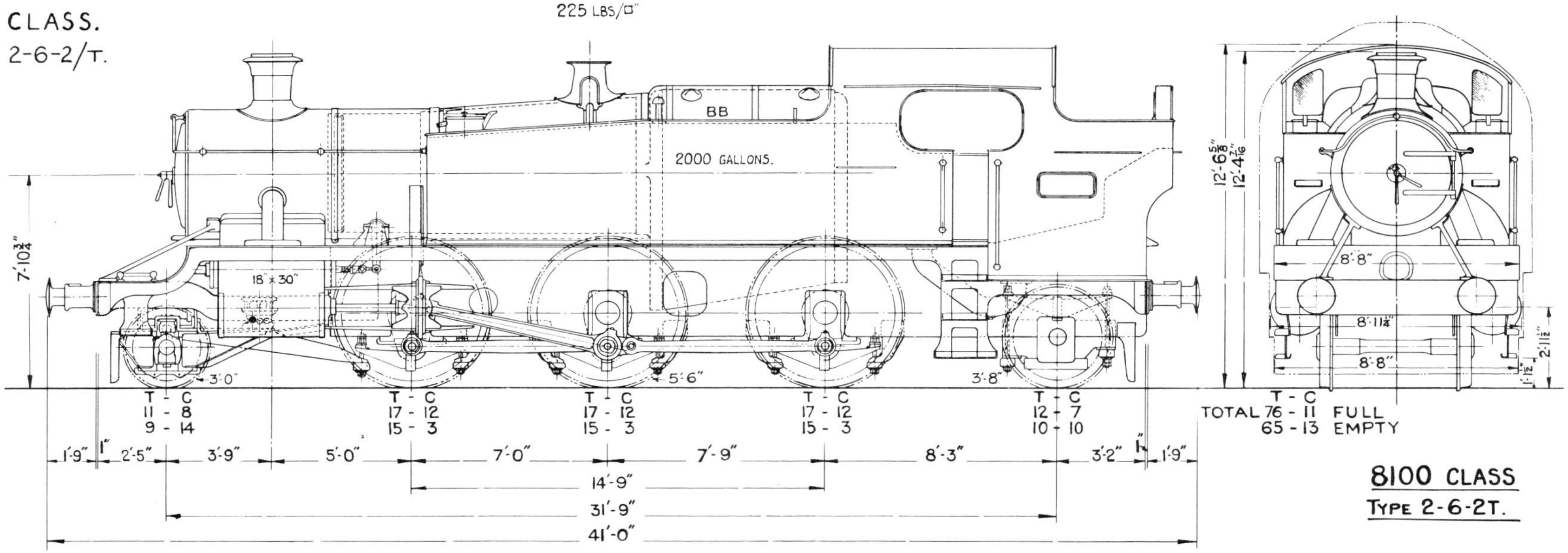

Two drawings of the '81XX' class, showing both sides of the engine. *Figure 548* is Colonel Templer's version of the right-hand side and *Figure 549* is the Swindon official *Diagram A.12.* Notice that both types of chimney are shown.

Figure 549

Figure 550

Figure 551

Figure 552

The '28XX' class has already been illustrated briefly on page 77, these being the first 84 engines built between 1903 and 1919. A gap of twenty years passed before any further additions were made to the series, and then in 1938, No. 2884-99 appeared, followed in the next four years by Nos. 3800-3866.

Although very like the earlier '28XX's in appearance, the 2884 class was nevertheless up-dated considerably. They were slightly heavier engines, and were fitted with large windowed cabs, outside steam pipes, and short safety valve bonnets. The framing and motion plate were also changed slightly to accommodate the fire-irons in a steel casing on the left-hand side only. However, not many firemen used the casings, preferring the old position on top of the tender, because, not only do habits die hard, but with a long red hot pricker, it was easier to swing it around, than back up into the tender before poking it in the casing.

A.T.C. was standard on this series of engine, and one can see the battery box in the detail shot of *Figure 550*.

No. 2889 is shown in *Figure 551,* No. 2884 in *Figure 552* and No. 3819 in *Figure 553.*

Figure 553

Twenty of the '28XX-38XX' class were converted to burn fuel oil in the years 1945 and 1947, and when this was done the first number was changed from 2 and 3, to 4, so making them '48XX's, and so causing the small Collett 0-4-2T's to lose their serial numbers, starting with '48XX' and going to '14XX'. However, the experiment did not last long, and although several expensive oiling bays were built at many depots, by 1950 all the engines had been reconverted to coal burning. *Figure 554* is a close-up detail of the air pump on the '38XX' class. The diagram for this series was *M* and is shown in *Figure 555.*

Figure 554

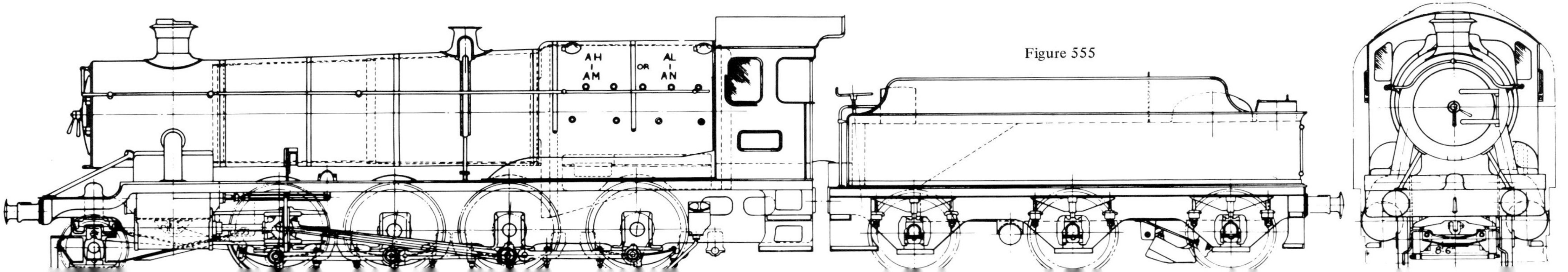

Figure 555

Figure 556

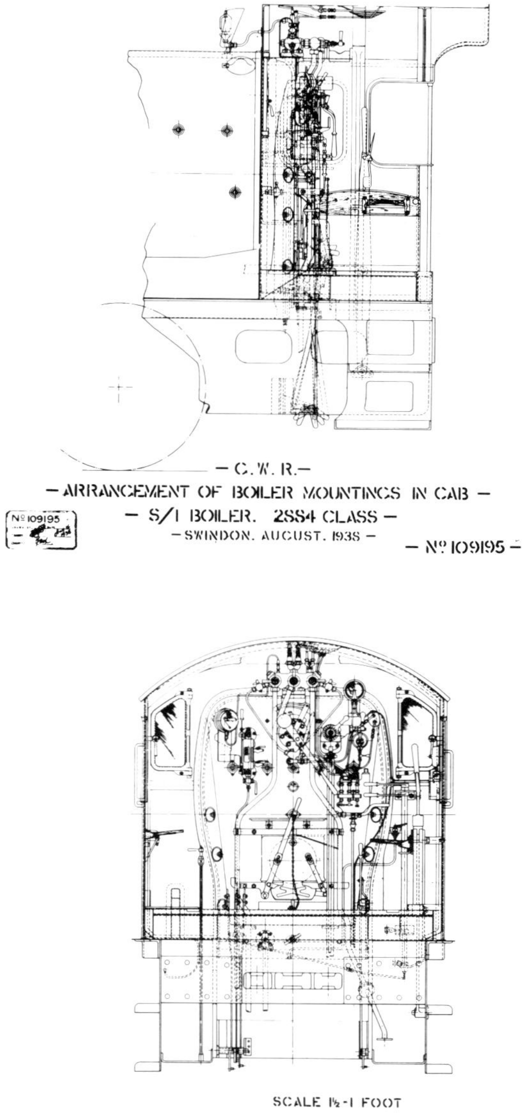

Detail of the crosshead, slide bars, valve rods and pump rod of the '2884' class can be seen clearly in *Figure 556*.

Figure 557

Figure 558

Here we see three pictures of the '38XX' class at work. *Figure 557* is of No. 3864 heading a 'C' headlight fitted freight on the up relief line at Sonning Cutting in 1948. *Figure 558* shows No. 3835 passing through Oxford in 1952 with a 'light' load of just one van. (Note that the safety valve bonnet is missing!) Finally, in *Figure 559* we see No. 3836 at Banbury Junction in 1946 with a train of coal empties for Woodford Halse.

Figure 559

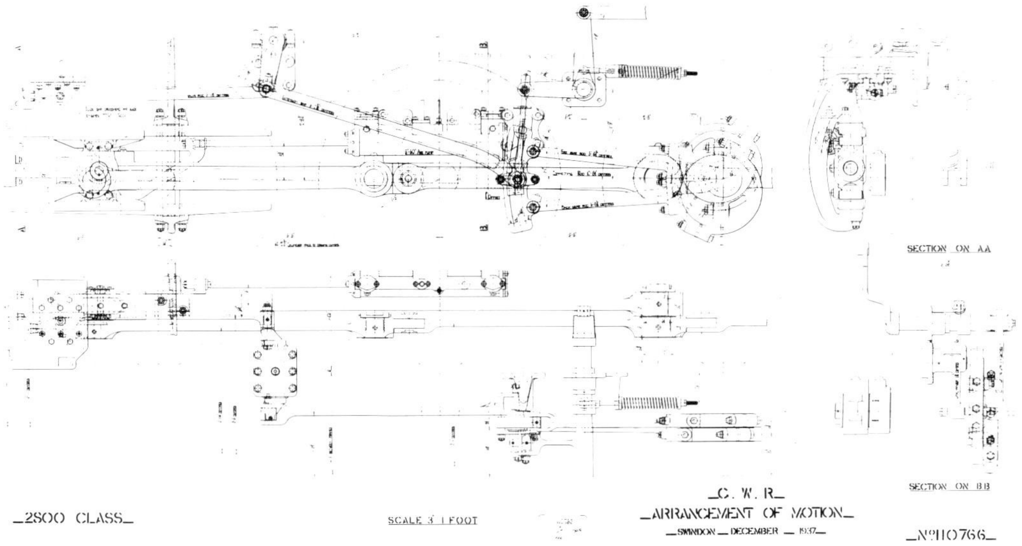

As both the 'Halls' and 'Granges' were too heavy for the 'blue' routes on the Great Western, a lighter passenger engine was needed to cover the routes still operated by the 2-6-0, '43XX' class.

Still making use of the motion and wheels of some of the 'Mogul' class, a new lightweight boiler was designed to Standard No. 14 and at last the duties of the 2-6-0's and 4-4-0's could be handled by this new design, named after 'Manor Houses' in Great Western territory.

The first engine *Torquay Manor* No. 7800 is seen in *Figure 560* outside 'A' shop at Swindon in 1938, the year of building, and I can remember well this engine taking over the 'Barry', as the Newcastle-Swansea express via Banbury was known to railwaymen. It was quite an occasion here at Banbury, as the L.N.E.R. engine came off the train, and at precisely 3.37 p.m. the spanking new engine steamed off via the Banbury-Cheltenham line to South Wales.

The diagram shown is the official Swindon *A.9*. Twenty of the class were built to *Lot 377* in 1950, Numbers 7800-19 and 7820-9.

A point worth mentioning is that *Torquay Manor* happened to be the residence of Sir Layland-Barratt, several of whose drawings appear in this work.

Figure 560

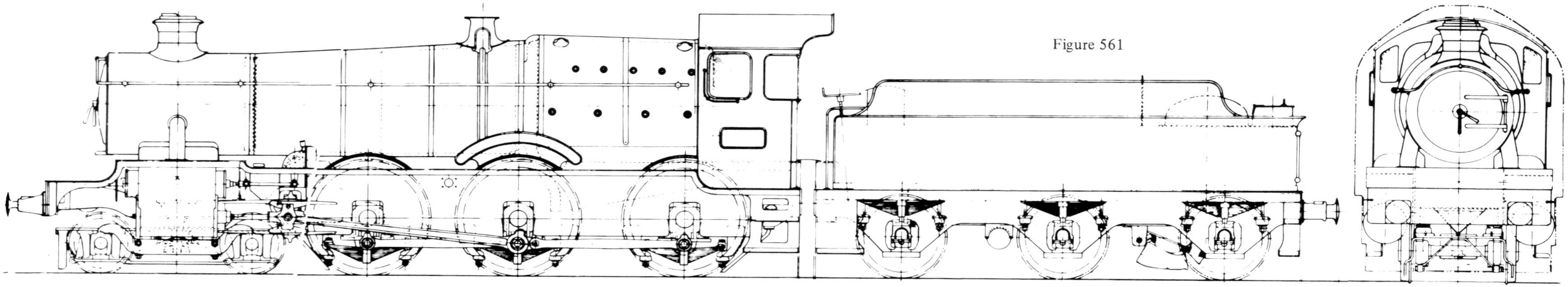
Figure 561

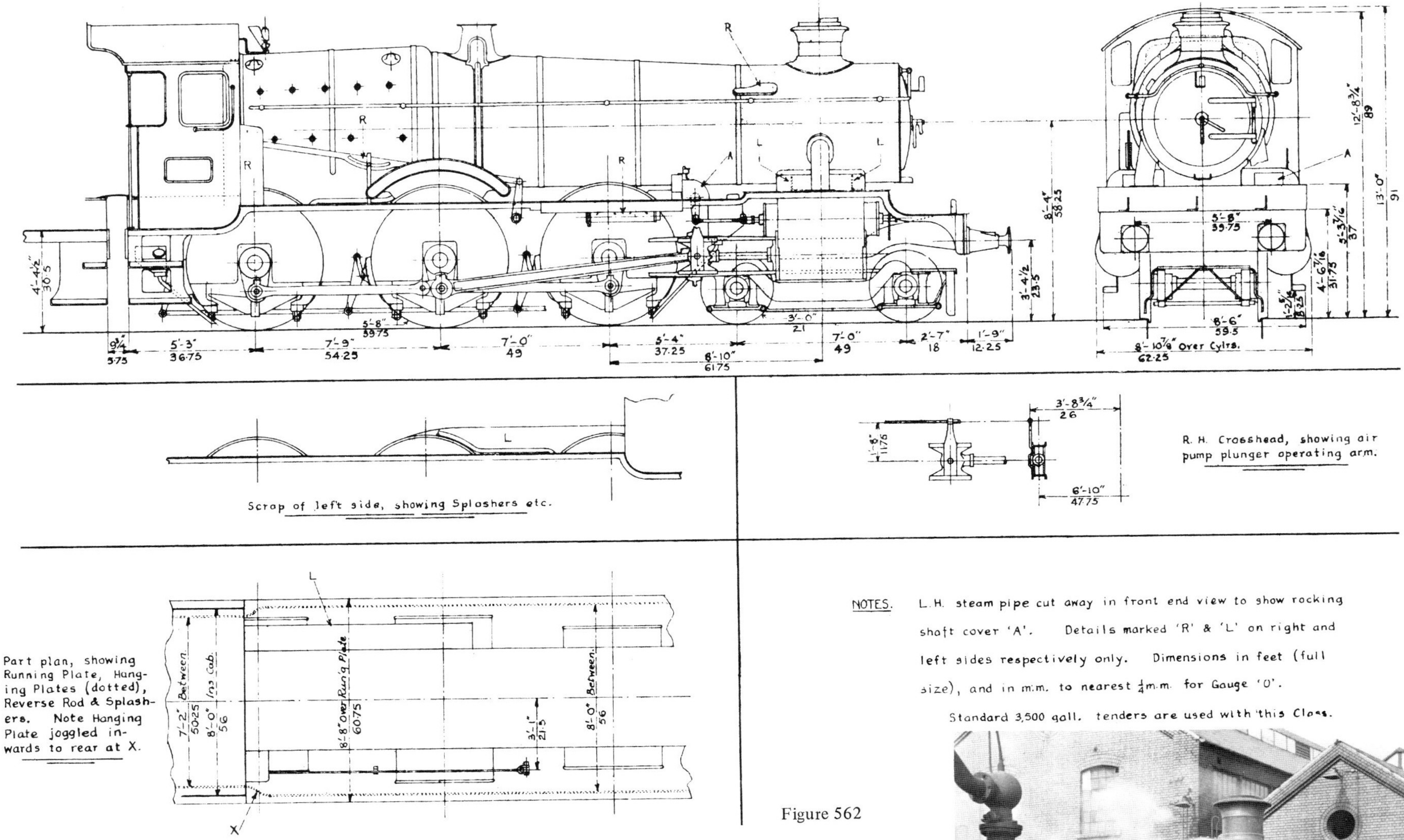

Figure 562

Figure 563

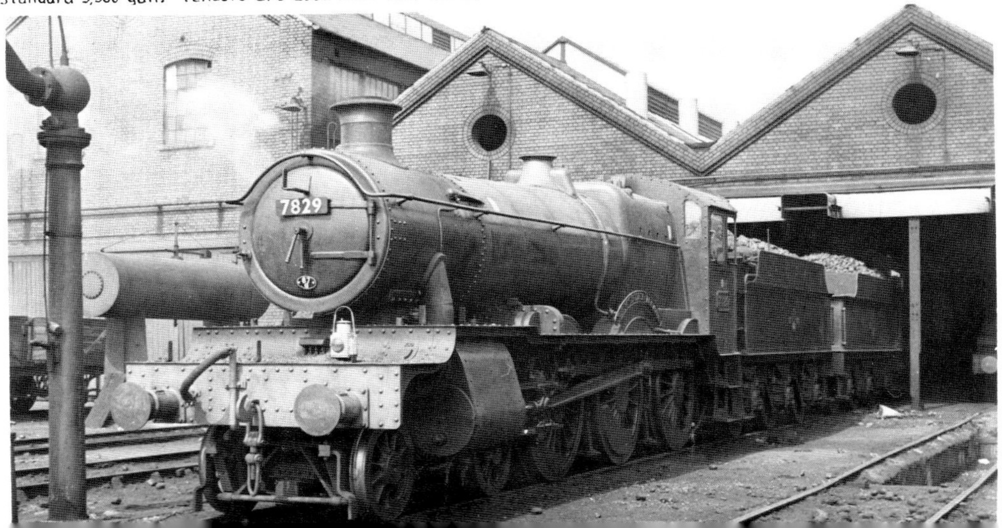

A modeller's drawing of the 'Manor' class is seen in *Figure 562.* This is the right-hand view of the series, and shows the reversing rod and air pump which were only on this side of the locomotives. In *Figure 563* No. 7829 *Ramsbury Manor* is seen; this was the last engine of the class to be built in December of 1950.

Figure 564

Two passenger locomotives in post war livery feature on this page, to show variations in class, livery and rebuilding. Both pictures were taken in 1946-7 period, and show in *Figure 564 Broome Manor* as reconditioned in 1946 with plain green paintwork, no lining and the simple G.W.R. on the tender.

In the lower photograph is seen a 1910 'Star' No. 4035 as she appeared on the occasion of her last major refit in 1946. Again in austerity plain green, with a 4000 gallon tender, and 'Castle' steam pipes, she still has an air about her, although only five years later she was cut up in the scrap yard. But the reason for these three illustrations is to show the family likeness which remained until the end.

Figure 566 shows once again the original engine from whence all these classes sprang. How close is the family likeness between No. 100 and No. 7805!

Figure 566

Figure 565

Figure 567

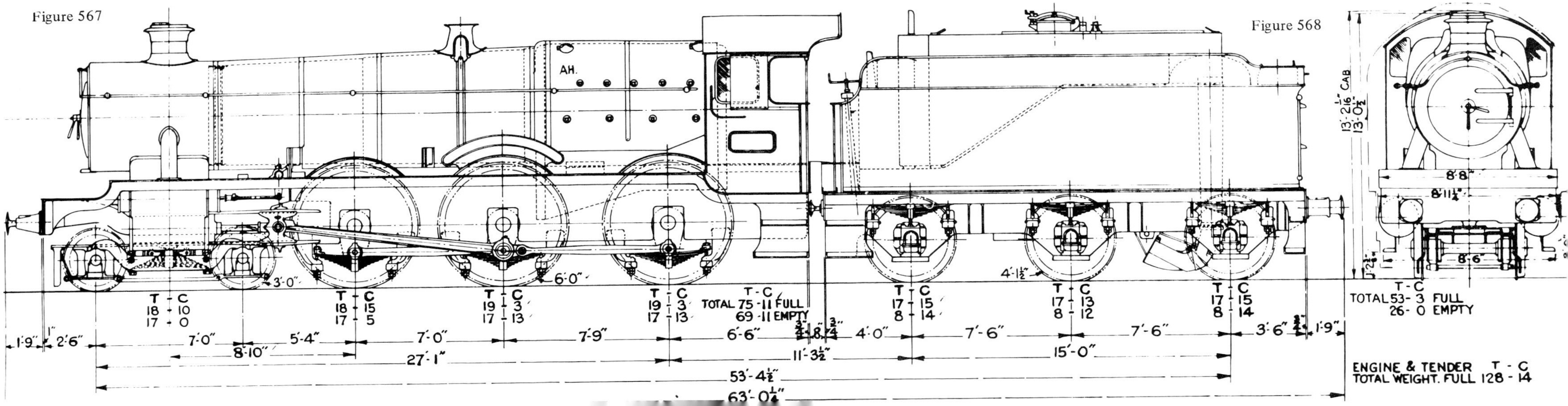

Figure 568

Figure 570

PAGE 220

Figure 567 illustrates *Ashwicke Hall* as converted for oil burning in 1947. Note the plain livery, but with the coat of arms positioned between the 'G' and 'W' on tender sides. Notice also the sliding shutter on the cab side window. The oil burning series were numbered in the '39XX's but reverted to '5976' in November of 1948. The diagram issued for this conversion was *A.21* as seen in *Figure 568.*

PAGE 221

The 'Hawksworth' Counties were the logical enlargement and development of the Great Western 2-cylinder express engines.

As the 'Kings' were to the 'Stars', so were the '1000' class to the 'Saints'.

These big 2-cylinder locomotives were the most powerful of their classification on the Great Western, and also were the last passenger design to be produced before nationalization. They were in fact a larger version of the 'Modified Hall' (*see page 225*), having plate frames throughout, a new boiler Standard No. 15 pressed to 280 lbs and a new driving wheel diameter of 6′ 3″. To go with this engine, Mr. Hawksworth designed a new flat-sided tender of 4000 gallons capacity and holding 7 tons of coal.

The first engine No. 1000 came out in 1945 unnamed, and with a copper-topped double chimney as per *Figure 569,* but the next to be built, No. 1001, had the single chimney very reminiscent of the 'King' pattern, see *Figure 570.*

The original drawing for this class shows that they were intended to be a '99XX' class!

Figure 569

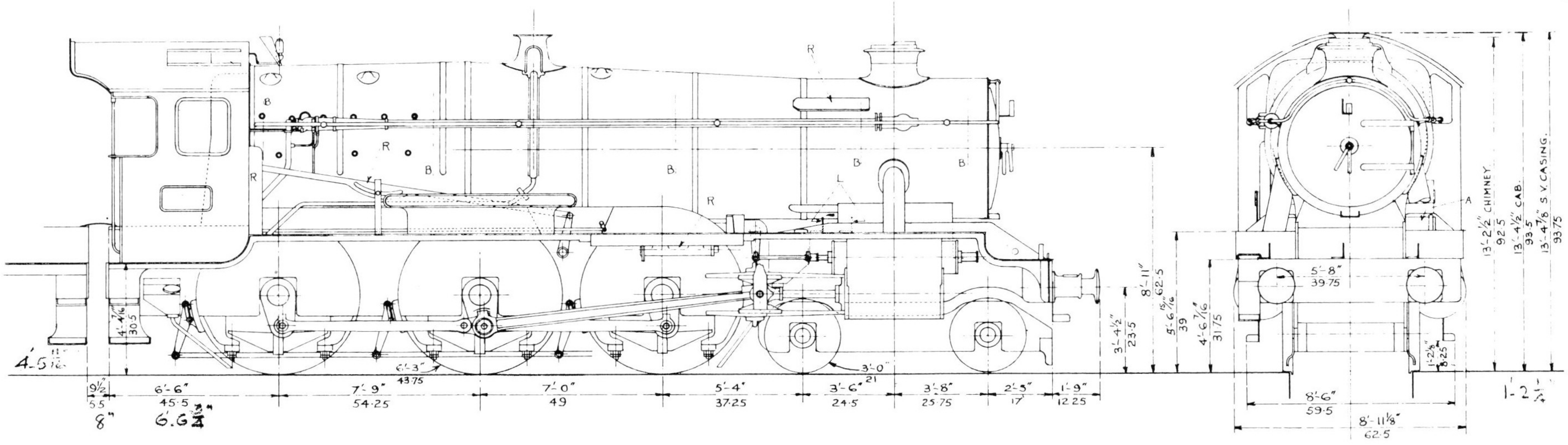

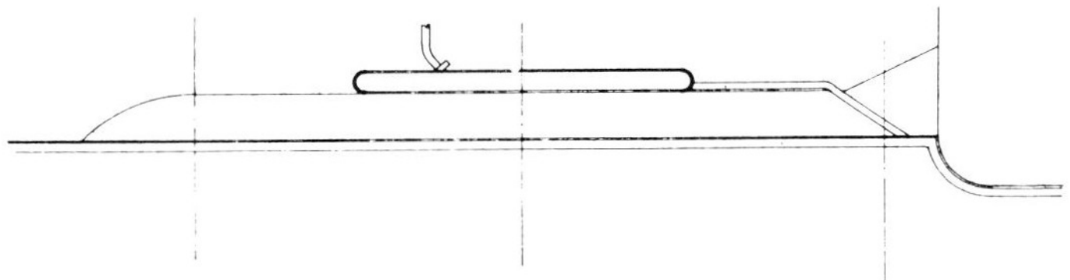

Scrap of left side, showing Splashers etc.

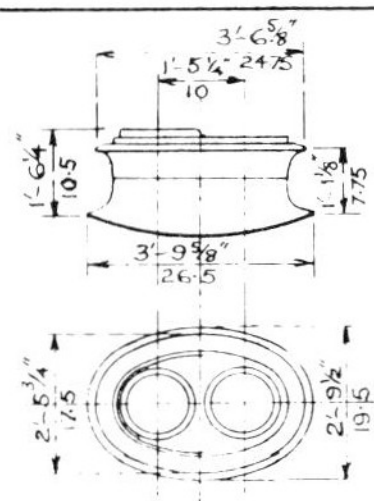

Double chimney fitted to No 1000. End view same as single chimney.

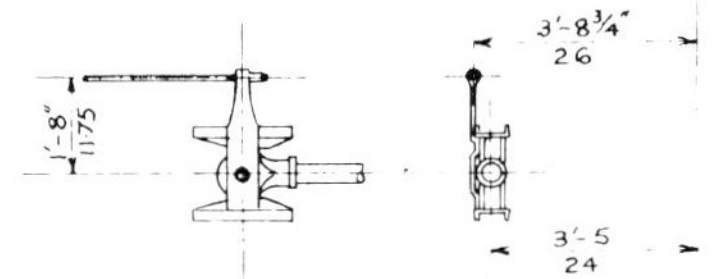

R. H. Crosshead, showing air pump plunger operating arm.

Figure 571

Part plan, showing Running Plate, Hanging Plates (dotted), Reverse Rod, Splashers & Name Plates. Note Hanging Plate joggled inwards to rear at X, and Running Plate widens at Y.

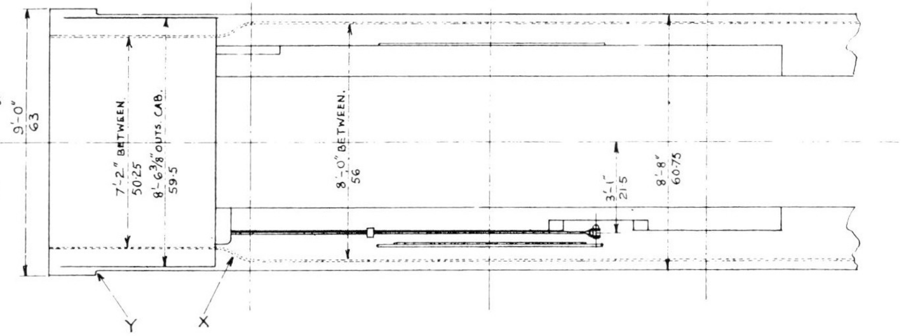

NOTES. L. H. steam pipe cut away in front end view to show rocking shaft cover 'A'. Details marked 'R' & 'L' on right and left sides respectively only. Centre lines 'B' show position of handrail knobs on left side. Dimensions in feet (full size), and in m.m. to nearest ¼m.m. for Gauge '0'. New pattern 4000 gall. tenders are used with this class.

G. W. R.	1000 "COUNTY" CLASS. TYPE 4-6-0.	*Scale 4m.m. = 1foot. Reduced from official drawings.*

This drawing of the '1000' class by Colonel Templer will be useful to modellers. When completed in 1946, Colonel Templer and his colleague Sir Layland-Barratt sent the original to Mr. Hawksworth at Swindon with their signatures and compliments. One unusual feature of these engines was the long single splasher over the driving wheel, and the step just alongside the front left buffer.

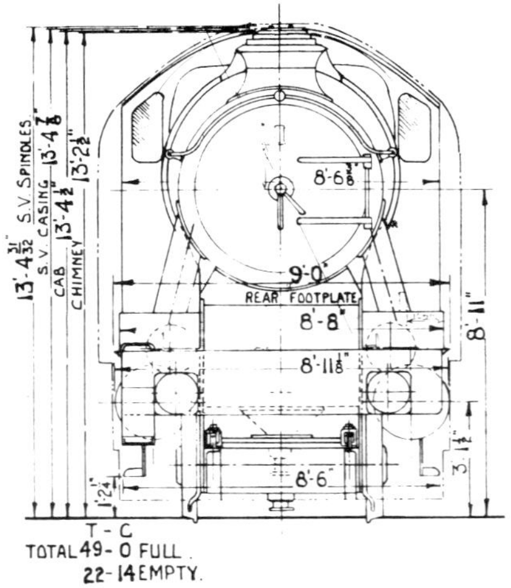

ENGINE & TENDER T - C.
TOTAL WEIGHT FULL. 125-17

1000 CLASS. (1ST ENGINE ONLY.)
TYPE 4-6-0

Figure 572

Figure 573

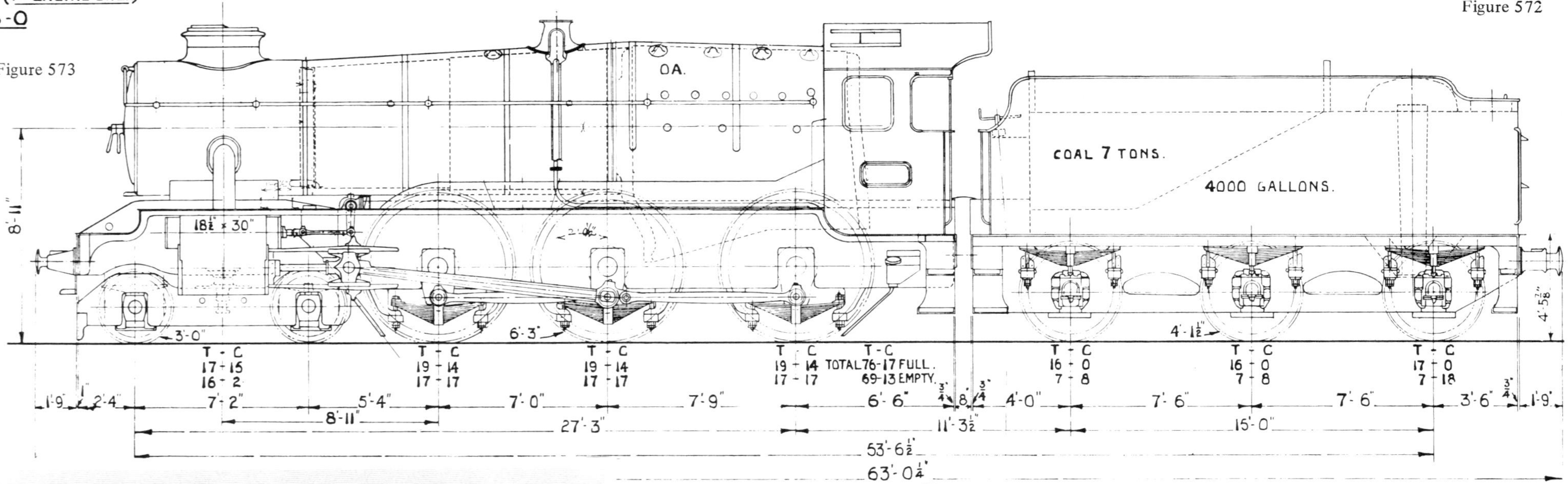

TRACTIVE EFFORT 32580 LBS

Figure 574

The first eighteen engines came out without names, but in March 1946 No. 1000 was given plates *County of Middlesex* and from then on all the rest of the class being built were issued with names of English and Welsh counties. These unnamed engines in service received theirs as they passed through Swindon on overhaul.

Altogether thirty of the class were constructed between 1945 and 1947, but although powerful locomotives, they were not liked by either enginemen or the Engineering Department. The latter disliked them because of the heavy hammer blow effect they had on the track. Classification was Red, commenced in E group, but reduced to D with X which allows a slight overloading.

Figure 572 illustrates *County of Worcester* as she was turned out of Swindon in April 1947, and was the last in the class to be built. The drawing is the official *A.17* and shows the double chimney with which most of these engines were later fitted. *Figure 574* shows No. 1027 in British Rail days.

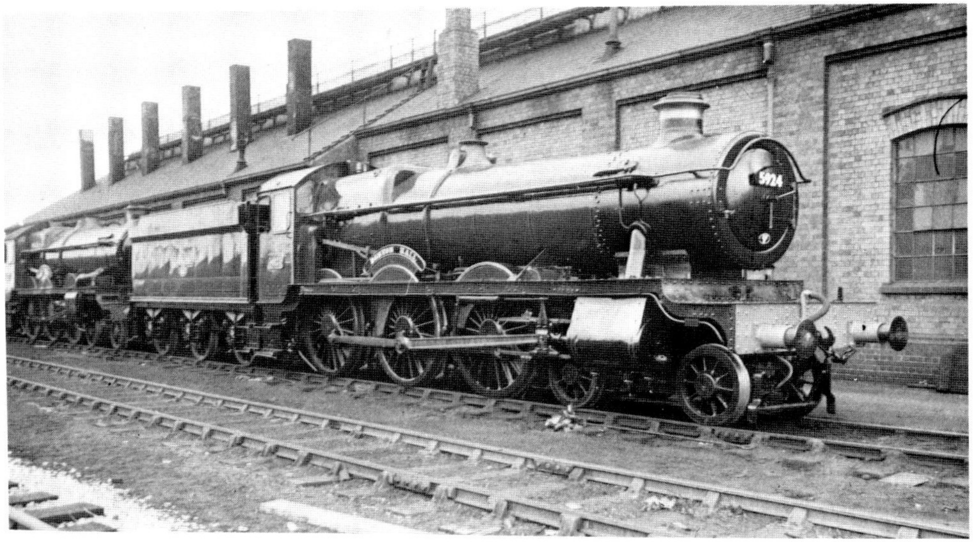

Figure 575

Figure 576

The photographs on this page are included to show the development of the 2-cylinder engines in the last years of the Great Western Railway. *Figure 575* shows No. 5924 *Dinton Hall* at Swindon in 1962, *Figure 576* shows No. 6874 *Haughton Grange* at the same place and date, whilst *Figure 577* shows No. 7808 *Cookham Manor* (now preserved) on S.L.S. duties in 1962 and *County of Warwick* is shown at Paddington in 1948 in *Figure 578.*

Note the differences in the chimneys, but similarity in the general arrangement.

Figure 577

Figure 578

This was Banbury Shed's first 'Modified Hall' and I took this photograph of her standing outside the Gasworks in 1948. Note the plate frames extending to the buffer beam, and the plate framed bogie, with wheelbase increased to 7′ 2″. The 6′ coupled wheels have the filled in web just below the crank pin, and the engine is coupled to the slab-sided flat-bottom tender.

The diagram for this engine was *A.25* seen in *Figure 580*.

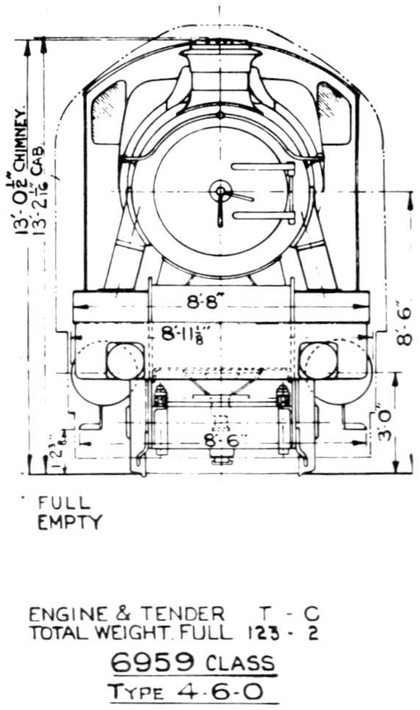

Figure 579

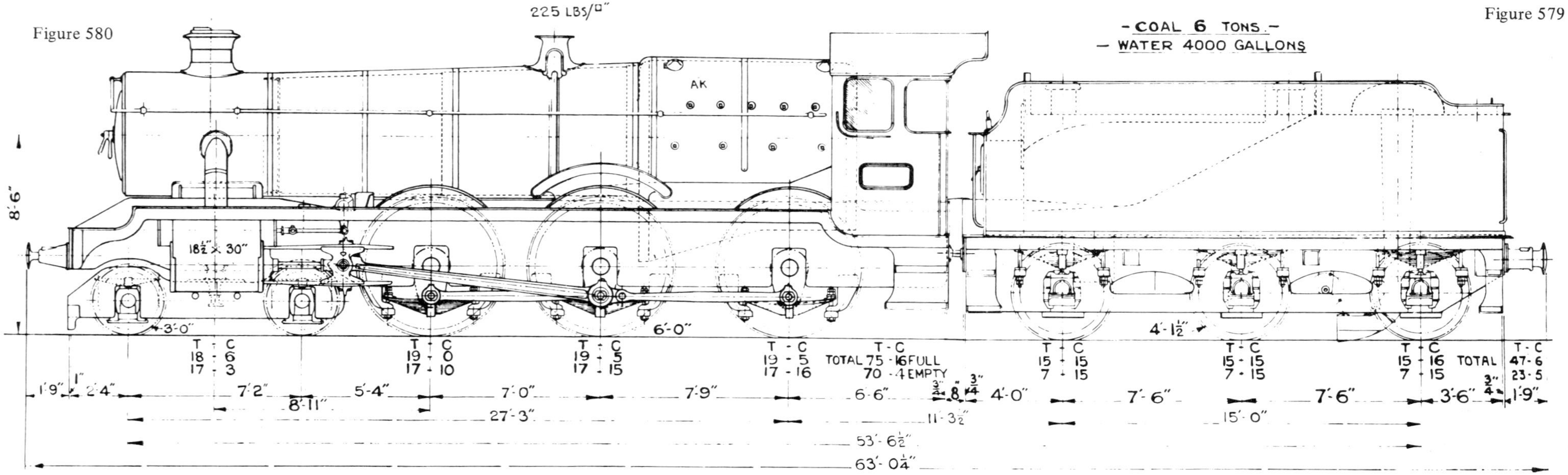

Figure 580

Figure 581

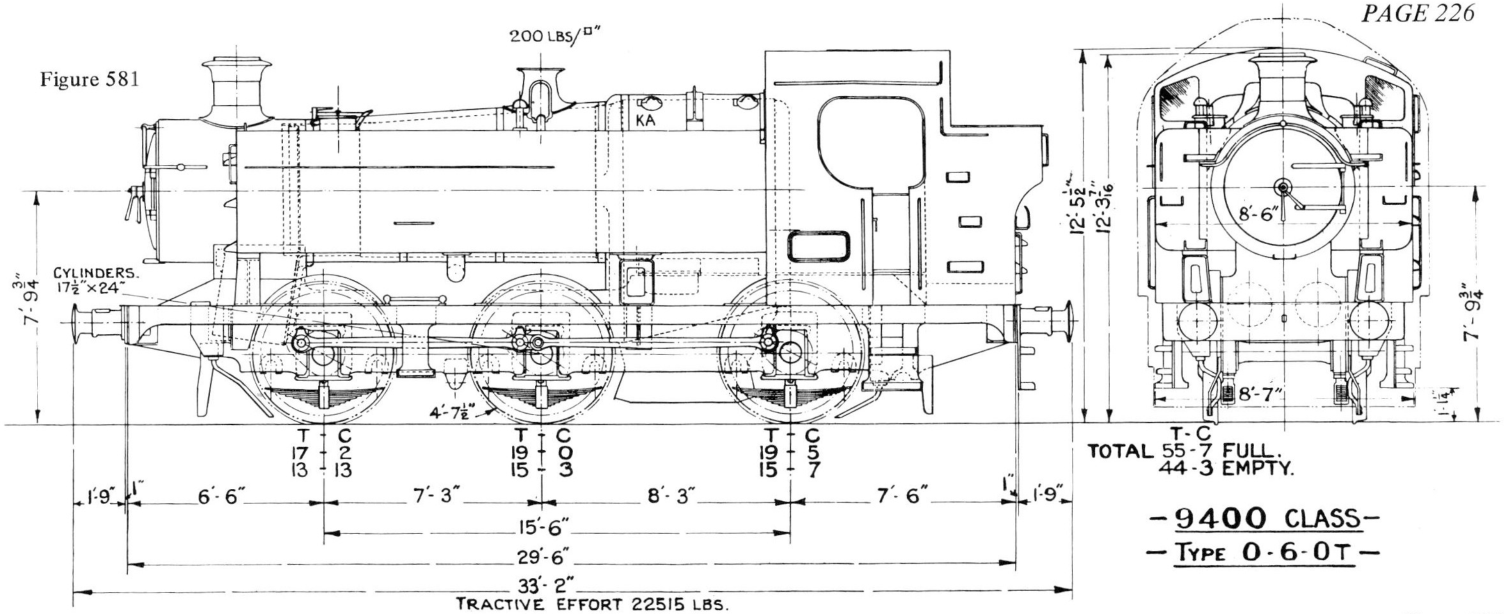

The '9400' class was the tank version of the Collett '2251' 0-6-0 tender engine. Only ten of the series were built by the Great Western at Swindon, but in all 200 were constructed by three outside contractors, namely Messrs. Bagnall, Yorkshire Engine Co., and Robert Stephenson & Co. It is odd to think that Stephenson's built the first locomotives for the Great Western in 1835 and here they were building the last Great Western design in 1950.

The numbers ran thus.

No. 9400-9	built by	Great Western at Swindon Lot	365	1947
No. 9410-59	”	R. Stephenson	382	1950-1
No. 9460-89	”	R. Stephenson	383	1950-3
No. 8400-49	”	Bagnall & Co.	384	1949-54
No. 8450-79	”	Yorkshire Engine Co.	385	1949-52
No. 8480-99	”	R. Stephenson	386	1952
No. 9490-99	”	Yorkshire Engine Co.	387	1954-5
No. 3400-9	”	Yorkshire Engine Co.	387	1955-56

Figure 581 shows the Swindon *Diagram B.78*

Figure 582

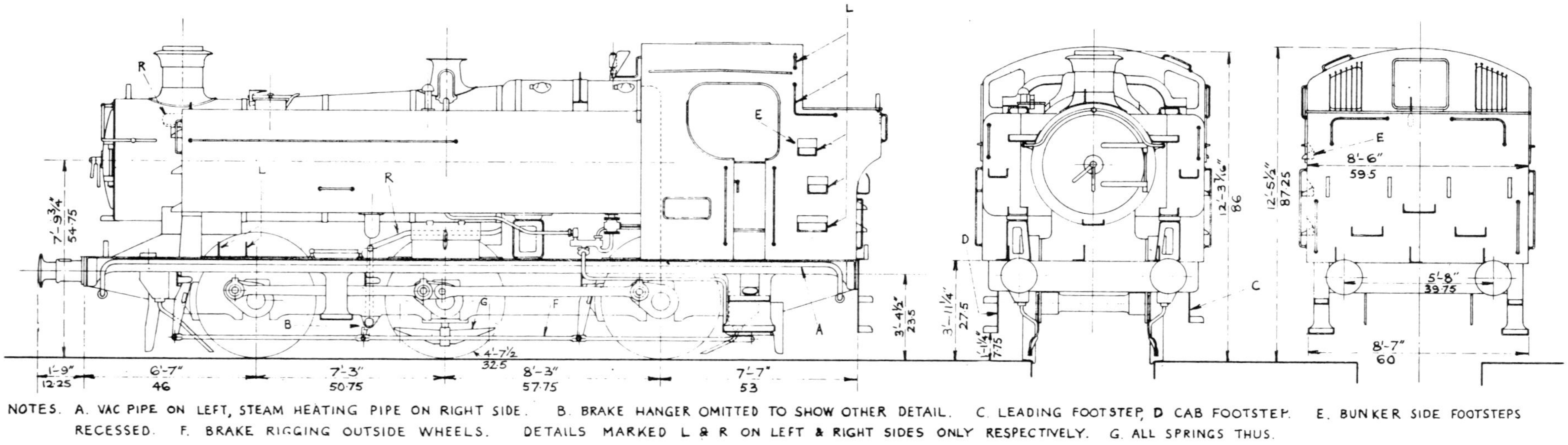

Figure 583

Figure 584

The final Colonel Templer drawing on this page gives the dimensions in feet and inches for the full size engine and in millimetres for 7m/m scale modellers. Back and front elevations are shown, which gives most of the necessary detail and measurements. In *Figure 584* No. 9409 is seen in the official photograph of the class, before being allocated to London duties. Note the 'PDN' on the motion step, an indication that the home shed was Paddington (Old Oak Common). There were no more Great Western *built* locomotives, but two more of Great Western *design* should be mentioned.

Ten engines, built in 1949 on Swindon *Lot No. 373* were different to any design seen beforehand. They were 0-6-0 tank engines, similar above the running plate to the '94XX' class, but below they had outside cylinders, with Walschaerts valve gear driving piston valves, no running platforms and a lot of welding together of parts instead of rivets. The wheelbase was very short being a total of 12′ 10″ so that the engines could negotiate curves of 3½ chains.

Most of their work was done on the Paddington carriage shunting, to and from Old Oak Common yard. Diagram was *B.80* as seen in *Figure 586*. This particular engine has been successfully modelled in 5″ gauge live steam by many people. Nicknamed 'Speedy' it performs as well in model size as it did in the full size locomotive.

Figure 585

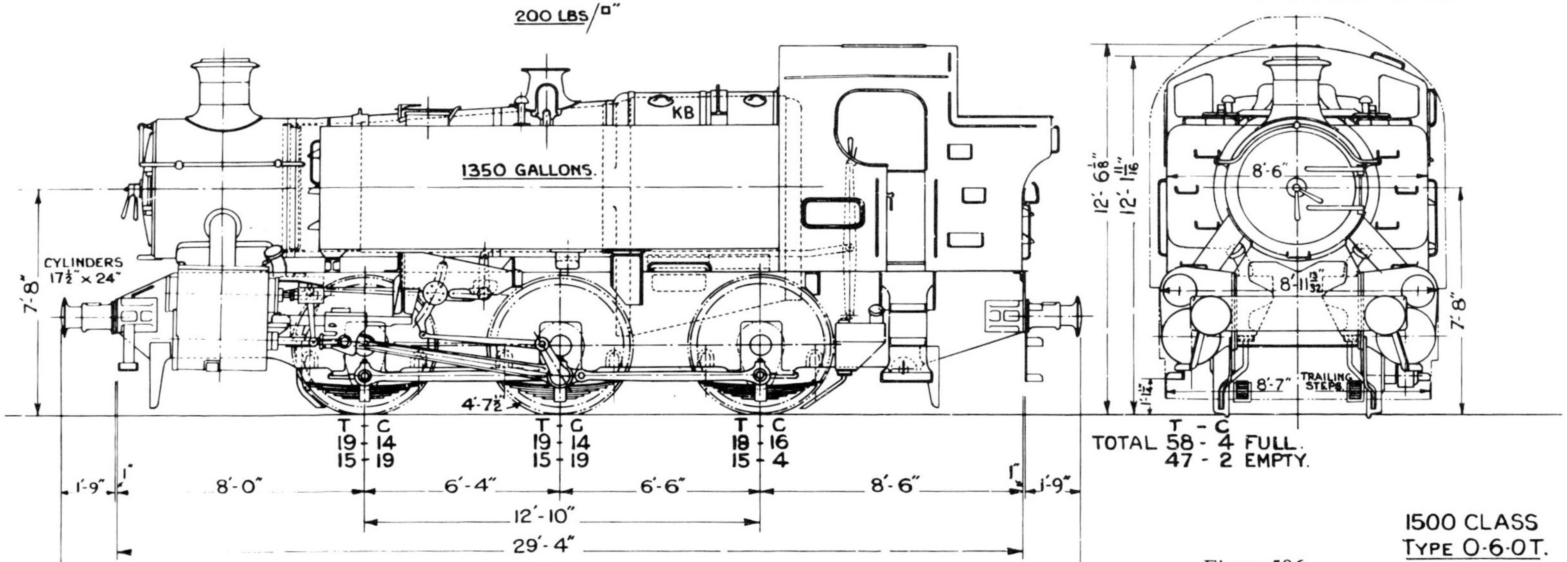

Figure 586

Figure 587

Figure 588

These were interesting little engines, but with a comparatively short life. In 1962, I saw a few on their way to be withdrawn. However, should any modeller be tempted, I include this excellent official shot of the valve gear on the '1500' class (*Figure 588*).

Power group was 'C' and the route colour was red, as there was more than 19½ tons on the two leading axles.

The boiler was the Standard No. 10 KB Group 23 and wheelbases 6′ 4″ + 6′ 6″, wheels 4′ 7½″ diameter.

Figure 589

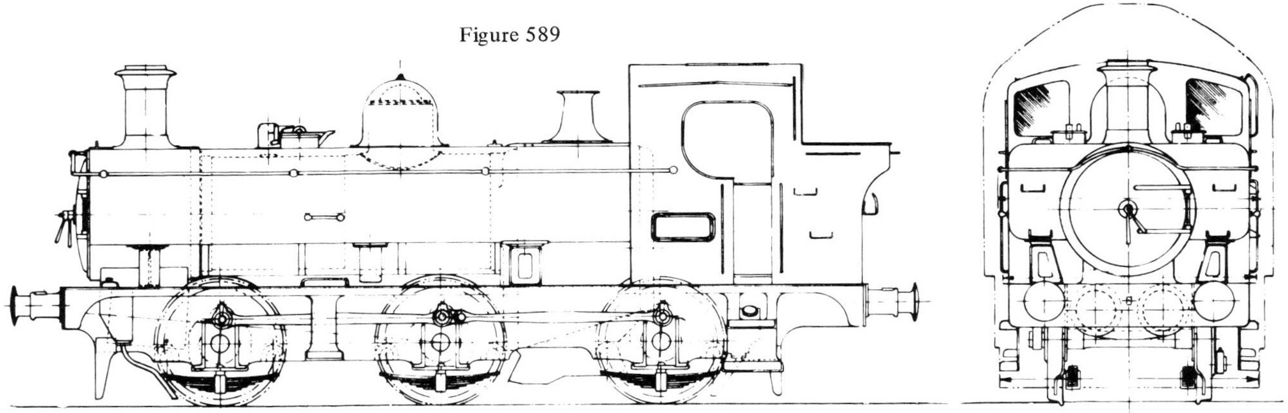

Figure 590

Figure 591

Figure 592

The last engine class to be illustrated is the '1600' class, a direct descendent of the old '2021' class of 1901.

Seventy of these little 0-6-0 pannier tanks were built in British Rail ownership, but the style is pure Great Western and indeed represents the last independent Great Western design, and was it pure chance that they were numbered in the same serials as the Swindon '1134' class of 0-6-0T's of 1874-81? They were quite small locomotives, having 4′ 1½″ diameter driving wheels, and a Standard No. 16 boiler. The height was kept to a minimum, which made them available for routes with low clearances, and as there was less than 14 tons on any axle, they were of the uncoloured class. The photographs here show No. 1604 top left, No. 1634 top right, and No. 1609 in the official photograph below. The diagram was *B.80* and is seen in *Figure 589*.

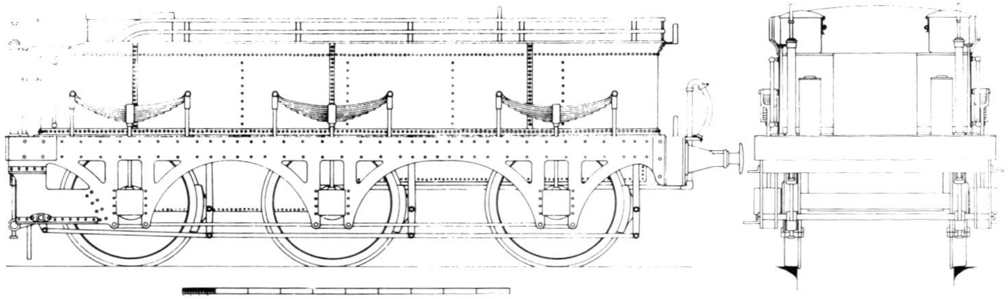

Figure 593

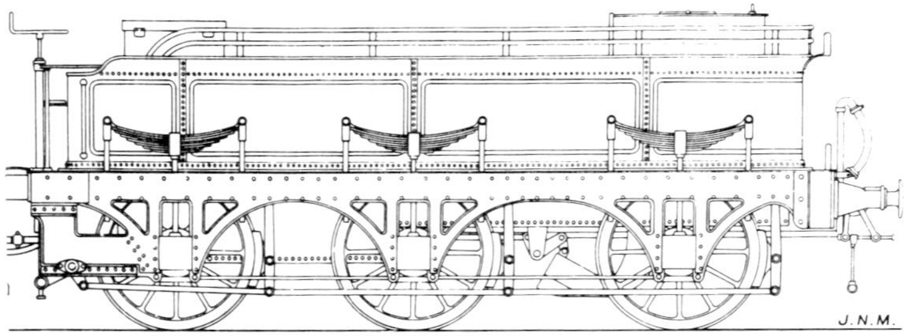

Figure 594

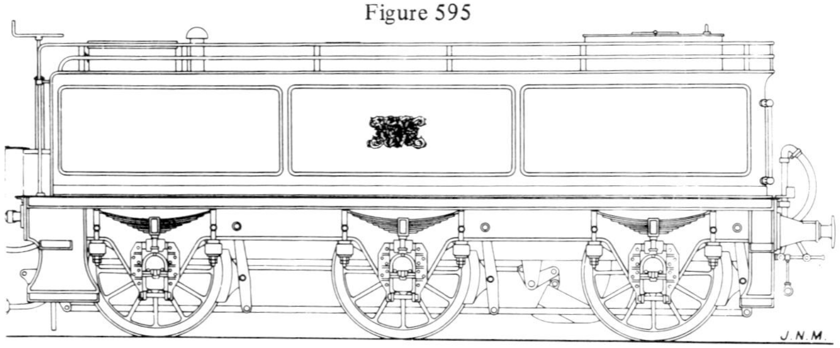

Figure 595

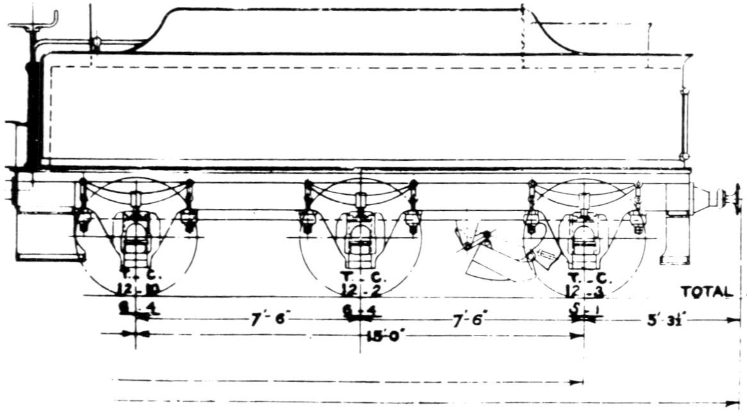

Figure 596

Over the years, not only did the engines themselves enlarge, develop and change, but so did the vehicles which were coupled to them for the purpose of carrying water and coal. Therefore the next few pages are devoted to illustrating some of the varying designs of tenders.

On this page, *Figure 593,* is shown the early 1880 type of tender with no water pick-up arrangement and in *Figure 594* the similar vehicle fitted with the scoop.

Figure 595 shows the 1890 tender as fitted to the 'Singles' and engines at the turn of the century. Next in *Figure 596* is the modification showing side plates instead of coal rails, and having separate filler and water dome.

The tiny tender in *Figure 597* was made especially for the restricted turntables in the West Country, and has a very short wheelbase. *Figure 598* shows the Churchward 3500 gallon tender with the dome and filler having a gap between them. *Figure 599* is a Midland and South Western Junction tender which came with the absorbed engines from that line, and lower right is one of the Robinson design R.O.D. tenders which ran with first the '30XX' class 2-8-0's, and later with some 'Aberdares' (*Figure 600*).

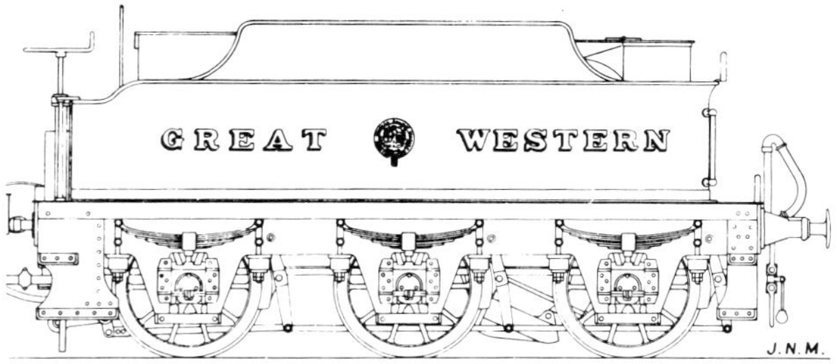

Figure 597

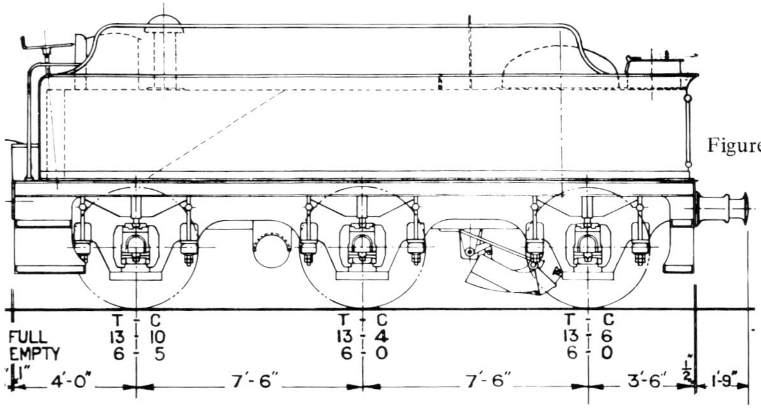

Figure 598

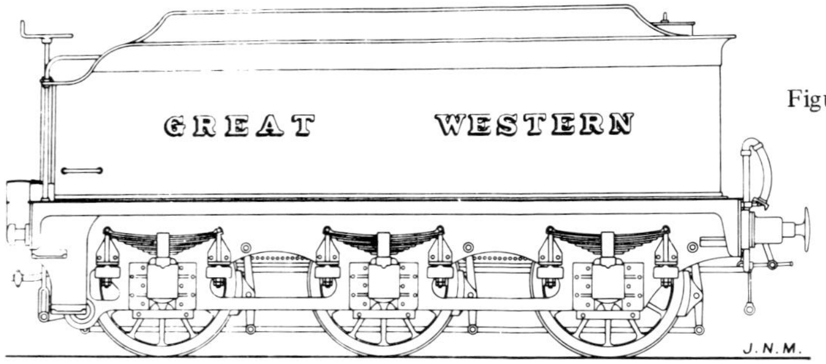

Figure 599

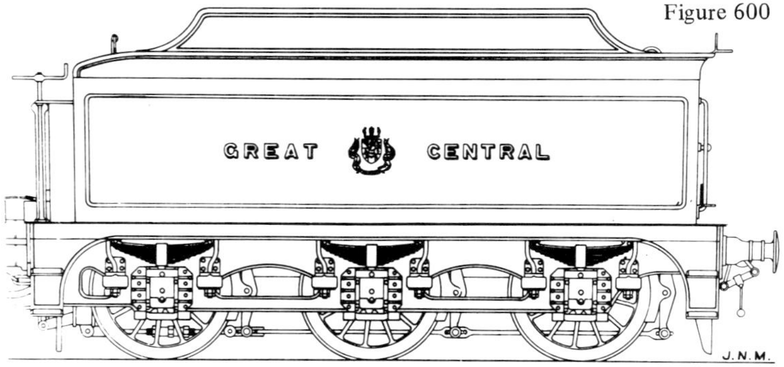

Figure 600

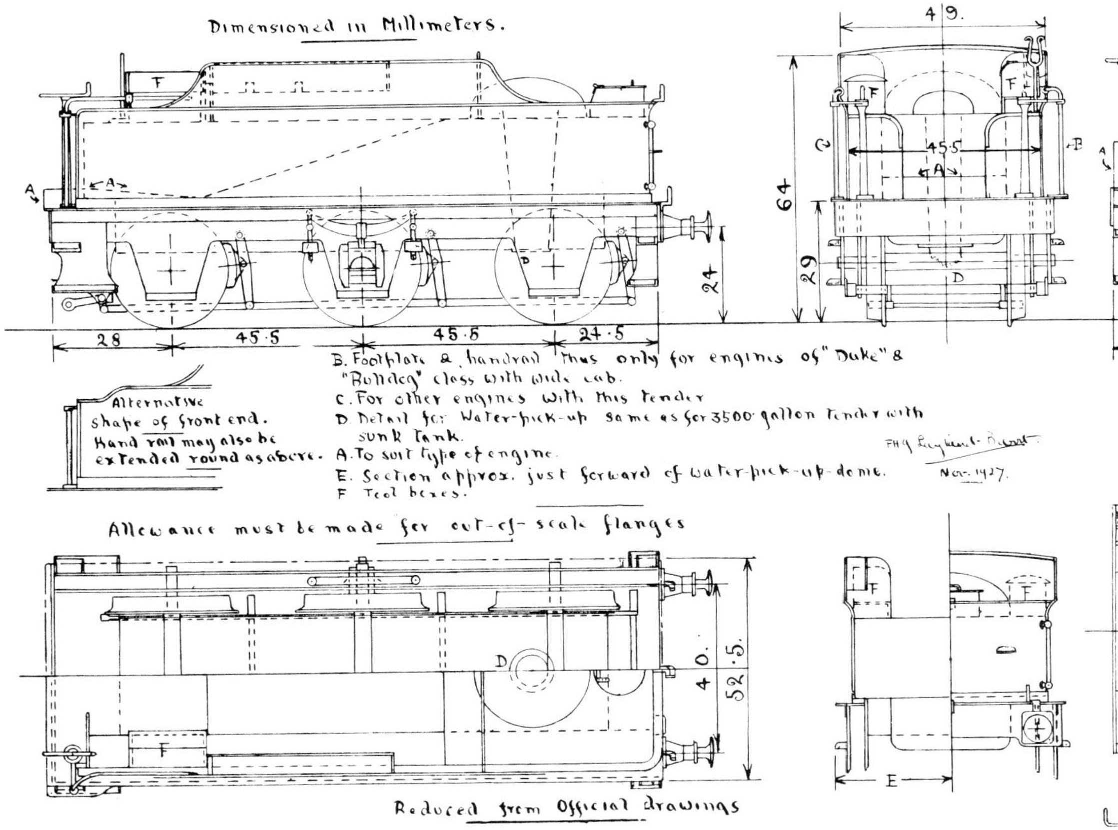

Figure 601

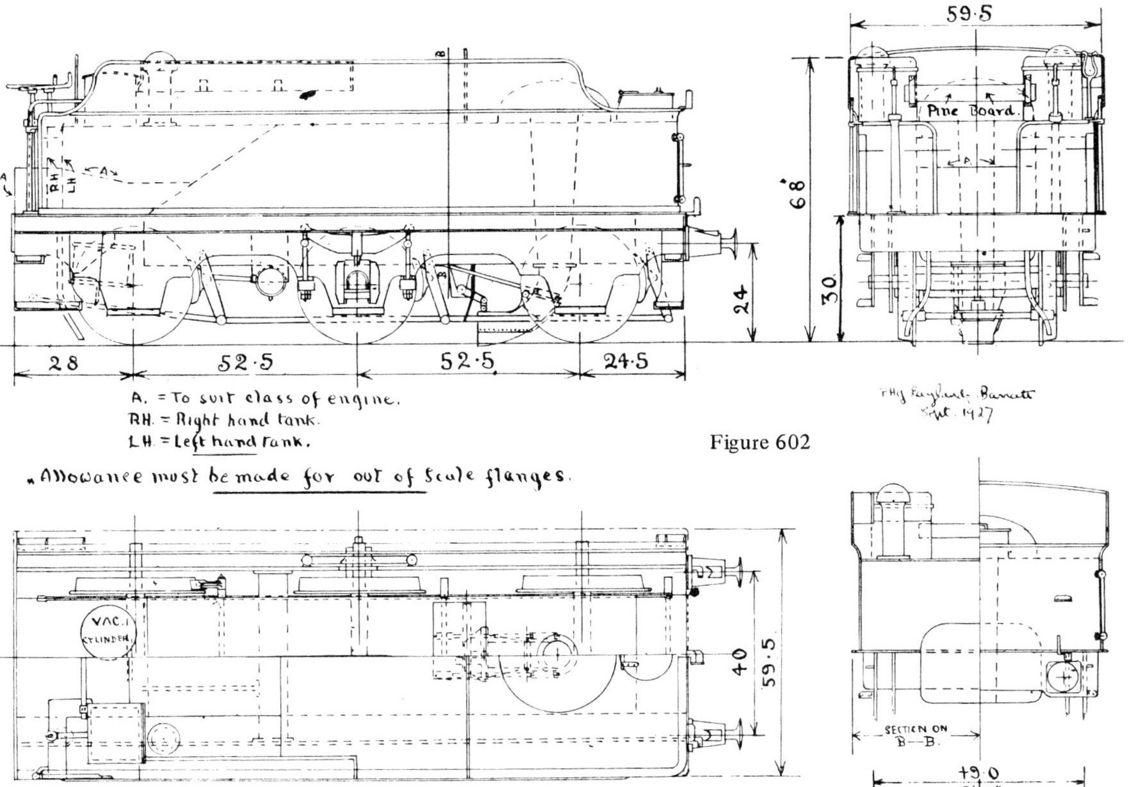

Figure 602

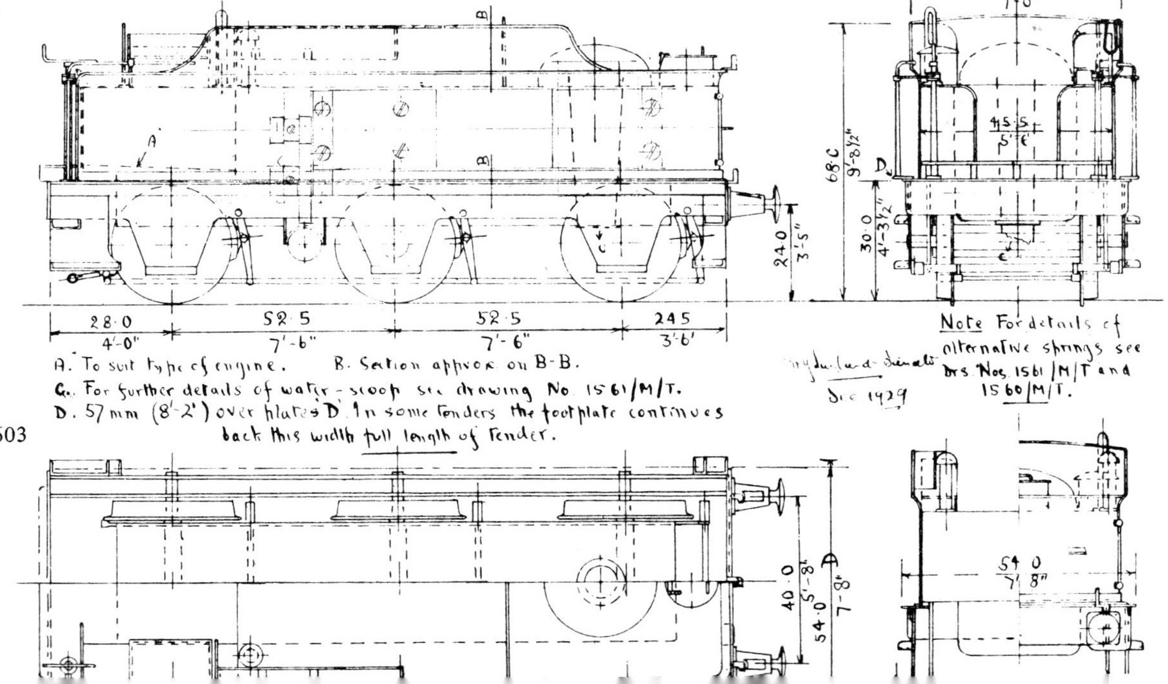

Figure 603

Three drawings of the Standard Great Western tenders especially for modellers drawn by Layland-Barratt in 1927. On the left the 3000 gallon short wheelbase pattern, and bottom right the 3500 gallon larger design as attached to the '43XX' class etc. In *Figure 602* is seen the Collett tender as used on the '2251' class.

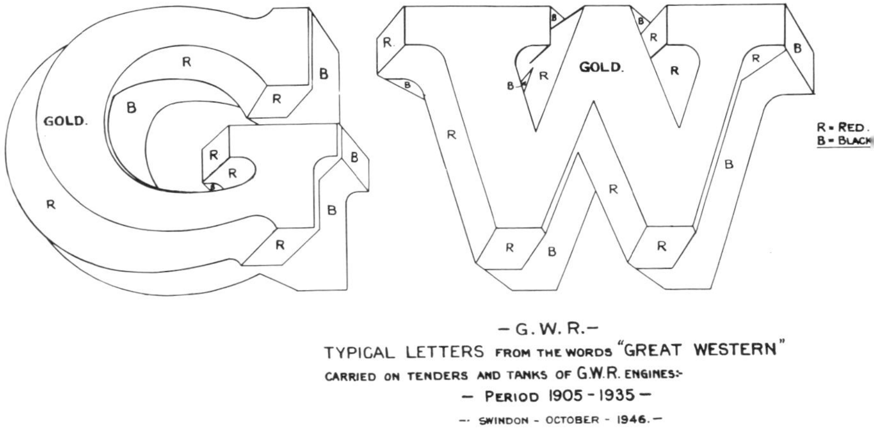

One of the largest passenger tenders is shown on this page, again by Sir Layland-Barratt, drawn as long ago as 1929. It is reproduced to 4m/m scale but the dimensions are for 7m/m scale.

Figure 604 shows this large 4000 gallon tender fitted to 'Kings', 'Castles', etc. from a high viewpoint and many hidden details are revealed.

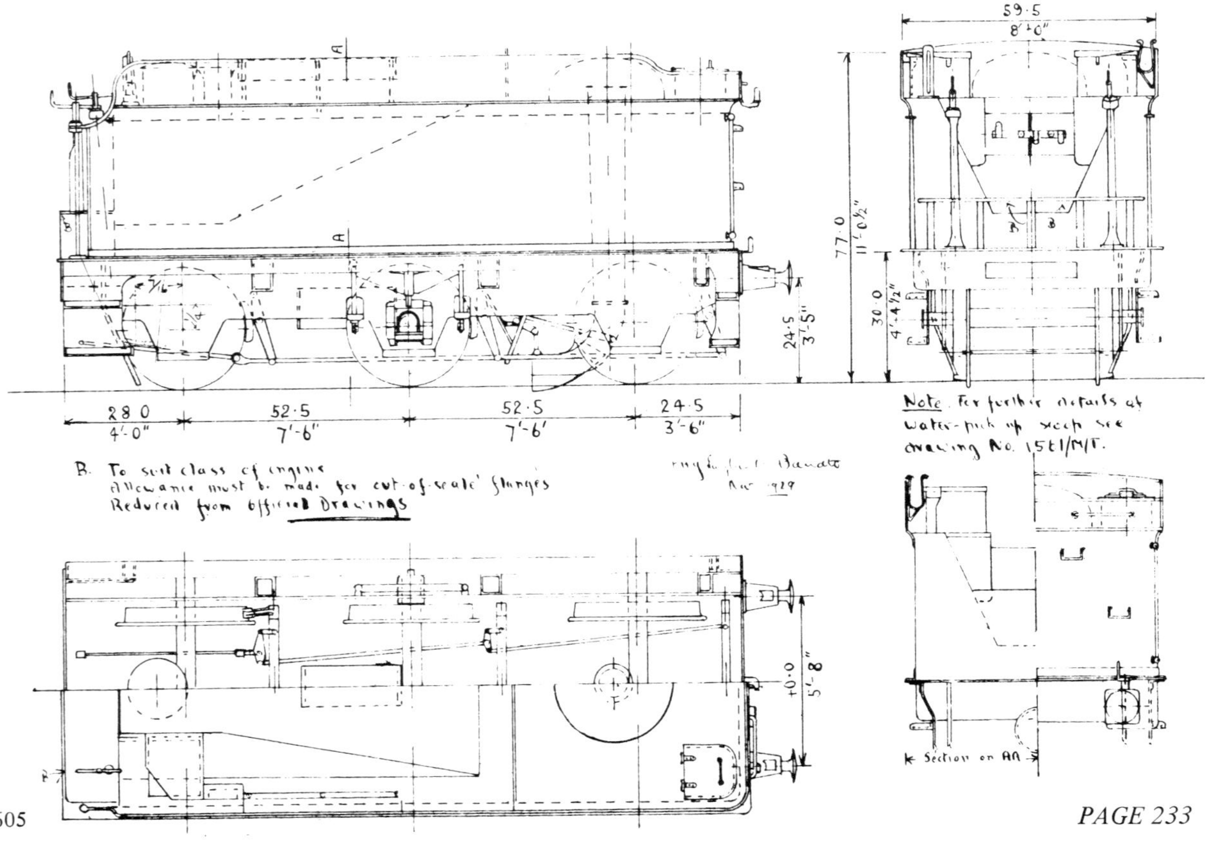

Figure 605

Figure 606

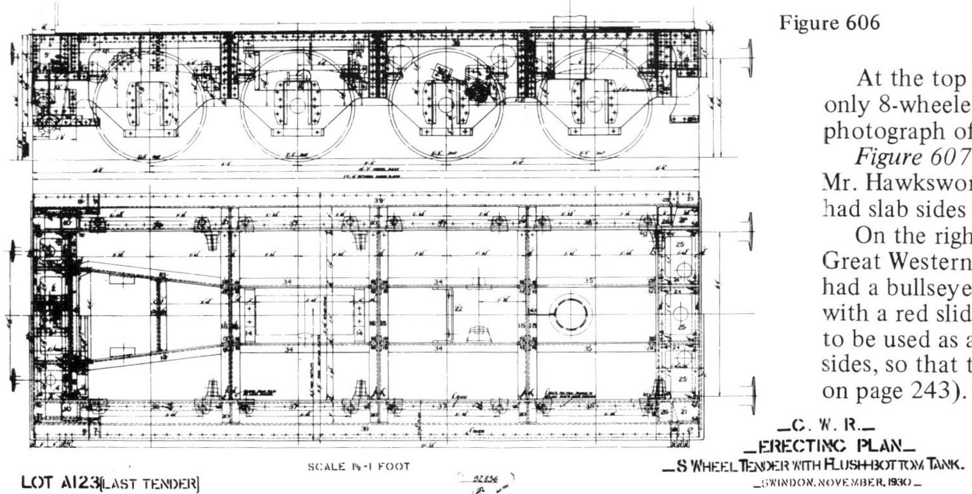

At the top left (*Figure 606*) is shown the frame plan of the only 8-wheeled tender, designed in 1930, and bottom right a photograph of this vehicle.

Figure 607 is the last tender to be designed at Swindon by Mr. Hawksworth in 1945 for the 'County' class. This vehicle had slab sides and a flat bottom.

On the right is a small picture which might prove of use, a Great Western locomotive headlamp, for modellers. This lamp had a bullseye in front and at the rear, both being white but with a red slide which could be slipped in to enable the lamp to be used as a rear light. Flat sockets were affixed on both sides, so that the lamp could be turned around (see drawing on page 243).

Figure 608

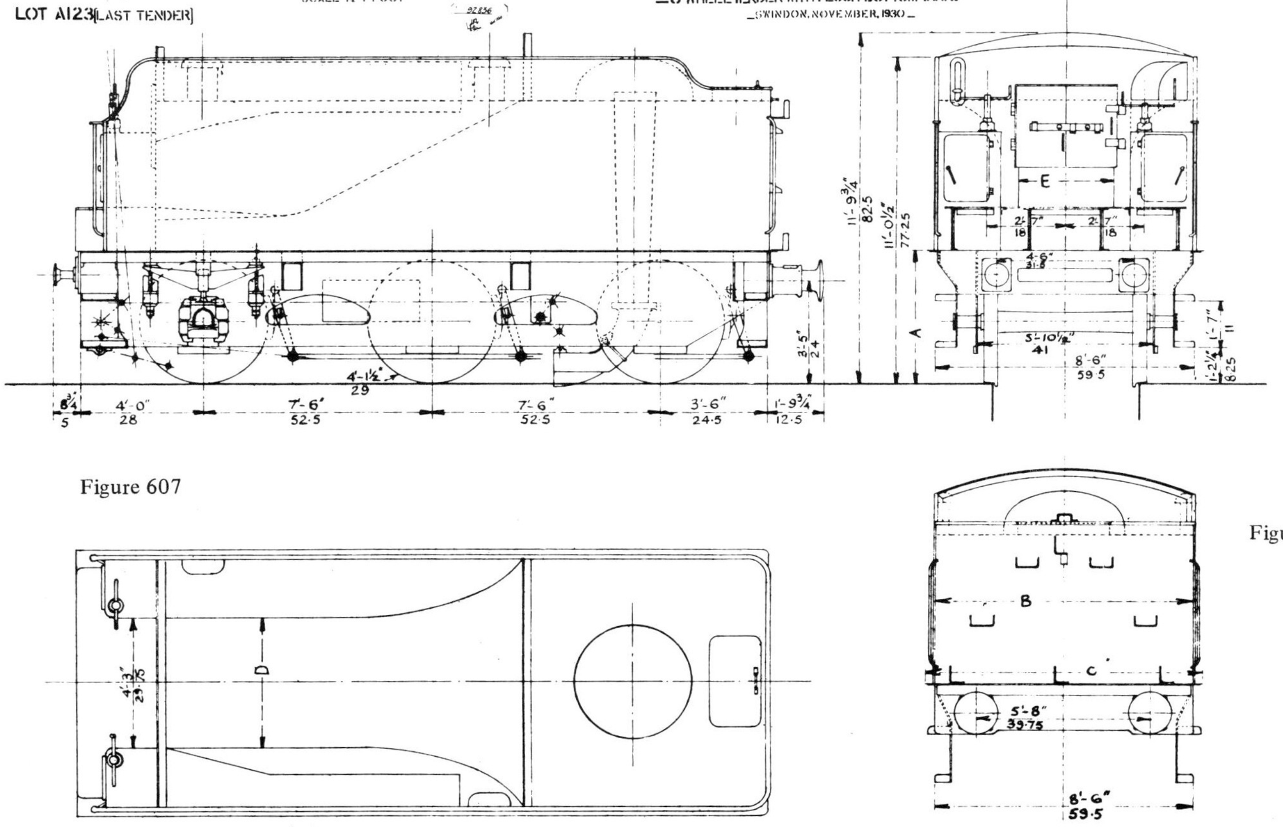

Figure 607

NOTE. THIS TENDER WAS FIRST DESIGNED FOR THE 1000 CLASS, AND DESIGN WAS LATER MODIFIED TO SUIT THE "CASTLE" CLASS. THE IMPORTANT DIMENSIONAL DIFFERENCES BETWEEN THE TWO TYPES ARE TABULATED BELOW. DIMENSIONS IN BRACKETS ARE M.M. FOR GAUGE "O".

TENDER FOR	A	B	C	D	E
1000 CLASS	4'-5⅜" (31.5)	8'-6" (59.5)	9'-0 (63)	4'-3" (29.75)	3'-2" (22.25)
"CASTLE" CLASS.	4'-4½" (30.75)	8'-0 (56)	8'-8" (60.75)	3'-9" (26.25)	2'-9" (17.25)

Figure 609

Figure 610

Figure 611

Figure 612

A page of tender details. On the left (*Figure 610*) is the rear view of the 'Hawksworth' 4000 gallon tender in all its stark severity. Top right is a Great Western water scoop, and lower right a tender axlebox and vacuum reservoir (*Figure 612*).

Figure 613

Figure 614

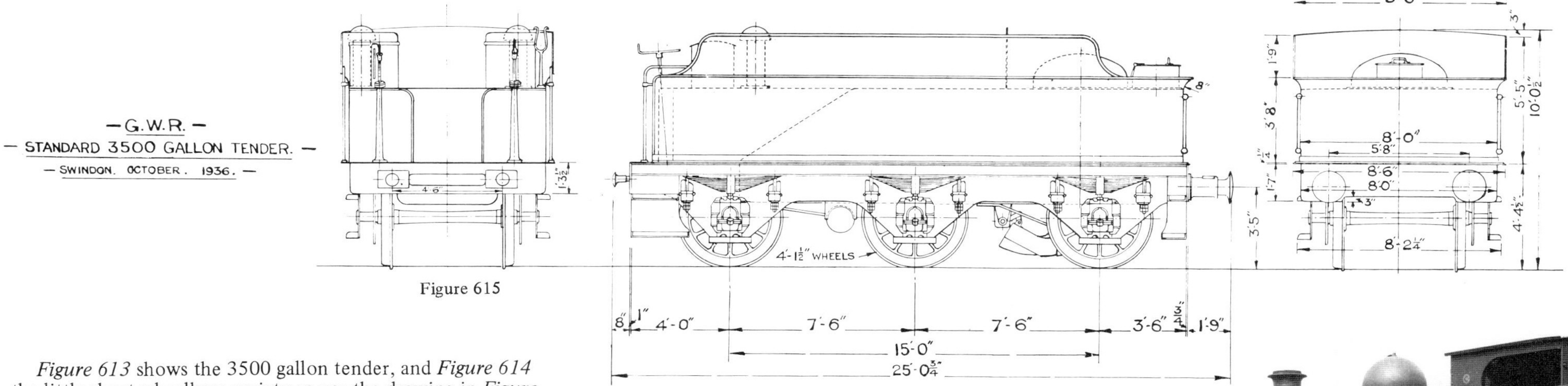

Figure 615

Figure 616

Figure 613 shows the 3500 gallon tender, and *Figure 614* the little short wheelbase variety as per the drawing in *Figure 597*. (The late Mike Longridge can be seen at top right.) In *Figure 615* the 3500 gallon tender used behind the '2251' class, this had the extra long coal rails, and was designed by Mr. Collett.

Also I include a picture showing what happens to old tenders when taken off their engines. Some were adapted for use to carry poison, which could then be sprayed on to the track whilst the train is in motion. *Figure 616* shows a weed killing train at Taunton in 1937.

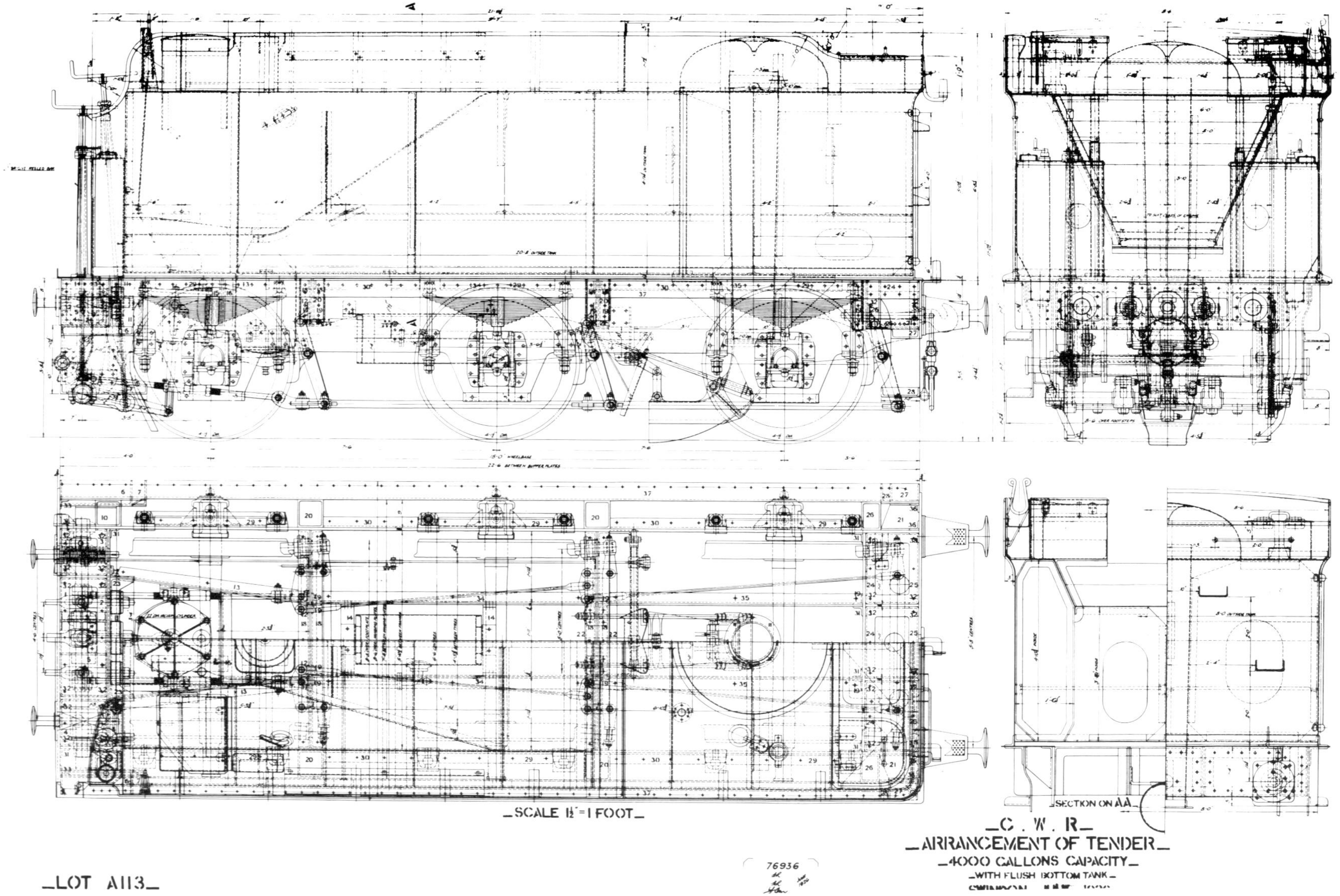

Figure 617

A 'general arrangement' drawing of the first pattern of 4000 gallon tender made at Swindon in July of 1926. This was the prototype of the Collett designed high-sided vehicle, made for the express passenger engines, giving them a greater range than the much smaller Churchward type. Not that this original pattern had sand boxes with pipes leading to the two front wheels.

All four of these last drawings are reproduced to 7mm scale, not only for the benefit of 'O' gauge modellers, but to enable readers decipher the very small dimensions which appear on the full-size Swindon plan. For reference see photograph on page 168.

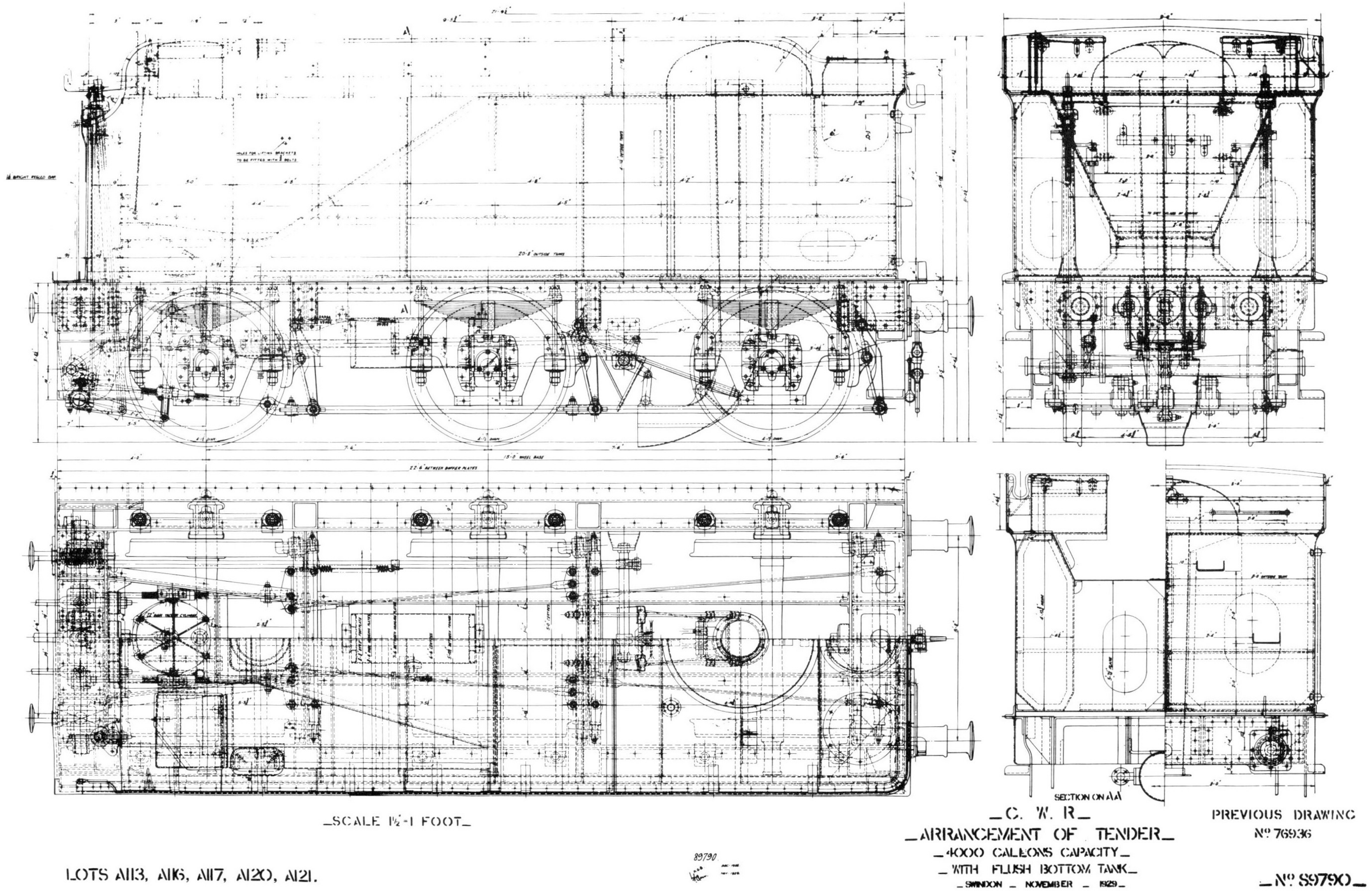

Figure 618

Dated November 1929, this drawing is the development of the large 4000 gallon tender. It will be seen that although very similar to drawing No. 76936, there are many changes, the sanding apparatus has gone, parallel buffers have taken the place of the taper-shanked ones, hand-brake and scoop crank handles are on the same level, and the fire-iron retainers are now recessed into the sides instead of being above the coal rails. (For reference see photograph in *Figure 565*.)

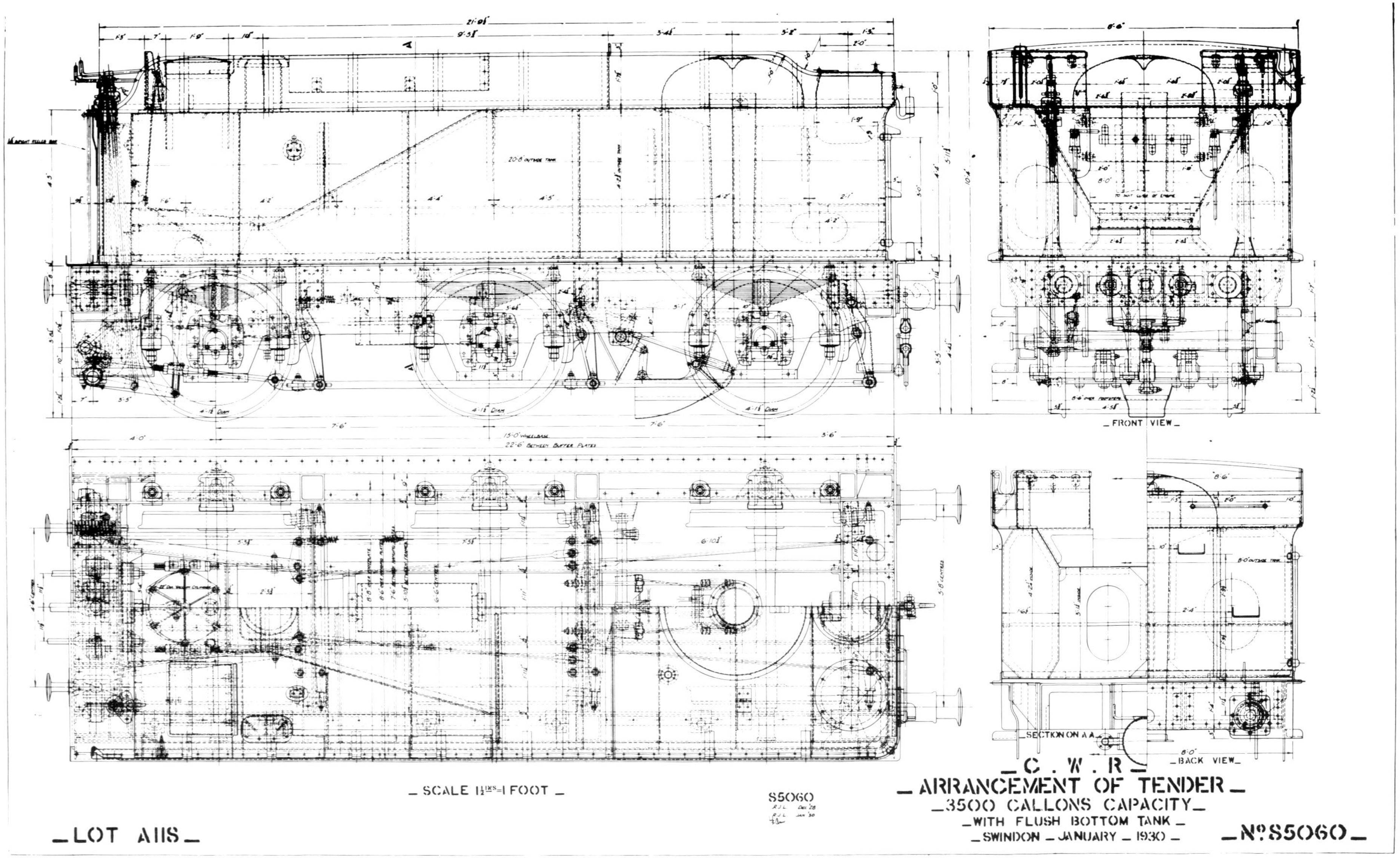

Figure 619

Although at first glance, this tender is identical to that on the previous page, it is in fact only of 3500 gallon capacity against the 4000 type, and consequently smaller. The sides are much lower in this design, being 7″ less in height than that in drawing 89790. (For reference see photograph in *Figure 576.*)

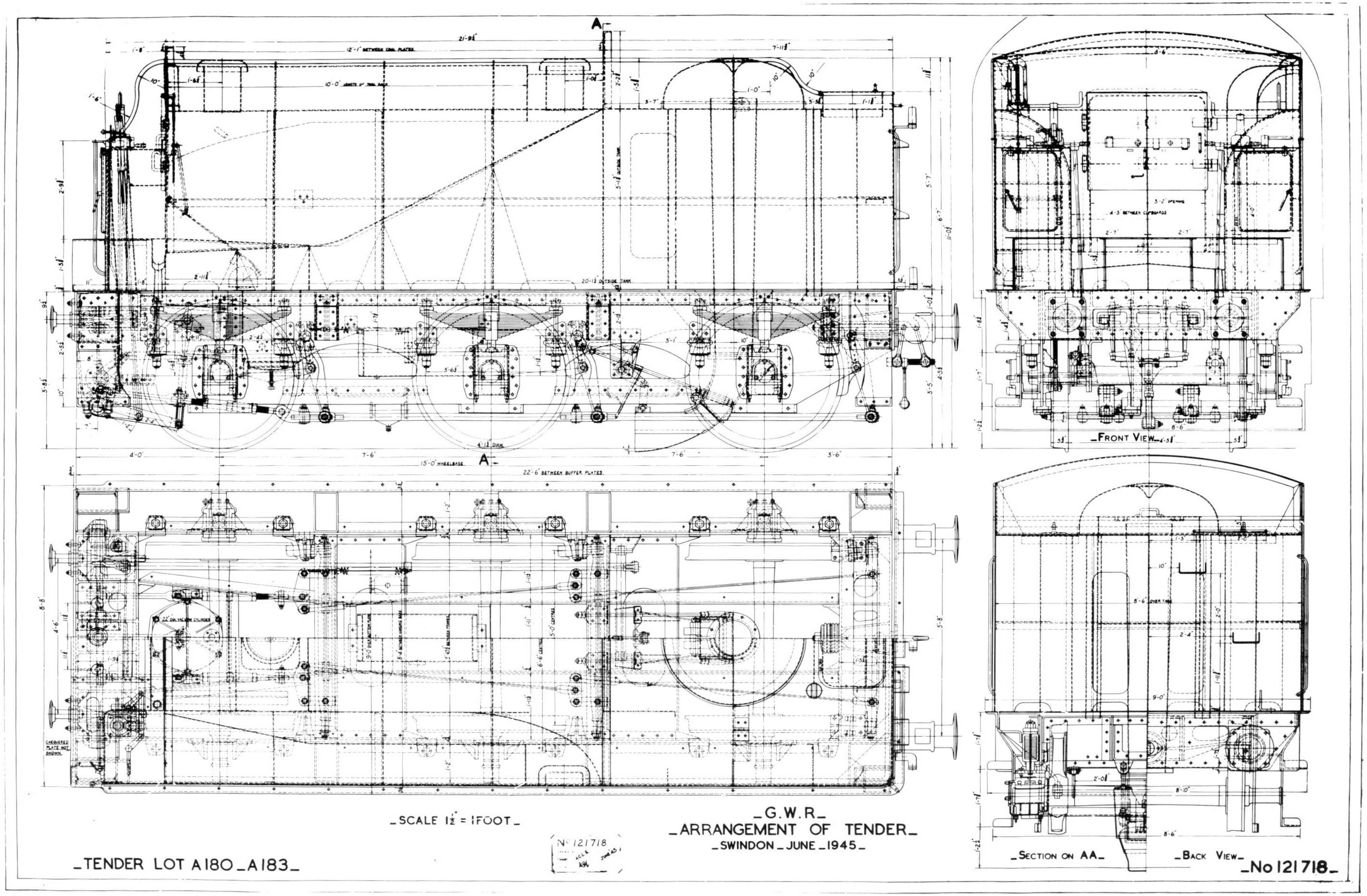

Figure 620

Finally this design of Mr. Hawksworth, dated 1945, is the style first used on the 'County' Class, '1000' series of 4-6-0. 2-cylinder passenger engines. It can be noticed that not only has this vehicle flat sides and rear, but also the framing is much changed, being deeper, with holes cut out between the horn guides. There are also coal gates at the cab end, and a locker is provided on each side of the footplate. (For reference see photograph on page 150 and 221.)

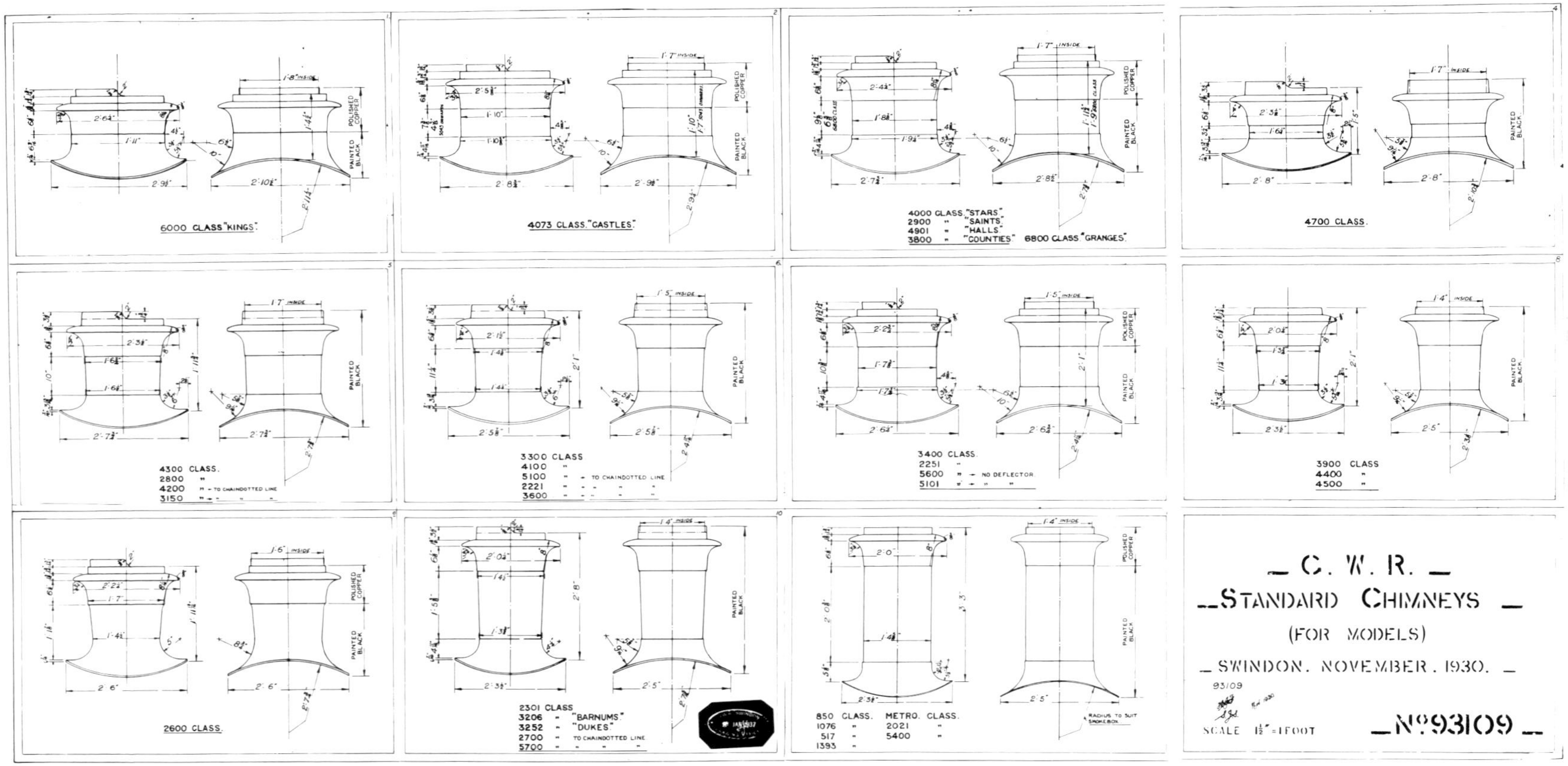

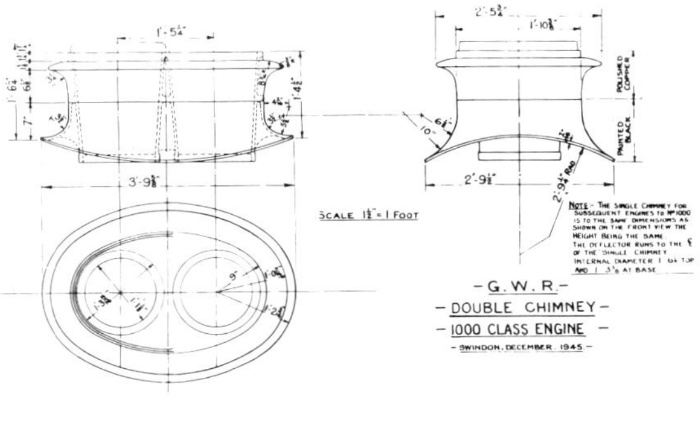

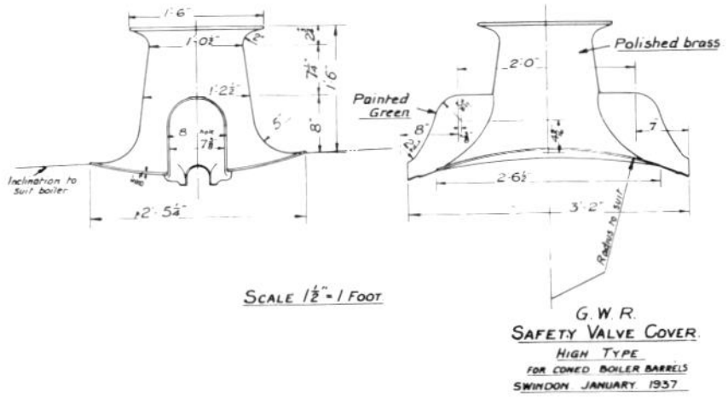

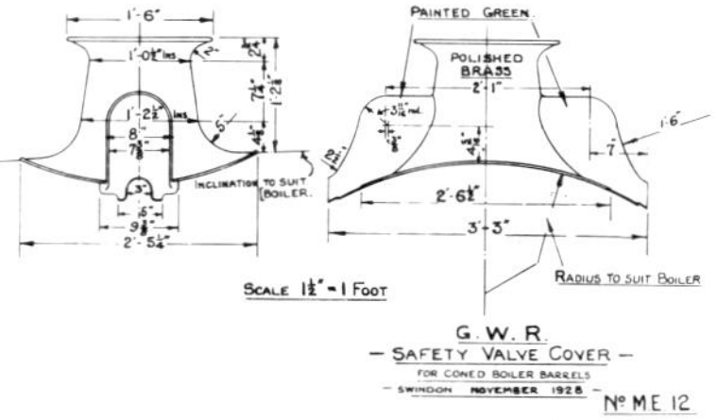

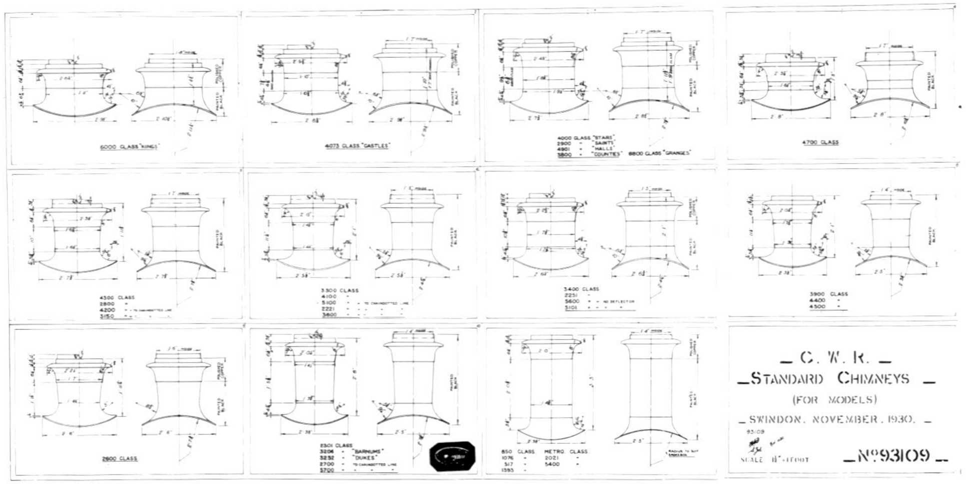

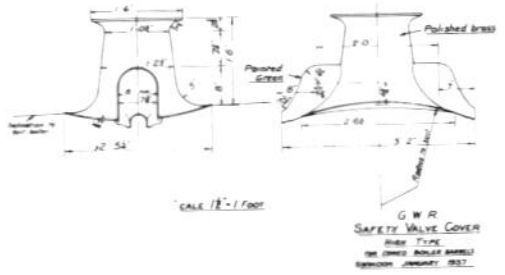

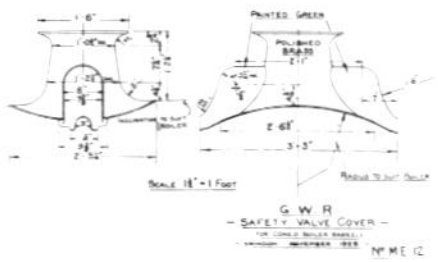

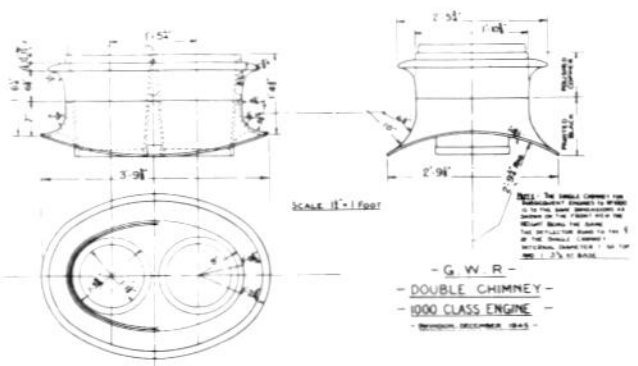

A page of Great Western pattern chimneys and safety valves shown in two scales. These were specially prepared for model makers by Swindon drawing office in 1930, and shows most of the standard classes of boiler mountings. They are illustrated here in 7m/m scale and 4m/m scale, not only for the benefit of the modeller, but because in the smaller gauge the dimensions are too small to decipher.

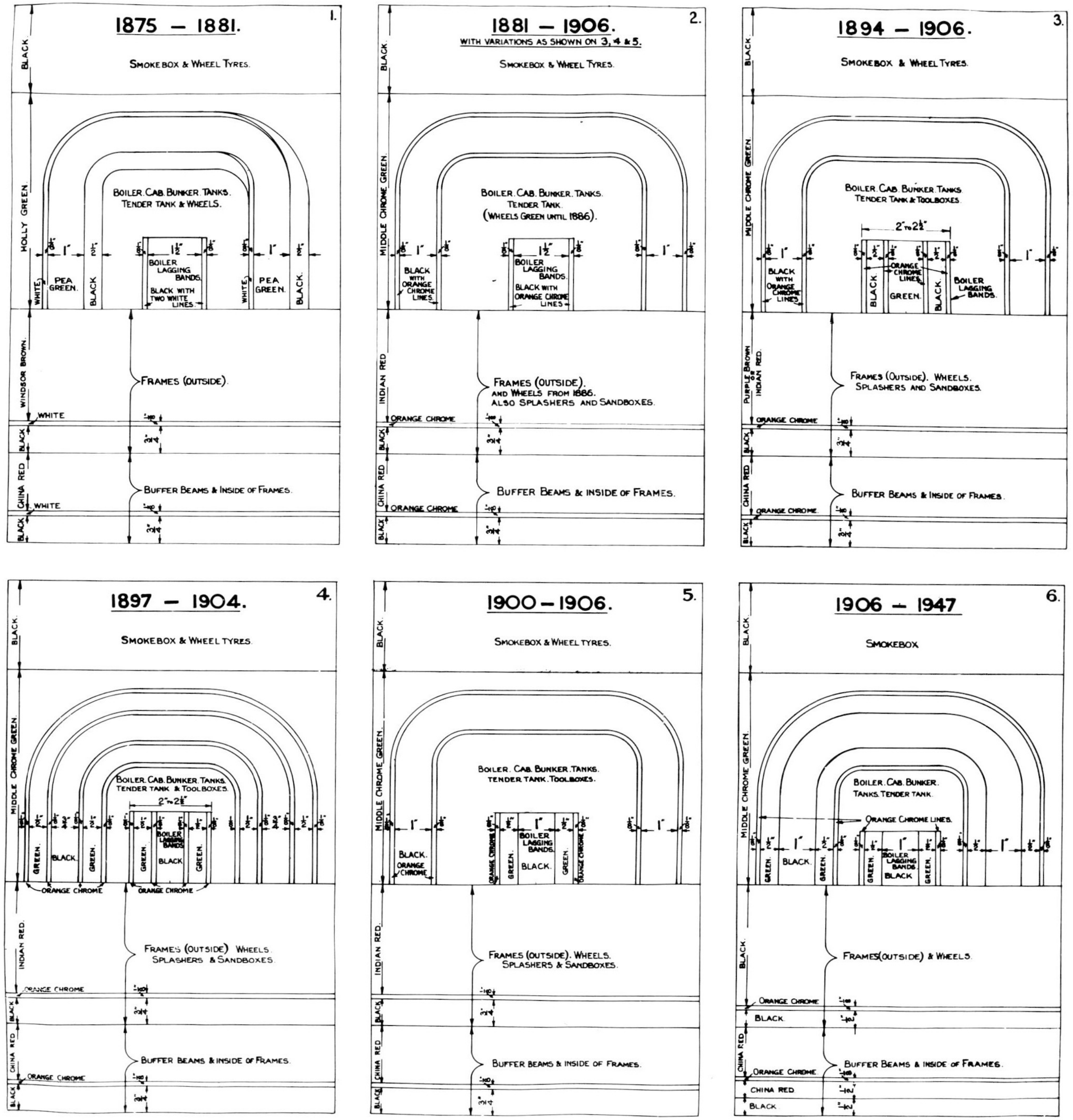

METHOD OF PAINTING GREAT WESTERN RAILWAY LOCOMOTIVES. Nº 97520A
SWINDON - JANUARY - 1954.

Last of all, a drawing in six parts, showing the painting of Great Western locomotives from 1875 to 1947, according to Swindon Paint Shop at 1954. This diagram is reduced from a large 20" x 30" sheet, and much of the lettering is of necessity very small, and an enlarged version of plans 1, 2, & 6, which was drawn in 1936, can be found on the last pages of Part 1 of this work. Note that wheels over the years have been, in turn, holly green, Indian red, and finally black!

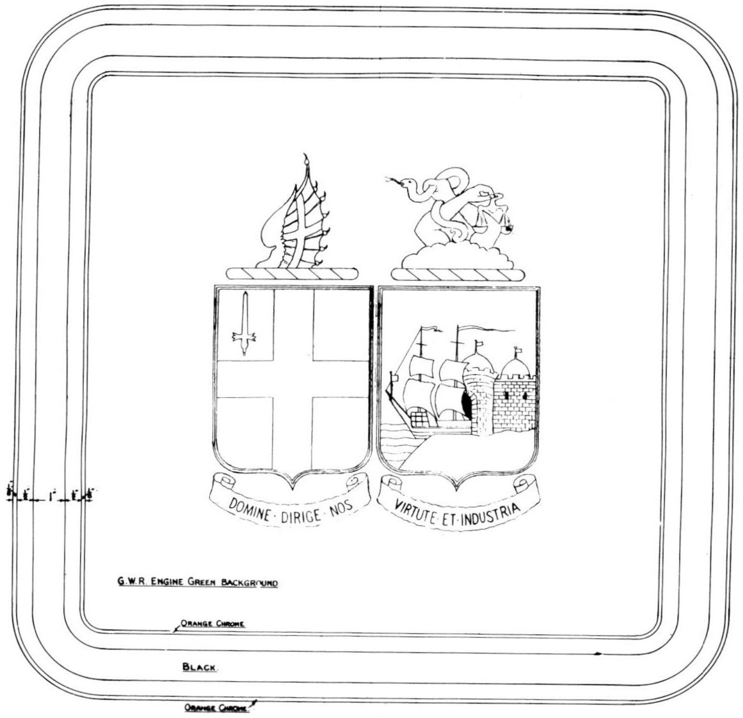

A drawing of the mock-up 'example' panel used by Swindon works to show lining and crests for Great Western tenders.

Bits and Pieces!

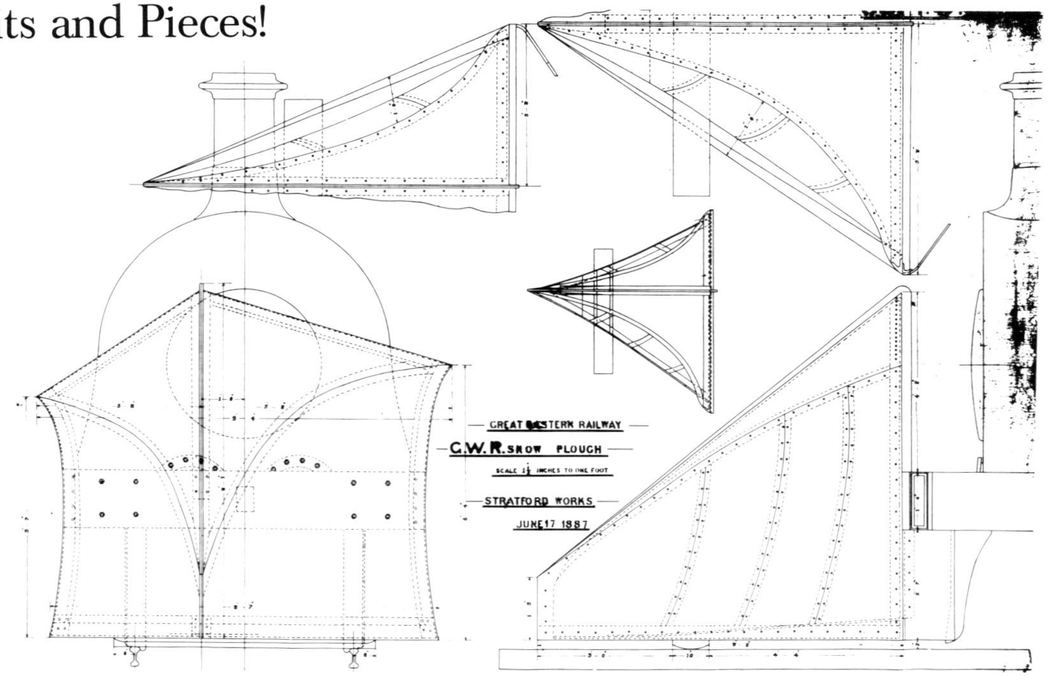

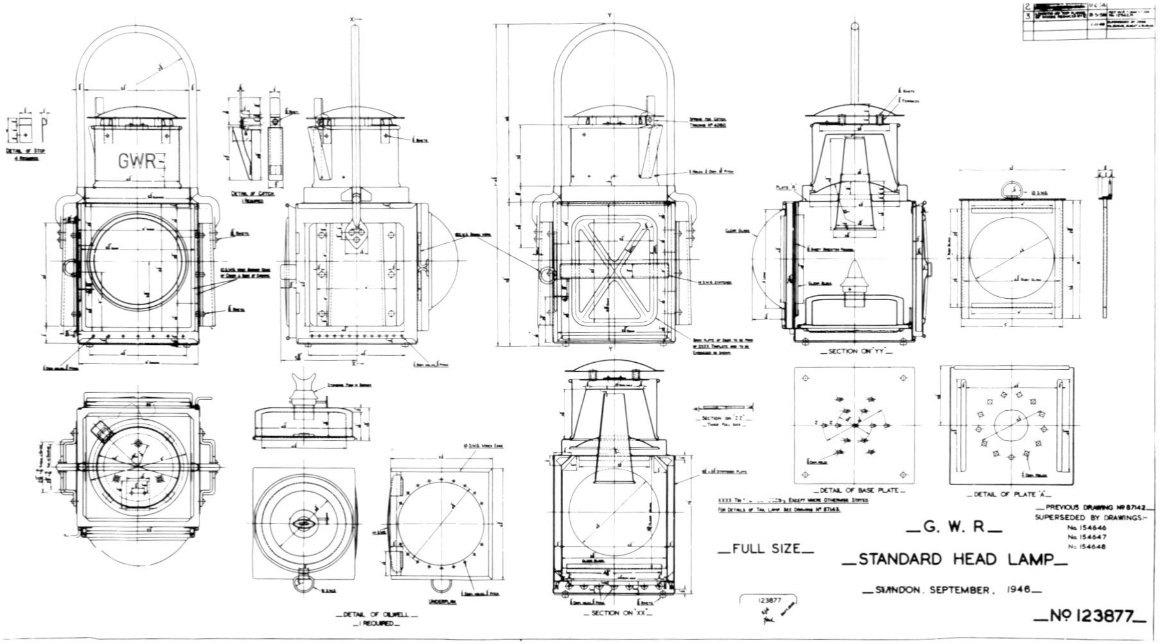

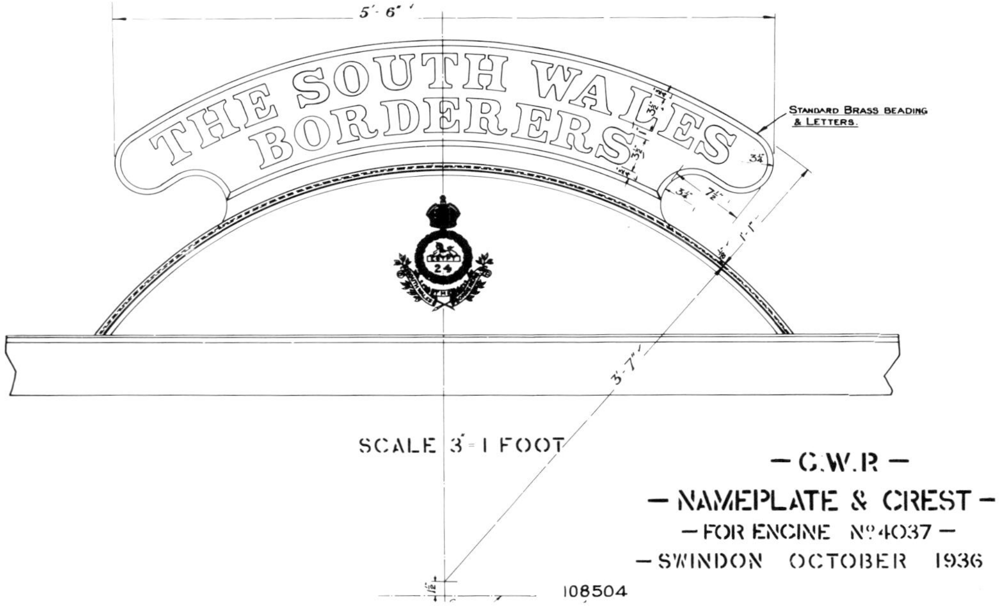

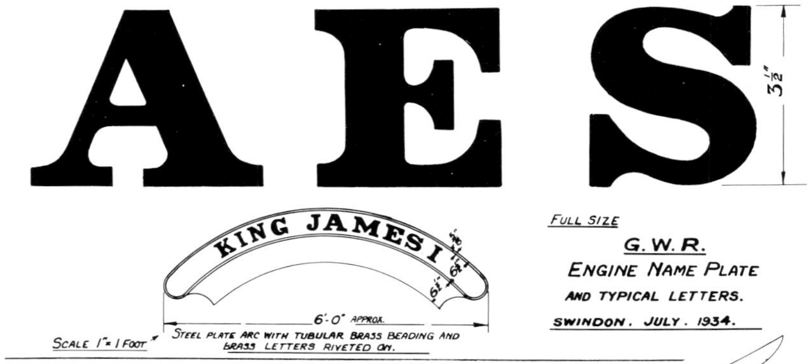

Examples of Locomotive Lettering

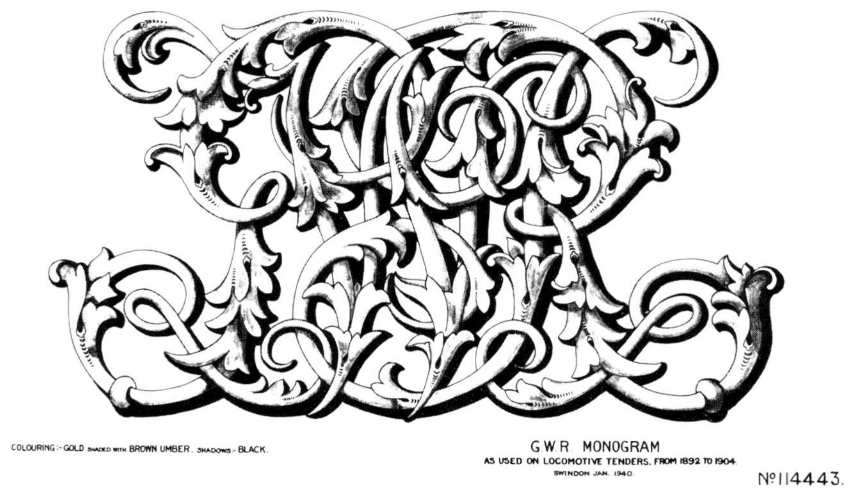

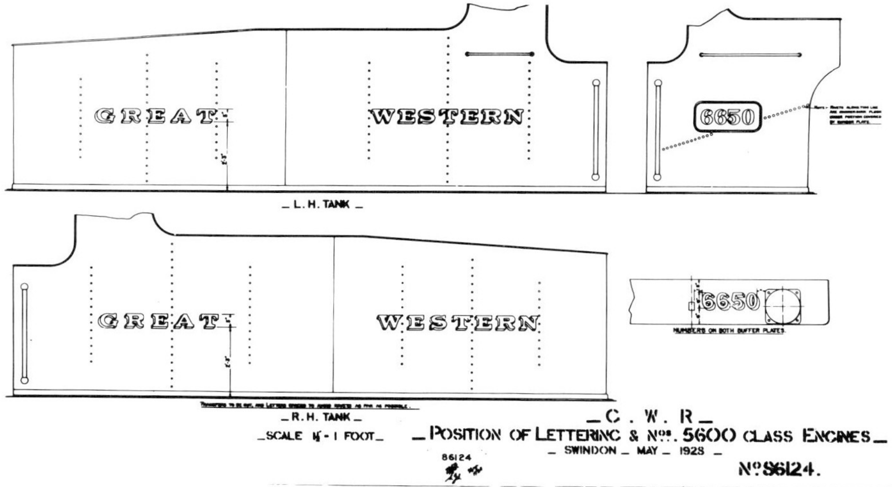

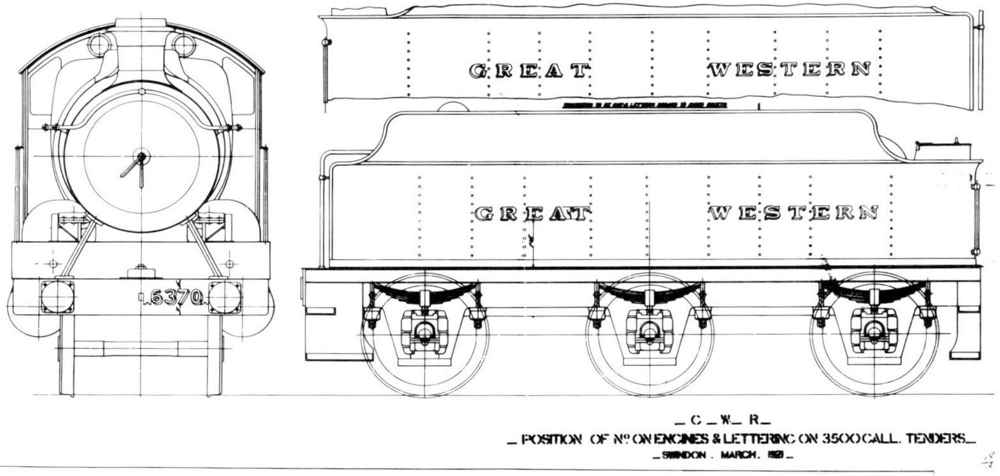

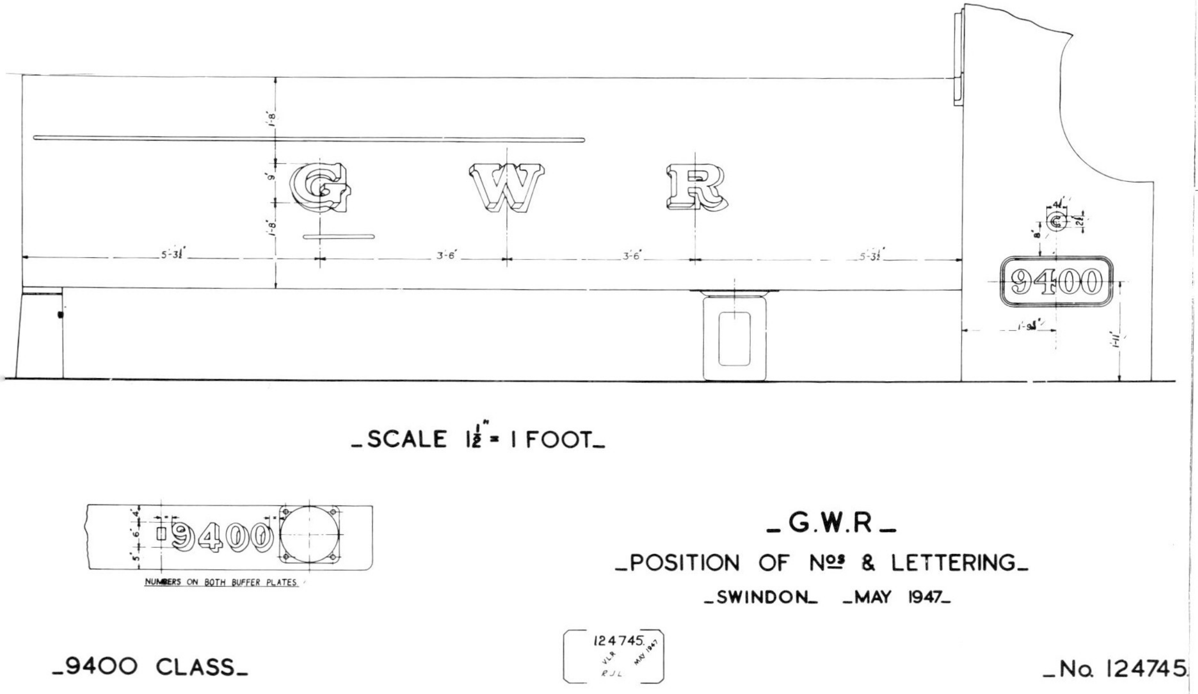

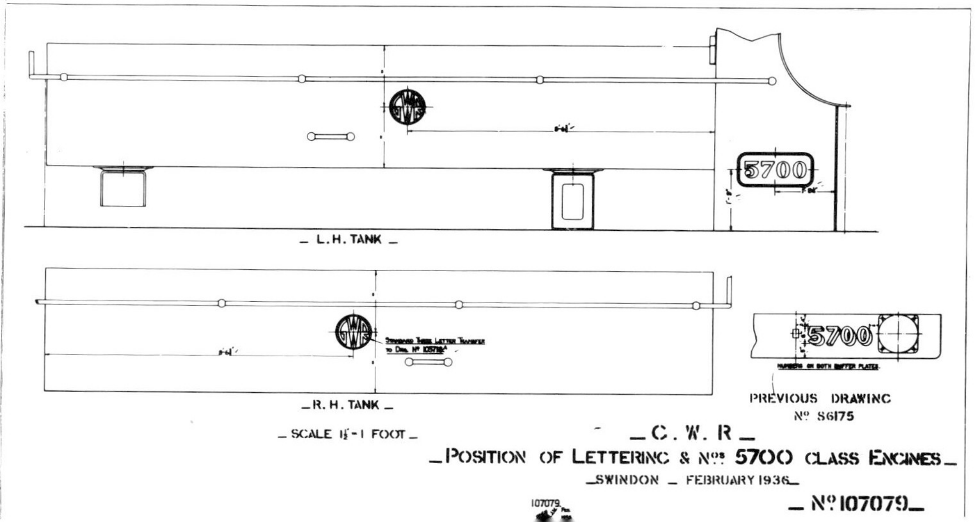